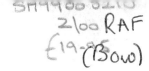

# THE INDIVIDUAL AND THE POLITICAL ORDER

*THIRD EDITION*

# THE INDIVIDUAL AND THE POLITICAL ORDER

## An Introduction to Social and Political Philosophy

*THIRD EDITION*

NORMAN E. BOWIE AND ROBERT L. SIMON

ROWMAN & LITTLEFIELD PUBLISHERS, INC.
*Lanham • Boulder • New York • Oxford*

ROWMAN & LITTLEFIELD PUBLISHERS, INC.

Published in the United States of America
by Rowman & Littlefield Publishers, Inc.
4720 Boston Way, Lanham, Maryland 20706

12 Hid's Copse Road
Cumnor Hill, Oxford OX2 9JJ, England

British Library Cataloguing in Publication Information Available

Library of Congress Cataloging-in-Publication Data

Bowie, Norman E., 1942–
    The individual and the political order : an introduction to social
and political philosophy / Norman E. Bowie and Robert L. Simon. —
3rd ed.
        p.   cm.
    Includes bibliographical references and index.
    ISBN 0–8476–8780–5 (paper)
    1. Liberty.   2. Equality.   3. Justice.   I. Simon, Robert L.,
1941–   .   II. Title.
JC571.B675   1998
323'.01—dc21                                              98–4965
                                                              CIP

ISBN 0–8476–8780–5 (pbk. : alk. paper)

Printed in the United States of America

♾ ™ The paper used in this publication meets the minimum requirements of American National Standard for Information Sciences—Permanence of Paper for Printed Library Materials, ANSI Z39.48–1984.

To Maureen and Joy

For their suggestions, their patience, and their understanding

# Contents

Preface ix

Acknowledgments xi

Introduction 1

1. Love It or Leave It? Individual Conscience
and Political Authority 7

2. Utilitarianism 23

3. Human Rights: Meaning and Justification 41

4. Justice 67

5. Liberal Justice and Its Critics 101

6. Democracy and Political Obligation 117

7. Liberty 145

8. Law and Order 179

9. An Evaluation of Affirmative Action 201

10. Ethics and International Affairs 229

Postscript 253

Index 255

About the Authors 267

# Preface

*The Individual and the Political Order* is now in its third edition. We were naturally disappointed when our original publisher let it go out of print, but we were heartened by the encouragement for producing a third edition that we received from a number of political philosophers, as well as from numerous high school debate coaches. Accordingly, we were delighted when Rowman & Littlefield agreed to publish a new edition.

In this edition, we attempt to retain the style and format of the original. We continue to defend a rights-based approach, which we locate within the liberal tradition, as justification for, and limitation upon, state action. We realize this approach is much less fashionable than it was when *The Individual and the Political Order* first appeared two decades ago. Accordingly, we have tried to address more recent criticisms not only of our own approach but also of what might be broadly thought of as the liberal tradition in political philosophy. For example, we have added a new chapter on communitarian and feminist criticisms of liberals such as Rawls. Our own discussion of Rawls has benefited from the publication of Rawls's book *Political Liberalism*. In addition, we have added discussions of hate speech, multiculturalism in a democracy, our responsibilities to intervene in the affairs of other countries that systematically violate human rights, and a number of other new issues. We have also revised many other chapters, such as the examination of affirmative action, where appropriate. Study questions have been added to each chapter. Through these additions and revisions, we hope to have given consideration to most of the important issues that have received attention in recent political philosophy.

We owe a large debt to many who helped prepare the manuscript. Jeffrey Smith, a doctoral candidate at the University of Minnesota, read all the chapters and provided many valuable suggestions for improving our discussion. We also want to thank the reviewers for Rowman & Littlefield who read the second edition and made many important suggestions for additions and changes. Ruth Lessman provided invaluable assistance in preparing the manuscript, and we are especially grateful to her. Above all, we appreciate the support and patience of our wives, to whom this book is dedicated.

# Acknowledgments

The authors and publisher thank the authors and publishers for permission to reprint quotations from the following works.

"Bicentennial Blues in Boston" by Jonathan Kozol, copyright © 1975 by The New York Times Company. Reprinted by permission.

"Communitarian Critics of Liberalism" by Amy Gutmann (*Philosophy and Public Affairs* 14 [Summer 1985]). Copyright © 1985 by Princeton University Press. Reprinted by permission of Princeton University Press.

*Democracy's Discontent* by Michael Sandel, copyright © 1996 by Michael J. Sandel. Reprinted by permission of Harvard University Press.

"Ethnic Pluralism" by Orlando Patterson (*Change: The Magazine of Higher Learning* [March 1975]). Reprinted with permission of the Helen Dwight Reid Educational Foundation. Published by Heldref Publications, 1319 18th St. N.W., Washington, D.C. 20036-1802. Copyright © 1975.

*Innocence and Experience* by Stuart Hampshire, copyright © 1989 by Stuart Hampshire. Reprinted by permission of Harvard University Press.

"Justifying Reverse Discrimination in Employment" by George Sher (*Philosophy and Public Affairs* 4 [1975]). Copyright © 1975 by Princeton University Press. Reprinted by permission of Princeton University Press.

*Liberalism and the Limits of Justice* by Michael J. Sandel by permission of Cambridge University Press.

*Morality and the Language of Conduct* edited by Hector-Neri Castaneda and George Nakhnikian by permission of Wayne State University Press.

*Philosophical Arguments* by Charles Taylor, copyright © 1995 by Charles Taylor. Reprinted by permission of Harvard University Press.

*Plato's Crito,* trans. Hugh Tredennick in *The Collected Dialogues of Plato,* ed. Edith Hamilton and Huntington Cairns. Copyright © 1989 by Princeton University. Reprinted by permission of Princeton University Press.

*Political Liberalism* by John Rawls, copyright © 1993 by Columbia University Press. Reprinted with permission of the publisher.

*A Theory of Justice* by John Rawls, copyright © 1971 by the President and Fellows of Harvard College. Reprinted by permission of Harvard University Press.

"Toward a Deliberative Model of Democratic Legitimacy" by Seyla Benhabib (in

*Democracy and Difference*). Copyright © 1996 by Princeton University Press. Reprinted by permission of Princeton University Press.

*Utilitarianism: For and Against* by J. J. C. Smart and Bernard Williams by permission of Cambridge University Press.

# Introduction

In a moving article entitled "Bicentennial Blues in Boston," written in the mid-1970s, Jonathan Kozol describes an encounter with a poverty-stricken African American child in Boston.

> One day I am forced to realize that Peter is no longer growing at a normal rate. . . . Brain growth was impeded prior to birth or else in infancy: he will not grow to normal size. . . .
>
> The doctor is firm. We ask if this is common and we ask . . . what causes something of this sort. Prenatal care. The mother is poor, or ill or underfed. . . . Peter's mother was in fact extremely ill. His infancy was lived in almost unabated hunger.
>
> The doctor goes on, "It hardly happens in white neighborhoods. . . . It is a problem of the poor, of rural slums and of impacted sections in the cities. With the right kind of care this could be totally eliminated (someday)."
>
> Someday, but we are alive on this day. . . . And Peter will not be born someday, will not be crippled one day. He is a real boy in the real world with a real curse.[1]

Consideration of tragic cases such as this can lead us to examine and evaluate the social and political arrangements that may contribute to such evils. For example, does the state have a right, or even an obligation or duty, to take resources from the affluent and redistribute them to eliminate or reduce poverty? Would such a redistributive state, favored by some liberals, violate the property rights of taxpayers by unjustly confiscating their property? Would the government bureaucracy needed to implement antipoverty programs actually create more poverty than it would eliminate, perhaps by creating incentives for the poor to become dependent on handouts, as some conservatives claim? Whether or not there is a general entitlement to some form of welfare support or safety net, does government have a special duty to eliminate burdens that fall disproportionately on minority racial groups, perhaps because of the legacy of past racial injustice?

These and a whole host of related issues are hotly debated, not only in the press and by political leaders, but also by ordinary citizens. Very often, however, the important philosophical questions underlying such debates, rather than being clarified or examined, are obscured in the heat and simplistic rhetoric of political argument.

Political arguments of the kind in question rest on philosophical presuppositions that need to be clarified and evaluated. The price of failure to do so is that the heat of rhetoric replaces the clarity of analysis, and our real problems are shrouded rather than being understood and squarely faced. For example, consider the following dialogues.

1

**Citizen A:** The idea that I should pay taxes to cover the medical costs of others is wrong. It is unjust to tax me, which in a sense amounts to seizing the fruits of my labor, to care for others. Why don't they buy their own private health insurance just as I do?

**Citizen B:** But proper medical care is a necessity. Moreover, it's expensive and not everyone can afford to pay for private health insurance. Thus, children of poor parents can't be left with no health care. One of the obligations of living in a society is contributing so that the rights of others to basic necessities can be honored.

**Citizen A:** But it isn't the government's job to provide every good thing for its citizens. I may have a need to live in an aesthetically pleasing environment and get exercise every day, but others shouldn't be taxed to provide me with artwork or exercise equipment.

**Citizen B:** But access to adequate health care is a right.

**Citizen A:** How do you know? I say I have a right not to have others seize the benefits I worked long and hard to get. And if access to medical care is a right, why don't I have a right to good athletic facilities, or works of art, or one-month vacations, which I claim I need? How do you decide what is a right and what isn't?

**Citizen C:** All candidates for the position in our company are relatively well qualified, so either a woman or minority group member should be hired. Women and minorities faced systematic discrimination in the job market in the past and so are underrepresented in our company. Hence, assuming they are relatively well qualified, they ought to be hired first.

**Citizen D:** But that is unjust and seems to be a kind of racism and sexism. After all, if it's unjust to discriminate against women and racial minorities because of race and gender, it must also be unjust to discriminate against white males because of race and gender.

**Citizen C:** You're confusing the issue. What I'm suggesting is not that we express prejudice against any group, as was the case in past discrimination, but that we take race and gender into account to overcome the effect of past prejudice based on those factors. I'm not prejudiced against white males. In fact, I am one. My point is that it is a kind of racism to ignore the past effects of racism.

**Citizen D:** I'm not saying we should ignore the effects of past discrimination. But if someone loses out simply because he is a white male, he has been discriminated against. People should not lose jobs because they belong to the "wrong" race or gender; that's unfair.

Debates such as these raise the kinds of issues that this book will address. In each exchange, fundamental philosophical issues are being discussed. But in each exchange, there also is the danger that the fundamental issues will be ignored as each side resorts to name-calling and mudslinging against the other. For example, in the first exchange, citizen A holds that there are moral limits to the domain within which government may exercise power over its citizens. These limits are set by the entitlements or rights of citizens, which include the right to control the fruits of their labors. Citizen B seems to agree that the rights of citizens are basic but believes in a wider set of rights than citizen A. According to B, these rights include entitlements to necessary benefits, and these entitlements do impose obligations on the more affluent to help provide necessities to others. It is all too easy in the actual political arena, where winning elections becomes paramount, or in the press, which often does not delve into such issues in depth, to fail to examine adequately the justifications that might be offered on behalf of different views. It is easier just to skim the surface, or to call opponents names, than to explore whether one side is supported by better arguments than the other.

Similarly, it is all too easy for different sides on debates over affirmative action simply to call names or declare those with different points of view to be advocating subtle or not so subtle forms of racism. However, as we hope the exchange between citizens C and D brings out, different sides have important points in their favor. Each citizen seems to appeal to an underlying conception of justice or fairness, but neither makes explicit what that conception is or how it is to be defended against other conceptions.

Political and social philosophy grapples with issues by clarifying different points of view on complex social and political issues, identifying and formulating arguments on different sides, and evaluating such arguments. It is primarily an exercise in moral evaluation of political and social issues, although political and social philosophers employ analysis and logic in their explorations. Thus, it is important to understand not only how the political order does work but also how it should work. Without such critical normative analysis, criticisms and defenses of current institutions may lack rational support, and discourse within the political arena runs the all too evident danger of becoming debased, so that it amounts to little more than emotional rhetorical appeals that may only contribute to, rather than help resolve, the very real political and social problems we all face.

Political philosophy can contribute to evaluation of the political and social order in at least two related ways. First, it can help clarify the concepts and arguments that are employed in political discourse. Unless such notions as "authority," "rights," "justice," and "liberty" are analyzed, it is far from clear that the parties to disputes such as those in our sample dialogues understand just what it is they are arguing about. Moreover, even agreement on terms of discourse can obscure fundamental disagreement. Thus, citizen C and citizen D might both be in favor of "equality," but one can understand equality in terms of fair opportunities to compete while the other might understand it as requiring compensation for disadvantages that may unfairly affect the competition.

This does not mean that philosophers clarify terms simply by reporting ordinary usage (although that may be relevant to their inquiries) or looking up words in dictionaries. Most often, terms like "equality," "fairness," "rights," and "liberty" are understood very differently by different people because they are embedded in different political theories. In effect, there are different conceptions or theories of how equality, fairness, rights, or liberty should best be understood. People who understand equality in terms of open access to fair competition alone have a very different normative conception of the political order than those who understand it in terms of fair representation of major ethnic groups and genders in our institutions. One of the tasks of political philosophy is to clarify and analyze the different theoretical explications of the major concepts of political thought.

While it is important to be clear about what we or others are saying, it surely is crucial to say something that is not only clear but also defensible or justified. Surely we want to know not only what is meant by liberty in a particular context but also how much liberty people are entitled to have. For example, is a law that regulates the sale of pornographic material morally defensible, or is it an unjustified restriction on personal freedom? Are regulations prohibiting and calling for punishment of so-called hate speech on college campuses necessary protections for minorities or unwarranted and dangerously vague intrusions on free speech and the uninhibited exchange of ideas in an academic setting? Political philosophy can contribute to the justification of political and social decisions, rules, policies, and institutions by formulating and critically assessing arguments of proponents and opponents alike.

Some readers may be skeptical about the second enterprise, asking "Who is to say which views are morally justified and which are not?" Unfortunately, this attitude leads to the kind of moral paralysis revealed by one of our students, who wrote in an essay, "Of course I don't like the Nazis, but who am I to say they are morally wrong?" In our view, all of us can make reasonable moral judgments by assessing the arguments for and against particular positions.

But isn't claiming that some positions are right and others wrong showing disrespect for others, perhaps by failing to recognize the cultural differences that may lead to moral disagreement? Isn't it demonstrating intolerance for the views of others? Those who ask such questions may fail to notice that the claims "We ought to respect the views of others" and "We ought not to be intolerant" are themselves moral judgments with which some other people may disagree. We also point out that taking moral positions does not require one to do so in a self-righteous or uncritical way and that perhaps the best way of coming to a reasoned moral view is through dialogue with those with whom one disagrees. Such moral disagreement, mediated by dialogue, can be among the highest forms of showing respect for others, since it recognizes the status of those with whom we disagree as thinking, rational persons who have the same opportunity to change our minds through argument as we have to change theirs. At the very least, such dialogue, even if it does not result in consensus, can lead to a better understanding of how reasonable people of goodwill can disagree on serious matters without either party being evil, although of course in some extreme cases, most typically that of the Nazis, dialogue might also expose the irrationality and moral evil that sometimes infect the political order.

As it sometimes is helpful to know where one is going before one sets out, we offer the following guide to subsequent chapters of this book. Our first task will be to evaluate the different accounts of the proper role of government and the proper limits to its authority over the individual. Suspicion of government is growing in contemporary America, and some Americans, such as the so-called extreme militia groups, go so far as to view their own government as their enemy. Does government have a legitimate function? If so, should its functions be limited to providing self-defense and ensuring fair competition on the free market, as libertarians claim, or is a more extensive government, such as the modern welfare state, not only desirable but also just and fair? Do modern liberal and libertarian theories overemphasize the rights of the individual and ignore the role of community and family values? Do all these theories reflect a kind of male bias, as some feminists charge, in overlooking the role or perspective of women in the political order or in emphasizing certain values over others?

As a result of considering these and related questions in the first five chapters, we will propose a perspective of our own that maintains that the government ought to be regarded primarily as the protector of individual rights and implementer of certain broad principles of justice and fairness, which can be applied to concrete policy issues.

The middle chapters of the book apply our general conception of the role of the state to more concrete issues of policy. Many of the questions in this section concern the conflict between individual behavior and institutions within the political order, such as the legal system. For example, what is the domain of individual liberty, and how is liberty to be reconciled with other values, such as security and respect? For example, should speech that insults or offends others be regulated? Should "hate speech" be permitted on college campuses?

Finally, in the last two chapters, we will examine two issues that concern the proper reaction to injustice and intense suffering: on one hand, the issue of international obligations and the obligation to relieve poverty and suffering in other lands; and, on the other, the obligation to remedy racial and gender injustice in our own country through various forms of affirmative action. Do we have a duty to alleviate starvation in other countries? Do we act wrongly by not giving to famine relief, or is giving a form of charity that it is good to do but not wrong to fail to do? If there is an obligation to relieve suffering by giving, isn't there also an obligation to intervene militarily on humanitarian grounds, for example in Bosnia or Somalia, when there is good reason to believe that military intervention will significantly alleviate human suffering? In our own country, is it permissible to take race into account in hiring and admissions decisions in order to make up for the evils of slavery, legally enforced racial segregation, and continuing racial discrimination?

Throughout our discussion, we will sometimes try to defend particular positions, but above all we will try to be fair to opposing viewpoints by presenting them in their strongest possible form. All too often in the actual political arena, views are caricatured by their opponents in a way that demonizes the opposition. "She's a heartless conservative" or "He's a 'tax and spend' liberal" function as epithets rather than arguments. (For example, what sane person would want to tax and spend for no purpose?) We hope, through fair consideration of opposing viewpoints, to enable readers to see what is good in opposing positions as well as to understand the weaknesses of different viewpoints. As a result, actual political dialogue between opposing viewpoints can be rational and informed. Perhaps we can even move beyond the kind of preaching to the converted, where each side talks only to those who already agree, that seems so prevalent not only in America generally but on college campuses in particular.

We also hope to defend a position that reflects and applies the principle so eloquently stated by John Rawls that "Each person possesses an inviolability . . . that even the welfare of society cannot override."[2] Accordingly, while we hope to provide an introduction to a wide range of views in political philosophy, our work also defends a perspective of its own. We hope, of course, that readers find that perspective plausible, but we hope also that we provide a fair enough account of other views so that the major objections to our own views are available for assessment. Whichever political position turns out to be most defensible, perhaps the study of political philosophy itself is of the highest value, for it can lead to critical and reflective evaluation of that great leviathan, the political order, that so significantly affects our lives, those of our fellow citizens, and those of our fellow inhabitants of the globe.

## Notes

1. Jonathan Kozol, "Bicentennial Blues in Boston," *New York Times*, 20 October 1975, 33. ©*New York Times*, reprinted by permission.
2. John Rawls, *A Theory of Justice* (Cambridge: Harvard University Press, 1971), 3–4.

# 1

# Love It or Leave It? Individual Conscience and Political Authority

We live in an age of great political conflict. Internationally, although the balance of nuclear terror between the superpowers has abated owing to major changes in what used to be the Soviet Union, famines, poverty in the Third World, wars, and international terrorism continue to threaten stability and disrupt the lives of millions. Domestically, controversies rage over the proper role of government in such areas as providing benefits for its citizens or in promoting important moral values. There is little consensus on how major social problems are to be solved. How can we best deal with crime in the streets or in the executive suites? Should the "war on drugs" be stepped up, or should use of certain drugs by competent adults be legalized? Is abortion a permissible exercise of individual choice or an assault on precious life? Does government have an obligation to promote "family values," or should it be neutral with respect to such matters as personal lifestyle and sexual preference?

The way such major social and political issues are dealt with will profoundly affect us all. The wise use of political power can benefit millions of people, while the unwise or immoral use of such power can seriously harm millions more. It is important, then, not only to describe how government does work but also to consider how it *should* work. One of the principal tasks of social and political philosophy is to formulate, clarify, and examine criteria for evaluating political institutions, such as government. Accordingly, political philosophy is a critical activity in at least the sense that it subjects political and social institutions and practices to intensive moral scrutiny.

It is characteristic of such institutions that they claim to have *authority* over individuals who stand in certain relationships to them. For example, a college or its faculty may claim the authority to establish requirements for graduation. A coach of a sports team may claim to have the authority to decide the lineup and determine who plays during games. To have authority in the sense in question is to have the *right* to make decisions in areas to which one's authority applies. Thus, authority differs from mere power in that authority is normative; the authority is not simply claiming to have more power than others but rather is claiming a right to decide or control.

The nation or state is perhaps the dominant political institution. States claim to have authority over their citizens in the sense of having a right to be obeyed. If states required obedience to law simply on the grounds that they are sufficiently powerful to make their subjects obey, they would differ only in scope from the biggest bully in the neighborhood. Their commands would lack moral legitimacy and be based only on force. Normally, states do not claim merely to be the biggest bully of them all. The United States government, for example, does not say it is up to each citizen whether he or she obeys the tax laws. This strong sense of authority in which the state's supposed right to command generates an alleged obligation to obey generates a major problem. The problem arises when the claims of the state to obedience clash with the consciences of its citizens.

The clash between conscience and authority can arise in a variety of contexts. Suppose, for example, that in a high school basketball game, the home team's worst foul shooter is fouled at a crucial point in the game. The coach notices that the referee is confused as to who was fouled and tells her best foul shooter to go to the line. The player is shocked and replies that she can't do that because it is cheating. The coach replies, "I'm the coach and I decide what you do during the game." If we take the coach as asserting a claim to authority and the player as responding that her conscience doesn't allow her to follow such directions, the kind of conflict we want to focus upon is at issue.

Moreover, in many cases of conflict between individual conscience and authority, it may not be so clear which side ought to prevail. Consider, for example, the problem of a hospital's ethics committee faced with the task of deciding which of two terminally ill patients receives the one organ available for transplant. According to the rules of the hospital, which have been accepted by the staff, cases that raise tough ethical issues are sent to the committee, whose decision is binding. In this case, each patient will die without a transplant, but not enough compatible organs are available to save both.

The first patient, A, must have the transplant almost immediately because his situation is very unstable. However, A would not have needed the transplant so quickly had he followed his physician's instructions about diet, medication, and exercise. Because of his own negligence, he needs treatment right now. The second patient, B, has been highly responsible and has postponed the need for treatment through good health habits. Furthermore, because B can be relied on to follow instructions, he could wait at least a short time in the hope that another organ will become available. While the odds are against another compatible organ becoming available, there is some chance that one will be found. Should the doctors give the organ to A, who will die imminently without a transplant, and hope that another organ will be found in time to save B, or should they save B on the grounds that A's predicament is his own fault, for which B should not suffer?

Suppose the committee decides that B should get the transplant because its members find A's behavior irresponsible, and further suppose that the physician who will perform the transplant believes that he cannot just stand by and let A die, especially when there is some chance that another organ will become available in time to save B.

One issue raised by this case concerns the justification of the decision by the ethics committee. Was its decision warranted?[1] A second issue concerns what the physician should do. Should he follow the directive of the committee and operate on B, or should he follow his own conscience and reject the committee's directive? It might not be easy to decide what the best resolution is to either issue.

In this chapter, we will focus primarily on the second issue, the apparent clash between the claims of authority and the claims of conscience, as well as some of the broader questions of political philosophy to which our examination leads. The twentieth century has seen horrible deeds committed by followers of charismatic leaders claiming authority. But at the same time, if we were never able to put aside our individual viewpoints and accede to the decisions of an authority, the result might well be chaos. Is there such a thing as legitimate authority? What is its moral basis or justification? Is it possible somehow to reconcile the claims of both authority and conscience and avoid the twin evils of social chaos and blind subservience?

In the political arena, many are inclined to give absolute authority to the commands of the state. Particularly in times of crisis, it is often felt that criticism of our leaders, let alone protests or disobedience of their commands, is disloyal, dangerous, and subversive. Thus, many Americans regard those who vigorously protested the Vietnam War, especially those who avoided military service, as having deserted, or even as having betrayed, their country in time of need. (Much of the hostility that portions of the electorate have directed at President Bill Clinton exists because he is seen by many as a draft dodger rather than as someone who perhaps felt unable to support a war that he may have regarded as ethically questionable.) On the political level, the slogan "Love it or leave it," which was so frequently directed at protesters against the Vietnam War, quite clearly expresses the attitude that criticism of the political order, particularly in time of crisis after a decision by authorities has been made, is incompatible with allegiance to it.

But while some are disposed to give absolute weight to the claims of authority, others are equally disposed to go the other way. Consider, for example, Henry David Thoreau's reaction to what he considered an unjust war. Rather than pay taxes that would have supported the Mexican War effort, he refused to pay and was imprisoned. Thoreau denied that his legal obligation to pay his taxes was a sufficient *moral* reason for obedience. In defense of his disobedience, Thoreau declared that

> Laws never made men a whit more just: and, by means of the respect for it, even the well disposed are daily made instruments of injustice. A common and natural result of an undue respect for law is, that you might see a file of soldiers . . . marching in admirable order over hill and dale to the wars, against their wills, ay, against their common sense and consciences.[2]

It appears that there is great tension between the claims to authority over citizens made by political and social institutions, particularly the state, and the claims of individual conscience and autonomy. As one contemporary writer puts it, "The defining mark of the state is authority, the right to rule. The primary obligation of man is autonomy, the refusal to be ruled. It would seem, then, that there can be no resolution of the conflict between autonomy . . . and the putative authority of the state."[3]

The implications of this apparent conflict are enormous. If the conflict is indeed genuine, we are faced with a momentous choice. If, on one hand, we are overly impressed by the need for order and stability that can be promoted by allegiance to a common authority, we may be led to stifle the exercise of independent critical judgment. But, as a result, we are in danger of ending up with the abhorrent picture of "good Germans" engaging in genocide under the commands of the Nazis. If, on the other hand, we assign absolute weight to individual autonomy, we may end up with the community in chaos, as individuals go their own way with no conception of the common good or common rules recognized as binding.

A major goal of political philosophy is to formulate defensible criteria for assessing the political order, particularly as embodied in the state. However, as the preceding discussion suggests, it is first imperative to consider what is involved in accepting political authority in the first place. Perhaps the costs of acceptance are prohibitive. For example, does acceptance of authority require us to abandon autonomy and disregard conscience? Under what circumstances, if any, are claims to political authority morally legitimate or justified? Is the only alternative to acceptance of absolute authority a kind of anarchy of individual conscience?

We will begin by considering a classic and highly influential defense of the necessity of absolute political authority provided by Thomas Hobbes. In particular, we will consider the kind of justification offered by Hobbes for recognizing the authority of the state. Then, we will consider the claim that our obligation to exercise our own critical judgment and be autonomous overrides any possible obligation to the state. Finally, in the concluding section of the chapter, we will suggest a strategy for evaluating the state, for distinguishing good states from bad ones, and for determining under what conditions the former might legitimately claim some form of authority over their citizens. That strategy will be developed, and contrasted with alternate approaches, throughout the book.

## The Grounds of Political Authority

### Thomas Hobbes (1588–1679): The Case for Absolute Authority

Hobbes's political philosophy reflects his horror of war, particularly civil war. This is not surprising in view of the tumultuous times in which Hobbes lived. He was born as the Spanish Armada was approaching England. The reigns of Elizabeth I and James I, the Civil War, the rule of Cromwell, and the Restoration all occurred within his lifetime.

Educated at Oxford in the scholastic tradition that he later repudiated, Hobbes spent much of his life as a tutor and later adviser to the children of the noted Cavendish family. His employment provided time for reading, writing, and thinking. Moreover, through the Cavendish family, he was able to meet many of the great thinkers of his time. Because of his political views, he feared the outcome of the Civil War and so, before the outbreak of the conflict, left England for Paris. There, he tutored the Prince of Wales who was later to become Charles II. However, the publication of his major work, *Leviathan* (1651), made Hobbes unpopular with the royalists because of its naturalistic, scientific, and rationalistic approach to political thought. So he made his peace with Cromwell and returned to England. When Charles II took the throne after the fall of Cromwell's government, he remembered Hobbes with affection. The last years of Hobbes's life were spent in philosophical reflection and conversation, with financial support provided by the throne.

**Hobbes's Political Philosophy.** In political philosophy, Hobbes's goal was to explain and justify a form of that great leviathan, the state, solely by reference to its elements, the individual persons of which it was composed. For Hobbes, human action was either largely or entirely egoistic, aimed ultimately at satisfying the desires of the agent or avoiding their frustration.[4] Agents normally are, and always have the potential to be, efficient rational calculators. They can select the most efficient means to reach their goals, which ultimately involve their own self-interest.

Here, then, is Hobbes's individualist starting point. It is a conception of how human nature would be in its pristine state, apart from the influence of the political order. The proper function of the state is to remedy the defects of the state of nature. The state is justified by appeal to the nature of life among the individualistic atomic individuals who would exist if human nature were left as it is apart from political and related institutional structures. Since the life of such individuals would be horrible and the state can remedy the defects that cause such horror, the existence of the state is warranted.

Hobbes is often criticized for exaggerating the extent of human egoism and for postulating an egoistic view of human nature without appropriate empirical evidence. We agree that these criticisms have some force, but it is important to note that they do not discredit Hobbes's approach to political philosophy. Thus, we doubt if psychological egoism—the view that human action always and everywhere is basically selfish—can be sustained in the face of counterexamples, such as heroism, the often unconditional love of parents for their children, and the countless acts that show concern for others that almost all of us engage in every day.[5] However, a Hobbesian could reply that at least some such acts are engaged in because we have institutions in place, such as the legal and educational systems, that protect us if our altruism makes us vulnerable and that tend to promote reciprocal altruism on the part of others. Even if not all human behavior was naturally selfish, prudent persons in the state of nature would have to take precautions against victimization simply because they would have no a priori method of distinguishing those who would exploit them from those who would not.

Perhaps more important, Hobbes may not be making claims about human nature in a straightforward empirical way. Rather, he may be suggesting that we ought to start our political philosophy not with optimistic assumptions about how nice we naturally would be to one another—for, given an assumption of universal niceness, many of the problems of political philosophy would not even arise—but with some more pessimistic assumptions whose implications we should examine. If we can solve many of our conflicts by finding points that even largely self-interested parties would agree upon, the solutions would rest on a much more powerful foundation than solutions based on a kind of "sweetness and light" view of human nature that, if true, makes it difficult to see how the problems ever got started in the first place.

Given Hobbes's assumptions, then, what would life without the state, in what he calls the "state of nature," be like? According to Hobbes, life in the state of nature would be "solitary, poor, nasty, brutish, and short."[6] If there were no state to preserve law and order, then given human selfishness, or at least the presumption of it, scarcity of resources, and approximate equality in strength, cunning, and personal resources, the result would be a war of all against all. If there were not enough to go around, and everyone, whether through strength or cunning, was a potential threat to everyone else, and if it would be prudent to assume the worst about the intentions of others, competition for the objects of common desire would be constant and often bloody. Consequently, given Hobbes's postulates—that humans are, or must be reasonably assumed to be, selfish; that not all selfish desires can be satisfied; and that humans are approximately equal in their capacities to harm one another—the conclusion that the state of nature would be one of anxiety, violence, and constant danger would seem to follow.[7]

Human beings, however, would not be stuck in the state of nature. On the contrary, Hobbes has described human beings as rational, as efficient calculators about how to reach their goals. Thus, people in the state of nature would realize that the war of all against all was contrary to their interests, particularly their overriding concern with self-preservation. For whatever else people want, and surely different individuals want diverse things, they all need personal security and continued existence as prerequisites for their enjoyment of anything else: "The passions that incline men to peace are fear of death; desire of such things as are necessary to commodious living, and a hope by their industry to obtain them. And reason suggesteth convenient articles of peace . . . which otherwise are called Laws of Nature."[8]

According to Hobbes, "A law of nature . . . is a precept or general rule, found out by reason, by which a man is forbidden to do that which is destructive of his life, or taketh away the means of preserving the same. And consequently, that every man ought to endeavor peace, as far as he has hope of obtaining it; and when he cannot obtain it, then he may seek . . . all help and advantages of war."[9] In other words, since the state of nature, being a state of war of all against all, is a disaster for all concerned, it is in the rational self-interest of the inhabitants to end the war by forming a state with the authority and power to limit conflict. Thus, the first law of nature, which enjoins everyone to seek peace, implies the second; namely, that when others are willing, all parties to the state of war contract together, or create a covenant, to set up a supreme authority over them all. By doing so, and (given the postulates about human motivation and scarcity) only by doing so, can the evils of the state of nature be avoided. The state, then, is an instrument to keep the evils of the unregulated pursuit of self-interest in check.

In fact, given his view of human nature, Hobbes concludes that only a state with absolute power over its citizens can provide security for them. For "covenants without the sword are but words, and of no strength to secure a man at all . . . if there be no power . . . every man will rely on his own strength and art . . . against all other men."[10] That is, if citizens are given some freedoms against the state, then given the initial assumptions about the pursuit of self-interest, they will use that freedom to advance their own ends and defeat the opposing plans of others. The state of nature will just reappear in a new guise. Since only an absolute power can prevent reversion to the war of all against all, that is exactly the kind of state that rational parties to the original covenant would create.

Hobbes's argument, as reconstructed here, does not presuppose that there ever actually was a state of nature. Hobbes can best be understood as presenting a hypothetical argument. If the political state did not exist, look how bad things would be. The actual existence of the state of nature is not required for the success of his argument.[11]

Hobbes believes, then, that the authority of the state cannot coexist with the individual autonomy of the citizens. Although rational inhabitants of the state of nature may autonomously agree to the covenant that creates the sovereign, the absolute state that enforces the peace, by creating that leviathan, they surrender their own power of decision making. Little if any room is left in the Hobbesian state for the kind of individual rights valued in liberal democracies. To Hobbes, the constant struggles between interest groups in the liberal state and the degeneration of political discourse into insult and invective are simply evidence of the inherent instability of liberal democracy and of the thin blue line that stands between such degenerate forms of the state and the war of all against all.

In spite of these gloomy conclusions, however, Hobbes's approach to political philosophy is of the greatest value. First, it is an attempt to explain not only the need for the political order but also the necessity for all rational individuals to assent to it, on the basis of minimal assumptions about human altruism or human kindness. The state is an instrument of mutual advantage. The political order is explained and justified in naturalistic terms without recourse to controversial moral assumptions or such metaphysical doctrines as the divine right of kings or the special fitness of one group of humans to rule all the others. Rather, what Hobbes has done is to isolate what he takes to be the basic unit of political and social analysis—the individual person—and ground his account of the political order upon it.

**Evaluation of Hobbes's Political Theory.** Hobbes views the state as an instrument for providing those basic primary goods without which a minimally satisfactory human life is impossible. These basic goods, according to Hobbes, are peace and security. In his view, only a state with absolute authority can provide them.

If we are to avoid Hobbes's defense of the absolute state, we must either reject his premises or his reasoning from premises to conclusion. Critics might begin by questioning Hobbes's pessimistic view of human nature. Even if it is true, as Hobbes seems to maintain, that humans always act to satisfy their desires, it doesn't follow that their desires always are *selfish*. Parents who act for the benefit of their children, soldiers who sacrifice themselves for their comrades, and teachers who give up their own time to help their students all count as examples of individuals who sometimes act for unselfish reasons. Of course, one could reply that the parents really act for the personal satisfaction they get from helping their children, the soldier really wants to be remembered as a hero, and the teachers are trying to avoid the pain of guilt they would experience if they did not help their students. But these replies are implausible. Why, for example, would the teachers even feel guilt unless they cared about their students and thought the students ought to get help?[12] It is difficult to believe that all apparently unselfish acts really are selfish ones, especially when one sees that the goals of avoiding guilt and receiving satisfaction presuppose that the agent thinks some ways of treating others are right and wrong independently of any personal benefit the agent receives.

Of course, it is always possible to discount a priori any data that conflict with one's pet theory. For example, one might argue that all human actions are really altruistic and that apparently selfish acts are really done to benefit the other in the long run. "That mugger was really trying to toughen you up and show you not to be so trusting." If such armchair psychology is implausible when arguing that all acts really are unselfish, it must be equally implausible when used to show that all acts are selfish. Consequently, Hobbes's apparent defense of psychological egoism, the view that all human behavior is selfish, seems altogether too extreme to withstand examination.

However, Hobbes might not need such an extreme view to make his point. Perhaps he could argue more modestly that (1) a good deal of human behavior is selfish; (2) selfish behavior is more likely to occur in the state of nature than in the state where political institutions control selfishness; and (3) in the state of nature, where any mistake could be deadly, it is simply prudent for each agent to *assume* that all other agents are acting only for their own good, even if each agent knows that is not always true. That is because one is more likely to be harmed or killed by mistaking an egoist for an altruist than by mistrusting everyone.

Let us suppose that Hobbes can make his argument work with this revised assumption about what it is rational to assume in the state of nature.[13] His view still faces serious difficulties. First, if we assume a general tendency toward selfishness, the Hobbesian state itself would seem to be an impossibility. For the sovereign state to have the kind of absolute power Hobbes thinks is necessary to keep the peace, it must have a powerful coercive apparatus under its control, for example, a strong police force or army. But given Hobbes's assumptions about human psychology, who will coerce the coercers? The police and soldiers will have a tendency to act in their own interest where it conflicts with that of the sovereign. That is, the sovereign and its agents will be in a state of nature with respect to one another. As a result, breakdown of the very coercive order that is supposed to preserve the peace is always a real threat. Even if we assume that many individual members of the sovereign's force have a disposition to do their duty and put aside self-interest, as suggested by the revision to Hobbes's theory proposed above, each may find it prudent to suspect the others. How could the kind of trust needed to preserve the state be generated? Hobbes's psychology, then, tends to undermine his political theory.[14]

A second problem is even more important, however. As the seventeenth-century philosopher John Locke argued, Hobbesian individuals in the state of nature would be irrational to set up an absolute sovereign state in the first place:

[T]hough men when they enter society give up the equality, liberty and executive power they had in the state of nature into the hands of society . . . yet it [is] only with an intention in every one the better to preserve himself, his liberty and property—for no rational creature can be supposed to change his condition with an intention to be worse.[15]

Surely it would be irrational to leave the approximate equality of the state of nature simply to create a sovereign more powerful than any of one's previous enemies. Given Hobbes's psychology of human nature, rational individuals would be prudent to assume that the sovereign and its agents will act for their own selfish purposes. If so, Hobbes's deduction of the absolute authority of the state over the individual seems invalid, since the Hobbesian covenant seems not only to make individuals no better off than they were in the state of nature but also to make them liable to a new and powerful threat, more dangerous than their enemies of old.

For Hobbes, at least as we have read him, power relations are central. The state is a mechanism for preventing the disastrous use of power by unconstrained individuals, all following their own self-interest at the expense of others. It is mutually advantageous for each individual in the state of nature to set up an absolute sovereign to end the war of all against all. However, Hobbes's argument as so understood may undermine itself, since, for one thing, it is hard to see how the different agents of the state could ever trust one another sufficiently to keep the state going and, for another, it is hard to see why the parties in the state of nature would ever find it rational to sign the social contract or covenant to begin with.

But we should not abandon what surely is one of Hobbes's major insights; namely, that the state is an instrument to secure some benefit to its citizens or to protect them from some evil. It should not be viewed as a private preserve divinely assigned to a ruler (the theory of the divine right of kings) or a resource to be exploited by the few at the expense of the many. Hobbes's insistence on mutual consent and mutual advantage suggests that the state's claims of authority could be justified if reasons were provided for accepting it that would be, or could be made to be, acceptable to everyone. Thus, we may want to follow Locke, whose views we will explore in chapter 3, in denying Hobbes's claim that absolute authority and power must be ceded to the state but accepting at least some of Hobbes's assumptions about the need to provide an argument for state authority that should be found acceptable or reasonable by all.

Thus, Hobbes's approach to political philosophy reveals both the dangers of submitting to an absolute authority, whose will would dominate the autonomy of individuals, and the possible benefits of grounding the authority of the state on considerations mutually acceptable to all. The first road, if we are not careful, may lead to dictatorship and tyranny, but the second may help ground the liberal democratic state. If so, in spite of the weaknesses of Hobbes's approach to political philosophy, some of his insights, suitably revised, might prove part of an acceptable approach to justifying the political order.

## Robert Paul Wolff: The Supremacy of Individual Autonomy

If one rejects the idea of an absolute and unquestionable authority, does it follow that one is thereby committed to rejecting political authority altogether? According to a contemporary philosopher, Robert Paul Wolff, there is an irreconcilable conflict between the claim that we ought to submit to authority at all and our duty to think for ourselves and exercise personal autonomy over our actions. As Wolff puts it in a passage quoted earlier, "The defining mark of the state is authority, the right to rule. The primary obligation of man is autonomy, the refusal to be ruled. It would seem, then, that there can be no resolution of the conflict between autonomy . . . and the putative authority of the state."[16]

Wolff's point should be familiar to those who have studied the catalogs of many of the best liberal arts colleges and universities in the United States. Such institutions claim to help students learn to think critically and develop and test their own system of values. But how can we both think for ourselves and judge the positions of others critically and at the same time simply obey the commands of an authority, especially the state? Wolff's claim is that it is impossible to do both, and as a result he concludes that "it would seem that anarchism is the only political doctrine consistent with the virtue of autonomy."[17]

Professor Wolff performs a valuable task in emphasizing the importance of individual judgment, conscience, and autonomy, features that the Hobbesian solution of the absolute sovereign state would require us to ignore. In fact, both Hobbes and Wolff accept the very same assumption: that autonomy and authority necessarily conflict. Hobbes, fearful of the state of nature, argues that the autonomy of individuals must be ceded to the sovereign, while Wolff, fearful that power corrupts and absolute power corrupts absolutely, argues for the retention of autonomy and rejection of authority. But both accept the same common assumption, the incompatibility of autonomy and authority, one which we believe should be rejected.

A reply to Wolff might start with the point that authority itself can be accepted by autonomous decision. That is, autonomous individuals might decide for themselves that living under an authority entitled to make decisions would be better for everyone than living in the kind of chaos that might result if there were no way of coordinating individual decision making or adjudicating conflicts among individuals. However, this point by itself is not enough. Wolff might reply that just as one can freely decide to sell oneself into slavery, one can autonomously decide to accept the authority of the state. But once the sale into slavery has been completed, freedom has been lost. Similarly, once the state's authority has been accepted, individual autonomy has been lost. From the fact that one can decide for oneself to regard the state's commands as authoritative, it does not follow that one can remain autonomous once such a decision has been made.

However, there appears to be a crucial difference between selling oneself into slavery and accepting the authority of certain kinds of political decision procedures. Once one is a slave, one has no say in formulating the master's commands. But a political decision procedure can itself be based on autonomous decision making by citizens. Thus, in the democratic state, the citizens determine the policies of the whole. Rather than abandoning their autonomy to the state, they express it through the very procedures that determine state policy.

If this suggestion has force, then perhaps Wolff's major mistake is his too-narrow conception of what it is to accept authority. According to Wolff, "Obedience is not a matter of doing what someone tells you to do. It is a matter of doing what he tells you *because he tells you to do it.*" On this view of obedience, we can see why Wolff regards authority with such distaste. Obedience does require individuals simply to let their own judgment be overridden by the commands of the authority. What this account leaves out, however, is, first, that there may be good reasons for accepting the authority that individuals themselves autonomously affirm; and, second, that the individual's own values may be given a fair and equitable voice in determining the policies of the authority. Advocates of the liberal democratic state claim that such an authority satisfies these two requirements and hence avoids Wolff's argument, at least in principle.

Wolff, however, might remain unconvinced and reply that even if one has some voice in democratic decision making, that voice is often very minimal. In particular, in today's representative mass democracies, the voice of the individual, particularly if he or she is not wealthy or influential, may be thought to count for very little. Moreover, the decision of the majority in the mass democratic state may run counter to the conscience of the individual. For example, the majority, or its representatives, may vote to send you to fight in a war that you think is morally wrong. Even if you had a voice, a vote, in the decision making, it would seem that obedience to the authority of the majority means rejecting the dictates of your own conscience and forfeiting your autonomy to decide for yourself what to do.[18]

This rejoinder has force, and we will try to discuss it more thoroughly in our chapter on democracy. For now, we suggest that two points need to be considered. First, in a democratic state, one does not have to defer blindly to the majority when one thinks it is wrong. Rather, one can attempt to change others' minds, support organizations that favor one's own point of view, and try to bring about change through democratic institutions. Second, in extreme cases, one might practice principled civil disobedience against laws or policies one regarded as seriously unjust, as advocated by thinkers such as Gandhi and Martin Luther King Jr. That is, allegiance to a democratic authority does not require blind, unquestioning obedience to its commands, and it does not necessarily require obedience no matter how seriously unjust the commands of the authority may be thought to be.

Of course, all of this requires fuller development than we have given it in this chapter. In fact, much of the book will be devoted to examining principles for evaluating the political order. Our task will be to justify conditions under which the state and other political institutions justifiably can call for our commitment and under which we retain a significant degree of autonomy and decision-making power. What we do want to suggest for now, however, is that we need not be forced to embrace either acceptance of absolute authority, and the danger of tyranny it carries with it, or total rejection of authority, with its loss of the advantages of the political order. These two extremes might not be the only possibilities open to us.

Of course, the mere possibility that there may be other alternatives does not show what they are, let alone that any actual state can justifiably claim authority over us. However, it does indicate that an inquiry into the conditions under which the state can justifiably claim authority is not necessarily pointless.

## Authority and the Neutral State

Suppose we are able to develop a plausible argument justifying the claims to authority of certain kinds of states, say, democratic ones. Issues would still remain about the extent or proper domain of the authority such states would wield. For example, should states have the authority to promote certain religious views, to redistribute wealth, to promote "family values," or to prohibit behavior that they regard as immoral but that does not necessarily harm other individuals—for example, the use of certain birth control devices?

One important view central to liberal democracy is that the authority of the state should be limited by the freedom of the individual. But how much freedom should the individual have?

The liberal tradition in Western thought has tended to defend two very important principles in this area. The first is that the freedom of the individual is limited only by the threat of harm to others. The mere fact that my behavior might offend others or violate their moral principles is no reason for restricting my liberty as long as my behavior is not harmful to others. Second, liberals often argue that the state should be neutral with respect to different theories of the good or proper life. That is, it may be the state's role to protect individuals from harm, or safeguard their rights, or provide a fair and just framework for individual choice and development. But it is not the state's business, on this view, to tell individuals how they should live or what choices they should make, so long as no harm to others or threat to their rights is involved.

But is this liberal view sustainable? Does the kind of liberty and individualism it defends turn into license? Doesn't the state have a role in promoting values and in trying to produce individuals who will be good citizens rather than indifferent louts? As the great nineteenth-century conservative thinker Edmund Burke mused, "The effect of liberty to individuals is, that they may do what they please; we ought to see what it will please them to do, before we risk congratulations."[19]

Thus, contemporary critics of liberalism argue that the neutral state, if neutrality is really possible at all, gives its citizens no guidance on what choices to make and ends up with the bonds of community split asunder as individuals pursue their own goods in independent and often mutually antagonistic directions. For example, are pornography and rap music that are demeaning to women just goods to be pursued in the individual's search for private pleasure while the quality of public life and civic values degenerate? As contemporary writer George Will argues, "an aim of government—indeed, a prerequisite of popular government—must be a sense of community rooted in a substantial range of shared values and aims. . . . A democratic state has the power sufficient to administer policies regarding abortion, sexual relations and pornography less extreme than today's policies," policies that in Will's view suggest that "these matters touching the generation of life and the quality of life are matters of indifference to the community."[20]

On the other hand, do we want the state telling us what values we should hold and how we should behave, even in the privacy of our own homes? Clearly, the debate over the proper domain of state authority is not something that concerned only Hobbes's contemporaries. While few thinkers in today's Western liberal democracies favor Hobbes's view of absolute authority, many would reject the liberal ideal of the neutral state and suggest instead that the authority of the state should be used in morally acceptable ways to promote important ethical values and civic virtues.

Clearly, the debate between liberalism and its critics on the proper domain of state authority is sophisticated and important. This debate will be pursued in later chapters, and, as we will see, whether it is ultimately defensible or not, liberalism is a far more sophisticated and resourceful doctrine than the simplistic insults about "tax-and-spend liberals" found in the political arena would lead people to believe.

## Evaluating the Political Order

Even if acceptance of political authority does not entail commitment to authoritarian rule, it does not follow that any actual political institutions can justifiably claim authority over individuals. Consider, for example, that all too many great evils, including the practices of genocide and slavery, have been carried out with the direct support of the state. Democracy itself is not immune to the grave misuse of power, either through the manipulation of the citizenry by unscrupulous leaders or through the ignorance or immorality of the majority. Accordingly, it is crucial that the state and its claims to authority be subject to critical scrutiny.

As we noted above, one strategy for justifying the state and its claims to authority over individuals is to consider the purpose of the state, what functions it can serve, or what individuals might get from belonging to a state that they would lack without it. We can then consider whether it is morally permissible for the state to serve such a function and whether the means it might need to do so are morally permissible as well.

In our own time, much of the debate in the United States over the function of the state has centered on its role in providing minimal material prerequisites of well-being for its citizens. The extent of poverty in an affluent society has aroused considerable concern. Moreover, African Americans, Native Americans, and members of other minority groups have borne a disproportionate share of the burdens of poverty, unemployment, and ill health. In response, many liberal advocates of the welfare state have supported Great Society programs as part of a war on poverty. On this liberal view, although government should be neutral concerning what sort of life people should choose to lead, it does have the obligation to provide a fair framework within which people can develop their abilities and talents. Thus, under the influence of this form of welfare liberalism, the United States government has sponsored food stamp programs, welfare, unemployment compensation, and Medicaid, to name just a few of the campaigns in the assault on poverty.

Others have objected to what they regard as big government, a dangerous threat to individual freedom. These critics, including libertarians as well as many conservatives, may share the liberal belief in the neutral state (although, as we will see, other conservatives, such as those on the religious right, pursue an agenda of values that they wish the government to support) but unite in regarding many government programs not only as violating individual liberty but also as wasteful and inefficient. Many of these critics argue that welfare provides incentives for the poor to remain in poverty, and so, on their view, the program perpetuates the very conditions it was designed to overcome.

Thus, in our own society as well as in others, there is considerable disagreement over what the purposes of government should be and how well government is fitted to carry them out. Our first task, then, is to ask what purposes the state should serve. Moreover, if good states are those that perform their functions well, good states may have the strongest claims to have authority over their citizens, at least under certain conditions. It also seems plausible to think, at least at the start, that the limits of the state's authority are set in great part by its function. In all other areas, individuals would be free of obligations to the state. Accordingly, we propose to begin by investigating what the proper function(s) or goal(s) of the state might be.

In the course of dealing with this question, we hope to shed light both on the contemporary debate over big government and on the claim that the state should be neutral among rival conceptions of the good life found among its citizens. Thus, if one set of questions concerns the ground or justification for the state's claims to authority, a second set concerns the domain or limits to that authority.

Finally, there is the issue of how the state should deal with injustice and violation of law. Injustice, of course, can be perpetrated by the state itself. Laws mandating slavery and racial segregation were at one time enforced by the government of the United States. Racial segregation in the public schools was not officially declared unconstitutional until the *Brown* decision by the Supreme Court in 1954. What are the duties of the state when such injustice has taken place? Is it enough just to end the injustice? Should some compensation be made to the victims? Should social policies be put in place that would help nullify the effects of the injustice and prevent existing manifestations, such as continuing racial discrimination? Much of the controversy over such questions has been focused on the justifiability of contemporary affirmative action policies, which we will examine in detail in later chapters. What about those, such as Martin Luther King Jr., who violate the law, not for criminal purposes and personal profit, but to protest injustice? How should the state react to civil disobedience of its laws?

In this section, three distinct lines of inquiry concerning the authority of the state have been identified:

1. Under what conditions is the state's claim to authority justified?

2. How far does that authority extend?

3. What is the state's proper response to unjust conditions or practices it itself has tolerated or promoted?

It is important to consider these questions in depth not only because of their own importance but also because they lead to other equally important questions. For example, suppose it is suggested in answer to the first question that only the just state has authority over its citizens. This will naturally lead to an inquiry into the nature of justice, a question just as important as the one with which we started. Indeed, an inquiry into justification of the authority of the state can be expected to broaden into an examination of most of the major questions of political and social philosophy.

In the next few chapters, we examine various criteria for evaluating the state. One criterion often appealed to is social utility. The good state is one whose actions or policies produce consequences as good as, or better than, those of alternate acts or policies available to it. It is to the ethical theory of utilitarianism and its application to political philosophy that we now turn.

## Notes

1. Similar issues are raised in other areas of medicine whenever goods or services available are insufficient to meet crucial needs. There is an extensive discussion of such issues of allocation in the literature on medical ethics. A selection of articles relevant to the issue can be found in Thomas A. Mappes and Jane S. Zembaty, *Biomedical Ethics* (New York: McGraw-Hill, 1991), 545–620, as well as in other widely used anthologies on medical ethics.

2. Henry David Thoreau, "Civil Disobedience," in *A Yankee in Canada* (Boston: Ticknor & Fields, 1866), 125. Thoreau's essay is widely reprinted and is available, for example, in Hugo A. Bedau, ed., *Civil Disobedience: Theory and Practice* (New York: Pegasus, 1969).

3. Robert Paul Wolff, *In Defense of Anarchism* (New York: Harper & Row, 1970), 18.

4. The issue of whether Hobbes believed all human action was selfish is complex. For discussion, see Jean Hampton, *Hobbes and the Social Contract* (New York: Cambridge University Press, 1986), esp. 19–24.

5. Often, egoists reply that such apparently unselfish acts are really selfish after all, since they are done to avoid the pain of guilt the agent would have felt otherwise. But as a philosophical tradition going back at least to Bishop Joseph Butler (1692–1752) replies, a truly selfish agent would not feel guilt in the first place. The fact that we often feel guilty for harming others, rather than showing we are selfish, shows we are concerned for others and sometimes count their interests as equal to, or even more important than, our own. After all, if we didn't feel we had done something wrong in harming others, why would we feel guilty?

6. Thomas Hobbes, *Leviathan,* in *Hobbes Selections,* ed. Frederick J. E. Woodbridge (New York: Scribners, 1930), 253. Originally published in 1651.

7. The idea that all humans are equal threats to one another in the state of nature does not imply that they are all equal in one quality, say, physical strength. Rather, it is that advantage in one area, say, strength, does not make one invulnerable to the power of others. Thus, an especially strong individual can be brought down by a group of weaker but more cunning individuals.

8. Hobbes, *Leviathan,* 257.

9. Ibid., 269–70.

10. Ibid., 335–36.

11. Hobbes does suggest that the nations of the world are in fact in a state of nature with respect to each other, since there is no common power above them.

12. As pointed out in note 5, this line of argument goes back at least to Bishop Butler (1692–1752).

13. An alternate and perhaps equally plausible assumption is that all humans have an innate tendency toward reciprocal altruism. That is, people might obey minimal guidelines of fair behavior toward those who obeyed such guidelines toward them. Some sociobiologists have argued that genes promoting such reciprocal altruism might confer survival advantages on their bearers, since any sacrifices required would benefit a greater number of bearers of the genes. Whether the genetic argument is plausible or not, parties to the state of nature who tried to behave ethically toward those who would respond by behaving ethically toward them might actually do better under some conditions than those who presumed no one else ever was to be trusted. Of course, such an assumption might not work in single encounters where a failed experiment might mean death, but it might lead to the development of ties of trust under circumstances where encounters could be repeated over time. For discussion, see Robert Axelrod, *The Evolution of Cooperation* (New York: Basic Books, 1984).

14. Moreover, any attempt to minimize the influence of egoism among the rulers also casts doubt about the extreme effects of egoism in the state of nature postulated by Hobbes.

15. John Locke, *Second Treatise of Government* (1690), chap. 9, sec. 13 (9, 13). Available in many editions, e.g., that by Thomas P. Peardon (Indianapolis: Bobbs-Merrill, 1952).

16. Wolff, *In Defense of Anarchism,* 18.

17. Ibid., 18.

18. Wolff does agree that authority and autonomy can coexist in a direct democracy in which unanimous votes are required for decision making but denies that any other kind of democracy, particularly indirect representative democracy, reconciles authority with autonomy for the reasons given in the text. See *In Defense of Anarchism,* 22 ff.

19. Edmund Burke, *Reflections on the Revolution in France* (1790; reprint, ed. Conner Cruise O'Brian, Harmondsworth, England: Penguin, 1969), 91.

20. George Will, *Statecraft as Soulcraft: What Government Does* (New York: Simon & Schuster, 1983), 149, 151.

## Questions for Further Study

1. Explain the difference between the normative analysis of political institutions and descriptive and explanatory analyses of them.

2. Explain the alleged conflict between authority and autonomy. Why do some theorists, such as Robert Paul Wolff, think that an autonomous individual cannot recognize the claims of authority?

3. Why does Hobbes believe we must accept a virtually absolute authority rather than retain our autonomy? How would you reconstruct his argument for such a conclusion?

4. Hobbes appeals to the idea of the state of nature. Do you think the state of nature, as described by Hobbes, ever existed? How would you defend your view? Do you think Hobbes's argument can have force even if the state of nature never existed? Why or why not?

5. Be able to explain and evaluate at least two criticisms of Hobbes's approach. Are these objections successful? Be prepared to defend your view.

6. Be able to explain and evaluate at least two criticisms of Wolff's view that authority and autonomy are incompatible. Are these objections successful? Be prepared to defend your view.

7. Do you agree that anarchism is the only form of social organization compatible with human autonomy and respect for the conscience of the individual? How would you argue for your view?

8. How would you explain the idea of state neutrality toward conceptions of the good? In what way might a neutral state be compatible with individual autonomy?

# 2

# Utilitarianism

Suppose one were to ask the following question of a cross section of American society: "What should the United States government be doing for its citizens?" Many people would answer in specific terms. For example, some would say that the United States government should do more to protect the environment. Others would say that the government should lower taxes. Those who respond in more general terms, however, will say that the government should act in the general interest, the public interest, or that it should do what will benefit all Americans, not just the interests of business or labor, for example. Americans talk as if they want their elected leaders to serve all constituencies. A leader too closely identified with one faction or interest risks defeat at the polls. Many Americans, then, would argue that the purpose of government is to promote the general welfare or serve the public good.

Terms like "public interest" and "general good" have rich positive emotional associations. It may even be argued that such terms have more favorable connotations now than "motherhood" or "patriotism." Although everyone seems to be in favor of the public good or the general interest, it is very difficult to get everyone to agree as to what precisely promotes the public good. There is a tendency for each particular interest to claim that an activity or program that benefits its particular goal is really in the public interest, while the activity or program that benefits a competing particular interest is said not to be in the public interest. Each interest group has its own version of "What's good for business is good for America." Few, if any, interest groups have much of an idea of how to determine the public interest. However, there is a well-developed philosophical theory called utilitarianism that does have a carefully worked out program for defining the public interest. The public interest is defined as the sum of individual interests. By examining this theory in some detail, we will see some of the advantages and disadvantages of a theory that sees the function of the state as a means for providing the aggregate welfare or public good, conceived of as the greatest good for the greatest number.

## Historical Background

### Jeremy Bentham (1748–1832)

Jeremy Bentham was born in London and raised by a family with strict monarchical views. He studied law at Lincoln's Inn, where he was introduced to the contract theory of natural rights and obligations. However, he was also introduced to the legal works of the Italian writer Beccaria, the philosophical treatises of David Hume, and the economic writings of Adam Smith. As a result of these influences, he became skeptical of a social contract theory as the basis for the legitimacy of the state because there was no empirical justification for asserting that any social contract ever existed. In addition, he came to recognize that tradition, custom, and instinct had no foundation in reason. Indeed, Bentham concluded, blind adherence to tradition had created significant problems. Hence, Bentham saw his task as one of reform. His individualistic utilitarianism, he believed, was an appropriate tool for the reformation of the major political institutions of his society.

Perhaps we can best understand utilitarianism if we consider a question that a legislator might well ask: "From among these competing policies, how can I choose the best one?" Bentham's answer was clear-cut. The legislator ought to choose the policy that leads to the greatest good for the greatest number. Indeed, the test of the greatest good for the greatest number became Bentham's test for all social institutions. Upon applying his test, Bentham found many nineteenth-century English laws and institutions failing it. It is for this reason that Bentham's utilitarian principle was viewed as a principle of reform.

Bentham's earliest work, *Fragment on Government* (1776), provided a utilitarian critique of the British legal system and of its chief intellectual champion, Blackstone. In the criminal law, for example, Bentham believed that the traditional and formal classification of crimes and punishments should be given up. Crimes should be classified according to the amount of unhappiness they bring about. Punishments must be similarly classified to fit the crime. The basic rule is that the punishment must exceed the advantage gained by committing the offense. Penal institutions should make it likely that indeed crime does not pay.

Bentham's concern in punishment was not to set the moral order right, nor did he believe the infliction of punishment to be valuable because in some way criminals were made to pay for their crimes. Rather, Bentham argued that the infliction of pain was always an evil and hence was to be avoided unless it could bring about more good. One calculates the benefits of rehabilitation and deterrence that punishment effects and subtracts the pain that punishment causes. Punishment is justifiable only when the benefits exceed the pain. One should punish only up to that point where the infliction of pain brings about greatest benefits in rehabilitation and deterrence. Only in this way does punishment provide for the greatest good of the greatest number.

In order to apply utilitarianism, one must have an account of what is most valuable or intrinsically good. Bentham's view was based on his account of human psychology. He believed that human action was motivated by seeking pleasure and avoiding pain. He then concluded that individual happiness was the supreme good:

> Nature has placed mankind under the governance of two sovereign masters, pain and pleasure. It is for them alone to point out what we ought to do, as well as to determine what we shall do. . . . The principle of utility recognizes this subjection, and assumes it for the foundation of that system, the object of which is to rear the fabric of felicity by the hands of reason and of law. . . . By the principle of utility is meant that principle which approves or disapproves of every action whatsoever, according to the tendency which it appears to have to augment or diminish the happiness of the party whose interest is in question.[1]

Having decided on what was most valuable, it was easy enough to formulate a utilitarian moral principle that stated that the right thing to do was to maximize that which was most valuable, namely, happiness. On utilitarian morality, one ought to act so as to produce the most happiness, the greatest good for the greatest number.

**The Hedonic Calculus.** If one is to act on utilitarian morality, however, one has to have some way of measuring happiness so that the individual happiness or unhappiness created by any given act can be compared and summed up. Bentham is committed to a quantitative measurement of happiness whereby one computes the greatest total happiness by adding the quantitative units of individual happiness and by subtracting the units of individual unhappiness to arrive at a measure of total happiness. Bentham developed a device he called the hedonic calculus for measuring pleasure. The quantitative figure for any pleasurable experience is reached by considering its intensity, duration, certainty or uncertainty, propinquity or remoteness, fecundity, purity, and extent. Perhaps it is worth quoting Bentham's six-step process for evaluating any proposed action or event:

> To take an exact account then of the general tendency of any act, by which the interests of a community are affected, proceed as follows. Begin with any one person of those whose interests seem most immediately to be affected by it: and take an account,
>
> 1. Of the value of each distinguishable pleasure which appears to be produced by it in the first instance.
> 2. Of the value of each pain which appears to be produced by it in the first instance.
> 3. Of the value of each pleasure which appears to be produced by it after the first. This constitutes the fecundity of the first pleasure and the impurity of the first pain.
> 4. Of the value of each pain which appears to be produced by it after the first. This constitutes the fecundity of the first pain, and the impurity of the first pleasure.
> 5. Sum up all the values of all the pleasures on the one side, and those of all the pains on the other. The balance, if it be on the side of pleasure, will give the good tendency of the act upon the whole, with respect to the interests of that individual person; if on the side of pain, the bad tendency of it upon the whole.
> 6. Take an account of the number of persons whose interests appear to be concerned; and repeat the above process with respect to each. Sum up the numbers expressive of the degrees of good tendency, which the act has, with respect to each individual, in regard to whom the tendency of it is good upon the whole: do this again with respect to each individual, in regard to whom the tendency of it is bad upon the whole. Take the balance; which, if on the side of pleasure, will give the general good tendency of the act with respect to the total number or community of individuals concerned; if on the side of pain, the general evil tendency, with respect to the same community.[2]

We now have a means for evaluating matters of policy and legislation. In facing a problem of what to do—for example, staying with your sick mother or joining the Resistance to fight the Nazis—make your decision on the basis of the greatest happiness. Use the hedonic calculus to get a quantitative figure for the happiness of all relevant individuals affected by your act. Then, after adding the happiness and subtracting the unhappiness for each alternative act, perform the act that produces the most happiness.

**Criticism of Bentham's Utilitarianism.** Bentham's theory has been the target of vigorous and sustained criticism. We limit our discussion to three traditional critiques of Bentham's utilitarian political philosophy: a critique of its hedonism, a critique of its quantitative methodology, and a critique of utilitarianism as a normative test of state actions.

Bentham's hedonistic view that individual happiness was best understood in terms of pleasure soon came under ridicule. In fact, his philosophy was sometimes referred to as the "pig philosophy." The difficulty centered on a conflict between the logic of hedonism and some commonly held beliefs on matters of value. In point of logic, under hedonism the pleasures of artistic creation may be no better than, or may even be inferior to, the pleasures of wine, sex, and song so long as the happiness of the latter is equal to, or more than, the former. It is charged that on hedonistic grounds it is better to be a satisfied pig than a dissatisfied Socrates. To see the force of this criticism, the reader should ask whether he or she would willingly become a pig, even with an ironclad guarantee that the life of the pig would be happier. Those who are still with us can see that hedonism conflicts with our strong convictions that in fact some activities are better than others even if they are not more pleasurable.

It has also been objected that experiences of pleasure are not susceptible to quantitative measurement, that Bentham's hedonic calculus is really a useless device. How could one use the seven measuring devices of the calculus to compare quantitatively the pleasure of solving a difficult philosophical problem with the pleasures of a cool swim on a hot summer's day? Certainly Bentham's calculating tools are inadequate.

Even more serious are the moral objections that can be raised against utilitarianism. On moral grounds, utilitarianism provides neither necessary nor sufficient conditions for justifying either state action or any of the institutions of government.

Utilitarianism cannot provide sufficient justification because some government decisions cannot be made on utilitarian grounds alone. For example, suppose a government could choose between two possible programs:

|  | Program 1 | Program 2 |
|---|---|---|
| Citizen 1 | 3 units of pleasure | 4 units of pleasure |
| Citizen 2 | 3 units of pleasure | 5 units of pleasure |
| Citizen 3 | 3 units of pleasure | 0 units of pleasure |
| TOTAL | 9 units of pleasure | 9 units of pleasure |

Since the *total* happiness is identical for both programs, there is no basis on utilitarian grounds for choosing between them. However, other things being equal, most everyone would prefer program 1 on egalitarian grounds. Equality provides an additional condition for evaluation.

Moreover, the traditional utilitarian formula "the greatest happiness for *the greatest* number" can provide conflicting results. Consider the following two government programs:[3]

|  | Program 4 | Program 5 |
|---|---|---|
| Citizen 1 | 5 units of happiness | 3 units of happiness |
| Citizen 2 | 4 units of happiness | 3 units of happiness |
| Citizen 3 | 0 units of happiness | 4 units of happiness |
| TOTAL | 9 units of happiness | 10 units of happiness |

Program 4 makes more citizens happier than program 5, but program 5 provides the greatest total happiness. Which program should the government provide?

A more important problem can be raised when one considers questions of population control. Consider the following situation, which reflects problems in the real world. If the government takes no steps to control population, 1 million residents can be supported at a minimum standard of living. Let us say that such a minimum standard of living has a hedonic value of 10. Total utility for a population of 1million would be 10 million, with the average utility for each person equal to 10. Suppose the population were limited by government action to 750,000. This policy would enable each person to live a more comfortable life with an average utility value of 13. Total utility for the society would equal 9,950,000 utility units. Is it better to have a large population at a minimum standard of living or a small population that has a smaller total of happiness but where each person is happier on the average? Utilitarianism seems to have nothing to say here.

The reason for these paradoxes is clear. In providing his account of utilitarianism, Bentham did not indicate whether total or average happiness was to be used as the criterion for determining what should be done. Neither did he recognize that an appeal to equality or some other distributive principle might be necessary when two or more potential distributions of some goods yielded identical totals of utility. Most contemporary utilitarians have adopted the average-utility criterion, although there is controversy among utilitarians over which approach is best.

Some have also argued that utilitarianism is too demanding as a moral theory or, in other words, that it asks too much of us. It seems as if Bentham would require us to consider all the alternatives to any act that we undertake in order to determine which one leads to the greatest good. But surely that would be too demanding. In fact, common sense, as well as much nonutilitarian moral theory, regards many of our acts as morally neutral or without significant moral import. Surely when brushing our teeth, we need not consider whether there is an alternative action that would bring about a greater good.

Utilitarians could respond to this criticism by saying that experience has taught us that many actions lack consequences of moral significance and that in many circumstances alternative acts of significance are not open to us. Therefore, the greatest good is done simply through ordinary acts. Normally, we should just brush our teeth without worrying about whether an alternative action would bring about the greatest good. Indeed, ordinarily, spending all our time worrying about whether there is such a significantly better alternative actually may be harmful, as little will get done. However, a utilitarian also would insist that sometimes an ordinary act can have moral import. If a person is just beginning to brush her teeth and she hears a cry for help from next door, the utilitarian would say that she should investigate and try to help if aid is required.

From our point of view, one of the most important values omitted from Bentham's utilitarianism is the value of individual rights. Indeed, failure to consider individual rights is one of the chief criticisms of utilitarianism today. We can illustrate this point with one of the most common and most persuasive objections against utilitarian analysis, the so-called punishment-of-the-innocent example. Consider the following situation: A small city has been plagued by a number of particularly vicious unsolved crimes. The citizenry is near panic. All homeowners have guns; doors and windows are locked. The local police officer goes to the freight yards and arrests a homeless person who has taken shelter in an abandoned railway car. Investigation shows that although the accused, who has no family or friends, is innocent, he can be made to appear guilty. Utility, both total and average, could be increased if he were punished and the populace calmed. On utilitarian grounds, the innocent man should be punished. But should he be?

The point of this example can be generalized. None of our rights is safe from the measuring rod of utility. On the whole, our rights to freedom of the press, freedom of speech, and trial by jury are consistent with utilitarian considerations, but on occasion they are all subject to surrender. Indeed, under utilitarianism there is nothing inconsistent in saying that a slave society is the best society. All one would need to show is that the happiness (total or average) of the slave society exceeds that of the nonslave society. Most of us, however, would not declare that the slave society is better even if it is happier. The utilitarians' lack of concern with rights offends some of our more firmly grounded moral insights.

Early supporters of utilitarian theory denied that their theory had these undesirable consequences or claimed at least that Bentham's theory could be repaired so as to avoid them. These repairs began almost immediately and continue in the work of contemporary utilitarians discussed later in this chapter.

## John Stuart Mill (1806–1873)

John Stuart Mill was stung by the barbs about the "pig philosophy." One of his intellectual projects was to reformulate Bentham's utilitarianism so that it could avoid the objections of its critics.

Mill abandoned quantitative utilitarianism and the hedonic calculus that accompanied it for a qualitative utilitarianism. Mill vigorously maintained that some pleasures really are better than others. Pushpin (a popular parlor game) is not as good as poetry. A dissatisfied Socrates' life is qualitatively better than the life of a satisfied pig: "It is quite compatible with the principle of utility to recognize the fact that some kinds of pleasure are more desirable and more valuable than others. It would be absurd that, while in estimating all other things quality is considered as well as quantity, the estimation of pleasure should be supposed to depend on quantity alone."[4]

**The Panel of Experts.** Having introduced qualitative distinctions and having abandoned the hedonic calculus, Mill needed some other means for comparing and qualitatively ranking experiences. Mill claimed that we know one experience is better than another by consulting a panel of experts. Mill was not entirely clear as to how this panel of experts was to be composed, but one condition was that the members have had both the experiences in question. Having experienced both, they have met at least one of the conditions for making a qualified comparison:

> Of two pleasures, if there be one to which all or almost all who have experience of both give a decided preference, irrespective of any feeling of moral obligation to prefer it, that is the more desirable pleasure. If one of the two is, by those who are competently acquainted with both, placed so far above the other that they prefer it, even though knowing it to be attended with a greater amount of discontent, and would not resign it for any quantity of the other pleasure which their nature is capable of, we are justified in ascribing to the preferred enjoyment a superiority in quality so far outweighing quantity as to render it, in comparison, of small account.[5]

To those who might retort that such a panel of experts could not take the perspective of the pig, Mill argued that humans were qualitatively different from animals. Humans have a higher capacity that prevents them from desiring a lower grade of existence even if they would be happier. Mill refers to this capacity as man's sense of dignity. This sense of dignity provides the ground for qualitative distinctions among pleasures.

This reference to a human capacity might provide the clue to Mill's answer to the moral objections to utilitarianism. It may be that there are a number of human practices that, if followed, or human characteristics that, if developed, would lead to the greatest happiness. In other words, human rights are norms that are adopted because of their utilitarian value. It may well be that Mill was working toward a distinction that split utilitarianism into two camps. Today these two types of utilitarianism are most frequently referred to as act and rule utilitarianism.[6]

**Rule and Act Utilitarianism.** Act utilitarians, such as Bentham, argue that one ought to do those particular acts that produce the greatest good for the greatest number. On an act–utilitarian view, rules are mere shorthand devices that are suitable as rules of thumb but that are to be abandoned when following them would not lead to the greatest good for the greatest number:

> Does the utilitarian formula leave any place for moral maxims like "Keep your promises" and "Always tell the truth"? Yes, these maxims can be regarded as directives that for the most part point out what is a person's duty. They are rules of thumb. They are properly taught to children and used by everybody as a rough timesaving guide for ordinary decisions. Moreover, since we are all prone to rationalizing in our own favor, they are apt to be a better guide to our duty in complex cases than is our on-the-spot reflection. However, we are not to be enslaved to them. When there is good ground for thinking the maximum net expectable utility will be produced by an act that violates them, then we should depart from them. Such a rule is to be disregarded without hesitation, when it clearly conflicts with the general welfare.[7]

Under rule utilitarianism, however, rules have a very different status. On rule utilitarianism, the appropriate answer to the question "What ought I to do?" is "You ought to follow the appropriate rule for that type of situation." However, the appropriate answer to the question "What rules should one adopt?" is "One should adopt those rules that lead to the greatest good for the greatest number." Perhaps the difference between the two types of utilitarianism can be illustrated by an example. Consider the practice of grading college students for course work. Suppose that one of the rules for receiving a grade of A in Mathematics II is obtaining a 90 average or better on quizzes and examinations. An act utilitarian would treat the rule of 90 for an A as a rule of thumb. In circumstances where utility would be maximized, one could give an A for less than 90 or one could give a B for a grade of 90 or better. What determines each act of grading is the consequence of giving a certain grade in that particular case. The rule of A for 90 is a guide, but it is not authoritative. For the rule utilitarian, things are different. A student with an 85 could not argue for an A on the basis of the special circumstances of his or her case alone. Rather, he or she would have to show that the grading rule of A for 90 does not provide the greatest good for the greatest number. The task of the moral philosopher, on the rule-utilitarian account, is to formulate those rules that pass the utilitarian test. For example, perhaps the rule for giving an A that has the most utility should allow some exceptions for test performances that were affected by serious illness.[8] The rule utilitarian does not necessarily endorse following popular or fashionable rules but believes we should follow the rules that would maximize utility if generally complied with.

If Mill is interpreted as a rule utilitarian, individual rights can be construed as rules that protect individuals. These rights, however, are grounded on utilitarian considerations. Individual rights should be recognized only if by recognizing them the happiness of the greatest good for the greatest number can be secured. Whether or not Mill actually was a rule utilitarian is a matter of scholarly debate. However, interpreting him as a rule utilitarian enables us to see how Mill could construct a reply to those who criticized Bentham for ignoring moral rules, particularly rules for the distribution of happiness, and rules that protect individual rights. A society has such rules because they pass the utilitarian test.

Indeed, one can more readily understand some of Mill's remarks on liberty, representative government, and laissez-faire capitalism from this rule-utilitarian perspective. Mill saw the political philosopher's task as one of describing the procedures and institutions that make the realization of the greatest good for the greatest number most likely. In his writings on liberty, he attempted to describe the social and political conditions that must obtain if individual liberty is to flourish. In his economic writings, he attempted to describe what social and political conditions are necessary to overcome the evils of industrialization, that is, to increase the public good. For example, Mill's *On Liberty* discusses various institutional arrangements that support the free exchange of ideas. Mill was greatly concerned about the tyranny of public opinion—especially the tyranny of the opinions of the uneducated. Hence, one institutional safeguard he recommended in *Considerations on Representative Government* was weighted voting. The votes of the educated would count more than the votes of the uneducated.

In summary, one could argue that Mill strengthened utilitarianism by making qualitative distinctions among pleasures, by abandoning Bentham's simplistic hedonic calculus, and by finding a place for justice and individual rights within a utilitarian framework.

**Criticisms of Mill.** Mill's efforts, however, did not put an end to the critical commentary. Mill's critics argued that the attempt to make qualitative distinctions among pleasures was to concede that utilitarianism was inadequate. If the pleasure of listening to rock music is quantitatively greater than the pleasure of listening to Beethoven, even though Beethoven is better, what does the music of Beethoven have that rock does not have? Mill would say that Beethoven's music provides a higher pleasure. But surely Mill's response is deceptive. After all, how can pleasures differ except quantitatively? Beethoven's music must have some quality other than pleasure that makes us rate Beethoven's music higher than rock. Mill's appeal to higher pleasures is not an appeal to pleasure at all. Rather, by implication, Mill concedes that there are some qualities that have value in addition to pleasure. In other words, there are a number of goods, in addition to pleasure, that are valuable.

In the late nineteenth and early twentieth centuries some utilitarians, such as G. E. Moore, accepted this critique of Mill and formulated a new version of utilitarianism called ideal utilitarianism. Ideal utilitarianism asserts that there are many goods besides pleasure. What one ought to do is maximize the greatest goods for the greatest number. Ideal utilitarianism is not hedonistic, but it still subscribes to the principle of maxima. In this view, the function of the state is to maximize the total good.

Mill's substitution of the panel of experts for Bentham's hedonic calculus came under attack as well. Some argued that we could not say that the life of a dissatisfied Socrates is better than the life of a satisfied pig since we could not get the opinion of the pig. At this level, the objection misses the point, since Mill stipulates that the panel of experts must have had both experiences. Of course, the panel could not literally live the life of the pig, but, following Aristotle, the panel could contrast animal-like pleasures with the pleasure of rationality. This interpretation does not remove all the difficulties, however. Mill assumes either that the panel of experts will approach unanimity in their comparative judgments or that a majority opinion is sufficient to decide the question. Neither assumption would seem justified. Lifestyles are notoriously diverse even among the well-traveled and well-educated. There is no reason to think that a consensus would develop on anything but the most general value judgments. For example, most would probably say that the life of a dissatisfied Socrates is better than the life of a satisfied pig, but unanimity on much else is fairly unlikely. On the other hand, it is not self-evident that the device of majority voting is the correct device for deciding questions of this type. Finally, many objected to the elitism of Mill's panel of experts. Heavily influenced by the discipline of economics, which counted each person's desire as equal to every other, most utilitarians returned to a more refined hedonic calculus to measure and compare happiness. The economic theory of utility provided one such basis.

However, the most complicated and arguably the most important exchange of ideas concerned whether or not Mill succeeded in finding a legitimate place for rights and justice. Indeed, contemporary utilitarians have spent so much time discussing this issue that we should turn to their accounts of the matter. After a thorough analysis of these discussions we shall decide whether utilitarianism is able to provide the test for the justifiability of state actions.

## Utilitarianism and the Economists: Contemporary Discussions of Utilitarianism

Despite the shortcomings of both Bentham's and Mill's formulations of utilitarianism, the theory remains attractive to many and perhaps especially to economists. If utility were to refer to preferences expressed by consumer choice in the marketplace, utilitarians could avoid the issues involved in the measurement of such psychological states as pleasure and pain. Utility would be maximized when everyone made choices in a free competitive market. The competitive market assures that the highest average of personal-preference satisfaction is obtained. Preference utilitarianism also seems capable of mathematization, which gives it the appearance of rigor, a quality not often seen in ethical theories. In fact, John Harsanyi derived a rule utilitarianism that maximized satisfaction of personal preferences from the postulates of an important (Bayesian) account of rational-choice theory.[9]

However, in spite of its attractive features, the difficulties facing preference utilitarianism are at least somewhat analogous to those that plagued Bentham. Since all preferences are taken as given, nothing in the theory allows us to distinguish rational, refined, socially responsible preferences from irrational, crude, or antisocial preferences. The preferences of a social worker would count the same as those of a racist.[10]

> In utilitarianism the satisfaction of any desire has some value in itself which must be taken into account in deciding what is right. In calculating the greatest balance of satisfaction it does not matter, except indirectly, what the desires are for. We are to arrange institutions so as to obtain the greatest sum of satisfactions, we ask no questions about their source or quality but only how their satisfaction would affect the total of well-being. Social welfare depends directly and solely upon the levels of satisfaction or dissatisfaction of individuals. Thus, if men take a certain pleasure in discriminating against one another, in subjecting others to a lesser liberty as a means of enhancing their self-respect, then the satisfaction of these desires must be weighed in our deliberations according to their intensity, or whatever, along with other desires.[11]

Although economists have tended to accept the idea of preference neutrality, many moral philosophers, including Harsanyi, have not. Harsanyi, like most preference utilitarians, insists that only rational preferences should count. To avoid the problem presented by the racist, he also has stipulated that antisocial preferences should not count either.

Although these stipulations seem morally correct, in making them Harsanyi and other preference utilitarians may have moved beyond utilitarianism in a way analogous to Mill. Mill claimed to find a special quality in some pleasures that enabled him to say that the life of a satisfied pig could not be better than the life of a dissatisfied Socrates. But what could this quality be if Mill was to remain a hedonistic utilitarian? Similarly, Harsanyi argues for the principle of preference autonomy yet eliminates "irrational" or "antisocial" preferences from utilitarian calculations. But mustn't this involve the use of some other criterion of value or some other theory of the good than preference satisfaction, and, if so, how is this consistent with the kind of preference autonomy required by utilitarianism?

Contemporary utilitarians have not only discussed utilitarian theories of the good, such as the idea of preference satisfaction, but also have continued the debate between rule and act utilitarianism.[12] One of the challenges to contemporary utilitarians, which has engaged defenders of both act and rule versions of the theory, is to avoid counterexamples like the following:

> It [utilitarianism] implies that if you have employed a boy to mow your lawn and he has finished the job and asks for his pay, you should pay him what you promised only if you cannot find a better use for your money. It implies that when you bring home your monthly paycheck you should use it to support your family and yourself only if it cannot be used more effectively to supply the needs of others. It implies that if your father is ill and has no prospect of good in his life, and maintaining him is a drain on the energy and enjoyment of others, then, if you can end his life without provoking any public scandal or setting a bad example, it is your positive duty to take matters into your own hands and bring his life to a close.[13]

Act utilitarians believe that counterexamples like these are based on totally unrealistic situations. For example, it often is claimed that utilitarianism would justify convicting a friendless and homeless person of a crime, even though authorities knew him to be innocent, in order to deter criminals and reassure citizens, thereby maximizing utility but treating the victim unjustly. The act utilitarian might reply, however, that it is extremely implausible to think that the decision to punish a person known to be innocent could remain secret. In addition, long-term consequences, such as the erosion of the prosecutors' sense of justice, would work against the public interest.

On the other hand, suppose a careful act utilitarian does take account of such notions as justice, equity, and the dangers that result from breaking rules. Normally justice should be promoted, and well-entrenched moral rules should not be broken. But sometimes rules should be broken—namely, in those rare cases where utility is maximized by breaking them and all the consequences have been factored in.

But against such a response, consider that it may be extremely difficult to predict the consequences of acts, particularly those undertaken under pressure. Under pressure, it may seem efficient to ignore equity, fairness, justice, and rights and maximize utility, even though judgment about such factors is likely to be distorted by the pressure of the situation itself. At the very least, it seems to us that act utilitarianism does not offer sufficient protection for the innocent; the innocent are protected only insofar as complex calculations about consequences tend to come out the right way. And the very circumstances where the innocent, or unpopular individuals and minorities, most need protection are exactly those where utilitarian calculations are likely to be done carelessly or under the influence of pressure or bias.

Considerations like these have encouraged other contemporary utilitarians to reformulate Mill's rule utilitarianism. Richard Brandt's book *A Theory of the Good and the Right* is one such attempt. Brandt argues that utilitarians should advocate the adoption of a welfare-maximizing moral system (or code of moral conduct). The rules in such a system would be suited to the nature of human beings and would take into account the intellectual capacities of the average person as well as the negative qualities the average human being possesses—negative qualities such as selfishness and impulsiveness. The code of moral conduct must be teachable and should have fairly concrete rules for frequent situations.[14] Brandt thinks that utilitarianism should serve as the moral guide for deciding what moral rules should be included in a moral system. Utilitarianism also urges us to consider psychological facts about human beings as various rules are proposed. Only in this way can you have a welfare-maximizing moral system.

A similar argument can be made for the accommodation of individual rights. Such an argument is found, for example, in David Braybrooke's *Three Tests for Democracy*. Indeed, Braybrooke refers to rights as rule-utilitarian devices. The chief purpose of rights, in Braybrooke's view, is to forestall some of the difficulties that attend act utilitarianism:

> However, one of the basic principles behind the practice of asserting and heeding rights is precisely to forestall general considerations of happiness or well-being and the like from being freely invoked to decide the particular cases embraced by rights. Neither the person asserting the right nor the agent or agents called upon to respect it would normally be able in a particular case to review the alternative possibilities and their consequences really thoroughly. It would be dangerous to empower agents to act on such reviews as they can make: dangerous not only because the agents are liable to bias in their own interests, deviating from the demands of the asserted right in making the reviews; but dangerous also because the agents involved are out of communication with one another and do not have the information necessary to coordinate their actions.[15]

In this view, rights are institutional safeguards to protect us from our own shortsightedness and bias in considering individual cases; rights protect us from the frailty of human nature. Thus, in a world with no human frailty, that is, in a world of perfectly rational and knowledgeable impartial observers, there need be no rights at all. In the real world, utilitarians would admit that rare circumstances could arise in which we would want to say that rights should be given up since in those circumstances failure to give up such rights would lead to disastrous consequences. However, for a few rights, the probability that disastrous consequences would arise that would nullify the right is virtually zero. These rights, in Braybrooke's analysis, are inalienable and inextinguishable:

> Men may regard certain rights as inalienable, considering that the rights in question have emerged from profound social processes worth continuing respect. . . . There is, furthermore, an impressive empirical consideration that offers a strong defense, indefinitely continuing, for the inalienability of certain rights. Mindful of the weaknesses of human nature and aware of the imperfections of provisions for legislation, people believe that they will be safer if certain rights are kept out of reach. . . . Some rights, it might be said, are inalienable and inextinguishable for reasons that no empirical evidence could upset. Could the alienation or extinction of the right to a fair trial be accepted under any social conditions? . . . [I]f a society makes any use of the concept of rights to regulate its affairs then in that society there must be a right to a fair trial.[16]

Inalienable and inextinguishable rights are like other rights in having a ground in utilitarian considerations; however, they differ from other rights in that empirical circumstances that would enable us to give up the practice are not a realistic possibility. In this respect, inalienable rights are like basic laws of nature; falsification by empirical events is not to be expected.

The thrust of points of view like Brandt's and Braybrooke's is to find a place within the structure of utilitarianism itself for our commonsense convictions about rights and justice. Indeed, the convictions and corresponding rights structure arise because adherence to justice and individual rights does work for the greatest good for the greatest number. If a system of rights did not work for the greatest good of the public, it would soon be abandoned. Hence, the rights theorists are correct in emphasizing the importance of rights, but they are incorrect in making them independent. We do not use rights to constrain utilitarianism; rather, utilitarianism is the justification for having rights in the first place.

## Criticism of Contemporary Utilitarianism

Perhaps the place to begin this aspect of the debate is with a hypothetical but very dramatic example described by Bernard Williams:

> Jim finds himself in the central square of a small South American town. Tied up against the wall are a row of twenty Indians, most terrified, a few defiant, in front of them several armed men in uniform. A heavy man in a sweat-stained khaki shirt turns out to be the captain in charge and, after a good deal of questioning of Jim which establishes that he got there by accident while on a botanical expedition, explains that the Indians are a random group of the inhabitants who, after recent acts of protest against the government, are just about to be killed to remind other possible protesters of the advantages of not protesting. However, since Jim is an honored visitor from another land, the captain is happy to offer him a guest's privilege of killing one of the Indians himself. If Jim accepts, then as a special mark of the occasion, the other Indians will be let off. Of course, if Jim refuses, then there is no special occasion, and Pedro here will do what he was about to do when Jim arrived, and kill them all. Jim, with some desperate recollection of schoolboy fiction, wonders whether if he got hold of a gun, he could hold the captain, Pedro and the rest of the soldiers to threat, but it is quite clear from the setup that nothing of that kind is going to work: any attempt at that sort of thing will mean that all the Indians will be killed, and himself. The men against the wall, and the other villagers, understand the situation, and are obviously begging him to accept. What should he do?[17]

Before discussing this example, it should be pointed out that, as noted above, many contemporary utilitarians argue that it is not fair to use what R. M. Hare has called "fantastic examples."[18] After all, any ethical theory can be criticized by creating some far-fetched story that makes the theory look ridiculous but that resembles fantasy rather than reality. Ethical theories are designed to guide human conduct in the real world, and they should be tested against realistic rather than fantastic examples. Thus, utilitarians would argue that the story about Jim and the Indians never could happen and so does not constitute an example with which utilitarianism should be expected to deal.

Critics of utilitarianism might respond, with some justice, that something very much like Williams's example could happen in wartime. However, in fairness to utilitarianism, let us note the objection to the use of examples like this but use it nevertheless to illustrate some commonly held objections to the utilitarian theory.

It would seem that on any utilitarian analysis—even on the complex versions of Brandt and Braybrooke—Jim ought to kill one Indian so that nineteen others would be saved. A utilitarian of any stripe should find Jim's question rather easy to answer. A nonutilitarian might find Jim's question very difficult to answer, however. What makes the question difficult for the nonutilitarian is that something other than future consequences should be considered. Jim must consider not only the number of deaths that might result but also the fact that if he chooses one way, he is a killer, whereas if he chooses another way, he is not. If Jim kills an innocent person, then Jim himself has killed. However, if Jim refuses to kill an innocent person, then we cannot say that Jim has killed the nineteen other people who will die; perhaps we cannot even say that Jim caused the nineteen Indians to be killed. What we think Williams is driving at is the fact that one's position in a situation makes a difference. There is an integrity of a position or role that cannot be captured under the utilitarian umbrella.

Jim does not have the same responsibility to the twenty Indians that Pedro would kill as Jim does to the one Indian he would kill. Of course, it may be that he should kill one to save nineteen, but there are *complications* in that question that no utilitarian can understand.

The utilitarian's failure to consider the position or role one holds in the chain of consequences is symptomatic of a serious deficiency in the way utilitarians consider individuals. John Rawls—at one time an adherent of rule utilitarianism but now an adherent of an important nonutilitarian theory of justice that we will consider later—charges the supposedly individualist theory of utilitarianism with ignoring the distinctions that exist among persons. Since utilitarianism has traditionally been viewed as an individualist theory par excellence, how is it possible that it ignores personalities? Rawls says that utilitarianism extends to society the principle of choice for one man:

> It is customary to think of utilitarianism as individualistic, and certainly there are good reasons for this. The utilitarians were strong defenders of liberty and freedom of thought and they held that the good of society is constituted by the advantages enjoyed by individuals. Yet utilitarianism is not individualistic, at least when arrived at by the more natural course of reflection, in that, by conflating all systems of desires, it applies to the society the principle of choice for one man. . . . There is no reason to suppose that the principle which should regulate an association of men is simply an extension of the principle of choice for one man.[19]

What Rawls seems to be saying is this: Under utilitarian theory, each person strives to maximize his net happiness with due account given to the intensity of his desires. So far, the utilitarian analysis is individualistic in the accepted sense. We then ask what policies a society should pursue. At this point, the utilitarian treats society as a single person. The satisfactions and frustrations of desires of the individuals in society are summed up, with the frustrations of some individuals canceling out the happiness of others. The policy that ought to be adopted is the one that maximizes net happiness. This answer looks at society as an individual who has balanced the gains and losses in order to achieve the greatest balance of happiness. Note the contrast in point of view, however. When Jones's desire for a third martini is denied because Jones wishes to avoid a headache tomorrow, both the desire frustrated and the desire fulfilled are desires of the same individual. However, when policy X, which leads to the greatest happiness on balance, cancels out the wants of Jones in favor of the wants of Smith, the analogy with a single individual is no longer legitimate. The frustration of Smith is not like the frustration of Jones's desire for a third martini.

Even though rule utilitarians and some antiutilitarians might endorse the same rules, and even though some rule utilitarians might support individual rights, utilitarians and many of their critics look at the people governed by the rules in very different ways. The antiutilitarians do not treat people as means for achieving maximum net satisfaction.

Moreover, even though rule utilitarianism is presented as an approach that reconciles utilitarianism with a concern for individual rights, rule utilitarianism might not, in the last analysis, constitute a distinct position of its own. David Lyons has argued that ultimately there is no real difference between rule and act utilitarianism. Consider how

Lyons reduces rule to act utilitarianism. His main point is that if a rule turns out to permit bad consequences in a given situation, utilitarianism would require that the rule be modified to allow for an exception. For example, the rule against lying should allow an exception in cases where lying is necessary to save another person's life. Other exceptions surely will be needed as well. However, as the rule is amended to allow more and more exceptions, it looks more and more like a rule of thumb. Thus, when doubts arise about whether good consequences will follow from following the rule in a specific case, for all practical purposes, we might as well proceed as act utilitarians. That is, for all practical purposes, there is no significant difference between act utilitarians who treat moral rules as rules of thumb and rule utilitarians who allow exceptions to be built into the rule whenever a situation arises where following the rule leads to bad consequences.

If Lyons is right, then the appeal to rule utilitarianism in order to avoid objections to act utilitarianism will not work. Of course, the rule utilitarian could avoid the objection by not allowing exceptions and making the rules inviolable. However, rule utilitarianism will then be committed to rigid, inflexible rules that cannot be violated even when making an exception would produce far greater good than blindly following the rule. Thus, rule utilitarians may be trapped between the erosion caused by an indefinite number of exceptions, which may make the position indistinguishable from act utilitarianism, and inflexible rule worship.

## Conclusion

In general we have criticized utilitarianism for failing to give an adequate account of how to ensure protection of an individual's rights. The story of Jim's dilemma illustrates how utilitarians ignore the roles individuals play in the causal chain. One cannot say what a person ought to do by ignoring past obligations, commitments, and responsibilities. Neither can a state treat society as a superperson so that canceling a desire of Smith to fulfill a desire of Jones is analogous to an individual's frustration of one of his desires to fulfill another desire of his own. In addition, a state should not treat all desires of its citizens as equal. Moreover, it should not expect the less fortunate to make greater sacrifices for the more fortunate simply because total utility is thereby increased.

Utilitarians like Brandt and Braybrooke would respond that their more complex utilitarian formulas do take these complicating factors into account. They would argue that the more complex constructions of the utilitarian formula do not conflict with our widely cherished moral beliefs. For example, Brandt would argue that his formula allows utilitarianism to take account of such antiutilitarian sentiments.

Perhaps, assuming that rule and act utilitarianism really are distinct positions, one might refine utilitarianism so that rules and practices justified on utilitarian grounds were identical with the rules and practices that would be justified on some other, nonutilitarian ethical theory. In other words, utilitarianism and at least one of its main rivals would sanction the same acts as morally right and condemn the same acts as morally wrong. So it might appear that we have a case of the chicken-and-the-egg problem. However, that would be misleading. Even if the utilitarians and their rivals agreed about what was right or wrong, they would continue to disagree on the reasons. For the utilitarian, the rules and practices that protect individual rights are justified because such rules lead to the greatest good for the greatest number. Should the world change and such utilitarian results no longer obtain, the rules and practices that protect individual rights would be surrendered. For the antiutilitarian the fact that the rules no longer bring about utilitarian results need not be a reason for abandoning them. The question now becomes what perspective one should take toward rules that protect individual rights and specify how happiness should be distributed.

We believe that the utilitarian perspective is inadequate, and in the next chapter we develop a competing theory that places ultimate value on the rights of the individual. The answers to the questions of political philosophy are then assessed in terms of how well the rights of individuals are supported. Even if a sophisticated utilitarianism such as Brandt's or Braybrooke's could give the same answers to these questions that we do, we would prefer our rights perspective to that of the utilitarian for two reasons.

First, the utilitarian support for rights rests on too shaky a foundation. As we noted, Braybrooke argued that there is an impressive empirical consideration that offers a strong defense, indefinitely continuing, for the inalienability of certain rights. "Mindful of the weakness of human nature and aware of the imperfections of provisions for legislation, people believe that they will be safer if certain rights are kept out of reach." We suggest that this kind of protection for fundamental rights is too insecure. Let people's attitudes about the frailty of human nature become less pessimistic and human rights will be in danger.

Second, the very complexity of the utilitarian attempt to find a place for human rights suggests that we might do better to let human rights serve as the focal point at the outset. However, the reader is urged to wait until completing chapter 3 before making a final decision on the question. In concluding this chapter, let us return to at least two of our original questions concerning the state. Our first question asked under what conditions a state should actually have authority. A utilitarian would answer that the state should have authority to provide for the public good. Immediately one would then ask our second question: "What is the proper scope or extent of its authority?" To this question, a utilitarian would respond that the extent of the state's authority should be sufficient to enable it to provide for the public good as long as the cost of expanding state authority is taken into account. Let us now consider how an adherent of fundamental human rights would delineate the function of the state and the scope of its proper authority.

# Notes

1. Jeremy Bentham, *Principles of Morals and Legislation* (1789; reprint, Garden City, N.Y.: Dolphin Books, 1961), 17.

2. Ibid., 38–39.

3. This point, using the schema of both our examples, is made by Nicholas Rescher in his *Distributive Justice* (New York: Bobbs-Merrill, 1966), chaps. 2 and 3. This problem could be avoided if the utilitarian simply used the greatest good as the criterion. There is some evidence that Bentham actually gave up the double criterion of the greatest good for the greatest number. See Bhikhu Parekh, ed., *Bentham's Political Thought* (London: Croom Helm, 1973), 309–10.

4. John Stuart Mill, *Utilitarianism* (1863; reprint, Indianapolis: Bobbs-Merrill, 1957), 12.

5. Ibid.

6. Different philosophers sometimes use different terms to mark this distinction. Thus, J. J. C. Smart, a contemporary philosopher who has made important contributions to the development of utilitarianism, uses the term "extreme utilitarianism" to refer to act utilitarianism and "restricted utilitarianism" to refer to rule utilitarianism.

7. Richard B. Brandt, *Ethical Theory* (Englewood Cliffs, N.J.: Prentice-Hall, 1959), 384.

8. Some philosophers argue that a rule utilitarian who formulated the rules that pass the utilitarian test would justify the same actions as an act utilitarian who successfully measured all the consequences of any individual act. The most outstanding book arguing for this equivalence is David Lyons's *Forms and Limits of Utilitarianism* (London: Oxford University Press, 1965), which we will discuss briefly later in the text.

9. John C. Harsanyi, "Morality and the Theory of Rational Behavior," *Social Research* 44 (Winter 1977): 623–56.

10. Ronald Dworkin has discussed this problem under the heading of external and internal preferences in his *Taking Rights Seriously* (Cambridge: Harvard University Press, 1977).

11. John Rawls, *A Theory of Justice* (Cambridge: Harvard University Press, 1971), 30–31.

12. Thus, a contemporary act utilitarian counterpart to Bentham is J. J. C. Smart. A rule utilitarian counterpart to Mill is Richard Brandt. See Smart, "An Outline of a System of Utilitarian Ethics," in *Utilitarianism: For and Against,* ed. J. J. C. Smart and Bernard Williams (Cambridge: Cambridge University Press, 1973), 3–74; and Richard B. Brandt, *A Theory of the Good and the Right* (New York: Oxford University Press, 1979).

13. Richard B. Brandt, "Toward a Credible Form of Utilitarianism," in *Morality and the Language of Conduct,* ed. Hector-Neri Castaneda and George Nakhnikian (Detroit: Wayne State University Press, 1965), 109–10.

14. Brandt, *The Good and the Right,* 290.

15. David Braybrooke, *Three Tests for Democracy: Personal Rights, Human Welfare, and Collective Preference* (New York: Random House, 1968), 39.

16. Ibid., 42–43.

17. Bernard Williams, "A Critique of Utilitarianism," in *Utilitarianism: For and Against,* by J. J. C. Smart and Bernard Williams (New York: Cambridge University Press, 1973) 98–99.

18. See, e.g., R. M. Hare, *Moral Thinking: Its Levels, Method, and Point.* (New York: Oxford University Press, 1981), esp. 131–52.

19. John Rawls, *A Theory of Justice* (Cambridge: Harvard University Press, 1971), 28–29.

20. Lyons, *Forms and Limits of Utilitarianism.*

## Questions for Further Study

1. Bentham's version of utilitarianism has been criticized because it seems to say that it is better to be a satisfied pig than a dissatisfied Socrates. Explain the nature of the objection. Do you agree with it? Why or why not?

2. Hedonistic utilitarianism urges us to maximize happiness. Should we maximize total happiness or average happiness? Does it really make any difference?

3. Explain the "punishment of the innocent" objection to utilitarianism. Does rule utilitarianism avoid that objection? Why or why not?

4. Most philosophers agree that rules have an important role to play in ethics. How do act utilitarians and rule utilitarians treat rules? Which account is better, and why?

5. How did economists change the classical utilitarianism of Bentham and Mill? Does their reformulation enable them to escape the criticisms raised against Bentham and Mill? Why or why not? Is their version subject to new criticisms? If yes, what are these objections?

6. How do utilitarians account for human rights? Evaluate their account.

7. What is the point of the story of Pedro, Jim, and the Indians? Do our moral intuitions regarding that story undermine utilitarianism? Why or why not?

8. Is Lyons right in his claim that rule and act utilitarianism come to the same thing? Why or why not?

## Suggested Readings

Bentham, Jeremy. *Principles of Morals and Legislation.* 1789. Reprint, Garden City, N.Y.: Doubleday, 1961.

Brandt, Richard B. *A Theory of the Good and the Right.* New York: Oxford University Press, 1979.

Braybrooke, David. *Three Tests for Democracy: Personal Rights, Human Welfare, and Collective Preference.* New York: Random House, 1968.

Frey, R. G., ed. *Utility and Rights.* Minneapolis: University of Minnesota Press, 1984.

Gibbard, Alan. *Utilitarianism and Coordination.* New York: Garland Publishing, 1990.

Glover, Jonathan, ed. *Utilitarianism and Its Critics.* New York: Macmillan, 1990.

Hare, R. M. *Moral Thinking: Its Levels, Method, and Point.* New York: Oxford University Press, 1981.

Haslett, D. W. *Moral Rightness.* The Hague: Martinus Nijhoff, 1974.

Lyons, David. *The Forms and Limits of Utilitarianism.* London: Oxford University Press, 1965.

Mill, John Stuart. *Utilitarianism.* 1863. Reprint, Indianapolis: Bobbs-Merrill, 1957.

Regan, Donald. *Utilitarianism and Cooperation.* Oxford: Clarendon Press, 1980.

Sen, Amartya, and Bernard Williams. *Utilitarianism and Beyond.* Cambridge: Cambridge University Press, 1982.

Sidgwick, Henry. *The Methods of Ethics.* 7th ed. Chicago: University of Chicago Press, 1962.

Smart, J. J. C., and Bernard Williams. *Utilitarianism: For and Against.* Cambridge: Cambridge University Press, 1973.

# 3

# Human Rights: Meaning and Justification

The twentieth century unfortunately has seen some of the greatest evils of human history. During the Holocaust, millions upon millions of people were murdered as the Nazis attempted to carry out their goal of exterminating the Jewish people and eliminating other "undesirables" from their Reich. The racist policy of apartheid was a dominant system until recently in South Africa. "Ethnic cleansing" has claimed a still unknown number of victims in the Balkans. Indeed, it sometimes seems, even during the late 1990s, that abuse of our fellow humans is almost everywhere. In its 1996 report, Amnesty International describes violations of basic rights in virtually every corner of the globe. "Arbitrary killings by government forces and armed opposition groups go unpunished and unchecked. Torture is rife. Prisoners of conscience are confined behind bars. Political prisoners face trials that are a travesty of justice—or are jailed with no trial at all."[1] Although in our view the recent record of the United States is superior to that of most other countries, our own history includes a legacy of slavery, racial segregation, gross mistreatment of native peoples, and a continuing battle against racial discrimination.

Many of these gross violations are carried out by governments and other organized political groups. Individuals may be victimized because of their political views or simply because they belong to a racial, ethnic, gender, or religious group that has been targeted by oppressors. It is just this kind of inequality and degradation that the doctrine of human rights is intended to prevent.

The doctrine of human rights is designed to provide certain fundamental protections for individuals against the state, other political and social organizations, and other individuals as well. Such rights create basic protections for the individual that morally may not be ignored, even to provide gains for a greater number of people. Although, as we will see, human rights can be conceived of as devices that promote long-term utility, they may best be thought of as protections for individuals that are of sufficient moral weight to protect us against being sacrificed for the greater good of the greater number. On our view, the principal function of the state is to protect the human rights of its citizens. Unfortunately, as indicated above, states have often been among the greatest abusers of human rights. However, the doctrine of human rights, properly implemented by the state, can provide a powerful protection for all of us against the kind of systematic abuses that have been all too frequent throughout human history.

Our first task will be to clarify the notion of a human right. In particular, the concept of a right, and especially the concept of a human right, must be explained and examined.

## Analysis

### Rights

Compare two universities, university A and university B. In each, it is sometimes the case that a professor grades a student's paper unfairly. The reasons for this vary from case to case, and the incidence of unfairness is no greater at one institution than at the other. What does differ, however, are the methods and procedures for dealing with unfairness when it does arise.

In university A, if students believe their papers have been unfairly graded and if they wish to appeal, they must petition the professor who graded the paper for an appointment. According to the rules of the university, it is entirely up to the professor whether such petitions are granted. Even if the petition is accepted, the rules of the university leave it entirely up to the professor whose fairness is being questioned to decide whether the paper will be reviewed and the grade changed. There is no higher court of appeal. Of course, many faculty members at this university are conscientious and kind men and women. Most would not dream of turning down a student's petition for an appointment. However, according to the rules of the university, whether a professor chooses to act conscientiously and kindly is solely up to that professor. Students have no claim on the faculty, nor are they entitled to impartial review. If some professors choose to act properly and others do not, then, as far as the rules of the university are concerned, it is a matter between them and their own conscience. At university A, then, faculty consideration of student complaints is a gratuity that may or may not be dispensed at will.[2]

In university B, things are quite different. Student complaints of unfairness in grading must be dealt with through established procedures. All complaints must be investigated by faculty previously uninvolved in the case. In university B, it is not up to the professor involved to decide whether the grievance machinery is called into play. Rather, the student is entitled to impartial review upon request.

In university B, but not in university A, students have rights in the area in question. The example illustrates the difference between having and not having rights. The example also brings out the point that rights are entitlements. The students in university B are entitled to impartial review. Their claim to review is not dependent upon faculty goodwill or permission. Indeed, the domain of rights is to be contrasted with that of permissions, on the one hand, and benevolence, on the other.

The notion of an entitlement has justificatory import. If someone is entitled to something, his claim to it is justified, at least prima facie. The justification may be institutional, legal, or moral, depending upon the kind of right considered. Such a justification need not be conclusive. For one thing, rights may clash. My right to ten dollars from Jones and your right to ten dollars from Jones cannot both be honored if Jones has only ten dollars. Moreover, if Jones has only ten dollars, perhaps none of us is justified in claiming it in the first place, all things considered.[3]

If students in university B have a right to impartial review upon request, then they are entitled to such review. And if they are entitled to it, others—in this case, the faculty—are under at least a prima facie obligation to provide such a review. Rights imply obligations in the sense that if some person has a right to something, some other persons are under an obligation either to provide it or at least not interfere with the rights bearer's pursuit of it.[4]

While some philosophers believe rights can be defined in terms of the obligations of others, we suggest that it is of crucial moral importance to distinguish obligations that arise from rights claims from obligations of what may be a different sort, particularly those that arise from noblesse oblige or "one's station and its duties." A useful example has been provided by Richard Wasserstrom. Wasserstrom points out that during the civil rights movement of the late 1950s and early 1960s, white southerners frequently asserted that they had great concern for the welfare of "their Negroes." According to Wasserstrom, "what this way of conceiving most denies to any Negro is the opportunity to assert claims as a matter of right. It denies him the standing to protest the way he is treated. If the white Southerner fails to do his duty, that is simply a matter between him and his conscience."[5]

The white southerner of Wasserstrom's example views kind treatment of blacks as a matter of personal benevolence. If indeed there are any obligations involved, as Wasserstrom's (perhaps confusing) use of the word "duty" may suggest, such obligations do not arise from the correlative rights of the blacks themselves. If we view persons as possessors of rights, we view them as agents, as makers of claims, as beings who are entitled to certain considerations whether or not others feel like going along. It is this aspect of the emphasis on rights that, as we will argue later, accounts for the important connection between human rights, on the one hand, and human dignity, autonomy, and respect for persons, on the other.[6]

It may be objected that to explicate rights in terms of entitlements is to offer a circular account. For what can it mean to say that someone is entitled to something other than that he or she has a right to it?

However, even if the analysis is circular, it is not necessarily unhelpful for our purposes. For our goal is not to offer a formal definition but rather to demonstrate the normative function of rights talk; namely, to demarcate an area of individual inviolability that may not be invaded on grounds of benevolence, social utility, the public interest, or charity.

Perhaps a full analysis of rights would go on to explicate "X is entitled to Y" roughly as "X ought to have Y and it would be impermissible to deprive X of Y in the absence of a compelling justification." If moral rights were at issue, different kinds of moral theories could then provide different sorts of justifications for particular normative judgments about when X ought to have Y and why deprivations would normally be impermissible. Thus, rule utilitarians might see rights as institutional devices that forbid violation of the individual in direct pursuit of utility precisely because such a prohibition would indirectly promote the most utility in the long run. Others might argue, as we will do later in this chapter, that certain fundamental moral entitlements must be protected if persons are to be respected as rational autonomous agents.

For our purposes, then, rights are best construed as entitlements. Legal rights are entitlements that are supportable on legal grounds, while moral rights are entitlements that are supportable, perhaps in the ways suggested above, on moral grounds. What then are human rights? The idea of human rights evolved out of the older tradition of natural rights, which we will now consider.

## Natural Rights

The doctrine of natural rights evolved over a long period of time and was often the center of political and philosophical controversy. The roots of the doctrine go back at least as far as debates among the Sophists of ancient Greece over whether justice is conventional or objective and universal. Plato and Aristotle argued that the nature of justice could be discovered by reason and so was accessible to all rational persons. And the later

Stoic philosophers emphasized a natural law, binding on all men, that takes precedence over the particular laws embodied in human political institutions. As natural laws were held by the Stoics to be independent of existing legal principles, they constituted an Archimedean point from which the legal order could be evaluated.

The concern for the rule of law as manifested in ancient Rome led to further emphasis on the Stoic ideal of a law of nature. In 534 A.D., Emperor Justinian presided over the completion of the *Corpus Iuris Civilis,* a great codebook of Roman law.[7] This codification of the law of the Roman Empire was to have remarkable influence, for one of the great gifts of Rome to later civilizations was appreciation of the significance of the rule of law. Justinian's law books claimed universal validity and so reinforced the Stoic ideal of a law over and above the law of any particular community, applying equally to all. This conception of a "higher" law than that of one's community was acknowledged by many educated Romans during various stages of the empire's development. Perhaps none expressed the idea as well as Cicero, who declared: "There is indeed a law, right reason, which is in accordance with nature; existing in all, unchangeable, eternal. . . . It is not one thing at Rome, and another thing at Athens . . . but it is a law, eternal and immutable for all nations and for all time."[8]

This conception of natural law was further developed by Scholastic philosophers during the Middle Ages. The account defended by Thomas Aquinas has been especially influential. It fitted the Stoic belief in a rational moral order, analogous to an (allegedly) rational natural order, into the framework of Judeo-Christian theology, which sometimes identified moral laws with commands of God or with conceptions of human flourishing built into our very nature by God. Thus, some Scholastic natural law theorists, following ideas of Aristotle, regarded us as social beings by nature, so natural law would tell us that the good for human beings consists at least in part in living in a well-ordered society. Since the natural laws were identified with outpourings of divine reason, they were open to discovery by other rational beings. Aquinas maintained that

> it is clear that the whole community of the universe is governed by divine reason. This rational guidance of created things on the part of God . . . we can call the Eternal Law. . . . But of all others, rational creatures are subject to the divine Providence in a special way . . . in that they control their own actions. . . . This participation in the Eternal Law by rational creatures is called the Natural Law.[9]

Aquinas emphasized that this natural law is a higher law than that of such man-made institutions as the state: "And if a human law is at variance in any particular way with Natural Law, it is no longer legal but rather is a corruption of law."[10] This conception of natural law, like that of the Stoics, provides an external, rational standard against which the laws and policies of particular states are to be measured.

The Scholastic conception of natural law, however, was intimately tied to a theological foundation and tended to be embedded in a theistic political framework. Although natural laws were held to be discernible by reason, they were also held to be promulgated by divine will. The political order, in turn, was held to serve a function determined by that will; namely, the development of distinctively human nature within a given social framework. However, in the seventeenth and eighteenth centuries, growing rationalism and growing individualism led to revision of the classical account of natural law and natural right. Such documents as the French Declaration of the Rights of Man and the American Declaration of Independence asserted the rights of humans qua humans against the state. The foundation of natural law and of the rights of the individual was placed in reason alone, rather than in theology. The political order, in turn, was viewed as an instrument through which diverse and essentially egoistic individuals could pursue their private ends and not as an agency for socialization through which the citizen would become fully human. Natural rights were appealed to in defense of human liberty and autonomy against what came to be perceived as the potentially (and often actually) oppressive power of the state.

However, with the rise of utilitarianism in the nineteenth century, the natural rights approach no longer held a position of dominance in political theory. Utilitarians, with their forward-looking consequentialist ethical theory, regarded only the effects of action or policy as relevant to moral evaluation. Right and wrong were held to depend on consequences, not on allegedly preexisting natural rights. Thus, Jeremy Bentham attempted to relegate the doctrine of natural rights to the graveyard of abandoned philosophies when he held that "Natural rights is simple nonsense: natural and imprescriptible rights, rhetorical nonsense—nonsense upon stilts."[11]

But, as we have seen, a basic problem for utilitarian ethics is how to avoid permitting the oppression of a minority so long as the result is the production of the greatest overall good. The horrors of the Nazi Holocaust and the struggle for the civil rights of black persons in America seem to have motivated many to search for a normative political theory that asserts the inviolability of the individual. While utilitarianism, on any plausible interpretation, would condemn Nazi genocide, many reflective people have regarded the kind of protection utilitarianism provides for the individual as inadequate, resting at best on complex empirical calculations, and have tried to argue for the inviolability of persons on nonutilitarian grounds. Thus, the doctrine of natural rights has resurfaced, shorn of much of its excess metaphysical and theological baggage, in the form of a plea for human dignity and for the kind of treatment that makes possible at least a minimally decent human life. We will refer to the modern version of the doctrine as a doctrine of *human rights,* to indicate that the theoretical framework in which such rights are embedded and justified is independent of theology and of older accounts of natural law. We will reserve the expression *natural rights* for older historical versions of the doctrine.

How then are we to conceive of human rights? Traditionally, natural rights and natural law have been thought of as independent of any given social or political order. Thus, they can serve as external standards for the evaluation of such institutional frameworks. This explains the point of calling a certain class of rights natural. "Natural" has many opposites, including "artificial," "social," "conventional," "abnormal." In the context of natural rights, "natural" is in contrast with "social" and "conventional."

We will follow this account in explicating human rights. Human rights are rights that do not arise from any particular organization of society or from any roles their bearers may play within social institutions. They are to be distinguished from the rights of parents against children, teachers against students, and clients against their lawyers. Instead, they are rights possessed on grounds other than the institutional role of the holders or the nature of the society to which they belong. They belong to human beings as such.[12] Conversely, human rights impose obligations on everyone, regardless of rank or position. Since such rights are not held in virtue of social status, everyone is obliged to respect them.

Human rights also are thought of as morally fundamental. That is, the justification of other rights claims ultimately involves appeal to them. They are the most general of our moral rights. Thus, the right to pursue a hobby in one's spare time can be defended as deriving from a more basic natural right to liberty from interference by others.

Moreover, human rights are general rights, not special rights. Someone, for example, may have the right to limit your freedom because of some special arrangement to which you and he previously had agreed. Thus, if you promised Reed to carry his packages home, then he has the right to have you do your duty, even though you would rather do something else at the time. Such a right is a special right; one "which arises out of special transactions between individuals or out of some special relationship in which they stand to each other."[13] General rights, however, are rights that hold independent of the existence of such special arrangements. Human rights are general rights, then, in that their existence is not dependent upon special relationships or previous agreements that rights bearers may have entered into. Human rights are not only logically prior to social and political institutions, they are logically prior to human agreements as well.

In addition, many writers, including the authors of the Declaration of Independence, have held that such rights are inalienable. If this claim is taken to mean that it is always wrong to fail to honor a claim of human right, we suggest it is mistaken. Since rights claims can clash, situations may arise in which we can honor the fundamental rights of some only at the expense of failing to honor the equally fundamental rights of others. Although this is lamentable, it hardly can be wrong if some such rights are not honored in this sort of context. No other alternative is available.

However, more plausible interpretations of the claim that natural rights are inalienable are available. Perhaps they are inalienable in the sense that they must always be counted fully from the moral point of view, unless waived by the rights bearer under special sorts of circumstances. Thus, if there is a human right to life, perhaps it cannot legitimately be disregarded unless the rights bearer himself decides that life is no longer worth living. Or perhaps human rights are inalienable in the sense that even the rights bearers themselves cannot waive their claims of natural right. Thus, if someone were to say, "I give up my right to life, so go ahead and kill me," this would not entitle anyone to kill the speaker. However, requests for beneficent euthanasia in order to avoid the suffering of a terminal illness may constitute counterexamples to this formulation. Many of us are inclined to accept a waiver of the right to life in such circumstances. Perhaps, most plausibly, natural rights are inalienable in the sense that they cannot be waived except by the bearer and then only to protect another right of the same fundamental order. Thus, in the case of a request for beneficent euthanasia, we may view the patient as waiving the right to life in order to better implement the right to a minimal degree of well-being, which would be destroyed by purposeless suffering.

Someone has a human right to something, then, if and only if (a) he or she is entitled to it; (b) the entitlement is morally fundamental; (c) the right does not arise from the bearer's social status, the prescriptions of a legal system, or from any institutional rules or practices; and (d) it is general in the sense discussed above. In addition, human rights may be inalienable in one of the several plausible senses mentioned. Condition *a* places human rights within the broad category of rights, while the other conditions identify human rights as moral rights of a distinctive and fundamental kind.

## The State as Protector of Individual Rights

As we have seen, utilitarian theorists regard the state as a maximizer of utility. But, as we have also seen, it is far from clear that utilitarianism provides sufficient protection for the individual or, if it does, whether it does so for the right reasons. That is, human rights, as we will see, may be thought of, not implausibly, as rule-utilitarian devices for securing future utility, but this would call into question their fundamental character. They would be means to a more important end rather than rock-bottom protections for the inviolability of individual persons.

This leads to a nonutilitarian view of the state. For, from the point of view of the human rights tradition, it is the function of the state to protect and implement the human rights of its citizens.

Perhaps the most influential spokesman for this tradition in political philosophy was John Locke. Locke, like Hobbes, used the social contract as a device to show that if the state did not exist, we would need to invent it. However, unlike Hobbes, Locke did not view all political and social relations as power relations. For Locke, human behavior was morally constrained by claims of what he regarded as "natural" rights grounded in natural law. It was precisely the job of the state to secure such rights.

But just what rights do people have? It is an embarrassment to rights theory that its proponents have been unable to agree on just which natural or human rights people possess. For example, the American Declaration of Independence speaks of the rights to life, liberty, and the pursuit of happiness. The French Declaration of the Rights of Man speaks of the natural right to security. Many contemporary theorists defend rights to the material prerequisites of at least a minimal degree of well-being—for example, the right to a guaranteed annual income. The Universal Declaration of Human Rights of the United Nations even includes on its list the right to vacations with pay.

Part of this divergence doubtless can be attributed to the fact that not every list is presented as complete. In addition, many lists do not distinguish fundamental from derivative rights. Thus, the right to paid vacations listed in the Universal Declaration, to the extent that its inclusion can be defended at all, probably can be best understood as a derivative right necessary to implement the more fundamental right to the minimal prerequisites of well-being.

Although some disagreements among advocates of human rights can be explained away along such lines, deep differences remain. One such difference that is particularly fundamental concerns the shift in emphasis from negative rights to personal liberty— rights to be free of interference with one's person or property—to the positive rights to material prerequisites of well-being, which have been of concern to many contemporary defenders of human rights. Negative rights impose obligations on others to refrain from interfering with the rights bearer in the protected area. Positive rights, however, impose obligations to provide (or at least to support the sorts of institutions that do provide) those goods and services necessary to secure at least a minimally decent level of human existence.

As many persons regard positive rights with grave suspicion, primarily because they impose extensive obligations to provide things to others, it will be worthwhile to examine both kinds of rights.[14] The political philosophy of the seventeenth-century theorist John Locke is a paradigm example of a position that places nearly exclusive emphasis on negative rights. We will examine Locke's system to see whether such an emphasis is justified. After considering Locke's position, we will compare it with the expanded conception of natural rights suggested by the Universal Declaration of the United Nations. Next, we will consider the views of the critics of the modern expanded notion of rights. We will then be in a better position to decide just which fundamental rights, if any, the state ought to secure.

## John Locke and the Referee State

John Locke (1633–1704) was not only an important political thinker of the first order, indeed one of the founders of the liberal tradition, but he also made important contributions to epistemology and metaphysics. In particular, his *Essay Concerning Human Understanding* is one of the classic texts of the empiricist tradition. *Two Treatises of Government,* Locke's major work in political philosophy, is connected with the English Revolution of 1688, serving both as a stimulus to, and justification of, it. The *Treatises,* particularly the *Second Treatise,* have exerted an important influence on liberal thought up to our own day, particularly through the United States Constitution, which embodies many Lockean ideas.

Both Locke's empiricism and his political philosophy were bulwarks in the seventeenth-century struggle against the entrenched privileges of the monarchy and nobility. Each stresses the tests of experience and reason in an attempt to question dogmatism in both epistemology and politics.

Locke's method in the *Second Treatise* (like that of Hobbes, whom we discussed in chapter 1) is to postulate a state of nature within which no political sovereign exists. He then goes on to consider what sort of government the inhabitants of such a state could rationally establish. Locke may have thought that there actually was such a state of nature. After all, as he points out, the different nation-states can be regarded as being in the state of nature with respect to one another. This, of course, still may be the case. However, the actual existence of such a historical stage in human history is irrelevant to the force of his argument. Rather, as was the case with Hobbes, we can analytically reconstruct Locke's purpose as that of showing what problems would arise if there were no state and hence why it would be rational to create one. Locke, like Hobbes, argues that if there were no such thing as the state, it would be necessary to invent it.

**The Lockean State of Nature.** For Hobbes, the state of nature is one of war between each person and every other person. Life there is depicted as "solitary, poor, nasty, brutish and short." In contrast, Locke's state of nature "has a law to govern it which obliges everyone; and reason which is that law teaches all mankind who will but consult it that being all equal and independent, no one ought to harm another in his life, health, liberty or possessions."[15]

All men, then, are equal in possessing the human, or what Locke would call "natural," rights to life, liberty, and property antecedent to the establishment of government. These rights are negative in that they impose obligations on others to refrain from interfering in the protected areas. Each person is given a sphere of autonomy that others may not violate. However, even though others may not deprive anyone of life, liberty, or possessions, they need not in addition take positive steps to provide property, or maintain life, or supply the conditions under which liberty may be meaningfully exercised. It is one thing, for example, to say that we may not prevent you from seeing a particular movie. It is quite another to say we must provide you with the price of admission. The equality of the state of nature is of the former sort, consisting only of "that equal right that each has to his natural freedom without being subjected to the will or authority of any other man."[16]

Locke then argues that rational persons in the state of nature would establish the institution of private property. This is important, for, as we shall see, one of the terms of the social contract that establishes the state is that the state protect the private property of its citizens. The Lockean argument here is that the world is a storehouse created for the benefit of humans. Consequently, persons may appropriate the goods in the storehouse for their own use. The means of appropriation is labor, "for this labor being the unquestionable property of the laborer, no man but he can have a right to what that is at once joined to, at least when there is enough and as good left for others."[17] Property arises from labor, according to Locke. But, we are told, labor yields property only when there is "enough and as good left over for others." If we assume approximate equality of ability and need, this requirement seems to lead to a fairly egalitarian distribution of goods, where all those willing and able to work end up with about the same amount of possessions.

In the state of nature, the world is a storehouse for human use. If any person were to take more than he could use, his surplus would spoil, thus depriving others of their due. This spoilage problem could be avoided, however, if an imperishable medium of exchange were to be introduced. Money is precisely such a thing. If a farmer, for example, "would give his nuts for a piece of metal, pleased with its color, or exchange his sheep for shells, or wool for a sparkling pebble or diamond, and keep these . . . he invaded not the right of others."[18] For, as we have seen, Locke limits the property owner, not in the amount of possessions that can be accumulated, but rather to the accumulation of what will not spoil, so long as enough and as good is left for others. As long as one's possessions do not spoil and others have the liberty and opportunity to try to accumulate possessions of their own, no limit is set on the amount one might own. Consequently, "it is plain that men have agreed to a disproportionate and unequal possession . . . having by tacit and voluntary consent found out a way how a man may fairly possess more than he himself can use the product of by receiving in exchange for the surplus gold and silver."[19]

Through the introduction of money, the state of nature becomes one of unequal distribution in which some persons amass huge amounts of property through talent, effort, exchanges on the marketplace, and plain good fortune. Locke could have used his restriction on accumulation of personal property in defense of egalitarian distribution of wealth. Instead, he introduced inequality into the state of nature, thereby justifying inequality in civil society. Inequality results because people differ in talent, willingness to exert effort, business acumen in market transactions, and good fortune. Such differences produce unequal possessions. And since, as we will see, people enter civil society at least in part to preserve their property, this inequality will carry over into the state itself.

For Locke, then, inequality of possession is not necessarily injustice. An inequality might be unjust if, for example, it arises from one person stealing what another has legitimately acquired. But it is not unjust if it results from harder work, acuity in trade, or even good fortune.

The right to property, like the other Lockean rights we have considered, is negative. No one is obliged to provide property for anyone else. Rather, the only obligations are those of noninterference. Inhabitants of the state of nature are obligated not to deprive each other of the fruits of their labor or of possessions secured through contractual arrangements for the exchange of such possessions.

What rational consideration might induce an inhabitant of such a state to contract with others to establish political society? Locke cites several reasons, although he does not always clearly distinguish them. For one thing, there is no impartial judiciary to enforce the law of nature. Consequently, persons become judges in their own case. Moreover, after such "judges" hand down their decisions, there is no one to enforce them save the parties to the dispute themselves. This hardly makes either for fair and impartial decision making or for peaceful acceptance of decisions by all parties concerned. Even worse, everyone cannot be counted upon to obey the natural law at all times or to respect the rights of others. Indeed, any dispute might end in conflict. In fact, although the Lockean state of nature, unlike the Hobbesian one, is governed by a moral law, even well-intentioned people who wish to carry out that law might disagree upon its application and enforcement. Locke's state of nature is at best unstable and in danger of reverting to conflict. Consequently, "to avoid the state of war—wherein there is no appeal but to heaven and wherein even the least difference is apt to end where there is no authority to decide between the contenders—is one great reason of men's putting themselves into society and quitting the state of nature."[20]

However, since "no rational creature can be supposed to change his condition for an intention to be the worse,"[21] people do not give up all of their rights to the state. The Lockean state is not the Hobbesian leviathan. Rather, the individual, insofar as he is rational, only surrenders his right to executive and judiciary power. And he does so only on the condition that the state secure his own natural rights to life, liberty, and property.[22] Moreover, since for Locke the state is simply the community formed by the contract, the policy of the state is to be determined by the community or, where unanimous agreement is unobtainable, by a majority vote of the members.[23] Of course, such a majority vote cannot override the basic terms of the social contract; namely, that the individual surrender his right to interpret and enforce the laws of nature and that the state protect his rights to life, liberty, and property within a framework of public law governing everyone equally. The state, then, is the protector of the natural rights of its citizens. For, in Locke's view, it is only to form such a state that it would be rational to leave the state of nature in the first place.

Locke, then, like Hobbes uses a hypothetical social contract to justify a particular kind of state. The contract is hypothetical in that it is one we ourselves supposedly would have signed had we been in the state of nature, not one we actually did sign. Locke is justifying a certain sort of state not by its utility, which might benefit the majority at the expense of the minority, but by showing that all of us would agree to it if we were rational and in the appropriate position in the state of nature. It is our hypothetical consent and not the calculus of social interest that justifies the Lockean state. Of course, we would consent, because consenting is to our mutual advantage, but what justifies the state is the (hypothetical) consent of all rational persons, not that the state produces the greatest good for the greatest number.

The state's function, then, is to protect our fundamental rights. These natural rights, as Locke thinks of them, are primarily negative rather than positive. That is, the rights obligate others, not to provide essential goods and services, but simply to refrain from interfering with each individual's attempt to provide such goods and services for himself. Similarly, the state is conceived of not as a provider of welfare but as a referee. Its job (aside from providing defense against external enemies) is to regulate economic competition by making sure that each competitor respects the rights of others. The Lockean state is an umpire making sure that all citizens, in freely pursuing their own welfare, do not infringe on the similar free enterprise of others.

**Critique of the Lockean Position.** A principal objection to the Lockean account of the state is that it permits too unequal a distribution of economic wealth. As we have seen, inequality is introduced into the state of nature through the medium of money and is perpetuated in society through the social contract. Indeed, significantly unequal distribution of wealth is characteristic of many Western countries and of most other developed societies throughout the world.

In the ideal Lockean state, inequality of wealth arises basically from open competition on the free market. But, in competition for property, children of the previous generation's winners will have far more chance for material success than those of the previous generation's losers. So, in any generation after the first, many competitors will accumulate material goods at least partially because of their advanced starting position rather than because of their own abilities. Although all will have the right to property, they will be unequal in their actual power to amass it. Indeed, the rules of the Lockean free-market competition seem to allow a small group of successful entrepreneurs and their descendants to control indefinitely an overwhelming amount of property. Accordingly, critics of the Lockean minimal state argue that if defenders of an unregulated free market actually favor fair competition, they must supplement the rules of free-market exchange with some form of income, property, or power redistribution. This amounts to allowing other rights over and above the negative right to liberty and consequently entails abandonment of the referee theory of the minimal state.

It might be objected that if someone earns money, he or she is entitled to it.[24] Redistribution is unjust when it involves violation of rights, and persons surely have a right to what they earned. We will discuss this entitlement theory at length in chapter 4, but perhaps the following will suffice for now. For people to be entitled to what they acquire in the free market, the initial conditions under which bargaining takes place must be fair. But the initial bargaining positions are not fair if some people are so deprived of basic necessities and education that they cannot develop skills or compete with any real chance of success. Accordingly, the very idea of an entitlement presupposes at least a minimal welfare base that guarantees each competitor access to education, health care, and adequate diet and other necessities. Thus, the protest that redistributive measures fail to respect the entitlements of property owners is open to the objection that such entitlements can arise only when redistributive measures guarantee fair access to the competition for property in the first place.

The case that fairness requires more than minimal Lockean rights to liberty also can be based upon Locke's own model of the social contract. The usefulness of the contract model is that it can function as a test for fairness. If we ourselves would agree to a particular social contract under reasonable conditions of choice, the terms of the contract arguably are fair. Conversely, if the terms are such that it would be irrational for us to consent to them, they arguably are unfair. In order to test the fairness of Locke's minimal state, then, we can ask whether contract makers agree to the social contract that creates it.

Locke assumes that the contract makers would build the economic inequality found in the state of nature into the structure of political society. But surely this assumption is questionable. Why would the have-nots in the state of nature enter such an inegalitarian society in the first place? Surely, as Locke himself acknowledges, they would sign the contract only if they realized some gain from doing so. The rule of law, as Locke would argue, is indeed a gain, but it is much more of a gain for those who have property that the law can protect than for the poor. It seems plausible, then, that rational contractors would agree to enter the state only if they were guaranteed at least a minimal level of goods and services that would enable them to function as citizens and to benefit from the protection of the law in the first place.

In addition to redistributive arguments based on the requirement of fair competition (arguments that, on some interpretations of what fairness requires, may have quite strong redistributive implications), we can also argue that the very factors that guarantee Lockean rights to liberty also count in favor of positive rights to necessities. After all, liberty surely is important, because it allows us to determine the course of our own lives and to function autonomously. But, arguably, medical care, education, food, and shelter also are necessary if we are to develop as autonomous agents with plans for a life worth living.

Thus, even if people are entitled to what they earn, it does not follow that such an entitlement is absolute. For persons may also have positive rights to sufficient goods and services to make possible at least a minimally decent human existence. If so, persons may not have an absolute right to everything they earn. Rather, they may be obligated to contribute to efforts designed to satisfy the basic needs of others. Proponents of the entitlement theory, then, cannot simply assume that the only fundamental rights are Lockean negative ones.[25]

Consequently, defenders of the minimal state, which protects only negative rights to liberty, are open to the charges that (1) the economic competition it referees is unfair; (2) the inequalities it sanctions are not likely to be acceptable to all rational individuals under reasonable conditions of choice; and (3) the exclusive emphasis on negative rights is arbitrary.

We conclude that Locke's general account of the principal function of the state is sound. That function should be to protect the natural or human rights of its citizens. However, as our discussion suggests, it does not follow that the state's exclusive concern should be with negative rights to liberty, as exercised in the free market. As we have seen, there is a case for what might be called positive rights, rights to the receipt of basic goods and services, as well.

## Positive Rights: The Universal Declaration of Human Rights and the Welfare State

The Universal Declaration of Human Rights was adopted and proclaimed by the General Assembly of the United Nations on 10 December 1948. An examination of this document reveals that many of the rights included go far beyond the negative ones protected by Locke's referee state. For example, consider the following articles:

> Article 22: Everyone, as a member of society . . . is entitled to realization . . . in accordance with the organization and resources of each State, of the economic, social, and cultural rights indispensable for his dignity and the free development of his personality.
>
> Article 25: (1) Everyone has the right to a standard of living adequate for the health and well being of himself and his family, including food, clothing, housing and medical care and necessary social services. . . .
>
> Article 26: Everyone has the right to education. Education shall be free, at least in the elementary and fundamental stages.

Unlike Lockean rights, which obligate others not to interfere with personal liberty, the positive rights of the Universal Declaration require more. In addition, they obligate each of us to support or, where they do not exist, work for the creation of institutions that can provide the necessary goods and services. The state, which is presumably the fundamental political unit capable of guaranteeing such rights, becomes responsible for the welfare of its citizens as well as their liberty.

**The Critique of Positive Rights.** The concept of positive natural or human rights has been criticized on several grounds. We will consider some of the most important here, leaving a fuller account of other significant issues involved for later consideration.

A principal objection to the kinds of social and economic rights mentioned in articles 22, 25, and 26 of the Universal Declaration is that they do not fulfill some of the conceptual requirements for natural rights. The first requirement is that of practicality. As Maurice Cranston points out:

> The traditional "political and civil" rights can . . . be readily secured by fairly simple legislation. Since those rights are for the most part rights against government interference with a man's activities, a large part of the legislation needed has to do no more than restrain the government's own executive arm. This is no longer the case when we turn to "the right to work," "the right to social security," and so forth. . . . For millions of people who live in those parts of Asia, Africa, and South America where industrialization has hardly begun, such claims are vain and idle.[26]

Moreover, it is held that natural or human rights must be rights that impose obligations on everyone. Yet such rights as the right to work or to free education seem to be, at best, rights against one's government and not rights against all humankind.[27] Since social and economic rights fail these tests of practicality and universality, they cannot be natural rights.

Yet another objection rests on an alleged important conceptual difference between positive and negative rights. Negative rights, by definition, impose obligations to refrain from acting in proscribed ways. Positive rights impose obligations to act in a required manner. But, so the objection goes, no one is morally required to perform the kinds of acts enjoined. Such acts may be beneficent and altruistic and, as such, should be encouraged. However, they are not morally obligatory. Thus, it may be praiseworthy for a family to give half its annual income to those less affluent, but they are hardly blameworthy if they fail to do so. According to this objection, then, there are no positive natural rights. For if there were positive natural rights, people would be obligated not simply to refrain from harming others but to go out of their way to benefit others. And, it is held, there is no such obligation.

Sometimes positive rights are criticized on the grounds that their implementation is incompatible with the attainment of other important goods. Thus, it frequently is claimed that the implementation of positive rights would involve drastic and unjustified restrictions on liberty. For in order to appropriate resources needed to honor positive-rights claims, the state would have to limit the right of owners to do with their property what they will. One cannot spend for oneself that portion of one's income that the government taxes in order to make Medicaid or welfare payments to others. Indeed, some critics have gone so far as to characterize the welfare state as a near slave-master that in effect forces people to work so that it can appropriate earnings for the support of others.[28]

To review, positive rights have been criticized on the grounds that (a) they are impractical since they cannot be readily secured by fairly simple legislation, (b) they do not impose universal obligations, (c) they impose positive obligations to act when there can be no such obligation, and (d) their implementation would require extensive violations of the right to liberty. Are these objections decisive?

**A Response to the Critique.** While critics are right to worry that with the addition of positive rights, the idea of natural or human rights may become too bloated, their wholesale dismissal of positive rights is open to question. Indeed, some contemporary philosophers have argued that the whole positive-negative rights distinction is a confused one and that all rights have positive and negative elements. Thus, as Henry Shue argues, if the negative right to liberty is to be significant, citizens have a positive obligation to provide the resources to support the police and judicial system.[29] Similarly, all rights may sometimes require us simply to refrain from harming others and at other times to provide positive aid. Before deciding whether the distinction between positive and negative rights makes sense, however, we need to assess points *a–d* summarized above.

Consider the practicality objection. According to this objection, positive rights, such as a right to a decent standard of living, are impossible for less developed and less affluent countries to implement, and so such states cannot be obligated to honor them. It surely is true that poor nations will have a harder time satisfying social and economic rights claims than will rich countries. In some cases, they may find it impossible. However, note that exactly the same situation can arise with respect to negative rights. A technologically underdeveloped country may not have the efficient means of communication and transportation, or the legal system, so necessary to prevent acts of violence or even the extermination of one group by another. Here we should note that article 22 specifies that each country is obligated to honor social and political rights in accordance with its available resources. In other words, each state (and individual, for that matter) is obligated to do what it can in light of its individual situation.[30] This applies to negative and positive rights alike. Both kinds of rights need support if they are to be enjoyed.

What about the requirement of universality, which states that natural rights impose obligations on everyone? It supposedly follows from this requirement that positive rights cannot be human rights. For, in this view, the bearers of positive rights have claims only against their own governments, not on everyone wherever they may be. For example, if you have a negative right to liberty, everyone—even people on the other side of the world—is under an obligation to avoid illegitimate interference with your activities. There seems to be no conceptual difficulty here, for the obligation imposed does not call on anyone to perform any positive act but only to refrain from acting in certain proscribed ways. Suppose, however, you have the positive right to a free education. Surely, it is implausible to say that inhabitants of China have an obligation equal to anyone else's to provide you with the needed schools. Rather, it is up to your government to provide the needed institutions, and so the scope of your positive right is limited.

While we agree that rights claims can become unduly inflated and acknowledge that individuals should not be reduced to mere means for satisfying the positive rights of others, we suggest nevertheless that this objection to positive rights is overstated. The distinction it attempts to draw does not stand up under examination. True, it is the state's job to implement positive rights, but this is often true of negative rights as well. If you have a negative right to liberty, the primary obligation imposed is the negative one of noninterference. But, as in Lockean theory, it may be rational to delegate to the state the authority to enforce laws designed to protect liberty. Of course, it is one thing to say that the state ought to protect citizens from illegitimate interference with their activities and quite another to say that the state ought to provide positive goods and opportunities. But, in either case, the conceptual point remains the same. The special responsibilities of the state do not replace those of private citizens. Rather, the good state is an instrument through which citizens can most efficiently discharge their obligations. Thus, in the case of both negative and positive rights, such obligations are not restricted to one's fellow citizens. Moreover, while the state may be the primary instrument for discharging our positive obligations that arise from human rights, these obligations may not simply disappear at the nation's borders. The issues of ethics in international affairs are complex, however, and we will devote special attention to them in a later chapter.

What about claim *c,* which maintains that there can be no positive obligations? This claim seems simply to beg the very question at issue. Simply to assume that we can't be obligated to do something (rather than refrain from doing something) is just to state what is being argued for. One cannot establish that there are no positive obligations as a conclusion by simply asserting that very same point as a premise.

Finally, would recognition of positive rights require extensive violations of the negative right to liberty? Is it ever justifiable to infringe on someone's liberty to implement a positive right? This issue will be discussed more fully in chapter 4, but some important points need to be considered here as well.

There is a danger that positive rights can become so bloated that the individual becomes a mere resource for satisfying the claims of others. This is the worry of the libertarians who fear that the welfare state will turn productive citizens into natural resources for benefiting the less fortunate. We agree that there is a genuine problem in specifying just where positive rights claims become so extensive as to violate the liberty of others, but we suggest that the libertarian worry is not justifiable.

Thus, as Henry Shue points out, negative rights may also impose positive obligations that can threaten liberty.[31] How much can the state ask you to give up to support the police, who in turn protect others from coercion? Can't the state ask you to pay taxes to support the court and prison system that may protect citizens from assault by criminals? Negative rights, when enforced and protected by the state, impose positive obligations just as positive rights do. The very same problem arises for each kind of right.

Moreover, the right to a minimum standard of well-being requires no more than protection from the acts of others—just the kind of protection required for a right to liberty. For example, suppose a factory owner moves one of his plants to an even more profitable location. Since the factory to be closed is the chief industry in this small town, a large number of people will simply be unable to support themselves. Hasn't the right to a minimum standard of living been violated by the action of the factory owner in just the same way that a kidnapper violates a person's freedom?

Defenders of the traditional distinctions would say that there is a difference between actively and intentionally harming another and having the harm result as the unintended by-product of some other action. That reply might apply to a natural disaster, such as having a tornado destroy the factory. But moving a factory is not like having a factory destroyed by a tornado. Moving a factory is an intentional human action, and the owner may foresee the harm it causes (just as a violent criminal may know his action will cause harm). Of course, what distinguishes the owner from the criminal is intent and motivation. But perhaps basic rights need to be protected from violators with good or neutral motives as well as from those with bad motives. Otherwise, the rights would not be basic.

In our view, Shue's claim that the negative-positive rights distinction is a confused one does have force. Perhaps we should abandon the distinction and conceive of all rights as imposing both positive and negative obligations.

Whether or not the positive-negative distinction should be dispensed with, we conclude that arguments *a–d* against positive rights fail. Our discussion does call the wholesale critique of positive rights into question. Thus, either there is as good a case for positive rights as for negative ones, or, if Shue is correct, no rights are altogether positive or altogether negative. Rather, each right imposes both negative and positive obligations depending upon context. In either case, the Lockean's exclusive emphasis on the "negative" right to liberty has been misplaced. The case for the minimal state based on the assertion that the only human rights the state legitimately can protect are purely negative freedoms from interference by others is far from self-evident. This issue will be pursued further in our discussion of justice in the next chapter. However, our arguments so far strongly suggest that, on the contrary, claims to at least minimal levels of welfare warrant equal protection as well.

If these arguments have force, the real question is not whether we have positive as well as negative rights. Rather, the real question is what fundamental entitlements must be protected if our status as rational and autonomous agents is to be protected. Our discussion suggests, then, that if claims based on appeal to human rights are justified, these rights claims include entitlements to the basic necessities for a minimal standard of living as well as entitlements to be free of coercion by others. This does not mean that such economic and social rights must be given constitutional status, as in the American Bill of Rights, for, as we will argue later, they may best be implemented through the democratic political process rather than through the courts.[32] Nevertheless, we conclude that some claims made on the basis of positive human rights are as justified as some claims made on the basis of negative rights.

But are any claims of human rights justified? Let us now turn to the issue of whether any claim to a human right can be justified, warranted, or adequately supported.

## Justification

We can show that people have justified claims based on human rights by showing that they have fundamental moral entitlements of the kind specified in the first section of this chapter; namely, entitlements that are not due to social, institutional, or legal status or rules but are general and perhaps inalienable. In this lies the importance of analysis. If we do not have an adequate analysis, we cannot be clear about what conditions must be satisfied if a human rights claim is to be justified.

But how are we to show that claims that appeal to human rights are justified? That is, how can we show that the conditions specified in the first part of the chapter are satisfied? While a full treatment of the issue would require a long digression into ethical and metaethical theory, we believe that at least a plausible case for human rights can be developed here.

### The Egalitarian Argument

When unequal treatment is regarded as unjust, it is often because it seems to ignore the basic similarity of all affected. Those who receive beneficial treatment do not seem to be significantly different from those who do not, and so the inequality is held to be arbitrary and unfair.

This type of egalitarian argument is often employed in defense of human rights. The point of the argument is that in view of the factual equalities or similarities between persons, it is arbitrary to distinguish between them with respect to such rights. Since human rights are entitlements to those goods and opportunities that make a distinctively human sort of life possible, all humans are sufficiently alike to qualify as possessors. As John Locke puts it, "there [is] nothing more evident than that creatures of the same species and rank . . . born to all the same advantages of nature and the use of the same faculties should also be equal one amongst another without subordination and subjection."[33] Locke can be read here as maintaining that given that humans are basically similar (equal in fact), it would be irrational to regard some humans as having a greater claim than others to fundamental rights.

Unfortunately, there are difficulties with this type of argument. First, even if all humans are so similar that if anyone has human rights then everybody does, how do we know anyone has such rights in the first place? Second, although it may be conceded that humans are alike (equal) or nearly alike in some respects, they are notoriously different (unequal) in others. Locke's argument is that given human similarity, any presumption of superiority would be groundless. It is simply arbitrary, and hence irrational, to treat equals unequally. But are humans sufficiently similar or alike? The egalitarian must show that it is the similarities and not the differences that are relevant to justifying claims of natural right. Persecution of minorities, discrimination against women, slavery, and genocide all have been defended by reference to allegedly relevant differences between victims and oppressors.

The egalitarian surely will reply that it is the similarities and not the differences that are relevant where possession of human rights is concerned. Common human qualities that often have been cited as the grounds of such rights include rationality, the capacity to feel pain and undergo suffering, the ability to form a rational plan of life, and the need for affection and companionship. But even within these categories, people differ. How is the egalitarian to show that it is the differences that are actually irrelevant?

There are at least two problems, then, with the egalitarian argument. At best, it seems to show only that if anyone has natural rights, all relevantly similar beings have the same rights. Second, even if it can be shown that some persons have such rights, it still must be shown that all humans are relevantly similar to the rights bearer(s).

These problems are not necessarily immune to resolution. In what follows, we suggest lines of response that may be satisfactory. While no presently available defense of a fundamental moral outlook is philosophically uncontroversial, this applies as much to utilitarianism or other moral theories (as well as to moral skepticism and relativism) as to the human rights approach. In moral philosophy, the choice is probably not between strict knock-down, drag-out proof of one's moral position, on the one hand, and irrational whim, on the other. We hope that by developing lines of argument that can be advanced by proponents of human rights, we can show that there are good theoretical reasons for accepting human rights as fundamental elements of our moral system.

## Human Rights, Human Dignity, and Respect for Persons

Human rights, as we have indicated, might be compatible with a utilitarian framework. That is, some utilitarians might argue for human rights on the grounds that a moral system that provided such protections would produce more utility in the long run than one that lacked them. Sophisticated rule utilitarians might even agree that human rights function as trumps that can override the direct appeal to utility in judging individual acts, because in the long run it produces more utility to block such direct appeal in fundamental areas than to allow it. For example, if we were to try to decide in each individual case whether it promotes utility to prohibit a citizen in a democracy from speaking freely, we often would decide wrongly because we might be influenced by personal bias, our own political views, and the emotions of the moment in a crisis. A human right to liberty could promote utility in the long run by prohibiting such interference and allowing society to enjoy the benefits of open debate on issues.

However, even if, in spite of some of the criticisms of utilitarianism advanced in chapter 2, such a rule–utilitarian case for human rights can be made good, it does not make human rights fundamental moral commodities. Rather, such rights are regarded as means to the production of greater utility. Another approach to justifying human rights regards them as more fundamental, as protections for the fundamental dignity and respect due to all persons as human beings, as rational agents with goals and purposes of their own. It is this nonutilitarian approach that we will explore below.

**Rights as Fundamental Moral Commodities.** Consider a society whose moral code does not include the concept of a claim of right. People in it may act benevolently most of the time and are not cruel or unfeeling. Indeed, they may be imagined as kinder and more sensitive than the inhabitants of our own planet. What such a culture would lack is the notion of persons as makers of claims upon one another, as having basic entitlements that others are obligated to respect. And if occasional improper treatment occurs, there is no cause to complain: "The masters, judges and teachers don't have to do good things, after all, for anyone. . . . Their hoped for responses, after all, are gratuities, and there is no wrong in the omission of what is merely gratuitous. Such is the response of persons who have no concept of rights."[34] In a society without the concept of rights, we all would be in a position analogous to that of the students at university A or the southern blacks as viewed through the framework described by Wasserstrom in the examples we discussed earlier. We would lack the conceptual apparatus for asserting that some treatment was owed to us as a matter of right. If we are mistreated, that is a matter between our oppressor and his own conscience.

Rights, we are suggesting, are fundamental moral commodities because they enable us to stand up on our own two feet, "to look others in the eye, and to feel in some fundamental way the equal of anyone. To think of oneself as the holder of rights is not to be unduly but properly proud, to have that minimal self-respect that is necessary to be worthy of the love and esteem of others."[35] Conversely, to lack the concept of oneself as a rights bearer is to be bereft of a significant element of human dignity. Without such a concept, we could not view ourselves as beings entitled to be treated not simply as means but also as ends.

To respect persons as ends, to view them as having basic human dignity, seems to be inextricably bound up with viewing persons as possessors of rights, as beings who are owed a vital say in how they are to be treated and whose interests are not to be overridden simply to make others better off. Consequently, to opt for a code of conduct in which rights are absent is to abandon the kind of respect for persons and human dignity at issue. This price, we submit, is simply too high. Our answer to the questions of why people should be regarded as having claims of fundamental rights at all is simply that a world in which no such claims were ever made or ever regarded as justifiable would be a world that was morally impoverished, and very significantly so.[36]

**The Challenge of Elitism.** What if members of some special group were to accept the considerations cited above but maintain that only members of their elite or superior group possessed any rights at all? Others, perhaps blacks, perhaps Jews, perhaps women, perhaps the less intelligent, are held to be inferior or not fully human. In this elitist view, there may well be reasons for recognizing fundamental rights. But, the elitists hold, in view of allegedly significant differences among humans, no reason has been given for thinking such rights belong to all humans, that they are human rights rather than rights belonging to some elite subgroup.

In evaluating this kind of elitist challenge to equality, one must first get clear exactly what the ground of the proposed discrimination is supposed to be. Often proponents of an elitist morality will base their discrimination on alleged empirical differences between their own group and the supposed inferiors they victimize. For example, women have been held to be too emotional or too unaggressive to hold responsible positions. Slave-owners in pre–Civil War America argued that blacks were too simple and childlike to handle freedom, while allegations about differences in the brain size of white ethnics from Eastern Europe were used to justify immigration restrictions against them earlier in this century.

The proper line of defense against such elitists is to challenge their allegedly factual story of the difference between them and their supposed inferiors. That blacks are less sensitive than whites, that Jews are conspiring to control economic and political power, that women are unfitted for professional success, and other such elitist generalizations are blatant falsehoods that should have been laid to rest long ago. Moreover, elitism of this sort is often applied inconsistently. Thus, proponents of racial segregation in the South sometimes justified their view by appealing to unequal educational attainments of black and white pupils. Leaving aside the point that segregation itself, to say nothing of poverty and deprivation, may have been responsible for what differences there actually were, the most that such an argument justifies is segregation by educational attainment, not by race.

What if the elitist does not appeal to alleged factual differences between his group and those who are oppressed? What if the elitist instead simply asserts that his group, by virtue of its very nature, is superior—men, by their very nature, should be dominant; the more intelligent should control the less intelligent; whites (or blacks) just are the superior group? How can such elitist moralities be rationally discredited when they do not rest on empirical claims?

A particularly plausible response to such assertions is that they are arbitrary. They seem to be baseless assertions of purely personal preference rather than expressions of a reasoned moral position. As Bernard Williams has pointed out, "The principle that men should be differently treated . . . merely on grounds of their color is not a special sort of moral principle but (if anything) a purely arbitrary assertion of will like that of some Caligulan ruler who decided to execute everyone whose name contained three 'R's.'"[37]

But can't the elitist respond that if elitism with respect to rights is arbitrary, so too is the commitment to equal rights? Why should equality be in a privileged position? If "All persons are not moral equals" is arbitrary, why isn't "All persons are moral equals" arbitrary as well?

However, the egalitarian has a number of effective responses to this move. In particular, elitism of a fundamental kind may beg the question against its victims. Thus, it is important to note that within the elitist group itself, characteristics that all humans possess are accorded significant recognition. These include the capacity to experience pain and suffering, the desire to be treated with respect and dignity, the sense of oneself as a conscious entity persisting over time with distinctive wants, ideals, and purposes, as well as the ability to view the world from a distinctive, self-conscious point of view. Among themselves, white supremacists, for example, weigh these factors heavily. They do not inflict gratuitous pain on one another, destroy or enslave one another on whim alone, or regard each other's life plans as of no value whatsoever. Rather, they seem to hold that each member of the elite should be treated just as the egalitarian thinks all human beings should be treated.

But in view of the basic similarities among all humans, discrimination at the fundamental level seems ad hoc. It seems unintelligible that a mere difference in skin color
could by itself negate the importance of the factors enumerated above—the factors
whose importance is already acknowledged within the elitist community itself. Thus, it
hardly seems unreasonable to require the elitist to spell out the connection between any
proposed ground of discrimination and the worth of individual persons. Indeed, in view
of the great plethora of elitist positions—for example, anti-Semitism, sexism, various
forms of racism—it seems far from arbitrary once again to place the burden of proof on
the elitist.[38] In practice, elitists themselves give testimony to the arbitrariness of their
fundamental discriminatory principles, since they generally seek to justify their discrimination by appeal to principles intelligible to everyone. Thus, one is far more likely
to hear "Women should not hold responsible positions because they are emotionally fitted for raising children" than "Women should not hold responsible positions because
they are women."

Second, it is doubtful that elitist principles could withstand *impartial* scrutiny. Would
reasonable, impartial people find it justifiable to deny people the most fundamental of
rights on such grounds as skin color, religion, gender, ethnicity, or sexual preference? We
believe not. It seems far more plausible to think that people hold such elitist views
because they have not considered the matter impartially but only from their own perspective, usually that of the allegedly elitist group itself. Of course, actual elitists, such as
the Nazis or various contemporary racist groups, may refuse to view things impartially,
but then they must pay the philosophical price. That is, they cannot claim their position
is justifiable in the sense that it has grounds that can appeal to impartial, unbiased
observers. They have in fact opted out of the process of justification. While they may
continue to hold their position, they have forfeited any basis for claiming that their view
is defensible in the arena of public reason and debate.

The case for claiming that certain fundamental rights are human rights, equal rights
of all human beings as such, is that if there are such rights at all, the denial of such rights
on grounds such as race, religion, gender, sexual preference, and ethnicity is arbitrary and
cannot be supported from an impartial perspective. This does not imply the absurdity
that all people should be treated identically in all respects. For example, only the best
players ought to make the all-star team. However, it does suggest that attempts to
exclude some humans from the basic fundamental rights that ought properly to belong
to all of us should be condemned as among the most serious crimes against humanity.

## Summary

Our discussion suggests that human rights are justified as conditions that must be satisfied if humans are to live and develop as autonomous moral agents. They protect us from
being reduced to mere means in the pursuit of the overall social good and being victims of oppressive elitist moralities. While the claim that human rights are fundamental
requires more examination than we can give it here, we hope to have made a plausible
case for it. (Remember that human rights also might be viewed as rule-utilitarian
devices for securing the greatest good in the long run.) While it is doubtful whether
claims about human rights (or any other fundamental basis for morality) can be strictly
proved in any mathematical sense, a moral perspective based on rights does seem to cap-
ture our firmest intuitions about the foundations of our moral view. Those who demand
strict proof for everything probably will not find it in ethics, but they probably will not

find it in many other domains either. It is important, therefore, not to apply a standard to ethics that is so high that it would be judged absurd in other contexts. So while we clearly have not proved that some human rights claims are justified, we hope that we have advanced significant reasons for accepting such a conclusion, reasons that when fully developed and examined will indicate even more forcefully that all humans have fundamental rights that it would be terribly wrong to violate. Perhaps the ultimate justification of the human rights perspective, however, is its application in practice, a task to which we will turn in later chapters. Human rights in the actual world are sometimes implemented and, unfortunately, far too often violated by states. Accordingly, let us turn from questions of theory to issues of implementation and the role of governments in that process.

In our view, human rights are those entitlements whose protection and implementation are needed to safeguard human dignity, autonomy, and respect. In claiming that the human rights approach is warranted, we are claiming that it would not be discredited by extended evaluation of its theoretical justification and its implications for action and that it would survive such an examination at least as well as any of its competitors.

What are the implications of the human rights perspective for political philosophy? Surely, those who believe that humans should be regarded as possessors of fundamental rights, whether such rights are regarded as natural ones or as rule-utilitarian devices, would be sympathetic to the Lockean view of the state. According to Locke, the primary function of the state is to protect the fundamental rights of the individual. States can be ranked according to how well they fulfill this function. Moreover, the Lockean approach provides a framework for criticizing the excesses of the state. The state calls into question its own reason for being when it violates the fundamental rights of its citizens.

Unlike Locke, however, we argue for both positive and negative rights. Implementation of positive rights is just as much a prerequisite of promoting human dignity, autonomy, and self-respect as is implementation of negative ones. Accordingly, the proper response to a Lockean defender of exclusive emphasis on negative rights is that there seems to be no way of defending one kind of right without also defending the other. At the very least, perhaps the burden of proof has been shifted so that it is up to the defenders of purely negative rights to mount a defense of their position.

We conclude that the primary function of the state is to protect and, where necessary, implement the positive and negative human rights of its citizens. Although any attempt to list all human rights is likely to fail, surely any such list should include the rights to liberty and life, on the one hand, and to the material prerequisites of a minimally decent human life on the other. (The content of these rights will be discussed in the remaining chapters of this book.)

Moreover, rights can clash. Perhaps my right to well-being can be secured only by failing to protect your right to liberty. In cases of scarcity, it may not be possible to honor everyone's claim of right. Such conflicts among competing rights claims constitute especially poignant moral dilemmas, for any resolution is imperfect from the moral point of view. Thus, even a satisfactory human rights position is only a necessary constituent of an acceptable framework for adjudication of moral disputes. Where conflicts between competing claims arise, appeal is frequently made to social justice. Parties to the conflict may request, for example, that the dispute between them be justly settled. Accordingly, if one function of the state is to protect and implement natural rights, it is also plausible to think that it is the state's responsibility to adjudicate the clash of rights justly. In fact, the need for fair, just, and impartial adjudication of competing rights claims forms the basis in Locke's argument for the transition from the state of nature to the state of government. In the next chapter, we shall extend the human rights approach by examining issues that arise where just adjudication of competing claims is at issue. What is justice and how is to be understood?

## Notes

1. *Amnesty International Report, 1996* (London: Amnesty International Publications, 1996), 1.

2. Joel Feinberg, in "The Nature and Value of Rights" (*Journal of Value Inquiry* 4, no. 4 [1970]: 243–57), provides an example of a world without rights. We rely heavily on Feinberg's treatment here, particularly his claim that in a world without rights, good treatment would be regarded as a gratuity.

3. This has been pointed out by Joel Feinberg in "Wasserstrom on Human Rights," *Journal of Philosophy* 61 (1964): 642–43.

4. For discussions of rights and obligations, see, e.g., John Hospers, *Human Conduct* (New York: Harcourt, Brace & World, 1961), 386; and S. I. Benn and R. S. Peters, *The Principles of Political Thought: Social Foundations of the Democratic State* (New York: Free Press, 1964), 102.

5. Richard Wasserstrom, "Rights, Human Rights, and Racial Discrimination," *Journal of Philosophy* 61 (1964): 640. Our discussion of the nature of human rights is greatly indebted to Wasserstrom's article, which was particularly noteworthy for applying the insights of analytic philosophy to important social issues at a time when philosophy was dominated by the view that substantive issues were not within the scope of legitimate philosophical analysis conceived of as primarily linguistic and conceptual.

6. Even if, as some philosophers claim, rights are definable in terms of obligations, it does not follow that rights talk and obligation talk have the same practical or pragmatic consequences. Rights talk emphasizes the status of persons as active makers of claims, as possessors of entitlements that should be honored, rather than as passive recipients of the duties of others. Hence, there are practical reasons for adopting the vocabulary of rights even if rights are nothing but the reverse side of obligations. We doubt, however, whether rights can be fully defined in terms of obligations. As the example of the attitude of Wasserstrom's "white Southerner" illustrates, it seems possible that some obligations may not involve correlative rights. A related example concerns the possibility of obligations that arise from one's station and its duties. For example, the faculty of university A may have professorial obligations to hear student complaints fairly, but the students have no correlative right to such fair treatment.

7. See A. P D'Entreves, *Natural Law: An Historical Survey* (New York: Harper & Row, 1965), 17 ff. Our historical survey of the natural rights tradition relies heavily on D'Entreves's excellent study.

8. Cicero, *Republic,* trans. G. W. Featherstonhaugh (New York; G. & C. Cavill, 1829), 31.

9. Thomas Aquinas, *Summa Theologica,* 1ae, 2ae, quae 91, arts. 1 and 2.

10. Ibid., 1ae, 2ae, quae 95, art. 2.

11. Jeremy Bentham, *Anarchical Fallacies,* in *The Collected Papers of Jeremy Bentham,* vol. 2, ed. John Bowring (Edinburgh, 1843); reprinted in A. I. Melden, ed., *Human Rights* (Belmont, Calif.: Wadsworth, 1970), 32.

12. This is not to deny that such rights also may belong to wider classes of beings, such as higher animals or intelligent extraterrestrials. It also is meant to leave open whether they belong to potential humans, such as fetuses. Those issues are not central to our main task and so are not discussed here.

13. H. L. A. Hart, "Are There Any Natural Rights?" *Philosophical Review* 64, no. 2 (1955): 183.

14. Thus, if I have a positive right to education, medical care, and a minimal standard of living, you and other citizens may have an obligation to pay taxes to support the schools, pay for medical care, and provide a decent minimal standard of living, perhaps through a welfare system.

15. John Locke, *Second Treatise of Government,* 1690, chap. 2, sec. 6. All quotations are from Thomas P. Peardon's edition of the *Second Treatise* (Indianapolis: Bobbs-Merrill, 1952).

16. Ibid., chap. 6, sec. 54.

17. Ibid., chap. 5, sec. 27. See also chap. 5, sec. 26.

18. Ibid., chap. 5, sec. 46.

19. Ibid., chap. 5, sec. 50.

20. Ibid., chap. 3, sec. 21.

21. Ibid., chap. 9, sec. 131.

22. Ibid., chap. 2.

23. Ibid., chap. 8, secs. 95–99.

24. For an important defense of such an entitlement theory, see Robert Nozick, *Anarchy, State, and Utopia* (New York: Basic Books, 1974).

25. We consider the entitlement theory and the case for a relatively unregulated free market more fully in chapter 4.

26. Maurice Cranston, "Human Rights, Real and Supposed," in *Political Theory and the Rights of Man,* ed. D. D. Raphael (Bloomington: Indiana University Press, 1967), 50.

27. Ibid., 51.

28. See Nozick, *Anarchy, State, and Utopia,* 172.

29. Henry Shue, *Basic Rights: Subsistence, Affluence, and U.S. Foreign Policy* (Princeton, N.J.: Princeton University Press, 1980), 37–40.

30. D. D. Raphael makes a similar point in his chapter "Human Rights Old and New," in *Political Theory and the Rights of Man,* 63–64.

31. Shue, *Basic Rights,* 40.

32. For a fuller discussion of this point, see Brian Barry, *Justice as Impartiality* (New York: Oxford University Press, 1995), 93–99.

33. Locke, *Second Treatise,* chaps. 2, 4.

34. Feinberg, "Nature and Value of Rights," 247. See also Wasserstrom, "Rights, Human Rights, and Discrimination."

35. Feinberg, "Nature and Value of Rights," 252.

36. Here we are indebted to Feinberg's similar argument in "Nature and Value of Rights."

37. Bernard Williams, "The Idea of Equality," in *Philosophy, Politics, and Society,* 2d ser., ed. Peter Laslett and W. G. Runciman (Oxford: Basil Blackwell, 1962); reprinted in Hugo A Bedau, ed., *Justice and Equality* (Englewood Cliffs, N.J.: Prentice-Hall, 1971), 119.

38. Alan Gewirth has argued in a series of articles and books that it is the property of being an agent with purposes and goals that forms part of a nonarbitrary basis for human rights. While we question some specific steps in Gewirth's formal "dialectical" derivation of such rights, we agree that elitists claim such rights among themselves on just such a basis, and hence such common features provide a nonarbitrary basis for rights claims. While elitists might purport to claim such rights on some special basis, such as belonging to a particular racial group, their rights claims are related to their purposes and goals as agents. That is why it seems arbitrary for them to bring in a quality such as race to distinguish themselves from others who have similar purposes and goals. For Gewirth's ambitious and elaborate derivation of human rights, see his *Human Rights* (Chicago: University of Chicago Press, 1982), esp. chap. 1.

## Questions for Further Study

1. What distinguishes human rights from other kinds of rights? Can a right be a moral right without being a human right? Justify your view.

2. How would Locke argue that an unequal distribution of resources is not necessarily a violation of fundamental rights and is not necessarily unjust? Do you think his position is defensible? Why or why not?

3. Explain the distinction between negative and positive rights. State a criticism of the idea that positive rights are as morally fundamental as negative ones.

4. If one views the social contract as setting forth the terms that reasonable people would agree to live under within civil society, what arguments might be advanced to show that positive rights ought to be included in the social contract?

5. In what way are positive rights held to be threats to individual liberty and personal freedom? Assess the claim that positive rights should not be recognized because they represent a significant threat to personal freedom and individual liberty.

6. What is the egalitarian argument for human rights? What is its major weakness? How do you think this weakness might best be overcome?

7. Do you believe in fundamental human rights? If not, what reasons do you have for condemning such evils as Nazi genocide, racism, and discrimination on the basis of gender? If you think that there is no rational basis for condemning such evils, how would you justify your skepticism? Does the mere fact that Nazis might disagree with the moral criticisms made of their views show that their position is as justified as the belief that humans fundamentally are moral equals?

## Suggested Readings

### Books

Becker, Lawrence. *Property Rights: Philosophic Foundations.* Boston: Routledge & Kegan Paul, 1977.

Dworkin, Ronald. *Taking Rights Seriously.* Cambridge: Harvard University Press, 1977.

Gewirth, Alan. *Human Rights.* Chicago: University of Chicago Press, 1982.

Locke, John. *Second Treatise of Government.* 1690. (Widely available in a variety of editions.)

Nickel, James W. *Making Sense of Human Rights.* Berkeley and Los Angeles: University of California Press, 1987.

Lyons, David, ed. *Rights.* Belmont, Calif.: Wadsworth, 1979.

Raphael, D. D., ed. *Political Theory and the Rights of Man.* Bloomington: Indiana University Press, 1967.

Shue, Henry. *Basic Rights: Subsistence, Affluence, and U.S. Foreign Policy.* Princeton, N.J.: Princeton University Press, 1980.

Thomson, Judith Jarvis. *The Realm of Rights.* Cambridge: Harvard University Press, 1990.

Wilson, John. *Equality.* New York: Harcourt Brace Jovanovich, 1966.

### Articles

Berlin, Isaiah. "Equality." *Proceedings of the Aristotelian Society* 56 (1955–1956).

*Ethics* 92, no. 1 (October 1981). This entire issue is devoted to the topic of rights.

Feinberg, Joel. "The Nature and Value of Rights." *Journal of Value Inquiry* 4, no. 4 (1970): 243–57.

*Monist* 52, no. 4 (1968). The entire issue is devoted to human rights.

Nickel, James W. "Human Rights." In *Encyclopedia of Ethics,* vol. 1, edited by Lawrence C. Becker and Charlotte B. Becker. New York: Garland, 1992.

Phillips, Griffiths A. "Ultimate Moral Principles: Their Justification." In *The Encyclopedia of Philosophy,* vol. 8, edited by Paul Edwards. New York: Macmillan, 1967.

Wasserstrom, Richard. "Rights, Human Rights, and Racial Discrimination." *Journal of Philosophy* 61 (1964).

# 4

# Justice

When conflicting rights claims are pressed under conditions of relative scarcity, under which all claims cannot easily be met, problems of justice typically arise. Consider, for example, the problem of distribution of organs for transplant, a problem we discussed in chapter 1. More patients require organs than there are organs available. There simply are not enough organs from donors who are compatible with the needy recipients. Yet many untreated patients surely will die. How are the available organs to be allotted? What is the just distribution?

Considerations of justice might not be pressing if there were enough slots for everyone and if provision of sufficient organs were possible. Then, everyone could easily be treated and no problem would exist. Or, if some patients withdrew their claims to treatment so that all who demanded treatment could be treated, issues of justice would not arise. But when conflicts arise, we are often called upon to resolve them.

In the case of organ transplants, should organs be distributed by lottery? Such a procedure would at least count all applicants equally. But is equal treatment always just treatment? People often differ in merit. Perhaps organ transplants should go first to the most meritorious. Remember the case in which a patient requires treatment only because he disregarded his physician's orders. Is it just to count that patient the same as those who did follow orders, even at the cost of considerable hardship? Is need relevant? Suppose one patient is the sole support of several children while another is responsible only for himself. What if the patient who disregarded orders is the one with four dependents, while the patient who obeyed instructions has no dependents? How are need and merit to be traded off against one another? Indeed, perhaps the strongest argument for a lottery is the difficulty of assessing the weight to be assigned to other factors that seem significant.

Similar problems arise on a larger scale. Is it just to distribute wealth, honor, or positions on the basis of merit? After all, who is to say what merit is or who has more of it than another? Even if we could correctly identify the meritorious, what of those with great need but little merit? Are they to be left to starve in the streets? On the other hand, are all inequalities in wealth arbitrary? Don't those who work harder than others or who perform better deserve more of a reward? How are all these different values to be properly weighed on the scales of justice?

In this chapter, our purpose is to explain and evaluate several theories of the nature of justice. We begin by discussing a number of traditional accounts of justice. We then consider some important contemporary theories of justice and make some suggestions of our own for improving upon them. We will also apply our analysis to specific problems of economic justice. Later we will extend the analysis to issues of compensatory justice that arise in connection with current controversies over affirmative action, alleged preferential hiring and admissions policies for women and minorities, and global distributive justice among nations.

## Traditional Theories of Justice

### Formal Theories

One major distinction that divides theories of justice is the distinction between formal and material theories. A formal theory does not provide any content or substance to principles of justice. A material theory does. In the strict sense, a formal theory is one that insists only on the logical criterion of consistency. Any consistent theory of justice satisfies the formal criterion. Consider the following principles of justice:

1. If X is a just result, all situations relevantly similar to X are also just results.

2. If M is our justice-making characteristic, let the dispensing of justice be proportionate to the possession of M.

3. Justice is the treating of equals equally and of unequals unequally.

These principles are all formal in the strict sense. They meet the criterion of consistency. However, there is no material content. X and M are not interpreted in the formulas. We emphasize that (3) should be understood as a restatement of (1) or (2); be on guard against the philosopher who tries to smuggle some content into (3) by capitalizing on ordinary connotations of "equality." For example, it is easy to say, "Since you should treat equals equally, there should be equal income for equal work." However, this inference is invalid. The consequent is not deducible from the antecedent. One needs the additional premise that the appropriate criterion for pay is work performed. However, such a criterion would not be acceptable to some socialists who insist that equal income for equal need is the appropriate formula or to those who think seniority justifies greater pay for senior workers doing the same work as junior ones. A substantive conclusion cannot be derived from a formal premise. The formal premise tells us that equals should be treated equally but does not specify the criterion for determining who are equals or what kind of equality is relevant.

One must also be careful to distinguish formal theories from general ones. All formal theories are general, but not all general theories are formal. A general theory that is not formal has some content. Something is substituted for the variables X or M. For example, consider the formula, "Justice is giving each person an equal opportunity." This is a general theory but not a formal one. For X, it substitutes content, namely, equal opportunity. It is general in that it applies to everyone. For our purposes, any consistent justice formula using variables as the justice-making criteria is a formal theory. When norms are substituted for the variables, the theory is a material theory. The distinction should be kept clear. The socialist formula of distributive justice, "From each according to his ability, to each according to his needs," is a material theory, not a formal one.

The classical position on justice that best exemplifies the formalist perspective is that of Aristotle.[1] He maintains that just distribution is proportionate to the possession of some quality that serves as the justice-making characteristic. If A and B are equal with respect to this characteristic M, then their shares should be equal. If they are unequal with respect to M, their shares should be in proportion to M, and hence the ratio of their shares to the proportion of M should be equal:

$$\frac{\text{Share for A}}{\text{A's possession of M}} = \frac{\text{Share for B}}{\text{B's possession of M}}$$

The principle is formal because, as Aristotle points out, one can choose any criterion for desert one wishes. The principle is compatible with any criterion. The principle insists only that once the criterion has been established, the ratios should be equal.

The difficulty with formalism is that at most it gives a necessary condition but not a sufficient condition for justice. It certainly is not just that all Jews be put in the gas chamber, even if only Jews are put in the gas chamber and no non-Jews are put there. In other words, consistency is not enough. Nazism does not become just merely by being consistently applied. Thus, what the Aristotelian formula needs is some means for specifying what the justice-making characteristic, the characteristic M, should be. The formalist theory of justice must be supplemented by material considerations if the theory of justice is to be practicable.

## Material Theories

**Plato.** The earliest fully developed account of justice can be attributed to the Greek philosopher Plato. For Plato, justice involves giving all persons their due.[2] The problem is that of determining a person's due. Plato tries to resolve the problem by providing a functionalist analysis, an approach that in its essentials is shared by Aristotle. This approach is based on a teleological metaphysics, or view of reality, in which everything has a purpose or function. Justice is to be analyzed in terms of function. To assert of something that it is performing its function is the same as saying that it is performing justly. A sheepdog is just when it protects the sheep. A racehorse is just when it competes well in races. Human beings are more complicated creatures, since they have souls composed of appetite, will, and reason. A just person has a harmonious soul. This harmony occurs when each part of the soul performs its appropriate function. Since the rational part of the soul is the higher part, the proper function of reason is to rule appetite and will. When reason rules, the soul is harmonious. The individual soul is a microcosm of the state. A just state is a harmonious state where each class performs its appropriate function. The business class is analogous to individual appetite, the class of soldiers is analogous to individual will, and the ruling class is analogous to individual reason. Justice is the harmonious relationship that occurs when the members of the various classes act in accordance with their nature. For Plato, justice occurs when everything is in its proper place performing its proper function.

Plato's philosophy makes a classic case for meritocracy. A meritocracy, in the sense in which Plato might defend it, is an organization of society in which one's place in the social hierarchy is determined by one's ability and qualifications for work at that level. ("Meritocracy" also is used to refer to a society in which material rewards as well as positions are distributed according to ability and qualifications, as well as to a society in which the quality of past performance is the determining factor.) In the Platonic view, it is unjust and corrupt to place people in jobs they cannot handle well. Some of us are better than others at particular activities. Since ruling is the most difficult and most important human activity, only the best and brightest should rule. To a Platonist, the democratic method of choosing political leaders makes about as much sense as allowing someone who knows virtually nothing of basketball to select the players who make up the team. The just society, to the Platonist, is the one in which everyone gets his or her due. And one gets one's due if one is assigned to one's proper place in the meritocratic structure of society.

Plato's theory, then, is an important challenge to many of the egalitarian assumptions made by democrats of our own time. Plato does not think everyone is equally good at making political decisions any more than everyone is equally good at athletics, music, or mathematics. For Plato, to give every citizen one vote amounts to giving the ignorant, the lazy, and the malicious the same power to affect our lives as the well-informed, dedicated, and well-intentioned.

The Platonic analysis of justice is inadequate, however. For one thing, Plato's theory of justice does not seem even to apply to many issues that we would now say are issues of justice. For example, how does it help in the case of the two patients who need the organ transplant to say that each should get what is due or that organs should be made available according to the function of the individual patient? If it simply means that the patient with the most merit should automatically get the organ, it seems to ignore other relevant factors. For example, suppose patient A has slightly more merit than patient B, but patient B has young children while A has none, and that A is seventy years old and B is twenty-five. Is it so obvious that A should get the only available organ, especially if A is only slightly more meritorious than B? On the other hand, if saying each patient ought to get what is due means only that each should get what justice requires after all the relevant factors have been weighed or considered, the implication is empty because we have not been told specifically how to weigh or consider them.

Second, it is far from clear that people have functions in the way artifacts such as knives and forks or lawnmowers have functions. Michael Jordan arguably may be a better basketball player than either of the authors of this book, but it does not follow that it is his function to play basketball or that an injustice would have been committed if he had chosen a career as a philosopher instead! More important, people's abilities reflect the opportunities they have been given, at least to some degree. As we will see, liberal theorists such as John Stuart Mill argue that actual participation in democracy, along with education, helps people to develop their potential and become concerned citizens.

Perhaps most important, a principal objection is to the elitism of Plato's account. Plato's ideal state is unpalatable even if only wise philosophers were kings and only the unintelligent were slaves. What is objectionable is not only the practical difficulty of identifying the best and brightest, great as it is; rather, what is most seriously questionable is Plato's assumption that the best and brightest should have absolute authority.

Suppose, if only for the sake of argument, that some means existed for determining who is most fitted to rule. Plato's egalitarian critics would respond that it is incorrect to argue from

1. Jones is the best fitted to rule.

to

2. Jones ought to rule.

What is needed is some independent argument to show that those most fitted to rule ought to rule, or that justice requires such a result. Plato just assumes that the best and brightest ought to rule. And he is far from alone in regarding that assumption as virtually self-evident. However, we will question this assumption and argue against it in our later discussions of democracy.

We need not wait, however, to call Plato's analysis into question. Once we concede that the move from (1) "Jones is most fitted to rule" to (2) "Jones ought to rule" needs support, we can ask what kind of support is needed. Surely, we must consider the claim that those most fitted to rule ought to rule since they deserve to rule on grounds of justice. It is just that those with the best qualifications and most merit rule. However, such a move leads to vicious circularity. The circularity is made explicit when we realize what the Platonist has argued:

Justice is to be analyzed in terms of giving each person his due.

Giving each person his due is to be analyzed in terms of a person's function.

The nature of a person's function is to be analyzed in terms of the justice of what he is due.

Plato cannot say both that justice is giving each person his due and that what a person is due depends on the justice of the function the person serves.

In fact, this circularity reveals the need for a criterion of justice independent of who is best fitted to rule. This is because A can be better fitted to rule than B precisely because of unjust background conditions. For example, the group to which B belongs may be unjustly oppressed by the group to which A belongs, perhaps because of race, gender, or religion. In such a case, justice may demand, not that A rule B, but that the oppression be ended so that B can develop the capacity to rule as well.

This criticism at best refutes only one version of what counts as giving a person his or her due. It does not refute the general strategy of analyzing justice in terms of what persons are due. There are numerous other possibilities for analyzing "giving persons their due." But that is the problem. No one interpretation of "giving persons their due" will suffice. What a person's due is depends on highly complicated individual circumstances. Whether Jones ought in the name of justice to give Smith ten dollars depends on the circumstances. We can begin the list as follows:

1. Did Smith earn ten dollars working for Jones?

2. Did Jones promise to pay Smith ten dollars?

3. Is Smith the tax collector?

4. Is Smith holding a gun on Jones?

This list can be expanded almost indefinitely. In speaking of distributive justice, philosopher Nicholas Rescher discusses the canons of equality, need, ability and/or achievement, effort, productivity, social utility, supply and demand, and claims.[3] An informative analysis must acknowledge the various circumstances that affect any decision about what is just. Even if circularity is avoided, to assert that giving each person his or her due is justice is not an adequate analysis. For the formula "Give all persons their due" seems to collapse into arbitrariness if "due" is explicated in terms of only one value, such as ability, but it lacks concrete content if "due" is taken as shorthand for a complex but unspecified process for balancing out a whole series of often conflicting values, such as ability, need, desert, and contribution.

**Justice and Equality.** Another important tradition tries to explicate the link between equality and justice. The nature of this link varies from writer to writer, however. In fact, equality itself is an extremely fuzzy concept, and writers in political philosophy tend to blur the various meanings of the term together.

One branch of the tradition emphasizes the formula "treat equals as equals." Justice then is treating equals equally and unequals unequally. However, stated this way, this formula is the formal theory of justice discussed earlier. It demands that justice decisions be consistent but does not specify what the content of the principles should be. Thus, the interesting questions arise when one tries to give some content to the formula, that is, to specify the characteristics that one is to use in consistent justice decisions. Let us consider briefly some of the characteristics that have been suggested.

At one extreme is the radical egalitarian position.[4] Under such a position, it is argued that all people are significantly alike and hence the just society is the strictly egalitarian society. Everyone is treated in exactly the same way. The obvious difficulty with the theory is that the factual premise is false. People are not sufficiently alike to be always treated alike. Their needs, abilities, contributions, physical characteristics, and interests are not identical. To treat them as if they were identical would be to commit great injustice. For example, sex equality in sports such as basketball is taken to require separate competitions for men and women because of innate differences in size, strength, and speed rather than blindness toward sex differences. It is not that extreme equality is impractical but that it is unjust. Obviously the egalitarian position must be modified.

One modification directs attention away from equal results to equal treatments.[5] In this sense, we treat X and Y equally if our treatment of them shows equal concern and respect for their needs and interests.[6] If we are speaking about police protection, justice is not achieved by giving equal protection to everyone. Some citizens—for example, those threatened by criminals—need more protection than others.[7] Justice is accomplished not by equal police protection but rather by unequal protection based on the principle of equal treatment. Even though $1,000 is spent on the citizen threatened by criminals and only $100 for the average citizen, all citizens are receiving equal treatment. The greater need of the threatened citizen requires the much greater expenditures if all citizens are to be treated equally with respect to police protection, that is, according to the principle "protect each proportionally to his need for protection." For the remainder of our discussion we will be speaking of equal treatment that may or may not entail equal results, depending on the circumstances.

However, this modification in egalitarian theory is not without its own problems. For one thing, it is incomplete. How are we to distribute justly when we lack sufficient resources to make a proportional contribution to all? To this question, the theory of equal treatment provides no answer. Again, it is at least controversial whether equal treatment is always just. Suppose parents have $100 to spend on their two children. Susie requires $90 for music lessons while Pam requires $10 for golf instruction. Is the inequality of result that equal treatment would engender really fair? Is it fair that those with the most expensive interests get the bulk of society's resources? Surely, it is far from clear that the answer always will be affirmative.

Perhaps egalitarians will respond that what is just or fair will be clear in specific contexts. Justice may require one thing in one situation, another thing in a different context. Isn't it clear that the mayor's son should not be excused from paying a speeding fine just because he is the mayor's son but should be excused if he was racing to get a heart attack victim to the hospital?

However, this modification does not eliminate all the problems. Let us consider the practice of licensing drivers of automobiles. In this case, our situation is the driving of automobiles and the characteristic appealed to in the rule is that of being a driver of automobiles. Any person correctly described as a driver is required to have a license. Here is a paradigm case of equal treatment in a particular situation. However, consider the following amended rule: Any person correctly described as an automobile driver and who has blue eyes is required to get a license. Certainly people with identical characteristics, blue-eyed drivers of automobiles, are being treated equally, although this rule, unlike the former one, is clearly unjust. It is not enough that certain identical characteristics are used in specific situations. The identical characteristics being used as differentiating criteria must be *relevant* to the activity under consideration. If we are charged with dispensing antityphoid vaccine, the relevant characteristic is exposure to typhoid and not the possession of blue eyes. Our egalitarian account must be further amended. Justice in any situation is accomplished when the identical characteristics selected for differentiating criteria are relevant to the activity and when all people with the appropriate characteristic are treated equally.

Even this further modification does not settle all the problems. The typhoid situation might be handled in a straightforward scientific manner. The differentiating condition is obvious, since there is a causal relation between being exposed to typhoid and contracting typhoid and preventing typhoid by vaccination after exposure. Unfortunately, many of the situations where problems of justice arise bear no analogy to our typhoid case. A discussion of voting qualifications illustrates this point clearly. The franchise should not be extended to everyone. Certainly, infants, the severely retarded, and perhaps criminals should be excluded. The problem before us is this: What characteristics are necessary if one is to be entitled to vote? Until very recently, literacy was considered necessary. Although the literacy requirement was frequently used unjustly in southern states to illegitimately disenfranchise black voters, a defense of sorts can be made for the impartial application of a literacy qualification. The defense is that there is a correlation between literacy and responsible voting. If that correlation can be shown, then there is at least a prima facie reason to make literacy a qualification. However, there is also a prima facie reason not to make it a requirement, since even if some persons are illiterate, they still have interests that can best be protected in a democracy by giving them a voice in the political process. The crux of the problem is that in many situations it is not at all clear what the relevant characteristics are. Accordingly, even this most recently modified account of equal treatment is incomplete since what counts as a relevant characteristic is controversial in many contexts.

**Justice and Equal Rights.** Perhaps there is another way out of the difficulty. Situations in which considerations of justice are relevant are of two fundamentally different types. One type is like most of those we have been discussing. Some specific physical characteristic is the relevant one, and the decision can be made on fairly straightforward factual grounds. The dispensing of the antityphoid vaccine is a paradigm case. In the other type of situation physical characteristics are not the prime determinant. Often, in fact, they are hardly relevant at all. People are morally entitled to equal treatment, not on the basis of any specific physical characteristic they possess except that of being humans. All persons have a right to protection of life, liberty, due process of law, and the pursuit of happiness.

The result is a dual theory of justice based on a dual theory of equality. At the first level, everyone has equal rights. The possession of those rights morally entitles everyone to equal treatment as rights bearers. At this level we have a moral analogue to the extreme egalitarian theory discussed above. With respect to human rights, everyone is considered equal; the only relevant characteristic is that the person be a rights bearer. Just what qualifies persons to have human rights, what rights they have, and in what situations they have them depend on the human rights theory in question. A discussion of some of the issues involved is found in chapter 3. On our own theory, as developed in that chapter, every human being has a human right to liberty and the prerequisites of a minimally decent human life (or well-being).

However, how human rights claims are honored and how disputes between rights claims are resolved depend on specific situations. The implementation of rights claims constitutes the lower level. We use the word "lower" because the decisions made at this level implement the rights claims to which we are entitled at the higher level. For example, the dispensing of antityphoid vaccine to those and only to those exposed to typhoid is a working out in specific situations of the human right to well-being. It is at this second level that differentiation on the basis of physical or societal characteristics is required if justice is to be done. Medicine should go to the sick and not to everyone, food to the hungry and not to everyone, and so on. The differentiating criteria depend on the situation. However, whatever the specific situation, if justice is to be done, it must represent an attempt to implement a human right.

It also is important to note that just inequalities can arise through the free exercise of human rights. If Jones and Smith open competing bakeries in our town or neighborhood, and if Smith does better because consumers prefer his baked goods to those of Jones, no injustice has been committed. The inequality has arisen simply because of the free choice of the consumers and because of risks voluntarily assumed by both Smith and Jones. Inequality of outcome, therefore, is not to be equated with injustice.

**Objections.** This account of justice is still inadequate, however. First, the theory is not complete. Even if a theory of human rights is accepted, we still have the difficulties of implementation. To provide a minimum income level of $16,000 per year in the United States, for example, may be defended as implementation of the human right to well-being. However, since that program must be paid for by taxing the incomes of those above the standard, those taxed might well argue that their human right to freedom is being infringed upon.[8] The previously discussed problem of conflicts of rights is with us again. The struggle for an end to racial discrimination and for equality of opportunity in America was at the outset phrased in the language of rights, specifically the rights to liberty and well-being. Black citizens wanted to use the same public facilities as whites, attend the same public schools, and use the same transportation facilities (right to liberty), and they wanted their share of America's prosperity (right to well-being). However, some owners of private businesses resisted black demands for integration of their facilities. They did so in the name of property rights (right to liberty). In response, a significant segment of public opinion replied with the phrase "human rights over property rights." Here is a clash of rights that creates what we take to be a paradigm case of a problem of justice. Moreover, it is clear that we have not resolved the problems of relevance with the introduction of the two-level theory. To say that justice requires respecting equal rights equally does not tell us what to do when rights claims clash.

Thus, as the equality theory of justice is modified, it becomes more and more obvious that the concept of equality can at best provide necessary, but not sufficient, conditions for justice. An analysis of the concept of equality can never provide an exhaustive analysis of the concept of justice. To say, for example, that justice in any situation is accomplished when the identical characteristics selected for differentiating criteria are relevant to the activity and when all people with the appropriate characteristics are treated equally is to make justice depend on more than considerations of equality. At the very least, a theory of what qualities are relevant to treatment is also required.

We believe it is correct to say that everyone has equal rights to liberty and well-being and that no situation is just if at least one of these rights is not honored. In this respect, equality spelled out as a theory of human rights does provide a necessary condition of justice. However, this equality theory must be supplemented by a theory that enables us to resolve the conflicts that arise between human rights. Second, it is a necessary condition of justice that whatever principles are accepted for resolving these conflicts and whatever characteristics are accepted as relevant differentiating criteria in particular situations, equals should be treated equally. However, an analysis of equality will neither provide the principles for resolving the conflicts nor determine which characteristics are the relevant ones. Thus, as stated earlier, when properly understood, equality considerations provide necessary conditions for justice; they do not provide sufficient ones.

## Just Procedures and Just Results

A major distinction that might be of great use here is that between just procedures and just results. Ideally one prefers both just procedures and just results. However, sometimes one ideal must be sacrificed for the other. For example, in distributive justice one can achieve a just result—for example, providing a minimum standard of living for the poor—by unjust procedures—for example, by a confiscatory tax on producers. Or in retributive justice, a trial by a jury of one's peers may well be defended as a just procedure, even though it may lead to an unjust result. An innocent person may be found guilty, or a guilty person may be found innocent.

Let us examine the notion of procedural justice by supposing that three friends order a pizza. When the pizza arrives, how should it be divided? Barring special circumstances, such as one person contributing more than another to the cost, the result or outcome that seems most just is that each person receives an equal share. But what procedure should be used to ensure that result? An appropriate procedure for this purpose is to make the person cutting the pizza take the last piece. Thus, if one piece is smaller than the other, the person who created the inequality cannot benefit from his behavior by getting the largest slice without the consent of the others.

The pizza example provides an illustration of fairness in both procedures and results. In some cases, however, just procedures alone must be relied upon to determine just results. Consider a lottery as an example. It makes perfect sense to speak of the conditions of a fair lottery. But what makes it fair? Suppose that most entrants are poor, but the winner is an extremely rich man. Can we say that the lottery is unjust? Certainly not. As with horse races, we condemn an event that is fixed, but we do not condemn one where the rich are winners. In situations like these, as long as the procedures are just, the results too are just.

Many problems of justice that we must handle as a society are ones of designing a system or set of procedures that provides as much justice as possible. Once we agree on appropriate procedures, then as long as a person is treated according to those procedures, the procedure is just, even if it turns out to produce inequalities that seem by other standards unjust. If we think a jury trial is the best way of determining guilt or innocence in criminal cases, then the result of such trials can, at one level, be regarded as just in the procedural sense even if we think a guilty person has gone free—an injustice at a different level of analysis.

A final example of procedural justice is provided by the lottery example. In this case there are no independent results that serve as a test of the procedure. If the procedure is just, the results produced by the procedure are just as well.

Our discussion has distinguished three different types of procedural justice. With perfect procedural justice, the procedure always leads to just consequences, as in the pizza-cutting example. With imperfect procedural justice, as with the U.S. system of trial by jury, the procedure is imperfect because it does not always lead to just consequences. However, the procedure still qualifies as just because it is the best procedure we have for achieving just results. Third, as in the case of the lottery, there is no independent standard of justice outside the procedure itself. The concept of pure procedural justice has been found to be fruitful in developing theories of justice. Some economists and philosophers have argued that a truly competitive market provides distributive justice. Yet a second approach is provided by John Rawls, who argues that a suitably constrained ideal social contract can provide the basic principles of justice. We ourselves shall argue later that democracy, suitably constrained, serves as an imperfect procedure for achieving justice in balancing the conflicting rights claims of citizens within a state.

Let us evaluate each of these theories in turn.

## The Market Approach to Economic Justice

### Classical Laissez-Faire Economics

In classical laissez-faire economics, the problem of distributive justice was to be resolved by the automatic working of the marketplace. Defenders of the marketplace as the procedural mechanism for distributive justice have relied upon both utilitarian arguments and arguments based on human rights. The utilitarian arguments are most commonly associated with economists who have developed elaborate models to show that the competitive market is the most efficient way to maximize the production of goods and services. Indeed, utilitarian defenses are more common than defenses based on human rights. However, a rights-based defense is central to the work of the libertarian economists Milton Friedman and Friedrich von Hayek and has been passionately defended by the philosopher Robert Nozick.

Milton Friedman argues that the market mechanism enables us to exercise our human right to liberty in the following ways.[9] First, it guarantees freedom of property, including the right to spend our incomes as we see fit. Second, it guarantees freedom of occupation. Persons choose the occupation they most desire consistent with their ability to get hired. Third, it enhances freedom of development. Each person chooses his or her own lifestyle and is free to go as far as possible consistent with his or her abilities. Fourth, it enhances freedom of expression. Friedman argues that the competitive market protects the basic freedoms of communication by separating economic and political power and by decentralizing economic power. Freedom of speech is more valuable so long as alternative opportunities for employment exist, since workers who have no option but unemployment if they speak freely are unlikely to speak vigorously in the first place. But alternate opportunities for employment cannot exist if the government owns and operates the economy. Freedom of expression, especially freedom of the press, is also enhanced by the marketplace because ideas inconsistent with those of the government or a particular editorial board may still get published. The fear that a competitor may publish the work often overcomes the distaste for certain ideas. For this reason, contemporary libertarians decry the increasing centralization of industry, the growth of government influence, and the establishment of the business–government–university alliance that economist John Kenneth Galbraith has characterized as the New Industrial State.

Friedman's appeal to our human right to liberty is also a useful device to combat contemporary critics of the market in general and of American capitalism in particular. Consider the kinds of criticisms we hear of American life these days. First, many groups believe that their salaries are too low, especially in light of salaries in other professions. In the market, salary depends, at least to a considerable degree, on the demand for the product or services produced. Under market conditions, social workers and teachers may get paid less than bartenders and garbage collectors. It does not seem adequate to inform the former groups that their lower salaries are justified since their services are less in demand. What about the artist who is ahead of his time and finds that his creations are not in demand? Just how serious should the economic consequences be for those who find the goods and services they have to offer unpopular? Still other critics focus on quality of products. They argue that the major corporations do not have adequate concern for the durability or even the safety of their products. The developers of nuclear power plants are criticized for failing to have developed adequate fail-safe safety devices. Nearly every month, another product is added to the growing list of suspected causes of cancer. Surely the market is incapable of policing itself; outside regulation is needed. Or so the critics argue.

Friedman delivers an uncompromising reply to such critics. He thinks the notion of passing judgment on the quality or social desirability of goods is dangerous. Who is to decide whether or not a good is socially desirable? Certainly we would not want government officials, or psychologists, or even philosopher-kings making that decision. What the marketplace provides is a democratic vote: the supply-and-demand procedure is really a voting procedure for determining quality. What the critics of libertarianism are really attacking is the democratic determination of the marketplace. They are trying to substitute the voices of a few for the voices of all. Such an elitist attitude, reminiscent of Plato's dismissal of democracy, is (a) unjustified because there are no experts on matters of value and (b) dangerous because expert determination of product quality undermines the individual freedom of consumer choice, which the marketplace is designed to protect. The fact that bartenders are paid more than social workers is the price we must pay for our individual freedom. Hence the market solution, which rewards producers on the basis of demand, is the best method of distributing goods and services.

Moreover, in addition to protecting our natural right to liberty, the market enhances our natural right to well-being. Since the workings of the marketplace provide for maximum efficiency, the greatest amount of economic good for the greatest number is produced. To tamper with the market interferes with its efficiency, and the end result is a smaller aggregate amount of goods and services. Hence, the unfettered market provides the greatest gross national product from which rights to well-being can he implemented.

Critics of the market mechanism may reply that the market allows distributive patterns that would be intolerable from the moral point of view. On pure classical theory, individuals receive economic reward if and only if (a) they have contributed to the productive process or (b) they are voluntarily supported by a producer, either as a member of a family or by gifts through charity. Clearly, to the extent that individuals are unable, through no fault of their own, to contribute to the productive process, and to the extent that voluntary charity is unable to meet their basic needs, the distributive pattern is unfair. It does seem to be a fact that the innocent nonproductive, such as the aged, the ill, infants with disadvantaged single parents, the mentally defective, and those who in spite of their best efforts cannot find work when the economy is depressed, all too often receive marginal treatment at best.

The defenders of the market solution to the problem of distribution are quick to point out the dangers of any other approach, however. The distribution of goods and services is related to, and dependent upon, their production. Any distribution scheme that interferes with the optimal conditions of production is at least inefficient, in the sense that fewer goods and services would be produced than could have been produced. If the interference is especially severe, the total number of goods and services will actually decline. There are technical reasons why certain distributive schemes, for example, taxes, interfere with the optimal conditions for production. Unsophisticated but popular expressions of this argument abound: "Why should I work so hard if 30 percent of my income is taken up in taxes?" "Why bother with overtime? Most of the money I make goes to welfare." "Why should I work at all? I can do better on welfare." In fact, many sophisticated contemporary critics of a state-supported welfare system also argue that it provides a disincentive to work or engage in other forms of responsible productive behavior and hence causes great inefficiency as well as imposing unfair costs on taxpayers. As a result, economic growth slows, and in severe cases the absolute number of goods and services declines. Thus, according to defenders of the market, well-intentioned guarantees of living standards do more harm than good.

Rather than interfere with incentives, the defender of the market mechanism argues, one should let the rapidly rising living standards that result from an efficient economic system bury the distributive problem in a cornucopia of goods. A sketch of the argument follows:

1. In certain situations individuals suffer from an extreme scarcity of goods and services through no fault of their own.

2. However, such situations are inevitable in an economic system where supply and demand play a large part.

3. However, the results of the system as a whole are so beneficial that everyone is better off. For example, a system that produces the means for twenty-four units of happiness and distributes them unequally, twelve, seven, and five, is more just than a system that produces only six units of happiness and distributes them equally two to each.

4. Premise 3 is true even if we feel that the recipient of five units should have received more in that particular system.

5. Hence, problems of distributive justice must be seen in their total context.

6. Therefore, a given instance of an unjust distribution is not an effective counterexample against the theory. The procedure may make everyone better off, including the offended party, than any alternative system.

Here the laissez-faire theorists rests their case. They claim that the market implements the rights to both freedom and well-being—and, in fact, maximizes them. These arguments indicate how the adoption of the market mechanism maximizes overall welfare, measured in terms of both freedom and well-being.

Moreover, since the market is a mechanism, the classical laissez-faire theory of distributive justice serves as one of the most famous examples of procedural justice. Procedural justice is not concerned with determining the justice of each individual situation. Rather, it is concerned with a just procedure such that whatever the actual distribution, so long as the procedure is followed, the distribution is ipso facto just. This implementation occurs without human moral effort. In fact, such conscious effort would only work to the detriment of the implementation. Instead, the driving force is the desire to do well in the market, either for personal, egoistic reasons or to benefit one's friends and family, or to serve some cause. As persons try to achieve their own aims, including their own personal good, the greatest good for all is achieved. In a strange paradox, the pursuit of personal interest produces beneficence: a private vice produces public benefits.[10]

## Nozick's Entitlement Theory

Robert Nozick's *Anarchy, State, and Utopia* is a valuable contemporary addition to the traditional laissez-faire approach. He agrees with Friedman and others that the free market supports individual freedom. He also believes that the market really does operate as a procedural mechanism of justice. To understand Nozick's proceduralism, it is necessary to understand his distinctions between historical and nonhistorical, and patterned and unpatterned, principles of justice.

Nozick wishes to distinguish between historical principles of justice and nonhistorical principles of justice that he calls end-state principles. With respect to distribution, a defender of the historical approach would argue that in assessing the justice of a situation, it is not enough to see how the goods are distributed. We must also look at how the goods were produced and how the distribution came about: "historical justice holds that past circumstances or actions of people can create differential entitlements or differential deserts to things."[11]

The historical approach is to be contrasted with those theories that impose on any distribution a fixed end or goal. For example, the utilitarian theory is nonhistorical. It argues that each distribution should be arranged so as to maximize the greatest good for the greatest number. It is Nozick's point that nonhistorical theories are deficient as theories of justice because they ignore ethically relevant historical circumstances. One ought not place people in jail just because total utility would increase if they were jailed. Rather, placing people in jail should depend on the historical fact of their being tried and found guilty. We agree with Nozick that historical considerations cannot be ignored. But we do not think that historical considerations are decisive, as Nozick apparently does. We do not think that possession is nine-tenths of the law.

Another distinction Nozick makes is between patterned and nonpatterned principles of justice. A patterned principle selects some characteristic or set of characteristics that specifies how the distribution is to be achieved. Any formula that fills in the blank of "to each according to _____" is a patterned formula. Nozick writes, "Let us call a principle of distribution patterned if it specifies that a distribution is to vary along with some natural dimension, weighted sum of natural dimensions, or lexicographic ordering of natural dimensions."[12]

He finds any patterned principle objectionable because the attempt to have the distribution be in accordance with the pattern is an infringement on liberty. Nozick illustrates this point by considering how a famous athlete such as former basketball great Wilt Chamberlain can upset the pattern. Suppose we achieve our patterned distribution, which in this case is equal. Suppose also that there is such a great demand to see Wilt Chamberlain play basketball that people will pay him 25 cents of their ticket price to get him to play. Suppose that during one year one million persons pay him $250,000 to see him play. This gives Wilt Chamberlain far more than he would have received under the equal distribution formula. What do we do now? To maintain the pattern of equal distribution, we would have to interfere with the transfer of the 25 cents by those million persons. As Nozick says:

> The general point illustrated by the Wilt Chamberlain example . . . is that no end-state principle or distributional patterned principle of justice can be continuously realized without continuous interference with people's lives. Any favored pattern would be transformed into one unfavored by the principle, by people choosing to act in various ways; for example, by people exchanging goods and services with other people, or giving things to other people, things the transferrers are entitled to under the favored distribution pattern. To maintain a pattern one must either continually interfere to stop people from transferring resources as they wish to, or continually (or periodically) interfere to take from some persons resources that others for some reason chose to transfer to them.[13]

Nozick can then magnify these infringements on liberty. Suppose, for example, that we tax people in order to provide others with a better standard of living. What is the difference, Nozick asks, between forcing someone to work five hours for the benefit of the needy and involuntarily taxing someone five hours worth of work? Nozick claims that there is no difference. He maintains that taxation of earnings from labor is equivalent or virtually equivalent to forced labor. Hence, Nozick has two arguments to show how attempts to achieve patterned distributions result in an infringement on one's right to liberty.

As an alternative, Nozick develops a nonpatterned theory that he calls the theory of entitlements. In Nozick's view, a distribution is just if everyone has what he is entitled to. To determine what people are entitled to, we must discuss the original acquisition of holdings, the transfer of holdings, and the rectification of holdings. Nozick's theory of acquisition is a variant of a theory of property rights developed by the philosopher John Locke, whose views we discussed in chapter 3. For Nozick, any person has a right to any owned thing so long as ownership by that person does not worsen the situation of others. Suppose I farm a plot of land that is neither used nor owned by anyone else. I cultivate the land, plant the seeds, and weed and water the garden plot. Surely, I am entitled to the fruits of the harvest. What Nozick attempts to do is to accommodate all types of legitimate ownership to the case of the garden plot. We are entitled to what we have worked for or freely received by transfer from others.

The scarcity of goods and resources complicates Nozick's account. After all, whenever someone owns something, he usually diminishes the opportunity for someone else to own it. There are not enough resources for a swimming pool and two cars for all. It is the recognition of this problem that accounts for Nozick's addition of the phrase "does not worsen the situation of others."

That phrase needs considerable interpretation, however. For Nozick, someone's situation is not worsened just because his opportunities became more limited. At times Nozick speaks as if someone's situation would be worsened if he fell below a certain baseline.[14] It is tempting to think that the phrase "baseline situation" means something like "minimum standard of living" or "welfare floor." If this were the case, fairly extensive violations of liberty would be allowed to keep people from falling below the baseline. For example, taxes for the purpose of providing a social safety net might interfere with people's liberty to spend their income as they wished.

However, the examples Nozick chooses for discussion and other, more extensive comments that he makes indicate that his view of how one's ownership of something makes another worse off is far narrower. Nozick seems to indicate that we should compare the situation of the person as it would be with a system of property rights and as it would be without a system of property rights. If Jones acquires something, Smith is not made worse off unless Smith's situation deteriorates to the point where he is worse off than he would be in a system without property rights.

The end result of Nozick's discussion of how one person can be harmed by another's acquisition of property is that nearly everyone is entitled to everything he acquires so long as coercion or fraud is not involved. The theory is rounded out by the contention that what one has justly acquired, one is entitled to transfer to others. One can see why Nozick would adopt the slogan "from each as they choose, to each as they are chosen." A person is entitled to something if he acquired it without worsening the situation of others or if he received it as a transfer from one who had acquired it without worsening the situation of others.

Is Nozick's defense of the unrestricted free market acceptable? Before attempting to answer this question, it will prove useful to contrast Nozick's theory with the principal contemporary defense of welfare liberalism, that of John Rawls.

## John Rawls's Theory of Justice

Many philosophers would contend that John Rawl's book *A Theory of Justice* is the most significant work on the topic of justice written in the twentieth century. In *A Theory of Justice*, Rawls argues that the primary task of social and political institutions is the preservation and enhancement of social justice, which he understands to include both principles of individual liberty and principles of well-being or welfare. Rawls tries to develop a *procedure* that would yield principles of justice. These principles of justice would then serve as guides in the construction and evaluation of social and political institutions.

In Rawls's view, questions of justice arise when a society evaluates the institutions and practices under which it lives with an eye toward balancing the legitimate competing interests and conflicting claims that are recognized as legitimate by the members of that society. If we adopt the language of rights, we can say that Rawls sees problems of justice arising when legitimate rights claims come into conflict. Rawls does not view the citizens of a state as naive moralists searching for a utopian ideal. Rather, they are sufficiently self-interested to wish to pursue their own individual interests or those of their families and loved ones and achieve their own individual goals. Given inevitably competing interests and conflicts, Rawls's task is to attempt to provide a procedure that will enable the members of the society to adopt principles for resolving the conflicts and for adopting just practices and institutions. In other words, his question is this: By what procedure can self-interested persons with legitimate competing claims adopt principles for just institutions and practices?

Rawls's answer is to appeal to a contract process constrained by certain assumptions. This process is hypothetical, not actual. It is governed by certain assumptions that define the hypothetical state, called the original position, in which the contract process takes place. Several of the more important assumptions are: (1) that human cooperation is both possible and necessary; (2) that the contractees adhere to the principles of rational choice; (3) that all contractees desire certain primary goods that can be broadly characterized as rights and liberties, opportunities and powers, income and wealth—in other words, general goods that it is reasonable to think are necessary to the attainment of any other individual goods persons may desire; (4) that the contract process is constrained by a minimal morality that stipulates that principles adopted by the contractees be general, universal in application, public, and the final court of appeal for ordering the conflicting claims of moral persons; (5) that the parties to the contract are capable of a sense of justice and will adhere to the principles adopted.[15]

The force of these five conditions is to put moral limits on the kind of contract that can be produced. With these five conditions acting as constraints, Rawls's strategy is to ask us to conduct a thought experiment. What principles of justice would we come up with if we were placed behind a veil of ignorance with all other rational agents and instructed to devise a set of principles of organizing society so that justice in the society would be achieved? The key to understanding how the principles of justice are to be selected is the veil of ignorance, or ignorance principle. The ignorance principle states that the contract makers are to act as if they did not know their place in society. Such ignorance guarantees impartiality and prevents us from arguing on selfish rather than general grounds. This veil of ignorance would exclude knowledge of one's class position or social status (including the probability of occupying any position or having any specific degree of status), one's fortune in the distribution of natural assets and abilities, one's intelligence, one's physical strength, the nature of one's society, and one's individual conception of the good and other values. Operating in this way, none of the contract makers would have any special interests to defend, nor would they have any reasons to form alliances to adopt principles that work to the disadvantage of a minority of other contract makers.

In effect, as Rawls applies it, the ignorance principle tells us to act as if our enemy were to assign our place in society. For example, suppose the issue were the distribution of income. Since the veil of ignorance prevents you from knowing how wealthy you are or will be, and it prevents you from knowing your occupation and talents, what strategy would it be rational to adopt? Surely, Rawls argues, you would want to protect the position of the least well-off. Similar thought experiments would assure that there would be no racist principles for the organization of social institutions. After all, you cannot be sure that you would not be a member of the race that would be discriminated against. Since the contract makers are like rational egoists operating from behind a veil of ignorance, they would adopt the general principle of seeking to minimize their losses. Since they are ignorant of the probability of any specific outcome and know that some outcomes, such as being a member of a despised minority, are unacceptable, they would guard against the worst possible outcomes by making the people in the worst-off position as well-off as possible.

We can now see how unanimous agreement on the principles of justice is possible. Since everyone agrees that it is rational to reduce one's losses and since no one knows what position he or she holds in society, the following two principles would be adopted unanimously: (1) Each person is to have an equal right to the most extensive total system of equal basic liberties compatible with a similar system of liberty for all. (2) Social and economic inequalities are to be arranged so that they are both (a) to the greatest benefit of the least advantaged, and (b) attached to offices and positions open to all under conditions of fair equality of opportunity.[16] These principles, which are the result of the contract, are just because the procedure that produced them is just. Rawls's hypothetical contract is an example of pure procedural justice.

These are the principles that persons operating under the constraints of Rawls's original position behind the veil of ignorance would choose as requirements of justice. Since they do not know particular facts about themselves, they have no specific interests to protect. Rather, the concern is with those goods Rawls calls primary goods—general goods that are reasonably thought to be necessary to the attainment of any other individual goods persons may desire.

One of the most important of these primary goods is liberty, which is protected by the first principle. Since no one will know his or her place in society, it is in everyone's interest to adopt the first principle, which provides a system of equal liberty for all. Otherwise, one might turn out to be at the mercy of more powerful individuals or groups.

What are the constituent liberties that make up the system of liberty? Rawls answers this question by providing a list of basic liberties. This list includes political liberty (the right to vote and to be eligible for public office) together with freedom of speech and assembly; liberty of conscience and freedom of thought; freedom of the person along with the right to hold (personal) property; and freedom from arbitrary arrest and seizure as defined by the concept of the rule of law.[17]

The second principle is concerned with the primary goods of opportunities and power, income and wealth. What Rawls does is to consider his principle in contrast to several competing ones and then ask which principles would be chosen by self-interested persons constrained by the ignorance principle. Rawls first considers a system of natural liberty. In such a system, positions are open to those able and willing to strive for them. The principle governing the distribution of wealth in such a system is called the principle of efficiency. In terms of his theory Rawls defines the position as follows:

> Thus we can say that an arrangement of rights and duties in the basic structure is efficient if and only if it is impossible to change the rules, to redefine the scheme of rights and duties so as to raise the expectations of any representative man (at least one) without at the same time lowering the expectations of some (at least one) other representative man.[18]

Rawls argues that this principle of efficiency within a system of natural liberty would be rejected, however. If, after the initial distribution, someone has vastly more wealth than others, nothing could be done to correct the situation that would not run afoul of the efficiency principle. Moreover, the distribution of wealth at any given time has been strongly influenced by the cumulative effect of the natural and social contingencies of past distributions. Accident, past injustice, and good fortune play an important role in determining who is wealthy at any given time. Since the veil of ignorance prevents us from knowing our own fortune and since, according to Rawls, it is rational to seek to minimize our losses, the principle of efficiency would not be accepted in the contract. Rational contractors would seek to avoid the risk of turning out to be on the bottom in the efficient society.

Rawls has more positive reactions to the principle of equal opportunity. This principle asserts that people with the same ability, talents, and expenditures of effort should have roughly the same prospects of success in given fields of endeavor. One's family background, race, religion, sex, or social background should not act as an impediment to success. To assure equality of opportunity, society imposes heavy inheritance taxes, offers a broad public education, and passes antidiscrimination legislation. To the extent that such societal measures are successful, the distribution of goods and services depends upon ability, talent, and effort. This is an attractive principle that has been widely supported by broad segments of the American public.

However, in Rawls's view, the principle of equal opportunity is still not sufficient. Rawls argues that the distribution of talent, ability, and capacity for effort is just as arbitrary from the moral point of view as the distribution of sex, family wealth, and social class. Jones has no greater right to more money because he is smarter than Smith than he has to more money because he is of a certain religion.

In part, Rawls seems to be claiming that behind the veil of ignorance, it would be no more rational to gamble on being smart, talented, or dedicated than on being a member of a dominant group in other areas, so we would reason conservatively and try to protect ourselves against bad outcomes. However, he also seems to appeal to our considered ideas about fairness. Distribution is fair, in Rawls's view, only if human assets are treated as collective social goods. After all, none of us deserves to have been born into favorable circumstances or with personal traits such as a disposition to work hard. These are gifts, distributed at birth as if by a natural lottery, and are not earned by us as individuals. Moreover, the distribution of goods and services is a cooperative effort on the part of all. Given the cooperative effort and the morally arbitrary distribution of natural assets and favorable family circumstances, the fairest principle is the one that accepts inequalities only if the inequalities work to the advantage of the least well-off:

> It seems to be one of the fixed points of our considered judgments that no one deserves his place in the distribution of native endowments, any more that one deserves one's initial starting place in society. The assertion that a man deserves the superior character that enables him to make the effort to cultivate his abilities is equally problematic; for his character depends in large part upon fortunate family and social circumstances for which he can claim no credit. The notion of desert seems not to apply to these cases. Thus the more advantaged representative man cannot say that he deserves and therefore has a right to a scheme of cooperation in which he is permitted to acquire benefits in ways that do not contribute to the welfare of others. There is no basis for his making this claim. From the standpoint of common sense, then, the difference principle appears to be acceptable both to the more advantaged and to the less advantaged individual.[19]

What the quoted passage shows, Rawls would maintain, is that his principles of justice conform to our own considered judgments about justice, those judgments in which we place the most confidence. Perhaps what ultimately justifies the Rawlsian contract procedure is its ability to explain, support, systematize, and provide grounds for reconsideration of, our intuitive sentiments about social justice.

Unlike the defense of the free market, Rawls's theory of justice requires the state to provide for the least well-off, and indeed to make that group as well-off as possible. This is because the second principle, like the first, would emerge from Rawls's contractual procedure and because the procedure itself supports and systematizes our considered judgments about justice.

When fully spelled out, then, the Rawlsian argument is that the two principles of justice are justified because they and they alone would emerge from a fair procedure of rational choice. The procedure itself is warranted because of its coherence with our most firmly held considered judgments about justice and fairness. Finally, Rawls maintains that a society in which the political, social, and economic institutions were constructed in conformity with the principles of justice would be a highly stable one. The citizens of such a society would recognize that the society is basically just. These citizens themselves would desire to act as the principles of justice require and would be inclined to support society's basic institutions. Such a society would be well ordered and stable.

For much of the remainder of his book, Rawls applies his theory to the task of creating social institutions in accordance with the two principles of justice. The details of Rawls's analysis take us beyond the scope of this study, but we should point out that liberty is secured in the writing of a constitution and that the implementation of the difference principle is accomplished through the legislature.

## Nozick or Rawls?

Which theory of procedural justice provides the best account of economic justice, Nozick's market-based view or Rawls's social-contract view of justice as fairness? Has Nozick provided a satisfactory defense of the unregulated free market, or has Rawls made a better case for using the authority of the state to provide benefits for the worst-off?

### Evaluation of the Market

Defenders of the market, such as Milton Friedman, defend it in terms of both liberty and economic efficiency. As we have seen, they claim that the market promotes liberty by providing a realm of private interaction and exchange that is not controlled by the state. The market, on this view, provides a buffer zone of freedom protecting the individual from government. However, while we agree that the market does offer significant protections for liberty and often does promote economic efficiency, we deny that these protections are fully adequate to provide justice and to protect our human rights to liberty and well-being.

The basic criticism is that the market, as well as Nozick's defense of it through the entitlement theory, ignores or gives insufficient weight to our rights to well-being. Pure market theorists such as Milton Friedman take the distribution of income as a given. That is, the current distribution of income is taken as morally acceptable. But Rawls would insist that this assumption is unjustified. Here are some reasons why.

Defenders of the pure market claim that the market is analogous to democratic voting, but we find this analogy to be misleading and inappropriate. In a democratic voting procedure, each person has only one vote. However, in the marketplace, voting strength is a function of the size of one's income or one's wealth. A rich person bidding against a poor person for a good or service always will prevail. Such a situation could be just only if the inequality of income between the rich and the poor is just.

Market theorists such as Friedman reply that the initial inequality is just because salaries are a function of each person's productivity along with the market demand for one's skills. Income other than salary is regarded primarily as a reward for providing one's capital to business for investment and, in the case of stocks and bonds, for willingness to incur risks.

In response, some critics of the market reply that income derived from inheritance clearly does not fall into any of these categories. However, inheritance raises some difficult issues. Do critics of the market really want to say that dying persons who have worked hard all their lives cannot leave their estate to their children? Perhaps the justice of the situation depends on how much is at stake and whether the state has the right to some share of the inheritance through taxation.

Perhaps more important, market critics also point out that the market provides no protection for those whose skills are not in demand. It also provides no protection for persons who through no fault of their own cannot make a contribution to the economy—for example, the ill (both physically and mentally), the unemployed, and those who must care for young children, as well as the children themselves. The market, therefore, is not sufficient to honor every citizen's human right to well-being.

The classical response to the egalitarian critique of the marketplace is to bury the objection in a cornucopia of economic goods. The long-range growth of the economic system makes everyone better off in the long run. The moral problem centers around the expression "long run." As John Maynard Keynes so cheerfully reminded us, "in the long run we are all dead." It may be just to distribute eight units of economic welfare to one person and two units to another in order that tomorrow we can distribute twenty units to one and fifteen to the other. However, it seems unjust to distribute eight units to one person and two units to another so that their great-grandchildren may receive twenty and fifteen units respectively. The philosophical point is a simple one: It is simply not true that all unjust distributions can be rectified in the long run. Certain basic economic necessities ought to be provided now, not later. Thus, the future normally can justify the past only if the individuals are the same in both cases. For certain groups in our society, particularly African Americans, the long run has become very long indeed.

The market does considerably better with the human right to liberty, since buying and selling in the market often is taken to be the paradigm of a free transaction among consenting adults. However, while the pure market is often an important protection for human liberty, it alone is not adequate to protect fully our human right to liberty. For example, the market does not always protect our freedom to find jobs or to keep them in the face of arbitrary decisions by employers. In the classical model, there are no unions to protect employees from their employers. And most employees are not protected by unions in the real world, since fewer and fewer workers are covered by union contracts.

An advocate of the market might respond that employees who do not like their employers or who are dissatisfied with working conditions, as well as those who think employers are treating them improperly or unfairly, are always free to leave and take employment elsewhere. But lack of funds and opportunities for training, family ties, and social networks, as well as depressed job markets, often make it difficult if not impossible to find alternative work, especially if alternative employment requires a move to another part of the country. In times of high unemployment, as in a recession or corporate downsizing, there may not be feasible alternatives to one's present job. Remember also that on the pure market model, there will be no unemployment insurance or welfare to tide workers over between jobs. In such situations, the formal freedom to leave one job and search for another may be rather empty and of little value.

The market does reasonably well on utilitarian grounds since, in the ideal case, it maximizes the amount of goods available for consumption. But if one is a rights theorist rather than a utilitarian, the market fares less well since it provides insufficiently for our human rights of freedom and well-being.

## Evaluation of Nozick's Entitlement Theory

Perhaps Nozick's entitlement theory fares somewhat better. Nozick's account of acquisition is the key to his theory. In describing how a just acquisition is achieved, he emphasizes liberty at the expense of all other values. His central starting point is the right to liberty. [20] As we have seen, he rejects any principle of distribution that violates the right to liberty. He rejects as well any interpretation of his own principle that creates such a violation. But why should we build a theory of justice in terms of liberty alone? As a consequence of his position, Nozick believes it would be unjust for even a wealthy state to tax individuals in order to provide better food, clothing, or housing for the poor. In Nozick's view we are entitled (have a right) to our legitimate acquisitions, but the poor have no right to a minimum standard of living. In chapter 3, we examined defenses of human rights. If rights claims are justified on the basis of our recognition of the dignity and self-respect of every individual, then the right to a minimum standard of well-being is as firmly justified as our right to liberty. Nozick not only ignores our right to well-being but utterly annihilates it, as it comes into conflict with one's right to liberty. Such an extreme point of view needs considerable defense, which unfortunately Nozick does not supply.

The extreme flavor of Nozick's theory is clearly seen in his discussion of how A's ownership of X can worsen the condition of B. How does Nozick justify his suggestion about how people's condition can be worsened? In his view, people's condition is worsened only if they are worse off than they would be in a system without property rights. It is most remarkable that Nozick provides no defense at all for this interpretation of worsening. Surely it needs a defense, because it implies that workers laid off by a company that downsizes are not really made worse off since they would be even poorer in a system without property rights. Since Nozick's interpretation is so counterintuitive, surely some justification is called for.

Of course, our criticism of Nozick would be less severe if we could interpret more broadly how people's condition could be worsened. We might say that someone's condition is worsened when it falls below a certain baseline (social-welfare floor). In this way our liberty as expressed through property rights would not be rejected but would be checked or limited in the face of extreme need. This interpretation would be clearly inconsistent with most of what Nozick says, however.

Unfortunately, as Nozick himself seems to concede, he does not offer a full-fledged theory of acquisition, or indeed of what it means to own anything. With respect to the former, there is no discussion of what counts as fraudulent acquisition. Stealing is clearly illegitimate since it violates one's right to liberty. Is advertising legitimate? Even subliminal advertising? Can one prey upon the ignorance of the poor? Must products be proven safe? With respect to the concept of ownership, when does someone own something? Can property owners forbid jet planes to fly over their homes? Do the minerals at the bottom of the ocean or on Mars belong to the person who gets there first? If so, can an explorer come to own all of Mars by arriving five minutes before a second explorer? What account can be given of public goods or collective ownership?

Nozick's account of justice is severely limited in scope. By construing "worsening the situation of others" so narrowly, he allows nearly any acquisition or transfer to be just. By failing to place some constraints on the means of acquisition and by failing to define how someone can be said to own something, Nozick ignores many of the important issues.

Moreover, Nozick may ignore the point that many acquisitions result from what might be called moral luck and may be wholly or partially undeserved. Thus, a proponent of John Rawls's theory of justice may respond to the Wilt Chamberlain example by pointing out that Wilt is able to enjoy his success in part, perhaps in great part, because of his height, which resulted in part from a fortunate genetic endowment; therefore he may not deserve all his income. Since he is not responsible for all his assets, he may not deserve or be entitled to (all) the fruits of their employment either. While we suspect this Rawlsian point is not decisive and is sometimes overdrawn—we ourselves criticize it below—we also think Nozick and the libertarians need to pay more attention to the result of moral luck in the market and its implications for deserts and entitlements. Do we want an individual's fate to be largely determined by the luck of the draw in either genetic endowment or the distribution of the most favorable environments for growth?

Nozick's theory also has difficulties with fairness. Suppose, for example, that a first generation of colonists establishes a settlement in a new land. They operate according to the market where economic goods are concerned. As a result, some do far better than others economically, since their goods and services are more highly valued than those of the other colonists. What happens, however, to the children of the first generation? Some, through no fault of their own, are born into poverty, while others, with better luck, are born into affluent homes. Some have lost their parents to accidents or ill health. Others become ill and cannot work themselves. Is it *fair* that such individuals must depend on the charity of others?

Nozick might reply that, whether the situation is fair or not, to appropriate the products of the work of other people against their will in order to help the disadvantaged violates the human right to liberty of the property owners. However, our arguments in chapter 3 suggest that, on the contrary, the disadvantaged have a human right to a minimal standard of living, as well as a right to liberty. To deny such a right and opt for Nozick's unmitigated entitlement theory is to fall prey to the Rawlsian objection that an individual's fate should not be the result of accidents of birth or factors for which the person is not responsible.

As we have seen, this objection applies more generally to the market model of procedural justice as well as to Nozick's particular defense of it. Accordingly, although we think the market often is an important mechanism for securing individual freedom and well-being, it does not always protect such values and in some significant cases can undermine them significantly. Accordingly, we conclude that an unregulated market, by itself, is not adequate for securing social justice (although it may well be part of a broader procedure that addresses its limitations).

We now turn to evaluation of the Rawlsian alternative.

## Evaluation of Rawls's Theory of Justice as Fairness

**Criticisms of *A Theory of Justice*.** Since its publication, Rawls's book has been subjected to intensive analysis by philosophers, political scientists, and economists. Initial criticism of *A Theory of Justice* tended to focus on Rawls's contractual procedure. For example, many critics have charged that in specifying just what sorts of information the veil of ignorance keeps from us (what has been called its "thickness"), Rawls is stacking the deck. That is, his only reason for specifying the contract conditions as he does is that his principles of justice are then the only ones that could be chosen. This can be most clearly seen in his discussion of the adoption of the second principle, which requires maximizing the position of the least well-off. It is difficult to see why rational parties to Rawls's original bargaining position would unanimously adopt it. Wouldn't some be willing to take risks on getting the larger shares as an alternative to the difference principle? Surely some would gamble on a society where 90 percent of the people lived in affluence and the other 10 percent at a bare minimum over a society where 100 percent of the people lived in near poverty although above the bare minimum. To avoid this contingency, Rawls stipulates that in the original condition the parties are ignorant of the probability of any outcome. This along with other features rules out any propensity to take risks, since gambling would be irrational under such circumstances.[21] But surely this looks like an ad hoc stipulation designed solely to rule out a competing alternative.[22]

In other words, critics can argue that the only reason Rawls has to rule out gambling is that if he allowed it, the parties would agree upon principles of which he disapproves. Rawls might reply that the propensity to gamble is precisely the kind of individual trait the veil of ignorance is designed to rule out, since knowledge of our own characteristics might destroy impartiality, but critics can rejoin that Rawls has characterized impartiality in a controversial way that is itself not neutral and not fair to all conceptions of justice.

A second line of initial criticism focused on the adequacy of the two principles of justice. By ordering them lexically, Rawls is saying that the conditions of the first principle must be completely satisfied before one tries to satisfy the second condition. Rawls's ordering of the principles in this way has received widespread criticism. Surely such a lexical ordering would not be accepted by a unanimous vote of the contract makers, and surely such a priority rule would be unjust. In underdeveloped countries, it may be rational, at least sometimes, to sacrifice basic liberties for improved economic well-being. Although all too often such an argument is used by a powerful elite to deny others their rights, it need not always be without force. For example, sometimes it may be justifiable to restrict free choice of occupation in order to place key workers in crucial positions, if severe economic deprivation can be prevented by such a policy. Rawls himself seems to recognize the force of this point since he is careful to limit the range of applicability of the priority of liberty.

> The supposition is that if persons in the original position assume that their basic liberties can be effectively exercised, they will not exchange a lesser liberty for an improvement in their economic well being, at least not once a certain level of wealth has been maintained. It is only when social conditions do not allow the effective establishment of these rights that one can acknowledge their restriction. The denial of equal liberty can be accepted only if it is necessary to enhance the quality of civilization so that in due course the equal freedoms can be enjoyed by all. The lexical ordering of the two principles is the long-run tendency of the general conception of justice consistently pursued under reasonably favorable circumstances.[23]

Once the lexical ordering rule is compromised, however, Rawls must provide some indication of the principles for determining the guidelines of compromise. Under what conditions should the lexical ordering be given up? The necessity for some guidelines will become more evident if we can show that the exceptions to the priority rule are not isolated and unusual but rather are pervasive and quite normal. To what extent would nonaltruistic parties in the original position compromise liberty for economic betterment? Speculations here would surely be highly abstract, but evidence abounds that economic betterment is currently valued more highly than Rawls thinks. Indeed, tradeoffs are not limited to so-called underdeveloped countries but exist in even the most affluent societies. Even the most casual observer of the United States cannot help but be impressed by the apparent dominance of pocketbook issues over issues of liberty. When such attitudes prevail in the most affluent society, it will likely take a very long time for the society to develop to the point where the lexical ordering will prevail. If we look toward actual societies, the compromise of the liberty principle is very extensive indeed.

Rawlsians might well reply that current societal practices do not mirror the reflections that would be made by persons in the original position operating under a veil of ignorance or by ordinary people living in a society regulated by Rawls's two principles of justice. This point would be well taken, but then it is incumbent upon proponents of

Rawls's theory to indicate the point at which the lexical ordering of the two principles is in fact legitimate. Vague comments about "due course" and "a certain level of wealth" are at best only rough guidelines that cannot be directly applied to social issues.

We also question the plausibility of the second principle. Rawls argued that the difference principle is the principle that would be adopted by those behind the veil of ignorance. Rawls's analysis has been seriously challenged by Robert Nozick and David Gauthier.[24] Nozick's point is that the most able and talented would not agree to the difference principle since they make all the sacrifices and have little to gain. After all, who has the most to gain from social cooperation? Surely it is the least able and least talented. Hence the less able should be willing to agree not only to an equal distribution of the fruits of social cooperation but also to something considerably less than equality. For example, why wouldn't it be rational for those behind the veil of ignorance to argue for a compromise position; namely, that everyone should reach a welfare floor, which in affluent societies might be quite high, but after this floor has been reached, everyone should receive in proportion to his or her contribution as determined by the market? If such a proposal is irrational, we have not been shown why.

Moreover, Rawls's view that our talents, capacities, and even our character are the arbitrary results of a natural environmental–genetic lottery, and so are social assets, is vulnerable to the charge of being disrespectful to persons. For example, why should Rawlsians value protection of individual choice so much if what we choose depends on such "accidents" as our tastes, inclinations, and skills? Isn't this letting the natural lottery affect outcomes just as much as rewarding talents and abilities? Why shouldn't our kidneys be viewed as social assets, since the luck of the draw determines who has and who lacks healthy kidneys? What is left of the individual once skills, capacities, and character are stripped away? Perhaps Rawls is just as guilty as the utilitarian of not taking seriously the differences between persons. At least on the intuitive level, it often seems just, as in competitive athletics, to let outcomes be determined by individual skills, effort, and ambition, so long as such practices do not undermine the rights of others, positive and negative alike. Perhaps that is all Rawls means to say, but his remarks about the natural lottery and the reduction of individual characteristics to social assets suggest a deindividualized view of the person that seems morally unattractive.

The criticism that has had the most impact, however, is the claim that Rawls's theory is biased in favor of liberal, individualistic, Western values and so cannot succeed as a universal theory of justice for all.[25] This contention is based on Rawls's account of the nature of the good. In the original position, Rawls rules out any knowledge of what each of us considers to be the good life. Rather, our knowledge of our desires is limited to what Rawls calls the primary goods. Primary goods are goods like rights and liberties, powers and opportunities, income and wealth that every rational person should want since these goods are necessary for achieving any other goods. By limiting our knowledge of the good in this way, Rawls can argue that no one would choose a society where the pursuit of one nonprimary good prevailed at the expense of all others. For example, no one would choose a society where religious persecution was practiced, since behind the veil one does not know if one would be in the majority religion or not. But again, isn't this stipulation biased against individuals who hold alternative theories of justice in which one value, such as predominance of a religion, or a limited set of values is given preeminence? As several critics have indicated, Rawls's refusal to rank particular conceptions of the good implies a very marked tolerance for individual inclination.

In other words, Rawls has not shown that being neutral with respect to various theories of the good is itself a neutral decision. It reflects a built-in liberal, individualistic assumption that is undefended within the theory.

It is true that by not making judgments about competing theories of the good, Rawlsian theory shows tolerance for competing nonliberal conceptions. Rawls wanted to rely on what he called "a thin theory of the good" that was represented by his list of primary goods. Primary goods are goods that everyone would want regardless of the more comprehensive "thick" theories of the good they might hold, since the primary goods are means to achieving a wide variety of conceptions of the good life. Thus, whether one is or is not religious, one might want the liberty to live according to the beliefs one holds. But some critics argue that religious fundamentalists, for example, might not be tolerant of conceptions of the good that they found blasphemous. Put in Rawlsian terms, some religious fundamentalists might find a society that tolerates what they regard as blasphemy intolerable and might regard Rawls's thin theory of the good as biased against them. Toleration of differing conceptions of the good, according to this line of criticism, is a characteristic of Western liberal democracies but may not be acceptable to all traditions and so is not neutral.

For these reasons among others, many critics of *A Theory of Justice* concluded that contrary to Rawls's hopes and intentions, his theory is not a universal theory of justice for all times and places but is, at best, a theory of justice that applies to liberal democratic societies.

**Rawls's Recent Responses.** When these criticisms, along with many others, were published and debated, Rawls reflected upon them and began to respond. Many specific criticisms were from communitarians and feminists, and Rawls's responses to them will be considered in the next chapter. In what follows, we will evaluate Rawls's response to the sorts of general criticisms of his theory considered above.

After nearly twenty years of debate over *A Theory of Justice,* Rawls published many of his responses in a new book, *Political Liberalism.* In this later book, Rawls revised many of his responses to published criticisms and tried to place them in a coherent order of argument rather than simply respond point by point to specific objections. Thus, *Political Liberalism* is an important contribution in its own right to theorizing about justice.

Significantly, Rawls agrees with his critics that his theory applies only to liberal democratic societies.[26] *Political Liberalism* should be seen not only as an attempt to expand on the work of *A Theory of Justice* but also as an attempt to limit its application to liberal democracies.

Toleration and stability are central themes of this later work. In *Political Liberalism,* Rawls holds fast to his belief that modern liberal democracies are characterized by intense competition among different, often conflicting theories of the good. How can people who hold these competing conceptions get along? As Rawls says in the introduction to *Political Liberalism,* "The problem of political liberalism is: How is it possible that there may exist over time a stable and just society of free and equal citizens profoundly divided by reasonable though incompatible religious, philosophical, and moral doctrines?"[27] Of course, there can be a modus vivendi where people agree that it is better to grudgingly accept one another than to fight. A tense stalemate is better than the Hobbesian war of all against all. However, a modus vivendi is inherently unstable, since it will tend to break down once one side has sufficient power to impose its will on others with impunity.

Rawls himself believes that his revised theory of justice can provide something more than a modus vivendi. It can provide an overlapping consensus constituted by the implementation of certain principles of conducting and carrying on debate that anyone with a reasonable conception of the good could accept. True to his procedural inclinations, Rawls believes that people with competing conceptions of the good can nonetheless accept certain common political ground rules. In that way, we have an overlapping consensus on these ground rules rather than an unstable agreement of convenience or modus vivendi. *Political Liberalism* can be seen as a series of essays that develop this central idea.

If this Rawlsian project is to succeed, there has to be some limit to the conceptions of the good that can be tolerated. Those who have no wish to get along with others and actively seek to eliminate adherents of competing ideas of the good, say those with different religious or moral beliefs, seek to impose their will on other citizens. Imposition of a conception of the good through coercion surely cannot be just. Thus, the Rawlsian democratic society tolerates only reasonable conceptions of the good. But what counts as a reasonable conception? Rawls must come up with criteria for what counts as a reasonable conception of the good. He attempts to accomplish this in two ways.

First, he provides a normative characterization of the citizens in a democratic society. Rawls is asking how we should view ourselves in the political arena. This is one of the ways the revised theory attempts to be political rather than metaphysical. It does not tell us what we are really like. Perhaps we are in reality divine beings with immortal souls, or perhaps we are purely material mortal beings. Rawls's theory does not attempt to adjudicate such complex metaphysical issues but tries to exclude from political discourse debate over such perhaps unanswerable, highly divisive metaphysical questions. It attempts to say how we may present ourselves in political interchange. Thus, a citizen should be committed to the use of public reason. That is, a citizen as citizen is committed to the use of evidence and to procedural rules for settling debates rather than, say, divine revelation or psychic insight not available to other citizens or confirmable by public tests. In addition, a citizen should respect the reasonable conceptions of the good that other citizens might have, even when these conceptions are inconsistent with his or her own comprehensive view of the good. Citizens in a just democracy, then, are appropriately tolerant of the reasonable positions of others. Any comprehensive metaphysical view of the good that does not respect this normative component of citizenship and public debate would be seen as unreasonable.

Second, Rawls distinguishes the rational from the reasonable and provides a further set of criteria for the latter. He begins with the claim that all citizens are free and equal. They are equal in the sense that they all have the capacity to have a sense of justice and a conception of the good. They are free in the sense that they have the moral autonomy to form their own conception of the good, regard themselves as self-authenticating centers of valid claims, and view themselves as capable of taking responsibility for their choice of aims. By "the rational," Rawls refers to the selection of effective means to our ends, as well as to how ends are selected and given priority over one another. Rationality, then, has to do with our selection, ordering, and implementation of our own ends or goals. What is missing from the rational is a commitment to engage in competition on terms that others could reasonably be assumed to accept. Thus, not only should citizens be rational with respect to their own interests, but also they should be reasonable in the sense that they will try to achieve their goals in ways that appear reasonable to all. Conceptions of the good that reject the normative account of citizenship as involving equality and freedom, or that involve achieving goals in ways that others could not accept, are unreasonable.

Another constraint on our various conceptions of the good is that we must be willing to let political values have priority over other values in public life. Only in this way is an overlapping consensus possible. Political values are those that govern the basic structure of social life. They are constituted largely by the principles that Rawls developed in *A Theory of Justice*: equal political liberty; fair equality of opportunity; economic reciprocity, presumably implemented through the difference principle; and the social bases of mutual respect among citizens. In his later work, Rawls adds the values of public reason that, as mentioned above, are primarily guidelines for public inquiry and rules for assessing evidence. Rawls believes that any person with a reasonable conception of the good will accept these political values and their priority. Finally, by giving priority to the political, the citizen brackets his own individual conception of the good and does not allow it to play a role in political debate involving constitutional issues or basic principles of justice. In this way, an overlapping consensus on the principles of liberal democracy and social justice is possible.

Rawls, however, is not committed to broad pluralism if by "broad pluralism" one means that every conception of a comprehensive good deserves a voice in a democratic society. Rather, Rawls is committed to what he calls a reasonable pluralism, one in which those with competing comprehensive theories of the good are willing to compete with one another on terms that all are willing to accept.

Rawls's analysis at this point may seem unduly abstract. But he is trying to resolve the problem of how people with very different conceptions of how life should be led, perhaps based on different religious, cultural, or ethnic traditions, can all get along in one society under a common set of guidelines that all can reasonably accept. To illustrate how reasonable pluralism works, Rawls provides the following example:

> Now in holding these convictions, we clearly imply some relation between political and non-political values. If it is said that outside the church there is no salvation, and therefore a constitutional regime cannot be accepted unless it is unavoidable, we must make some reply. . . . We say that such a doctrine is unreasonable; it proposes to use the public's political power—a power in which citizens have an equal share—to enforce a view bearing on constitutional essentials about which citizens as reasonable persons are bound to differ uncompromisingly. When there is a plurality of reasonable doctrines, it is unreasonable, or worse, to want to use the sanctions of state power to correct, or to punish, those who disagree with us.[28]

Thus, those who want to impose their conception of the good on those who do not share it are being unreasonable. Rawls comes close to saying that comprehensive conceptions of the good that are not committed to the basic political values of justice and the regulation of public debate are not reasonable.[29]

But what if several members of the state do not want to be reasonable in the way Rawls defines it? They believe not only that their doctrine is true but also that it is right, even morally required, to impose it on others. Isn't a notion of an overlapping consensus utopian in light of such strong commitments?

Rawls, however, suggests that the development of an overlapping consensus is evolutionary. Societies in which the various parties wish to impose their conceptions of the good on others tend to be racked with violence. Eventually a stalemate is reached, and the warring parties, deciding it is better to live and let live than continue to struggle, draw up a constitution that guarantees certain political rights to all and provides some regulation of political life. At first, the parties accept the constitution simply because it is better to do so than to continue civil strife. As the parties live under the constitution and its rules, however, they gradually come to accept constitutional values in their own right. Finally, as time goes on, the citizens develop a political philosophy that provides a foundation for the constitutional values, even though the citizens continue to have differences regarding what nonpolitical values are good. Thus, in our own society, many of us are prepared to defend the right to free speech of many of those with whom we profoundly disagree.

Not surprisingly, Rawls's revisions have not satisfied most of his critics. Michael Sandel, an early and thorough critic of *A Theory of Justice*, rejects Rawls's separation of political values from other moral values, as well as the Rawlsian hierarchy in which political values are given priority over others. Sandel argues that the notion of justice is just as contestable in a pluralistic society as other moral values and should not be given privileged status. Second, Sandel maintains that when grave moral issues are at stake, our individual conceptions of the good should be brought to bear on political discourse. Sandel uses the issue of abortion to illustrate his point.

> But if the Catholic Church is right about the moral status of the fetus, if abortion is morally tantamount to murder, then it is not clear why the political values of toleration and women's equality, important though they are, should prevail. If the Catholic doctrine is true, the political liberal's case for the priority of political values must become an instance of just war theory; he or she would have to show why these values should prevail even at the cost of some 1.5 million civilian deaths each year. Of course to suggest the impossibility of bracketing the moral-theological question of where human life begins is not to argue against a right to abortion. It is simply to show that the case for abortion rights cannot be neutral with respect to that moral and religious controversy.[30]

We suggest that Sandel is persuasive here. Although we adopt much of Rawls's revised theory of justice, we depart from him on the separation of political and other values. However, while Sandel may be correct to suggest that political values do not automatically take priority over others, we also think Rawls is correct to emphasize reasonable public standards of debate. Free and equal citizens are owed reasons or justifications for policies that are debatable in the public arena, and so arguments offered must be those that can be publicly debated and scrutinized.

**Summary and Evaluation.** Sandel is only one critic among many. In the next chapter, we will consider criticisms of political liberalism from the perspectives of radical feminism and communitarianism. However, it will be useful at this point to comment briefly on Rawls's political liberalism and compare it to our own rights-based approach.

Rawls has attempted to provide a justification for the position known as political liberalism. Its central tenet is that the state should remain neutral among competing conceptions of the good life. The role of the political order is to provide a fair and just framework, neutral among competing conceptions of the good, within which citizens can choose for themselves how they wish to live.

In many respects, our own rights-based position can be characterized as a version of political liberalism. We agree that the state should remain neutral among competing conceptions of the good life so long as those conceptions respect the legitimate rights claims of citizens who have competing views about what constitutes the good life. Thus, on our view, the principal task of the state is to protect, sustain, and support the human rights of its citizens. Moreover, we also agree with the Rawlsian idea in *A Theory of Justice* that justice in the liberal state is primarily procedural since it is virtually impossible to determine what is just when each and every individual case is evaluated from scratch on its own merits.

Since we recognize that rights claims frequently conflict, as can be seen when the right to liberty conflicts with the right to a minimum standard of living, we maintain that it is the function of the state to provide morally acceptable procedures for adjudicating these conflicts. Since the adjudication of rights claims is what justice is all about, we conclude that a function of the state is to provide justice.

We also believe, with Rawls, that public debate in a democracy should be reasonable and tolerant and thus should be conducted in a manner that shows respect for our fellow citizens. As noted above, while we agree with Sandel that there can be no clear separation between political and other sorts of moral values in debate, we agree with Rawls that debate must be reasonable and public. The reasons provided must be subject to public analysis and criticism and not be the sorts of reasons—say, those based on an alleged private revelation from God—that other free and equal citizens cannot reasonably be expected to accept.

Our emphasis on procedural justice, however, does not imply that we fully endorse Rawls's use of the veil of ignorance and hypothetical contract. While we regard the veil of ignorance as a useful heuristic test for impartiality, we agree with the criticisms made earlier that the contractual argument does not yield determinate results, at least not unless controversial assumptions favorable to liberalism are accepted as part of the argument. In fact, Rawls himself seems to rely far less on the contractual argument and the veil of ignorance in *Political Liberalism* than he did in *A Theory of Justice*.[31] In later chapters, we will argue that a form of democratic voting, conjoined with other traditional democratic institutions, provides the best means for settling rights conflicts and hence for approximating justice. For Rawls's hypothetical contract, we substitute a form of democratic government.

We emphasize, however, that in our approach, the framework of individual rights puts considerable constraint on the types of issues that can be subject to democratic vote. The proper objects of state action are the implementation of individual rights and the resolution of conflicts between rights. The rights of individuals can be denied only on the basis of providing for or protecting the rights of other individuals. Appeals to the maximization of utility or to broader conceptions of the good life are out of place. Thus, our view is very much within the tradition that we have called political liberalism.

In one respect, our approach is closer to the universal conception of justice defended by the Rawls of *A Theory of Justice* than to the revised views of *Political Liberalism*. While we agree that the application of principles of justice can vary with circumstances, our broad principles of human rights are intended to apply to all societies. A society that violates human rights normally commits a terrible evil. Human rights are restrictions that apply to all societies, not an overlapping consensus that only those already committed to liberal democracy should accept.

Finally, although we agree with Rawls that individual liberty is important and that the plight of the least well-off deserves special attention, we reject the specific wording of Rawls's two principles and their lexical ordering. We suggest that the historical circumstances of a people are relevant in determining appropriate principles of justice. The existence of goods and resources and the state of technological advance are important determinants of the principles that should be adopted for implementing our right to well-being and for protecting our rights to liberty and privacy.

In summary our theory of justice is the following:

1. Problems of justice arise as individuals attempt to implement their rights.

2. The function of the state is to provide a mechanism for adjudicating the conflicts of individual rights claims and for implementing the claims.

3. Suitably constrained, a form of democracy is the appropriate procedure for providing justice.

4. Our individual rights framework provides some limitations on the kinds of questions that can be submitted to the democratic mechanism.

5. Other moral principles place additional constraints on the democratic mechanism, but these supplementary principles can be discovered only by analyzing particular problems in particular historical circumstances. We do not believe a set of lexically ordered principles can be derived independent of such particular historical circumstances.

We acknowledge, however, that our politically liberal, rights-based approach is highly controversial, not only because of problems discussed in chapter 3 that are involved in justifying a theory of human rights, but also because political liberalism has been highly criticized, especially by those identified as communitarians and radical feminists. Indeed, some feminists, such as Iris Young, have charged that liberal approaches have been too concerned with issues of distribution of resources and not enough with the elimination of oppression, while communitarians and some feminists as well have rejected liberalism because of what they regard as its excessive individualism. In the next chapter, we will consider these critiques and indicate how a political liberal might respond.

## Notes

1. Aristotle, *Nicomachean Ethics,* bk. 5.
2. Plato's theory of justice is fully developed in his *Republic.*
3. Nicholas Rescher, *Distributive Justice* (Indianapolis: Bobbs-Merrill, 1966).
4. This tradition is represented by the French egalitarian Gracchus Babeuf (1760–1797).
5. One of the most sophisticated discussions of equal treatment is by Ronald Dworkin, "What Is Equality?" parts 1 and 2, *Philosophy and Public Affairs* 10, no. 3 (Summer 1981); no. 4 (Fall 1981).
6. There is considerable contemporary discussion as to what preferences and/or interests should be legitimately considered. One discussion occurs in Dworkin, "What Is Equality?"
7. This example is taken from Gregory Vlastos's important article, "Justice and Equality," in *Social Justice,* ed. Richard B. Brandt (Englewood Cliffs, N.J.: Prentice-Hall, 1962), 31–72.
8. This criticism is developed by Norman Bowie, "Equality and Distributive Justice," *Philosophy* 45 (1970): 140–48.
9. For his own defense of his position, see Milton Friedman, *Capitalism and Freedom* (Chicago: University of Chicago Press, 1962).
10. For a delightful discussion of this paradox, see Bernard Mandeville, *Fable of the Bees* (Oxford: Clarendon Press, 1924). Strictly speaking, the theory of the free market need not presuppose that people always act selfishly, in the sense of aiming ultimately to benefit only themselves regardless of effects on others. It is perfectly consistent with capitalism and the theory of the market that a person operates as a rational consumer in order to maximize profits and then gives them away to charity or uses them to support a family. The assumption required is that agents act in economically rational ways, not they they use what they gain in the market for purely selfish ends.
11. Robert Nozick, *Anarchy, State, and Utopia* (New York: Basic Books, 1974), 155.
12. Ibid., 156.
13. Ibid., 163.

14. E.g., Nozick uses the idea of a baseline when talking of transferring property from one person to another. "This excludes his transferring it into an agglomeration that does violate the Lockean proviso and excludes his using it in a way . . . so as to violate the proviso by making the situation of others worse than their baseline situation." *Anarchy, State, and Utopia,* 180.

15. John Rawls, *A Theory of Justice* (Cambridge: Harvard University Press, 1971), 126–42.

16. Ibid., 302. Rawls provides more complicated formulations throughout his book.

17. Ibid., 61.

18. Ibid., 70.

19. Ibid., 104.

20. In part 1 of *Anarchy, State, and Utopia,* which we did not discuss in the text, Nozick argues that a minimal state that functions only to provide for defense and prevent coercion and fraud would evolve from the state of nature without violating anyone's right to liberty.

21. Rawls, *A Theory of Justice,* 172.

22. This point has been made by a number of philosophers, including Brian Barry, *The Liberal Theory of Justice* (Oxford: Clarendon Press, 1973), 96, 230; R. M. Hare, "Critical Study: Rawls's Theory of Justice II," *Philosophical Quarterly* 23 (1973): 247-51; Russell Keat and David Miller, "Understanding Justice," *Political Theory* 2 (1974): 25-27; Thomas Nagel, "Rawls on Justice," *Philosophical Review* 82 (1973): 229-30; and David Lewis Schaefer, "A Critique of Rawls's Contract Doctrine," *Review of Metaphysics* 28 (1974): 100.

23. Rawls, *A Theory of Justice,* 542 (emphasis ours).

24. Nozick, *Anarchy, State, and Utopia,* 183–97; and David Gauthier, "Justice and Natural Endowment: Toward a Critique of Rawls's Ideological Framework," *Social Theory and Practice* 3 (1974): 3–26.

25. Critics who develop this point include Barry, *The Liberal Theory of Justice,* 228–29; Maurice Mandelbaum, in his review essay in *History and Theory* 2 (1973): 240–50; and Nagel, "Rawls on Justice," 228. Rawls has attempted to answer this objection. See John Rawls, "Fairness to Goodness," *Philosophical Review* 84 (1975): 536–54.

26. Not all commentators regard this as an improvement. Thus, Brian Barry argues that Rawls's theory is strongest in the form published in *A Theory of Justice.* See Barry, *Justice as Impartiality* (New York: Oxford University Press, 1995), xi-xii.

27. John Rawls, *Political Liberalism* (New York: Columbia University Press, 1993), xviii.

28. Ibid., 138.

29. This idea is developed by Michael Sandel in his review of *Political Liberalism,* in *Harvard Law Review* 107 (1994): 1777–82.

30. Ibid., 1778.

31. However, Rawls does sometimes suggest that the original position and veil of ignorance model the overlapping consensus, that they are devices that help us determine what conclusions the overlapping consensus would reach. See Rawls, *Political Liberalism,* 24.

## Questions for Further Study

1. What is the difference between a formal theory of justice and a material theory of justice? Does a formal theory have any use, or is it just an empty formula? Explain.

2. What is right and what is wrong with the Platonic formula that justice requires that each person be given his or her due?

3. It seems wrong to say that justice requires that everyone be given or guaranteed an equal amount. On the other hand, equality does seem to be a requirement of justice. How is equality related to justice?

4. Explain the difference between just procedures and just results. When, if ever, is it

morally permissible to be satisfied with just procedures in the absence of just results?

5.  Is the operation of the free competitive market a good example of procedural justice? Why or why not?

6.  What is a patterned formula of justice? What is the point of Nozick's Wilt Chamberlain example, and is it successful in making its point?

7.  Evaluate Nozick's formula of justice, "From each as they choose, to each as they are chosen." Does adding the phrase "so long as you do not worsen the condition of others" strengthen or weaken Nozick's formula? Explain.

8.  What is the purpose of Rawls's "original position"? Does the notion serve its purpose? Why or why not?

9.  State and evaluate Rawls's two principles of justice.

10. Describe the changes Rawls has made in his theory as expounded in *Political Liberalism* compared with the earlier *A Theory of Justice*. Is Rawls's theory stronger or weaker as a result? Explain.

## Suggested Readings

### Books

Ackerman, Bruce A. *Social Justice in the Liberal State*. New Haven: Yale University Press, 1980.

Aristotle. *Nicomachean Ethics*. Translated by Martin Ostwald. Indianapolis: Bobbs-Merrill, 1962.

Barry, Brian. *Justice as Impartiality*. New York: Oxford University Press, 1995.

Blocker, H. Gene, and Elizabeth H. Smith, eds. *John Rawls's Theory of Social Justice*. Athens: Ohio University Press, 1980. A collection of essays.

Brandt, Richard, ed. *Social Justice*. Englewood Cliffs, N.J.: Prentice-Hall, 1962.

Daniels, Norman, ed. *Reading Rawls: Critical Studies of "A Theory of Justice."* New York: Basic Books, 1975.

Feinberg, Joel. *Social Philosophy*. Englewood Cliffs, N.J.: Prentice-Hall, 1973. Chap. 7.

Friedman, Milton. *Capitalism and Freedom*. Chicago: University of Chicago Press, 1962.

Friedrich, C. J., and J. Chapman, eds. *Justice*. Nomos 6. New York: Aldine-Atherton, 1963.

Kymlicka, Will. *Contemporary Political Philosophy*. New York: Oxford University Press, 1990.

Nozick, Robert. *Anarchy, State, and Utopia*. New York: Basic Books, 1974.

Pettit, Philip. *Judging Justice*. Boston: Routledge & Kegan Paul, 1980.

Plato. *The Republic*. Translated by Francis MacDonald Cornford. New York: Oxford University Press, 1967.

Pogge, Thomas. *Realizing Rawls*. Ithaca, N.Y.: Cornell University Press, 1989.

Rawls, John. *A Theory of Justice*. Cambridge: Harvard University Press, 1971.

————. *Political Liberalism*. New York: Columbia University Press, 1993.

Rescher, Nicholas. *Distributive Justice*. Indianapolis: Bobbs-Merrill, 1966.

Wilson, John. *Equality*. New York: Harcourt, Brace Jovanovich, 1966.

## Articles and Essays

Berlin, Isaiah. "Equality." *Proceedings of the Aristotelian Society* 56 (1955–56): 301–26.

Dick, James C. "How to Justify a Distribution of Earnings." *Philosophy and Public Affairs* 4 (1975): 248–72.

Katzner, Louis. "Presumptivist and Nonpresumptivist Principles of Formal Justice." *Ethics* 81 (1971): 253–58.

Kaufmann, Walter. "Doubts about Justice." In *Ethics and Social Justice,* edited by Howard E. Kieter and Milton K. Munitz. Albany: State University of New York Press, 1968.

Keat, Russell, and David Miller. "Understanding Justice." *Political Theory* 2 (1974): 3–31.

Sandel, Michael. Review of *Political Liberalism,* by John Rawls. *Harvard Law Review* 107 (1994): 1777–82.

Schaefer, David Lewis. "A Critique of Rawls's Contract Doctrine." *Review of Metaphysics* 28 (1974): 89–115.

Wood, Allen W. "The Marxian Critique of Justice." *Philosophy and Public Affairs* 1 (1972): 244–82.

# 5

# Liberal Justice and Its Critics

The liberal theory of the state and political justice has been strongly criticized by a group of thinkers who are commonly referred to as communitarians, although there is no established "orthodox" communitarian doctrine and many of those characterized as leading communitarians have not adopted that title. Social scientist Amitai Etzioni has embraced the term, and Robert Bellah and his colleagues are sympathetic to it. However, when political philosophers refer to communitarian writings, they most frequently refer to the writings of such contemporary political philosophers as Michael Sandel, Alasdair MacIntyre, Charles Taylor, and Michael Walzer.

Although each of these individuals has a distinctive version of communitarian philosophy, some common themes seem to unite them. First, they agree that liberalism is too focused on the rights of individuals and that liberals do not focus enough on society and the bonds that are needed to hold society together. They point out that individuals receive a good part of their identity from being members of a particular society. They think that the liberal approach, including our own, of judging the legitimacy of social institutions by the extent to which these institutions protect or enrich human rights undermines the ties one has to society. Too often there is much discussion of rights against society but little, if any discussion of obligations to society. Second, communitarians argue that the liberal ideal of the neutral state is simply unattainable. What liberals call neutrality is a substantive way of life and thus a normative position as to what counts as a good life. As such, it must be explicitly defended against competing positions as to what constitutes the good life. Third, as a result of these considerations, communitarians tend to think that a substantive concept of the good is more central in political philosophy than the concept of rights or justice. In fact, communitarians claim, a concept of the good life (such as the liberal's emphasis on autonomy and individualism) is needed to decide what rights are basic. Finally, communitarians tend to look at specific problems differently from the way liberals do. Consider the debate over pornography. Liberals tend to discuss the issue in terms of whether the right to view pornography can be overridden by the obligation to prevent harm to others (assuming that there is such harm). Communitarians, on the other hand, tend to view the issue in terms not only of pornography's impact on the individual but also of its impact on the coarsening of community standards. With these general themes before us, let us consider the specific communitarian ideas of four philosophers.

# The Communitarian Critique of Liberalism

## The Communitarian Critique of the Liberal Self

Michael Sandel's book-length critique of Rawls, *Liberalism and the Limits of Justice,* established the theme for the communitarian criticisms of a liberal theory of justice. One of its criticisms of rights theorists and of political liberalism is that these theorists misunderstand the nature of an individual. The liberal notion of the individual is abstract. It is a kind of *x* that stands outside experience and decides what it will become. Some would criticize this account of the self by arguing that the content of the self, the what that the self chooses to be, is provided by society and that liberal political theory ignores this fact.

However, liberals have a reasonable response to this version of the critique. Of course the choices that are presented to the self are by and large provided by society. Nevertheless, people do change their religion or give up religion altogether; some people even emigrate to foreign countries. The fact that relatively few people do these things is immaterial to the liberal position. The fact that people can do these things and should have the right to do these things is what matters. Thus what the self decides to become need not be determined by society, although all liberals should acknowledge that the content of our choices comes from society.

Sandel's formulation of the argument cuts much deeper, however. Sandel admits that Rawls allows a greater place for community than laissez-faire economic liberals like Nozick. These laissez-faire liberals are instrumentalists with respect to the individual's relation to the state. An instrumentalist views the community as a means to one's ends. It is a resource upon which one draws, but it has no intrinsic value. Rawls explicitly rejects the instrumentalist view and adopts instead what Sandel refers to as the sentimentalist view. Rawls argues that in a just society, citizens are moved by a sense of community because they have shared final ends and a sense of cooperation. But Sandel thinks Rawls's account is still too individualistic because the starting point of the self is the individual. Sandel says that individuals are defined by community. An individual is the individual she is because of the relationships she finds herself in.

> A theory of the community whose province extended to the subject as well as the object of motivations would be individualistic in neither the conventional sense nor in Rawls'. It . . . would describe not just a feeling but a mode of self-understanding partly constitutive of the agent's identity. On this strong view, to say that the members of a society are bound by a sense of community is not simply to say that a great many of them profess communitarian sentiments and pursue communitarian aims, but rather that they conceive their identity . . . as defined to some extent by the community of which they are a part. For them community describes not just what they have as fellow citizens, but also what they are, not a relationship they choose . . . but an attachment they discover, not merely an attribute but a constituent of their identity.[1]

Charles Taylor, another theorist sympathetic to many communitarian themes, has developed his own criticism of the liberal self. He has characterized the liberal view of the self as monological. According to a monological view of the self, the essential characteristics of an authentic self cannot be socially derived; rather, they are internally generated and determined. Taylor contrasts this monological view of the self with what he calls the dialogical view. The dialogical view argues that a self becomes what it is in dialogue (broadly defined) with other human beings. Our identity is not self-determined, as on the monological view, but rather is determined in interaction with others. Taylor also notes as a matter of psychological fact that we cannot get the full enjoyment of some experiences unless we experience them with others. It is more fun to share. As Taylor says: "We define our identity always in dialogue with, sometimes in struggle against, the things our significant others want to see in us. . . . If some of the things I value most are accessible to me only in relation to the person I love, then she becomes part of my identity."[2]

We should note here that Taylor is making a stronger claim than merely asserting that the self we choose to be must choose characteristics from an existing society. One cannot choose to be an airplane pilot in a world where there are no airplanes. But of course the individualist liberal would concede this. Rather, Taylor is saying that the self who the individualist argues can choose is itself socially determined. There is no pure chooser. To the extent that a self chooses to be what it is, its status as a chooser is derived at least in part from its interaction with significant others. There is an important sense in which the self as chooser is already, at least in part, socially determined.

Michael Walzer also thinks Rawls and other liberals underestimate the importance of community and the social nature of the self. He takes the critique of the liberal self further to develop a second but related point, namely, that one's social relationships and circumstances play a crucial role in the development of the conception of justice that develops and applies in particular contexts.

Walzer begins his book *Spheres of Justice* by arguing that the liberals are mistaken when they try to develop principles of justice by abstracting away the particularities of individuals, thereby isolating them from their culture and other social relations. You cannot get principles of justice for real people in real historical circumstances by asking what would rational persons who knew nothing of their culture or other social relationships choose as principles of justice. Rather, people ask what is just, given our culture at this particular time. Walzer puts it this way:

> The greatest problem is with the particularism of history, culture and membership. Even if they are committed to impartiality, the question most likely to arise in the minds of the membership of a political community is not, What would rational individuals choose under universalizing conditions of such and such a sort? But rather, What would individuals like us choose, who are situated as we are, who share a culture and are determined to go on sharing it?[3]

Well, what would they choose? First they would recognize that goods are socially determined. Rawls thought that there was a list of goods that all rational people would want because they are the goods necessary for securing any other goods at all (primary goods). Walzer argues that what counts as a good depends on the culture one is in. All goods are good because they are shared with another group—in the widest sense, with a culture. Men and women take on the identities they do in part because of the way they relate to social goods.

Walzer then develops a normative theory for the distribution of social goods. He argues that there are many kinds of goods, such as money, free time, education, kinship, and love, to name but a few. What is important for justice is that no one good dominate another good. For example, not all goods should be reduced to money, and the economic sphere should not invade every sphere of our lives. Justice also requires that no one should be unequal across all goods in the sense of having dominant shares of a wide variety of different kinds of benefits. It is unjust that a person be rich, have great political power, be successful in love, have many fulfilling talents and abilities, and have lots of free time. These are the types of principles that are appropriate for dealing with the particularity of historical time and culture. Walzer also admits that three principles—free exchange, desert, and need—are relevant to issues of distributive justice but that no one of them should dominate the other for all goods. Thus it is not the case that all goods should be distributed according to the principle of need or the principle of desert.

Alasdair MacIntyre would likely agree with Sandel's critique of the liberal self and Walzer's critique of the liberal abstraction of justice from particular social contexts, but MacIntyre has much more to say about the social nature of the self than does either. MacIntyre argues that there is a narrative unity to a human life; man is a storytelling animal, but it is a story or stories that we enter from a point in time: "I can only answer the question, 'What am I to do?' if I can answer the prior question 'Of what story or stories do I find myself a part?' We enter human society that is with one or more imputed character-roles into which we have been drafted."[4]

Given the human condition, an individual begins his or her story with a certain social identity built in. As we move through life, we take part in traditions, which in turn are composed of practices. Both traditions and the practices that compose them are strengthened and sustained by the virtues appropriate to them. Each individual, then, is involved in a story in which he or she seeks the good for his or her own life. But the goods for a human life are embodied in practices—that is, in complex yet coherent sets of socially established cooperative activities through which human goods are realized. A tradition is a coherent set of practices that provide the unity of goods for a human life that is shaped and transmitted across generations. Thus the good for the individual is deeply embedded in socially established ways of life.

## Communitarian Critique of Liberal Neutrality

A second communitarian objection to liberal political theory is that the liberal state is not neutral among conceptions of the good, and as a matter of logic it could not be. Some religious views have as their essential characteristic a commitment to a conception of the good that rejects and refuses to tolerate certain competing conceptions of the good. Stuart Hampshire points this out in his description of the outlook of the Inquisitors, who, at the point of a sword, demand adherence to what they regard as the true religion:

> Your belief in forcible conversion as a duty follows from your conception of the good, and even when you want to be tolerant, you think you ought not to be, because you infer that it would be unjust—both to the faithful who would be scandalized, and to the infidel who would go to Hell. You are ready to argue against liberals in support of your conception of the good and of the consequent substantial conception of justice.[5]

Of course, one need not be intolerant to hold a nonliberal position. Many communitarians would argue that the state should not be neutral with respect to something as important to society as the stability of the family. Rather, they would argue that the traditional family should be favored under the tax laws and should receive benefits that nontraditional families or significant others should not receive.

Thus, communitarians argue that certain substantive positions about the good are required if the values of community are to be realized—positions that are inconsistent with the liberal procedural notion of the good. The communitarian is arguing in effect that the liberal cannot assert priority of the procedural account of justice over the communitarian's substantive account. Hampshire, in effect, is suggesting that Rawls's procedural notion of justice is itself a substantive position. Liberals claim that they are defending neutral procedures but in reality are themselves employing a disguised conception of the good.

Moreover, with respect to important moral issues, substantive matters of the good should be debated. As we saw in chapter 4, Rawls is willing to suspend debate on non-political matters of the good in order to attain an overlapping consensus on how politics should be conducted. Sandel disagrees with Rawls on this matter. Sandel points out that the setting aside (bracketing) of substantive moral issues was a major issue in the Lincoln-Douglas debates. Douglas argued that since there was substantive disagreement about slavery, it should be set aside (bracketed) and not made a matter of political debate. Lincoln argued the contrary position. Thus the liberals are aligned with Douglas and the communitarians with Lincoln.

However, as Sandel acknowledges, liberals can reply that slavery should not be bracketed because it is a violation of the requirement of equal respect for persons that constrains political debate. Slavery is inconsistent with the thin theories of liberal procedural justice. Sandel accepts this response for 1996 but argues that a liberal could not have made that response in 1856 because the issue was politically contested in 1856. But that is to make Rawls's political liberalism too historical. There are still positions that are unreasonable in the sense described in chapter 4. Thus, the suggestion that liberals could not contest slavery because that would be to raise a substantive rather than a procedural issue goes too far because it ignores the point that liberal procedures are based on such values as respect for all persons.

Sandel is on firmer ground when he discusses abortion. Many liberals argue that the issue of abortion should be bracketed and left to individual choice since its resolution depends on the solution of complex moral and metaphysical issues, such as the status of the fetus, that cannot be resolved by public reason. But surely this is to favor those who think that the fetus is not a person over those who think it is.

> Opponents of abortion resist the translation from moral to political terms because they know that more of their view will be lost in the translation; the neutral territory offered by minimalist liberalism is likely to be less hospitable to their religious convictions than to those of their opponents. For defenders of abortion, little comparable is at stake, there is little difference between believing that abortion is permissible and agreeing that, as a political matter, women should be free to decide the moral question for themselves. The moral price of political agreement is much higher if abortion is wrong than if it is permissible.[6]

Now liberals such as John Rawls and Ronald Dworkin, whose views on affirmative action will be discussed in chapter 9, do have a limited theory of the good. In *A Theory of Justice*, Rawls cites various primary goods that are necessary for the pursuit of any good whatsoever. In *Political Liberalism*, Rawls cites certain procedural conditions that must hold if one is to have an overlapping consensus rather than simply a modus vivendi. Communitarians argue, against Rawls and other liberals, that the procedural notions designed to separate the political from the civil and provide an overlapping consensus are too thin. Communitarians argue that a viable democracy must be based on a thicker theory; a viable democracy needs a commonly recognized definition of the good life.[7]

Thus, in *Democracy's Discontent*, Sandel has argued for a republican (and here we refer to civic republicanism, not the policies of the contemporary Republican Party) conception of the state rather than a liberal one. Civic republicanism emphasizes the life of participation in political institutions as part of the human good. Thus, Sandel argues that the participation by the citizen in the affairs of the state is a comprehensive theory of the good that a state should strive to achieve. Liberalism, on the other hand, has no place for such a general obligation; if citizens want to participate actively in the state, they of course have a right to do so, but there is no obligation to do so. Moreover, on the republican conception, part of the activity of participation in civic affairs involves engaging in debates about the common good. Sandel puts it this way:

> To share in self-rule therefore requires that citizens possess, or come to acquire, certain qualities of character or civic virtues. But this means that republican politics cannot be neutral toward the values and ends its citizens espouse. The republican conception of freedom, unlike the liberal conception, requires a formative politics, a politics that cultivates in citizens the qualities of character self-government requires.[8]

Sandel would take exception to our own construal of the purpose of the state as the protector of individual fundamental rights. We see the state as a protector of the right to liberty, a right that can be overridden only by another human right. Sandel argues that the right to liberty emerges from democracy and is in some sense dependent on it. For Sandel's version of civic republicanism, a citizen is free as a participant in a free political community that determines its own fate. Freedom, on this view, is participation in civic affairs and decision making (in other words, in helping to rule) rather than simply abstract freedom of choice. Sandel points out that there is a strong and a weak interpretation of the claim that freedom is participation in civic affairs. For Aristotle, participation in civic affairs is a necessary condition for freedom. On this strong (more demanding) Aristotelian interpretation, a person who does not take an active part in the polis is not really free. The weaker interpretation of this claim is that participation is instrumental to the exercise of liberty. Participation in the polis and public service help preserve liberty and thus strengthen it.

For civic republicans like Sandel, the liberal theory of freedom is too weak to sustain itself. People might use their freedom simply to get high on drugs or watch *Beavis and Butthead* reruns all day. At the very least, freedom is of value only when combined with correlative responsibilities to participate in the political life of the state and develop the civic virtues necessary to the good functioning of democracy.

However, we are concerned that the republican conception of freedom leaves fundamental human rights unprotected. Sandel seems close to admitting that in a democracy where all citizens actively engage in the political process, the state may adopt a notion of the public good that is shared by a majority. On certain issues, such as how much to spend on national defense and how much on welfare, we have no quarrel with this conception, so long as the amount spent for defense in peacetime does not deprive a family of the human right to a minimum standard of living. Yet we think there is a danger in Sandel's view that an active republican democracy could pass legislation that would in fact deprive a minority of basic human rights, such as the right to a minimum standard of living.

Moreover, if political participation is an important part of freedom, either intrinsically or instrumentally, does the state have a right to coerce us to be free, to force us to cultivate the civil virtues? We think Sandel would have to answer that question in the affirmative. We find the dangers of state coercion and oppression to be greater than the danger that citizens in a democratic state might neglect civic participation to an extent that threatens democracy itself. While we are alarmed at the cynicism that the American public has toward politics and by the declining percentage of the population that votes, be it in presidential or local school board elections, we do not believe that mandatory participation in the political process is the answer.

To summarize, both Taylor and Sandel have argued that participation in government is a good in itself. Both defend a vision of civic republicanism in which the impact of political and economic arrangements on the quality of political and social life must be considered. According to communitarians, liberals ignore these impacts but republicans do not. In embracing substantive conceptions of good citizenship as enforceable by the state, communitarians reject the liberal idea of neutrality toward conceptions of the good life.

Taylor has gone on to defend a notion of the right of a culture to survive. From the perspective of the culture, survival is a public good and a public good so important that it permits the violation of the right to equal treatment in certain cases. As an example, Taylor considers the concern of French separatists in Quebec, Canada, who are afraid that their French culture will be assimilated into an English Canada and disappear. As a result, the Quebec provincial government has passed a number of laws that might seem to violate liberal norms of equal treatment. French-speaking people and immigrants are not allowed to go to English-speaking schools, the operative language in businesses employing more than fifty people must be French, and all commercial signs must be in French. Taylor defends these laws on the basis of the public good of cultural survival. On this issue the state cannot be neutral with respect to two competing theories of the good. As Taylor says:

> Political society is not neutral between those who value remaining true to the culture of our ancestors and those who might want to cut loose in the name of some individual goal of self-development. . . . It is not just a matter of having the French language available for those who might choose it. . . . it also involves making sure that there is a community of people in the future that will want to avail itself of the opportunity to use the French language.[9]

This quotation from Taylor points to a potential difference between liberals and communitarians. For most liberals, it is individuals rather than cultures that have moral standing. In the language of this book, cultures do not have rights, including the right of survival.[10] But a few liberals have parted company with the tradition on this point. Some, like Will Kymlicka, have tried to integrate a concern with cultural survival into the liberal position.[11] Kymlicka has argued that persons, as individuals, have a right to have their culture protected. If Kymlicka's argument is successful, then he might accept Taylor's defense of the Quebec government's restrictions on traditional liberal rights, but on liberal rather than communitarian grounds.

Kymlicka's attempt to establish a right to cultural survival is an interesting one. Some liberals would argue that cultures do not have moral standing, that only individuals do. Such a position is consistent with the traditional emphasis on individuals as the locus of moral rights. We do not categorically rule out the notion of a culture having rights, but our attempt to accommodate the notion of cultural rights is more modest than Kymlicka's. First, we point out that liberalism does not require assimilation. A traditional liberal would argue that an individual should be free to assimilate or not. Liberals also see value in cultural diversity. Seeing issues from different perspectives contributes to the individual growth of all. On the other hand, we do see dangers in an overemphasis on groups and cultural rights. Too much emphasis on groups can lead to pressures of conformity within the group—a conformity that could undercut the rights of the individual. Moreover, an emphasis on group differences conjoined with an emphasis on loyalty to the group could create competition among groups that would tear society apart, undermining liberal democratic protections for all.

## Feminist Critiques of Liberal Justice and Rights

### Feminist Themes

Although there are similarities between the feminists and the communitarians, there are important differences as well. Both are critical of the liberals' attempt to be impartial and neutral. Both wish to situate the subject in historical space and time. But feminists tend to reject the republican notion that a state should seek a unified conception of the public good. Feminists fear that if such a conception were adopted, the opinions of certain groups, especially women, would be marginalized. In expressing this fear, the feminists have something in common with the liberals. Many feminists would agree with Amy Gutmann, who said of communitarians:

> The communitarian[s] . . . want us to live in Salem but not to believe in witches. Or human rights. Perhaps the Moral Majority would cease to be a threat were the United States a communitarian society; benevolence and fraternity might take the place of justice. Almost anything is possible, but it does not make moral sense to leave liberal politics behind on the strength of such speculation.[12]

The guiding philosophy of feminist ethics is that the marginalization and oppression of women are wrongs that ought to be corrected. That conviction is shared by all feminists. However, feminists differ on what is needed to correct the wrongs that are committed against women. Feminism is a diverse movement, and feminist theorists differ significantly among themselves over the extent and nature of oppression of women and over the proper remedies.

Liberal feminists have argued that women have been treated unequally from men and that justice requires that this unequal treatment cease and that genuine equal opportunity prevail. Liberal feminists do not reject liberal theory but want a fair and full application of it. To make the transition from unequal to equal treatment, many liberal feminists maintain that there will need to be a time for affirmative action and preferential hiring. Men and women are not fundamentally different, and both should have the same opportunity to become doctors or nurses, to serve in the armed forces, or to be physicists. To achieve that kind of opportunity, inequality in family life has to be addressed. So long as women bear unequally the responsibilities of family life, then equality in the workplace cannot be achieved.

Susan Moller Okin is one of the best known liberal feminists. She was the first major feminist, in her book *Justice, Gender, and the Family,* to challenge the Rawlsian position.[13] She argued that Rawls had ignored the family and that as a result of ignoring what she regards as the great inequalities in the division of labor between men and women in sustaining the family, he had perpetuated this injustice in his own theory. Okin believes that liberal projects like Rawls's can be corrected to take care of these inadequacies.

Many feminists have come to reject this liberal version of feminism. Some have argued that there are important psychological as well as physiological differences between the genders. Men and women really are different in some significant ways. As a popular book puts it, "Men are from Mars, women are from Venus." Lawrence Kohlberg, a psychologist of moral development, at one time interpreted data from his studies of moral development as suggesting that the most advanced stages of moral development emphasized impartial evaluation of the sort found in utilitarianism but especially Kantianism and the views of justice, such as that of Rawls, that developed in part from Kantianism. However, his former colleague, Carol Gilligan, argued in her influential book *In a Different Voice* that, on the contrary, women tend to reason differently from the impartiality perspective rather more often than men and that this alternate perspective, that of caring, is often ignored by Kohlberg and many traditional male philosophers.[14] Men argue abstractly, emphasizing impartiality, rights, and justice. Women, on the other hand, value the importance of relationships in the moral life, and the primary virtue for sustaining relationships is caring. Since Kohlberg, being male, undervalued caring, women scored lower on the moral development tests. In any case, some feminists emphasize giving equal respect and significance to the special ways that women contribute to our society or to correcting the special problems women face, sometimes as a result of sexism—for example, an alleged lack of attention by medical researchers to women's medical needs.

In line with Gilligan's work, other feminist theorists, such as Nel Noddings, have attempted to build a full-blown ethical theory of caring. Central to Noddings's notion of caring is "apprehending the reality of the other." This can be done only by apprehending the other person in all her particularity. Thus, a math teacher who appreciates the situation of a child who fears math reflects caring. You can't simply treat all math students alike. Some fear math and some do not.

Feminists have reacted in different ways to the notion that there is a distinctively feminist ethics of caring. Some have argued that any fully developed ethical theory must contain both an ethics of caring and an ethics of rights and fairness. Such a well-developed ethical theory would be neither distinctively feminine nor distinctively masculine. Thus, ethical theory would in fact become gender neutral. Jean Grimshaw is a good spokesperson for that point of view:

> The idea that women 'reason differently' from men about moral issues should be questioned. Insofar as there are differences between men and women, it is better to see these as differences in ethical concern and priorities, rather than as differences in mode or style of reasoning. The idea that women 'reason differently' rests on problematic oppositions between such concepts as 'abstract' and 'concrete' or on the notion that a morality of 'principles' can be sharply opposed to one in which judgement is contextual.[15]

Other feminists have argued that the traditional theories of rights and fairness, theories that emphasize impartiality, are mistaken. These traditional theories need more than supplementation. They need to be replaced. Feminists who think this way have tried to develop alternative feminist ethical theories that include more than an ethics of care. Since we are defending a theory of ethics based on individual rights, it is important that we consider carefully the feminist critique of traditional theories like ours and, if possible, spell out responses to those critiques.

The communitarians have criticized the notion that the state can be neutral with respect to competing theories of the good. Some feminists also have challenged the neutrality of liberalism at a deeper level. Specifically, they have argued that the notion of impartiality that is at the center of so much of ethical theory is itself biased and, moreover, biased in a way that undercuts the plausibility of the ethical theory upon which it is based. Thus, Iris Marion Young begins an important section of her book *Justice and the Politics of Difference* by saying, "A growing body of feminist inspired moral theory has challenged the paradigm of moral reasoning as defined by discourse of justice and rights."[16]

Young has been perhaps the most noted and radical critic of liberal ethical theory. She charges that liberal theorists' use of impartiality is seriously flawed for three reasons. First, traditional theory is overly abstract; it denies the particularity of situations; it treats all situations according to the same moral rules. Second, it seeks to eliminate feeling from discussions of politics and justice. Third, it reduces the plurality of moral reasons to one impartial point of view.

Young's first point, about abstraction, has been developed by Jean Grimshaw, who has argued that the charge of overabstraction can be made in two distinct ways.[17] First, abstraction does away with the concrete, unique particularities of each situation. In order to make comparisons, to apply a rule, what is unique about what is to be compared is discounted. But what is discounted is often what is most important from the ethical point of view. Thus a morality based on rules and principles misses something important from the ethical point of view. Second, a person can make a decision from a distance and thus not be able to imagine the consequences of that action. To be distanced in that way is to be abstract from the situation. Bomber pilots are trained to abstract themselves from their bombing missions in just that way. Because they are unable to see the direct results of the bombing, they are able to distance themselves from the harm their actions cause. Foot soldiers who confront the enemy face to face are unable to abstract in that way.

Young's second charge is that this excessive abstraction leads liberals to value detached reasoning too much and to ignore the role of feeling and emotion in moral life. Moral claims become like moves in an abstract chess game and lose all life and power.

Third, Young maintains that the liberal emphasis on the impartial point of view blurs the complexity of many moral situations and the very different factors that might apply to them. For example, the injunction simply to be impartial seems of little help when we must weigh a variety of competing factors in deciding whether more of our own personal resources ought to be spent saving for our children's education or helping our neighbors, the victims of a nearby tragedy such as a flood, get back on their feet.

## A Liberal Response

Are these charges of excessive abstraction and emotional detachment justified? Certainly liberal theorists like Rawls have tried to eliminate particularity and have emphasized reasoned discourse over emotion. The point of the veil of ignorance in the original position is to eliminate knowledge of our particular selves. Other liberal theorists such as Ronald Dworkin and Bruce Ackerman have used other metaphors to the same end. Certainly liberal theorists have emphasized rational discourse and argument as the appropriate means for determining principles of justice. So liberal theorists are more than willing to plead guilty to the first two complaints.

Why? Because liberal theorists are seeking to eliminate bias from the process for determining the principles of justice. Rawls and most other liberal thinkers assume that if particularity enters in, people will try to invoke principles of justice that benefit themselves. Rich people will propose principles that benefit rich people, members of particular racial, ethnic, or religious groups might well propose principles that benefit their group more than others, and so forth. By abstracting away these particulars, we are less inclined to be biased in the selecting principles.

Similar considerations account for the devaluing of the emotions. Liberal theorists seek principles that are acceptable to all. Getting universal or near universal agreement on basic principles is extremely difficult, since people initially tend to disagree over many basic principles. What is required in such circumstances is rational argument. Each citizen tries to persuade others as to the merit of the principles each proposes. Emotion is ill suited to accomplish this. When people's emotions get in the way, positions tend to harden and be less amenable to change. And when emotional appeals do succeed in getting people to change their minds, the change of mind seems not to be totally legitimate. People should accept moral principles or principles creating the just state on the basis of reason rather than emotion. Rational persuasion functions as a deliberative ideal of objectivity.

Young's response to the liberal's rejoinder is that as a matter of fact, eliminating emotion and particularity does not eliminate bias. The liberal's emphasis on rational discourse and the elimination of particularity is ideological in the sense that "belief in it helps reproduce relations of domination or oppression by justifying them or by obscuring more emancipatory social relations."[18] How does it do this? Sometimes Young and her allies point to the facts of domination or oppression that exist in the liberal state. The United States has oppressed blacks, and all industrial societies have oppressed women. Even if that allegation is accepted as absolutely and unqualifiedly correct, the liberal would argue that such oppression is not caused by liberal doctrines. Rather, oppression in liberal states is to be explained by the failure of the state to be liberal enough. Where discrimination and oppression can be shown to exist, the liberal is committed to removing them.

But Young would argue that such a response misses her point. The liberal doctrine itself, not the failure to implement it fully, is at fault. Why? One reason that Young gives is that liberalism legitimates bureaucratic authority. It does this because liberalism grants the state the power to oversee and referee in matters of conflict.

Presumably both conflicts of self-interest and competing views of the good are characteristic of a pluralistic society. If the state is not to be the referee, liberals ask, how are such conflicts to be decided? Young seems close to being in the tradition of a group of political philosophers who defend deliberative democracy—a group that includes many whose thought would not be classified as feminist. These thinkers include Seyla Benhabib, Joshua Cohen, John Dryzek, Amy Gutmann, Dennis Thompson, and Melissa Williams. Benhabib's characterization of deliberative democracy is representative:

> According to the deliberative model of democracy, it is a necessary condition for attaining legitimacy and rationality with regard to collective decision making processes in a polity, that the institutions of this polity are so arranged that what is considered in the common interest of all results from processes of collective deliberation conducted rationally and fairly among free and equal individuals.[19]

Those who support deliberative democracy criticize Rawls and others for developing principles of justice without getting the input of real citizens. The principles of justice should not constrain democratic decision making as Rawls would argue; rather, the principles of justice evolve from democratic decision making itself. Deliberative democrats would also take exception to our view that there are human rights that can be identified by political theorizing, independently derived rights that limit state power in advance of any discussion.

Although Young thinks deliberative democracy is a step in the right direction, she would prefer communicative democracy. She believes that deliberative democracy shares with liberalism a bias toward the rational. In deliberative democracy, those with the gift of speaking well have an advantage over those that do not. Young also believes that differences in the ability to speak are culturally related; that is, speaking skills are less valued in some cultures than in others. For example, deliberation privileges male over female ways of speaking.[20] Those without such a gift are devalued and marginalized. Thus justice requires that equality of participation be broadened from equality to deliberate to equality to communicate, where, in addition to standard discourse, greeting, narrative, and rhetoric are given standing as legitimate means of communication. We are familiar with many forms of greeting, such as "Hello" and "How are you?" Young thinks that forms of speech like these encourage the willingness for discussion and thus play an important role in communicative democracy. So do narratives that provide personal accounts of the needs and values of the speaker; for example, a member of the Lakota tribe explains why the Black Hills of South Dakota have such meaning.

We agree that deliberation should be given more importance than it is by Rawls, and we even accept Young's notion that greeting and narrative deserve standing in an expanded notion of citizen discourse. (We are less willing to accept rhetoric, on the grounds that rhetoric aims to persuade even with arguments that are without merit.) But in both deliberative democracy and communicative democracy, decisions have to be made. Once everyone who is affected and wishes to have a say has had it, what then? Must the resulting decision on a law or policy be unanimous, or is a majority vote good enough, or should some people or groups of people have a veto power? Neither deliberative nor communicative democrats are as clear as one would like here. With respect to general principles (general rules of action and institutional arrangements), Benhabib seems to lean toward unanimity—at least a unanimity by all those affected by the consequences of such general principles. Later on in the same article, Benhabib characterizes majority rule as a fair and rational procedure.[21] If unanimity is required, what are the chances that radical feminists, Rawlsian liberals, religious fundamentalists, and followers of David Duke can reach agreement? And if it is a majority vote, what is to ensure that a just result is reached?

Both feminists and deliberative democrats are committed to equal voice. But is that egalitarian commitment really justifiable? Should the voice of the racist count equally with the voice of a Native American seeking to protect tribal fishing rights? Should the voice of a religious fundamentalist count equally with the voice of a scientist in deciding whether creationism should be required in the schools? These are difficult questions that liberal theorists at least try to answer with their notions of impartiality and rights. Young's communicative democracy has no way of dealing with this problem. Indeed, she seems to have little room for impartiality and notions of rational deliberation such as Rawls's notion of public reason.

In fact, as Benhabib has argued, Young's own account requires a commitment to impartiality: "Without some such standards, Young could not differentiate the genuine transformation of partial and situated perspectives from mere agreements of convenience or apparent unanimity reached under conditions of duress."[22] Young herself at times seems to accept the force of this criticism, because she sees the necessity for some commonly accepted standards (unity) even in communicative democracy. Young says:, "The members of the polity . . . must agree on procedural rules of fair discussion and decision-making. These three conditions—significant interdependence, formally equal respect, and agreed on procedures—are all the unity necessary for communicative democracy."[23]

Young thinks that her account is thinner than the requirements for unity in deliberative democracy, but whether she is correct in that assessment depends on the content of such phrases as "formally equal respect" and "agreed on procedures." We suggest that spelling out those two phrases will move Young much closer to views like Benhabib's.

In addition, Young thinks liberals like Rawls marginalize African Americans, Native Americans, women, and Jews and other nondominant groups. But what would happen in a majoritarian state controlled by religious fundamentalists of the far right and supporters of David Duke? What worries liberals is that if there are no preconditions on discussion and no human rights that are not specifiable in advance, then there is the danger that individuals will be unjustly treated. Whereas Young sees the liberal theory of rights and impartiality as the cause of marginalization, the liberal sees these constraints as the means for preventing and eliminating marginalization—at least to the extent that human frailty allows. The rights theorist believes that some things should be off the table, or at least part of a nearly universally uncontested background, if justice is to prevail. A set of human rights is necessary to protect individuals from unjust state action. Melissa Williams characterizes this approach as putting the juridical over the political.[24] In an attempt to remove preexisting conventions of impartiality and rights in order to increase the voice of certain minorities, Young threatens their rights even more than they are threatened now.

Interestingly, some deliberative democrats agree with these liberals' concerns. Benhabib says, "The liberal concern about the corrosive effect of unbridled majoritarian politics is I believe incontrovertible."[25] Benhabib's solution ironically is to appeal to a set of moral rights.[26]

Moreover, we doubt that liberal emphasis on impartiality leads to viewing all problems from one perspective, that of the dominant. Impartiality, properly applied, requires each of us to consider the viewpoint of others and to give no special weight to our own. Moreover, impartiality need not lead to simplistic and highly abstract rules. Liberal impartiality, as Brian Barry has argued, is a second-order notion requiring that the major rules governing the political order be reasonable for all to accept, but it does not require that the rules themselves be simple or few in number.[27] On our view, which we regard as a form of liberalism, especially complex political issues sometimes may need to be resolved by suitably constrained democratic procedures that allow for the play of a variety of different perspectives in mutual dialogue.

So where does that leave us? We think that the feminists are right to point out the failures of liberal theory in the real world. Despite the claims of impartiality, much injustice still exists in the world, and it is statistically correct to say that injustice falls disproportionally on certain groups. However, we are not convinced that this failure results from any errors of logic in the rights-based theory of the state. Where violations of human rights or justice occur, we remain committed to corrective action. Feminist theories have sensitized us to potential blind spots, but they have not shown that rights-based theories of the state are fundamentally flawed. Indeed, if Benhabib is right, and we think she is, feminism itself needs a rights-based ethical theory.

Many "postliberal" thinkers tend to condemn or reject liberal attempts to ground political argument on impartial, neutral, or relatively objective grounds because they believe that such notions presuppose a "gods-eye view," or neutral perspective of impartiality and objectivity that humans cannot attain. Often, these critics view liberal attempts to be rational and impartial as ideological, in the sense that the liberals tend to protect their own controversial views from criticism by dressing them up in the supposedly objective language of neutrality, impartiality, and objectivity.

However, while we agree that the language of impartiality, neutrality, and objectivity often can be misused, we suggest that it is not so easy to dispense with such notions. Unless there are acceptable points from which reason can proceed, impartial ground rules common to all parties, it is hard to see how people on any side of a dispute can persuade those who disagree with them. Thus, the social criticisms of feminism itself could be dismissed as proceeding from a limited and biased viewpoint. Debate would lack all rational ground rules and degenerate into a struggle for power. Thus, while we agree with proponents of deliberative democracy that actual debate is an important way of resolving substantive disputes, such debate itself requires fundamental ground rules about what counts as a contribution, who can speak and when, and what counts as evidence and what does not. Debate itself can count as rational only if constrained by prior norms about what makes debate rational and moral. This is why even the critics of liberalism such as Young need to bring in their own conceptions of impartiality by the back door.

## Notes

1. Michael J. Sandel, *Liberalism and the Limits of Justice* (New York: Cambridge University Press, 1982), 150.

2. Charles Taylor, "The Politics of Recognition," in *Multiculturalism,* ed. Amy Gutmann (Princeton, N.J.: Princeton University Press, 1994), 33–34.

3. Michael Walzer, *Spheres of Justice* (New York: Basic Books, 1983), 5.

4. Alasdair MacIntyre, *After Virtue* (Notre Dame, Ind.: Notre Dame University Press, 1981), 201.

5. Stuart Hampshire, *Innocence and Experience* (Cambridge: Harvard University Press, 1989), 154.

6. Michael J. Sandel, *Democracy's Discontent* (Cambridge: Harvard University Press, 1996), 20–21.

7. Charles Taylor, *Philosophical Arguments* (Cambridge: Harvard University Press, 1995), 182.

8. Sandel, *Liberalism and Limits,* 5–6.

9. Taylor, *Philosophical Arguments,* 246.

10. We do not mean to rule out altogether the possibility of nonreducible group rights or responsibilities. But a culture seems too poorly defined to constitute the sort of entity that can have collective rights. In any case, not all cultures seem to have justified claims to survival. For example, would an evil culture have that right? Would a culture have such a right even if all of its members wished to become assimilated into a broader group? For a thoughtful recent discussion of collective responsibility, see Larry May, *Sharing Responsibility* (Chicago: Chicago University Press, 1992).

11. Will Kymlicka, *Liberalism, Community, and Culture* (Oxford: Clarendon Press, 1989).

12. Amy Gutmann, "Communitarian Critics of Liberalism," *Philosophy and Public Affairs* 14 (Summer 1985): 319.

13. Susan Moller Okin, *Justice, Gender, and the Family* (New York: Basic Books, 1989).

14. Carol Gilligan, *In a Different Voice* (Cambridge: Harvard University Press, 1982).

15. Jean Grimshaw, *Philosophy and Feminist Thinking* (Minneapolis: University of Minnesota Press, 1986), 224.

16. Iris Marion Young, *Justice and the Politics of Difference* (Princeton, N.J.: Princeton University Press, 1990), 96.

17. Grimshaw, *Philosophy and Feminist Thinking,* 204–15.

18. Young, *Politics of Difference,* 112.

19. Seyla Benhabib, "Toward a Deliberative Model of Democratic Legitimacy," in *Democracy and Difference,* ed. Seyla Benhabib (Princeton, N.J.: Princeton University Press, 1996), 69.

20. For a complete account of Young's argument here, see her "Communication and the Other: Beyond Deliberative Democracy," in *Democracy and Difference,* ed. Benhabib, 120–35.

21. Benhabib, "Deliberative Model," 70.

22. Ibid., 82.

23. Young, "Communication and the Other," 126.

24. Melissa S. Williams, "Justice toward Groups," *Political Theory* 23 (February 1995): 68.

25. Benhabib, "Deliberative Model," 77.

26. Ibid., 78.

27. Brian Barry, *Justice as Impartiality* (New York: Oxford University Press, 1995), esp. chap. 9.

## Questions for Further Study

1. Communitarians argue that political philosophers like Rawls have a distinctive notion of the self. What is that notion, and why are the communitarians critical of it? Do you agree with their criticism? Why or why not?

2. What is the theory of justice proposed by the communitarian Michael Walzer? Evaluate his theory.

3. What is the basis of the communitarian critique of liberal neutrality? Do you agree with the critique? Why or why not?

4. Should there be a right to cultural survival? Why or why not?

5. What objections might a feminist political philosopher bring against the communitarian perspective of community? Evaluate those objections.

6. Why would some feminists be opposed to the philosophies of such feminist thinkers as Carol Gilligan and Nel Noddings? Which feminist perspective do you think is more nearly correct?

7. Is liberal political theory guilty of excessive abstraction and emotional detachment? Explain.

8. Define deliberative and communicative democracy. Which theory of democracy is the most adequate? Are they both inadequate? If so, why?

## Suggested Readings

### Books

Barry, Brian. *Justice As Impartiality.* New York: Oxford University Press, 1995.

Gutmann, Amy, ed. *Multiculturalism.* Princeton, N.J.: Princeton University Press, 1994.

MacIntyre, Alasdair. *After Virtue.* Notre Dame, Ind.: Notre Dame University Press, 1981.

Okin, Susan Moller. *Justice, Gender, and the Family.* New York: Basic Books, 1989.

Sandel, Michael. *Liberalism and the Limits of Justice.* New York: Cambridge University Press, 1982.

Taylor, Charles. *Philosophical Arguments.* Cambridge: Harvard University Press, 1995.

Walzer, Michael. *Spheres of Justice.* New York: Basic Books, 1983.

Young, Iris Marion. *Justice and the Politics of Difference.* Princeton, N.J.: Princeton University Press, 1990.

## Articles and Essays

Benhabib, Seyla. "Toward a Deliberative Model of Democratic Legitimacy." In *Democracy and Difference,* edited by Seyla Benhabib. Princeton, N.J.: Princeton University Press, 1996.

Gutmann, Amy. "Communitarian Critics of Liberalism." *Philosophy and Public Affairs* 14 (Summer 1985).

Taylor, Charles. "The Politics of Recognition." In *Multiculturalism,* edited by Amy Gutmann. Princeton, N.J.: Princeton University Press, 1994.

Williams, Melissa S. "Justice toward Groups." *Political Theory* 23 (February 1995).

# 6

# Democracy and Political Obligation

"Democracy" is an honorific term. Normally, to call people democrats is to praise them, while to call people undemocratic is normally to suggest that their political morality is questionable. So powerful have the honorific connotations of "democracy" become that even totalitarian states have taken to calling themselves "true" or "people's" democracies.

But if the meaning of "democracy" is stretched so wide that virtually any government counts as one, the word is trivialized. In calling a state democratic, we would not be ruling out any particular way it deals with its citizens. So if any examination of the purported justifications of democracy is to prove fruitful, it is important to be clear about what is and what is not to count as a democracy.

Such clarity is especially important because of the prominent place given democracy in the writings of such theorists as Locke, Madison, Rousseau, and Rawls. Moreover, we have argued that states or governments are to be evaluated according to the degree to which they satisfy two fundamental criteria. First, they must protect and, where appropriate, implement the natural or human rights of their citizens. Second, they must institute just procedures for the adjudication of conflicting claims of right. We maintain that, at least in countries whose population exists significantly above the subsistence level, democracy, as suitably constrained by individual rights, is the principal procedure for adjudication. Hence, we need to ascertain how democracies are to be distinguished from other forms of government.

Any account that purports to provide necessary and sufficient conditions for democracy is likely to be controversial. To avoid such lengthy controversy, it seems useful to provide, not an exhaustive list of defining conditions, but rather an admittedly incomplete list of paradigm features of democracy. By a paradigm feature of democracy is meant a feature so characteristic of democracy that (1) one would point to it in teaching a child the meaning of the word "democracy" and (2) to the extent that any government fails fully to exemplify the feature, then to that extent it becomes less clear that the government in question is a democracy. Thus, a paradigm feature of baseball is that it is played by two teams of nine players each. However, if we were to witness a sandlot game in which each team had eight players, we would still call it baseball. Presumably, if there were only two on a side, we would be quite reluctant to call what was going on a game of baseball. Perhaps we would say that the players were only practicing. Similarly, a government may still be a democracy even if it does not fully exemplify a paradigm feature of democracy. However, any government that fails to a significant extent to exemplify one or more features is no democracy at all. As with the baseball example, borderline cases are also possible.

Three characteristics that seem to be paradigm features of democracy are (a) the holding of regular elections, whose results can genuinely alter policy and the people who make it; (b) the existence of virtually universal suffrage; and (c) the provision of civil liberties essential to the election process itself. Let us consider each of these characteristics in turn.

The first excludes from the category of democracy those states whose rulers claim to follow the will of the people but never allow that will to be expressed in genuine, periodic elections. In particular, genuine elections must be a contest between different points of view, such that the election results can alter policy and the people who make it. One-party "elections" are not genuine in this sense.

The second condition, virtual universal suffrage, rules out a state where a significant number of persons are denied the franchise for morally unacceptable reasons. Thus, a state in which women are denied the vote is an elitist state, not a democracy. Paradigm cases of justified exclusion include disenfranchisement of young children, the psychotic, and the severely retarded. Exclusion of criminals might well constitute an arguable borderline case. In view of the arguments of chapter 3, factors such as race, religion, sex, or ethnic or social background cannot justify exclusion.[1]

The third requirement, provision of democratically required civil liberties, distinguishes the democratic from the majoritarian state. Majoritarianism is the view that all political issues ought to be settled by a majority vote or by those elected officials who have received majority support.[2] Historically, however, democracy has been thought of as containing built-in safeguards for individual rights. The United States Constitution's Bill of Rights is an example. Such checks are justified as safeguards against the dictatorship of the majority, a group that can be as tyrannical as any individual despot.[3] At the very least, a democracy must protect those procedural rights, such as the right to vote and the right to free speech, without which elections become a mockery.[4]

It is the violation of these procedural rights that makes such features of many actual democracies as excessive government secrecy or harassment of dissenters so reprehensible. By depriving the citizenry of information needed for intelligent voting or by intimidating or harassing those who dissent from official policies, such abuses undermine the democratic process itself. And, as we will see, where the democratic process is significantly undermined, the obligation to abide by the dictates of so-called democratic decisions becomes weaker. Exactly where the point of vanishing obligation is to be located is controversial. Surely, however, the officials of a democratic government have a special obligation not to undermine the very process they have sworn to uphold.

Each of these features—regular genuine elections, universal suffrage, and protection of individual rights—is a paradigm feature of democracy in the sense already explicated. The dispute over whether or not a given state is democratic is not merely verbal. As will be argued later, the extent to which a state is democratic determines the extent to which we ought to support it and perhaps even whether we are under any special political obligation to respect its authority. Let us now consider what, if anything, might justify allegiance to democracy.

## The Justification of Democracy

### Utilitarian Arguments

Utilitarian arguments for democracy are those that argue from the good consequences promoted by democracy to the desirability of democracy as a form of government. In this context, the utilitarian is concerned with the consequences promoted by the workings of an institution and not with those of any one action. The utilitarian is evaluating the system of democracy rather than any individual act performed within the system and so is employing a form of rule rather than act utilitarianism. The utilitarian arguments we will consider below are individualistic, because, like the arguments of Bentham and Mill, the good consequences to which they appeal are individual goods for individual persons. In the next section, we will consider the arguments of collectivists or holists, who appeal to a group or the general good.

Here, as elsewhere in this book, it is understood that the utilitarian cannot appeal to considerations of justice or natural right as last resorts in political argument. Rather, the utilitarian must base natural rights and justice on their utility.

One kind of utilitarian defense of democracy appeals to the material benefits enjoyed by citizens of the Western democracies. It is true that at present most, or at least a great many, citizens of such states enjoy a higher standard of living than do most citizens of most other countries. So, in political argument, the democratic form of government is sometimes defended by appeal to the material benefits that accrue to those who live under it.

However, this argument is far from decisive. It is unclear, for one thing, whether the standard of living in a democracy is a result of its being a democracy, of its economic system, of its exploitation of other countries, of its plentiful natural resources, or of a host of other possible explanatory factors. Thus, in the absence of detailed support, the inference that a country's wealth is due, or even largely due, to its political system is questionable. While proponents might respond that the liberty enjoyed by citizens in a democracy leads to wiser choices by investors, consumers, and managers and so promotes greater economic efficiency (a view we considered in chapter 4), it is not clear that specifically democratic institutional arrangements rather than other factors are the major contributors to economic success.

More important, proponents of such an argument, by their own logic, would be forced to admit that if a totalitarian country did come to enjoy a higher standard of living than a democracy, there is a stronger reason for preferring the former to the latter. But surely a ruthless totalitarian government does not become morally acceptable just by making its citizens (those it does not oppress) rich. In fact, as subsequent arguments will show, there are good moral reasons for preferring democracy to other forms of government, even at a significant cost in material wealth.

A second utilitarian argument maintains that a democracy, by distributing power among the people, is most likely to avoid the abuses of power that result from its concentration in too few hands. If any group of leaders does misuse its power, in a democracy there are regular procedures that the people may use to separate such leaders from their power.

This is indeed a strong argument for democracy. In a great many contexts, the abuses of power may be avoided by distributing it to the people. Perhaps one example was democratic protest against the American government's involvement in the Vietnam War during the late 1960s and early 1970s. Although, in retrospect, some of the rhetoric and forms of dissent used by the protesters may have been ill conceived, the growing dissatisfaction with the war and doubts about the existence of any moral basis for the involvement of the United States led millions of Americans to question their government's participation and played a significant role in changing policy and bringing the conflict to an end.

We should point out, however, that the argument that democracy provides a check on the abuse of power is two edged. The totalitarian can reply that the very success of democracy in curbing the abuse of power, or at least acting as a check to abuse, may also be its Achilles' heel. For when quick, effective use of power is needed, democracy may not be able to supply it.

Although we agree with the utilitarian that the misuse of power is generally more to be feared than failure to use it, this conflict cannot be fully resolved within a utilitarian framework. Both sides are appealing to consequences. The issues between them are the empirical ones of whether misuse of power is worse than failure to use it in various contexts, or whether one is more likely to occur than the other. In a later section of this chapter, we will argue that power ought to be distributed among the people, not simply to maximize want satisfaction and minimize want frustration, but because the people have a right to such a distribution. Thus, we will maintain that democracy is best justified from the point of view of equality, justice, and rights rather than that of utility and efficiency.

Perhaps the most effective utilitarian defense of democracy in terms of its consequences was provided by John Stuart Mill. In his *Considerations on Representative Government,* Mill argued that participation in the democratic process developed the intellectual and moral capacities of citizens, while under other forms of government, the citizens—or, more accurately, the subjects—remained passive and inert.[5] In a democracy, according to Mill, people are encouraged to understand issues, develop and express points of view, and implement desires through political involvement. In a despotism, however, citizens are passive receptors for the will of the elite. Therefore, Mill maintains, those who value individual development are committed to valuing the form of government that best fosters democracy. Employing this argument, Mill broadens the conception of utility from the idea of individual happiness and personal pleasure to include development of important human capacities and talents as well.

While we are very sympathetic to Mill's approach here, some qualifications must be made. First, precisely because Mill transforms what counts as utility, it is not clear that Mill's position is genuinely utilitarian. In emphasizing the development of each individual's intellectual and moral capacities, and in de-emphasizing such quantitative factors as production of pleasure, Mill has moved a great distance from classical utilitarianism.[6] Instead, Mill seems to have shifted to a self-realizationist or "perfectionist" perspective where the goal is to promote the rational development of persons, to achieve a perfected or improved idea of human development.

One problem with such a view is that of determining how any one ideal of human nature or development can be shown to be better than any other. Another is that even if one conception of the human good can be shown to be most defensible, why should it be made the basis of public policy in a pluralist society in which many citizens hold opposing conceptions of the good? For this reason, as we have seen in chapters 4 and 5, many liberals advocate state neutrality toward conceptions of the good.

However, in defense of Mill, it can be argued, along lines suggested earlier, that one can never be justified in abandoning rational discourse. Since justification requires giving reasons, the claim that one is justified in abandoning reasoned discourse is incoherent. It amounts to claiming that one has reasons for not having reasons. In this interpretation, Mill's self-realizationist ethic can be grounded on the same foundation that supports one of our arguments for natural rights. It, like part of our own view, rests on the imperative to be rational, an imperative that can be rejected only by those who are willing to lead the unexamined and therefore unjustifiable life. Thus, it is plausible to think that the ideal of developing human rational capacities and talents is not just another conception of the good but rather is a prerequisite for even considering the questions of political and social policy, including evaluation of conceptions of the good, in the first place.

Mill's argument is that participation in the democratic process promotes rational development. However, actual democracies may not have as much of an effect on individual development as Mill expected. Mill's empirical claims about how individuals develop in a democracy may not hold when politicians market themselves as products (much as cornflakes are presented to the public) and rational discussion in the media and among the citizenry is notable largely for its absence. For this reason, a democrat might be wary of basing too much of his case on Mill's argument. People may not react to the actual democratic process as Mill thought they would to an ideal one. Mill could reply with force, however, that if any form of government is to develop human capacities for rational thought and action, democracy is the most likely to succeed. If democracies in practice encourage mindlessness, that is a reason for getting them to live up more fully to democratic ideals, not for abandoning democracy altogether.

Accordingly, some of the utilitarian arguments for democracy have considerable merit. In some if not all cases, democratic checks on power function effectively. Moreover, democracy may have some effect, and perhaps a large one under certain conditions, in developing the rational capacities of many citizens. Surely, democracy does better than totalitarianism in promoting such a goal.

However, utilitarian arguments for democracy do not tell the whole story. By the very logic of utilitarianism, if a totalitarian state were to produce the greatest good, that state would be rated best. If the utilitarian were to reply, following Mill, that dictatorships do not contribute to the rational development of citizens and so cannot produce the greatest good, then critics would claim with some force that a new nonutilitarian value, rational development, has been introduced into the argument. What counts, in this view, is the development of the individual, not extrinsic goods that the static individual can enjoy. Accordingly, this Millian defense of democracy rests on the assumption that the individual person is morally significant. This indeed is an important claim, but there is nothing distinctively utilitarian about it. As we shall see, the assertion of the importance of the individual is central to the egalitarian defense of democracy—a defense that is distinctively nonutilitarian in character.

At best, then, classical utilitarian defenses of democracy provide an important but only a contingent defense of democracy. Where other political systems provide good results, those systems pass the utilitarian test as well. On the other hand, insofar as utilitarian defenses of democracy are modified along lines suggested by Mill, it is doubtful to what extent they remain utilitarian. It is evident, then, that while utilitarian and modified utilitarian defenses of democracy are important, other kinds of justifications of democracy also merit serious consideration.

## Nonindividualistic Defenses of Democracy

So far, democracy has been evaluated by an individualist standard, that is, according to the benefits democracy provides for individual citizens. Even Mill, who emphasized the socializing and humanizing effects of democracy as a social process, was basically part of the individualistic utilitarian tradition. What such an approach may ignore is the role of the group in human life. To bring out such a role, two nonindividualist approaches to democracy will be considered, that of the pluralists, on the one hand, and that of the eighteenth-century French philosopher Jean-Jacques Rousseau, on the other.

**Pluralism.** Pluralism can be conceived of as a descriptive account of democracy advanced by analytical social scientists and as a normative justification of democracy as well. It has its roots in the *Federalist Paper 10* of James Madison. Madison accepted the basic Hobbesian account of human nature, that persons are basically selfish and take any opportunity to dominate their fellows. In order to prevent dominant individuals or groups from controlling the political process, Madison thought it necessary to distribute power widely. Democracy was the form of government that best accomplished this end.

Madison's approach is called pluralism because he advocated multiple centers of power. Wide distribution of power, rather than constitutional checks and balances, was, he believed, the best protection against tyranny. It is the pluralistic society that prevents despotism. Democracy, by allowing for the give-and-take of bargaining between competing centers of power, promotes pluralism.

So far, Madisonian pluralism resembles the utilitarian argument for the wide distribution of power that was considered earlier. Indeed, Madison is perhaps the finest articulator of that argument. What is of interest here is the union of this pluralistic approach with an emphasis on the role and value of group life in a democracy.

What the major modern pluralist theorists add to the Madisonian account is an emphasis on the importance of interaction between groups and an emphasis on extraconstitutional checks on the accumulation of power. The two additions are related in that it is the competition and compromise between groups that constitute the extraconstitutional checks on government, such as the decision of a legislator from Maine to support a program for Alabama on the understanding that the representatives from Alabama will support a project that benefits the citizens of Maine.

Individualists tend to view persons as egoistic utility maximizers. Recall Hobbes's view of human nature and Bentham's claim that pleasure and pain dictate what persons will do as well as what they ought to do. Critics of individualism, however, would question how successfully people can function as autonomous, isolated, atomic individuals. Indeed, as sociologist Emile Durkheim argued, isolation and rootlessness themselves are the source of many psychological and social problems.[7] Moreover, it is empirically doubtful that people do frequently function as isolated utility maximizers. Rather, it is as members of groups, coming out of traditions, embedded in a social structure, that we actually find individuals. By raising the ethnic and religious group to the center of attention, the pluralist theorists have provided the framework within which a theory of democracy based on group interaction can be constructed.[8]

In the pluralist view, the democratic process is a set of ground rules within which different groups can pursue their particular interests. Ground rules are necessary, for without them we would revert to a Hobbesian state of nature, a war of every group against every other group. Within the ground rules, the plurality of groups provides a check on the power of any one element in society. What we have is a shifting majority made up of many minorities temporarily voting alike in the pursuit of their share of the pie. "Constitutional rules are mainly significant because they help to determine what particular groups are to be given advantages or handicaps in the political struggle. . . . Thus the making of governmental decisions is not a majestic march of great majorities united upon certain matters of basic policy. It is the steady appeasement of relatively small groups."[9] It is this competitive extraconstitutional balance of power among groups that protects us from despotism.

Such a view has several advantages. In particular, it incorporates the importance of tradition, identification with a group, and social structure in the life of individuals. A significant loyalty of many individuals is to the group with which they identify. Moreover, pluralism incorporates this emphasis on the value of group life, on community rather than possessive individualism, into a traditional defense of democracy as a check upon tyranny. However, regardless of its merits as a descriptive theory about how democracy works, pluralism has serious weaknesses as a normative theory about how democracy ought to work.

In particular, critics have emphasized that, regardless of the intentions of the pluralists, pluralism has unacceptably conservative implications. As one critic, Robert Paul Wolff, has argued:

> the application of the theory of pluralism always favors the groups in existence against those in the process of formation. . . . The theory of pluralism does not espouse the interests of the unionized against the non-unionized, or of the large against small business; but by presenting a picture of the American economy in which those disadvantaged elements do not appear, it tends to perpetuate the inequality by ignoring rather than justifying it."[10]

As a theory, pluralism views democratic society as a common ground where groups pursue their interests within a mutually acceptable procedural framework. But critics charge that in practice, pluralism counts some groups as more equal than others. "The very passivity of government as 'referee' suggests that the 'game' is likely to be dominated by the oldest and strongest players."[11]

The pluralists themselves are not unaware of this difficulty. Robert Dahl, one of the leading pluralists, acknowledges, for example, that "if a group is inactive, whether by free choice, violence, intimidation, or law, the normal American system does not necessarily provide it with a checkpoint anywhere in the process."[12] While the system often has expanded to include previously unrepresented groups, it need not do so, nor need it provide opportunities for new groups to be heard or recognized. Accordingly, a major disadvantage of a normative defense of democracy based on pluralism is that pluralism contains no built-in protections for emerging or less powerful groups. Democracy should encompass more than simple power relationships, whether it is relationships between individuals or between groups that are at issue.

A second difficulty with pluralism arises from the competitive picture it paints of the democratic process. With each group struggling to attain its own interest, there is no incentive for any group to defend the common or public interest. Each party to the political struggle can hope that the common good will be taken care of by others and concentrate its energy on securing its own private benefit:

> America is growing uglier, more dangerous, and less pleasant to live in, as its citizens grow richer. The reason is that natural beauty, public order, the cultivation of the arts, are not the special interest of any identifiable social group. . . . To deal with such problems, there must be some way of constituting society as a genuine group with a group purpose and a conception of the common good.[13]

This is the very problem Rawls tried to deal with in *A Theory of Justice* and especially in *Political Liberalism* with his idea of a just framework and an overlapping consensus to which all groups committed to respecting persons as free and equal individuals in a democratic order could subscribe. However, Rawls's vision is a moral one, not simply a framework for nonmoral competition among groups.

The pluralists have certainly made a major contribution to the theory of democracy.

As political scientists, they have presented an interesting hypothesis about how democracy actually works, one that surely warrants extensive consideration. However, pluralism is at best incomplete as a theory of how democracy ought to work. It is true that the importance of groups is too often ignored by the individualist, and yet it is of the highest value to many persons. But even if we accept that the group is the proper unit of analysis here, pluralism contains no account of the fair or just apportionment of power among groups. Moreover, it seems to replace the individualist picture of society as composed of isolated, competing atomic individuals with the hardly more edifying picture of isolated, competing groups. In each case, the common values that are essential to all are left out of the picture. It is precisely these problems that the philosopher Rousseau hoped to avoid.

**Democracy and the General Will.** Perhaps the difficulties noted above arise because the assumption on which they are based—that democracy involves conflict between different interest groups—is itself faulty. An alternative account of democracy can be based on the views of the French philosopher Jean-Jacques Rousseau (1712–1778). In his book *The Social Contract,* Rousseau formulates the problem of justifying the state's claim to authority over the individual as follows. The problem is to determine if there is "a form of association which will defend and protect with the whole common force the person and property of each associate and by which each person, while uniting himself with all, shall obey only himself and remain as free as before."[14] Rousseau is asking the question we considered in chapter 1: How can the individual retain autonomy while acknowledging political authority?

Rousseau's solution is in the social-contract tradition that we have already encountered in the work of Locke, Hobbes, and, in contemporary form, Rawls. But while Hobbesian contractees give all their power up to a sovereign to enhance security and Lockean contractees give up some rights to better protect others, Rousseau's associates give up all their rights to enhance personal autonomy. They do this by ceding their rights to the association or community. Since each is an equal member, none is disadvantaged more than any other. Each is to have the same voice in group decision making.

Rousseau is making the important point that equality is a fair compromise between parties contracting to create a collective-decision procedure. If no party has any threat advantage over any other and if principles are not arbitrarily tailored to favor any particular group, then equality—one person, one vote—seems to be the favored result. (Rousseau seems to have anticipated the kind of contractual argument employed by Rawls. Rawls himself has acknowledged a great debt to Rousseau.)

But how is Rousseau to deal with the problems plaguing pluralism? The answer lies in Rousseau's conception of the political community. For Rousseau, the community is not simply an aggregate of individuals to be swayed by majority vote, as in Locke's conception, nor is it a disunited collection of competing groups. On the contrary, the parties to the contract could not retain their autonomy, Rousseau argues, if they were to accept the Lockean conception of majority rule. Majority rule, in its usual sense, implies that the minority should abide by the policies supported by the majority even when the minority opposes such policies. Submission to majority rule involves abandoning autonomy since one suspends one's individual judgment when it is not in accord with the majority view.

Rousseau's contractees, unlike Locke's, surrender all their rights to the community only because it is the function of the community to pursue the common good. Hence, each individual remains "as free as before," since, unlike what happens in the case of majority rule, no individual's or group's good is to be subordinated to any other's. The community, guided by its general will, is to pursue the general or common good, which is as much any one citizen's good as any other's.

Rousseau, like Hobbes, Locke, and Rawls, should not be read as offering a historical account of a social contract. Rather, Rousseau is exploring the rational basis of the state by asking under what conditions reasonable persons could accept the political order. His answer is that it is rational to acknowledge the authority of the state only if the state is a political community, not merely an aggregation. In the latter, each individual or group selfishly pursues its own interests, leading to the kinds of problems facing pluralism. A community, on the other hand, is not simply an aggregation of egoists. Rather, it is a group with a common goal: securing the common good for its members.

But how is the common good to be discerned? Rousseau believed that the *general will* of the community could discern the common good. This general will is to be distinguished from particular wills, even when the particular wills of all citizens agree: "There is often a great difference between the will of all and the general will; the general will studies the common interest while the will of all studies private interest, and is indeed no more than the sum of individual desires."[15] Individuals express their particular will when they vote their own personal preferences and desires. The general will is expressed only when citizens assume an impersonal standpoint and vote to secure the common good. One votes the general will when one abandons one's own selfish perspective and attempts to see things from a point of view common to oneself and others.

It is the merit of Rousseau's approach that he focuses our attention on the common good and the public interest, on what unites a collection into a community rather than an aggregation of competing individuals or interest groups. In such a state, no individual or group can be dominated by another, for the only interests the state can legitimately pursue are the interests of all. Rousseau's political philosophy serves as a counterweight to competitive individualism and pluralism alike—to a world where some affluent egoists or groups live in private splendor while such public goods as parks, clean air and water, and a beautiful and healthy environment vanish. But while Rousseau's emphasis on the common good is valuable, his approach is open to serious criticism on a number of points.

**Evaluation of Rousseau's Position.** Rousseau's argument, as presented above, can be stated as follows:

1. A political association has authority only if it preserves the autonomy of the associates, that is, keeps them "as free as before."

2. It preserves the autonomy of any given associate only if it does not subordinate the pursuit of his or her interests to the pursuit of those of others, for he or she could not rationally consent to such a system.

3. Such subordination can be avoided only if the association is restricted to pursuing only the common interests of the associates.

4. Therefore, a political association has authority only if it restricts itself to pursuit of the common interests of its members.

5. The general will and only the general will discerns the common interest.

6. Therefore, a political association has authority only if it allows for expression of the general will, that is, for democratic voting in which each votes from the point of view of all.

How is this argument to be evaluated? One problem is presented by premise 5. Is it really true that if voters try to discern what is in the common interest, they will succeed in doing so? On the contrary, it can be argued that there is little reason to think that the majority will usually perceive the common good, or wherein the common good lies, let alone that it will always do so. Indeed, critics contend that Rousseau's apparent assumption of the infallibility of the general will is actually dangerous to civil liberties. Rousseau has argued that those who oppose the general will must be "forced to be free."[16] Since only the general will expresses the common good, and since each rational citizen has consented to pursue the common good, each rational citizen has consented to obey the general will. Hence, in forcing the citizen to abide by its dictates, we really are carrying out the dictates of the citizen's rational self and so are not really coercing him after all.

As critics have pointed out (see the first section of chapter 7), this argument confuses satisfaction of rational wants with freedom. Coercion in people's interest, even coercion designed to get them what they would want under certain conditions, is still coercion. It is hardly forcing people to be free.

Rousseau assumes that the general will is infallible, or at least is likely to be correctly expressed on any given occasion. Hence, there is no need to protect individual rights; such rights are not needed as checks against a mistaken majority since the majority cannot be wrong. But since this assumption of the infallibility of the majority surely is mistaken, individual rights need to be protected against the tyranny of the majority. Indeed, if the considerations presented in favor of natural rights have force, claims of natural rights ought to be honored even if the majority is infallible. If a physician knows that informing a patient of a diagnosis of cancer will severely depress that patient, it does not follow that the patient ought not to be told. The patient's right to control his or her own life may be paramount. Indeed, if Y has a natural right to liberty, such paternalistic interference may be in violation of it.

If individual rights are honored, then a sphere of individual, private entitlement is protected. Within that sphere, individuals may follow their own possibly selfish judgments. It seems that we can eliminate such pursuit of private ends only by ignoring claims of individual right as well. Accordingly, Rousseau's view of the state is open to the criticism that pursuit of the common good is allowed unduly to dominate the pursuit of individual interest:

> Political problems very often demand a choice between conflicting interests. And though there may be good reasons for a given choice, it can rarely be one in which all interests are harmonized. Again, even where the objective is of general benefit, a truly "common good," it does not follow that it should therefore override all other claims; yet this is precisely what Rousseau felt about the common good.[17]

This is not to deny the importance of the common good or the public interest.[18] However, the common good or public interest does not automatically take precedence over all other values in all other contexts. Surely, a healthy environment is in the public interest if anything at all is. But suppose that we could prevent a 1 percent increase in cancer caused by pollution only by suspending basic civil liberties for an extended period of time. Or suppose we could prevent the increase in cancer only by severely limiting each individual's pursuit of private interest. Whether the gain is worth the loss is at least controversial. Rousseau's emphasis on the common good remedies a serious deficiency in pluralist theory but perhaps at the price of going too far in the opposite direction. In accepting premise 3, that the state avoids subordination of some citizens to others only by pursuing the common good, Rousseau opens himself to the objection that the common good should not always take precedence over the pursuit of private satisfactions. Rousseau thinks he has eliminated subordination but actually subordinates private interests to those that everyone has in common. By insisting that the general will represents the real will of each individual, he overlooks the private wants of the actual individual. Conflicting interests seem to be a central feature of political life. Rousseau obscures this conflict and so provides no mechanism for dealing with it.

A second problem with Rousseau's argument arises in connection with premise 2. This premise states that any citizen's autonomy is preserved only if the political association never subordinates the individual's interests to those of others, that is, if it pursues only the common good. However, while a majoritarian democracy often pursues some people's interests at the expense of others', it may well be in everyone's rational interest to consent to a decision procedure that allows just that to happen. Rousseau may not have given adequate weight to the distinction between (a) adoption of a decision procedure being in everyone's interest and (b) the actual decisions resulting from its application being in everyone's interest. Where (a) holds, it may be rational to consent to the procedure in spite of the fact that its application may not always work to everyone's benefit. Imagine, for example, two children who constantly quarrel over who is to make the first move in a board game. Rather than constantly fight, it may be rational for them to agree to a rule determining who goes first. Perhaps the rule is, "Each participant shall roll a die and the one with the highest number on the face of the die shall move first. In case of ties, the procedure is to be repeated until a winner emerges." On any given occasion, one child will lose if the rule is followed. Nevertheless, it may be rational for them both to adopt the rule and avoid interminable quarrels. Accordingly, premise 2's identification of an autonomous decision with one that never leads to the subordination of interests confuses the rationale for consenting to a decision procedure with that for evaluating the outcome of individual decisions. As in the case of the children, it may be rational to allow for some subordination of interests in the application of a procedure when it is significantly in everyone's interest to adopt such a procedure. (See chapter 1 for a discussion of this point.)

In spite of these criticisms, Rousseau has called our attention to the importance of common interests and the value of community. Moreover, Rousseau leaves democrats with some perplexing questions. If each group is to pursue its own interests, as the pluralists suggest, how are permanent minorities—groups that can always be outvoted by the others—to be protected? And how are egoistic individuals or groups to protect public interests as well as private ones? Rousseau may have unduly subordinated the private to the public, but critics, with some force, have pointed out that our society tends to do the opposite. How is a proper or appropriate balance to be achieved? Even if the criticisms of Rousseau's approach are decisive, the problems he set out to solve still remain.

## Democracy as a Requirement of Equality

Our own approach is in the egalitarian tradition of contractarians such as Locke and Rawls. Social-contract theorists begin with the model of equal parties arriving at an agreement rationally acceptable to all. We, too, begin with the assumption that each individual counts equally as a possessor of fundamental rights. Now suppose that such individuals need a decision procedure for resolving conflicts that arise among them. Since it is impractical to handle each case on a purely individual basis, what they need is a system of generating rules, laws, and judicial institutions. It is these rules, laws, and institutions that will be applied to particular cases. But how are they to be arrived at?

Since all citizens possess equal rights, no citizen has any special or superior moral standing that others lack. This does not mean that all are equally worthy morally, since clearly some people behave much more ethically than others; rather, it means that all count as equals with respect to fundamental rights. Jones may be a more ethical person than Smith, but they each nevertheless have an equal right to liberty, unless one or the other forfeits that right through wrongly harming others. Since each is a possessor of equal rights, neither starts out under the authority of the other. But since all citizens are equal, and equal cases should be treated equally, it is plausible to think that each citizen should count for one and only one in the process of generating rules, laws, and institutions for conflict resolution. According to this view, democracy is justified as a fair compromise between equals for sharing of decision-making power.[19]

A similar conclusion arguably would be reached by Rawlsian deliberators behind the veil of ignorance. For Rawls, "the constitutional process should preserve the equal representation of the original position to the degree that this is feasible."[20] In ignorance of who they are, what they value, and to what society they belong, persons are left with no rational basis on which to discriminate. Accordingly, the rational vote is for equality in the decision-making process.

Many critics of democracy will find this sort of equality to be its greatest weakness. Plato was able to dismiss democracy as "a charming form of government, full of variety and disorder, and dispensing a sort of equality to equals and unequals alike."[21] In Plato's view, ideal government is government by the best and brightest. The attributes of a good leader include wisdom, sensitivity, integrity, and the ability to inspire others. But democracy, so the argument goes, counts everyone equally and so reduces leadership to the lowest common denominator. To avoid this, Plato, in his *Republic,* advocated the formation of a guardian class, which was to include those citizens best equipped to lead the state. The guardians were to be trained especially for leadership, while members of the other classes—for example, warriors and artisans—were to be trained to carry out the tasks they performed best. In the ideal state, each component would perform the function for which it was best fitted.

Democrats and their critics alike can agree that not everyone is equally suited for political leadership. After all, one can be committed to democracy without believing that all people are likely to be equally good presidents of the United States. What democrats will want to stress, however, is the value of counting people equally for purposes of political decision making. Pluralists, for example, will deny that just because some people may make better leaders than others, the selection of leaders ought to be removed from the populace. The pluralists will argue that any self-perpetuating governing class is likely to rule mainly in its own interest. Hence, there is a need for a plurality of centers of power, either at the individual or group level, as a check against just the sort of tyranny to which Plato's system can lead.

But still, critics may object, isn't democracy just forced on us by practical difficulties? If we could produce wise and benevolent leaders, shouldn't all power be turned over to them? Democracy, in this view, is not the best form of government, all things considered. Rather, it is the best we can do, given our limitations.

Even if the critics were right here, the case for democracy would still be strong. After all, it is the real and not the ideal world that we are worried about. But ideals are important, if only as guides to improvement, as signals indicating in which direction we should move. Therefore, we should face squarely the elitist claim that if we could select the wisest and most benevolent among us, then they and they alone should rule.

There seem to be three key assumptions underlying the elitist case. These are that (1) the value of a form of government is determined by the wisdom of the political decisions to which it is likely to lead; (2) wise and benevolent political leaders are likely to make wise political decisions without being accountable to the people; and (3) when the first two assumptions hold, all power should be given to the wise and benevolent.

The democrat will argue against each assumption. In reply to the first assumption, Mill's case for the effect of democracy upon participants can be emphasized. On this view, the value of democracy lies as much in the development of the best that is within each particular person as it does in the outcome of the decision-making process. A benevolent dictatorship at its best is all too likely to reduce the citizenry to the status of satisfied pigs. Democracy at least aims at turning people into dissatisfied Socrateses.

Against the second assumption, democrats will deny that the good of the people can be identified independently of the expression by the people of their preferences through the democratic process. As one theorist recently maintained:

> in order to know which members of the community have the greatest capacities to contribute to the common good, we must know with some concreteness the forms that the common good will take. But what these forms will be cannot be known prior to the expression of the interests, needs and desires of the members generally. . . . In sum, the well being of a body politic cannot be ascertained in advance of the directive decisions made by its members, and therefore contributions to such well being, or the capacity so to contribute, cannot be used to determine who shall have a right to participate in those fundamental decisions.[22]

Indeed, even if a common good or public interest can be discerned independently of the expression of preference by the citizenry, it need not take precedence over the pursuit of private interest. And while in any individual case a wise and benevolent observer may know one's interest better than one does oneself, the democrat will argue that it is extremely unlikely that this would be true in any great number of cases. The dispute over assumption 2 is at least partially an empirical one between the democrat and the elitist. The former holds that, in general, the interests of the people cannot be discerned independently of their binding expression of those interests. The latter holds that wise and benevolent rulers can know what is good for the people better than do the people themselves. In the elitist's view, the people, in effect, are to be treated as children.

Suppose, for the sake of argument, that assumptions 1 and 2 of the elitist antidemocrat are granted. Often, the invalidity of the inference that therefore all power should be given to the wise and benevolent is not noticed. Thus, if X is selling his house, even if an outside observer Y could get a better price for it, it does not follow that X must turn over the selling to Y. For it is X's house and he has the right to sell it, even if he does not get the best price available. Similarly, if X were to place his life in Y's hands and follow Y's directives, X might have a happier life than would otherwise be the case. However, X has the right to run his own life.

As we just argued, the inference from "Y can make better decisions about X's life than can X" to "Y has the right to make decisions about X's life and X does not" is fallacious. Greater wisdom does not entail the right to rule. Indeed, if each citizen is a possessor of fundamental individual rights, each is equally entitled to rule. The strongest moral foundation for democracy lies in the importance of the individual. Whether one starts out with a theory of natural rights as developed earlier or regards individual rights as rule-utilitarian devices, it is the moral equality of individuals that justifies the democratic process.[23] Accordingly, the critics of democracy have not justified assumption 3. Rather, democracy is justifiable on grounds of fairness. Even if it does not always yield the best decisions, it is a procedure for collective decision making that not only counts equals as equals and respects individual rights but also is a major means for implementing those rights and resolving conflicts among them. Hence, we are entitled to reject the elitist case against democracy, even under those ideal (if unattainable) circumstances in which the wisest and most benevolent among us can be identified and brought forth.

Nevertheless, a number of problems remain. Suppose, for example, that in a democracy all procedural rights are implemented, yet one group is continually outvoted. Its interests are continually ignored over a long period of time, and it becomes a permanent minority. Second, suppose voters continually ignore the common good and the public interest, choosing only to satisfy their own personal wants instead. Can the democratic theorist deal adequately with the problems of oppressed minorities and the common or public interest?

## Democracy and Groups

**Oppressed Minorities in a Democracy.** Critics of democracy sometimes point to the fact that under such a political system, majority interest groups can unite at the ballot box to repress permanently the interests of minorities. Many would argue that in the United States, blacks and the poor have constituted just such a permanent minority group on election day. When such charges are true, they constitute a serious objection to democracy. Although every person has one vote under such circumstances, some people, because of the groups to which they belong, lack significant protection for their interests. Their votes are not important enough for politicians to worry about.

Now, there is nothing about democracy that rules out such unjust repression of a minority by the majority. A just procedure does not always yield substantively just results. Democratic theorists and policymakers alike have attempted to address this problem, but their attempts always have proved controversial. Consider the following issue. It is alleged that in contemporary American society, blacks will have difficulty being elected to public office in voting districts in which they are a minority. To enhance the possibility that some blacks would be elected, some states deliberately created districts where blacks constituted a majority, thus increasing the likelihood of having more blacks elected. Many of these specially created districts recently have been declared unconstitutional in a series of complex decisions handed down by the Supreme Court.[24]

However, even if such districts could pass constitutional muster, there is the practical difficulty that they may actually dilute the voting power of blacks rather than enhance it. By concentrating black voters in districts where they constitute a majority, elected whites from other districts may feel less of a need to respond to the concerns of blacks than they would if there were substantial numbers of black voters in their own districts. "Let the black officials look after blacks. My job is to look after my own constituents," such officials might respond. And there would be no political reason not to adopt such a position. Thus, even if structural revisions make a minority a majority in a local area, the group's minority status will reemerge in the larger system.

As a result, contemporary democratic theorists have focused on the importance of providing an effective voice for all constituents. These theorists, called participative democrats, were introduced in chapter 5. Surely, as they point out, more needs to be done so that the voice of those, like the poor, who tend not to participate in the democratic process is heard. However, we suggest that the mere failure of some groups to participate fully and actively in the democratic process may not always be a failure of democracy; in some cases the failure could be the responsibility of members of the group. The problem is not so much that democracies actively keep groups, such as poor people, from voting but rather that since some other groups, such as the rich, may have, or be perceived to have, disproportionate influence in the political process, members of less influential groups come to see themselves as relatively powerless and choose not to participate. In fact, the power of money to affect democratic procedures is well recognized, but, as the sad history of attempts at campaign reform show, correcting for the influence of money is difficult.

In addition, the participative democrats have no way to protect oppressed minorities once they get to the democratic bargaining table. Some participative democrats seem to believe that if the homeless had significant access to democratic forums of opinion and were able to tell their stories to the public at large, the majority would devote more resources to them. Perhaps, but isn't it equally possible that the majority might feel even greater contempt for the homeless once their story is told? Similarly, some social workers who deal with people on welfare believe that many of those on welfare do not deserve support. Of course, it may well be that morality requires that more resources be devoted to the poor and that the majority should change in order to meet the needs of oppressed minorities. But, as a practical matter, what can a democracy do when a majority holds incorrect beliefs?

When we reflect on the justification of democracy, we can formulate a response to these difficulties. On the natural rights view, democracy imposes moral limits on the majority. As all citizens of a democracy are counted as moral equals, on this justificatory approach, no citizen's rights should be overridden on the basis of mere power. Democratic government is not simply a matter of power but, as the exponents of deliberative democracy have emphasized, presupposes a model of critical rational dialogue among the citizens so that positions taken by some can be justified to others. While it is true that in actual democracies sometimes the majority simply imposes its will on the minority, ideally the majority should have a justification for its position that it believes the minority should at least find intelligible. While the minority should not be expected to agree that the majority is always right, the minority should at least be able to understand the reasons for the majority vote and be able to challenge them in open discussion. In this way, different sides have a fair chance to influence each other's supporters, and each side can grasp what considerations move its opponents. Of course, the whole process is conducted within a broader constitutional framework that protects the fundamental rights of all.

Although democracy can degenerate into the kind of interest-group egoism that critics describe, such egoism contradicts the very point of having a democracy. Equals should not be treated as mere means for the fulfillment of others' wishes. As the very point of having democratic procedures is to acknowledge the moral equality of others, it is surely morally self-defeating to use those same procedures to violate or ignore the rights of others. Of course, anyone is likely to be in a minority on some occasions. The concern here, however, is with a group whose interests have been ignored again and again. Any democrat should be prepared to lose on occasion, but no one should be a loser virtually all the time on a wide variety of issues. Hence, to the extent that a given democracy allows for the oppression of permanent minorities, the reasons for abiding by the democratic process are seriously weakened.

Thus, although we doubt that participatory democracy is a panacea for the problems of permanent minorities, we agree with the emphasis of many of the participative democrats on reasoned public discourse. If the moral basis of democracy is made clear to all and open dialogue on the problems facing different groups takes place, majorities can be challenged either to justify their views or to change them. However, it is important that such public dialogue go both ways. Majorities are not always wrong or oppressive, and minorities as well as majorities can be open to well-founded criticism. Perhaps the very point of open discussion and dialogue is to allow us to detect our errors and correct them. But just where change should be made or who is making the errors must emerge from the discussion and not be decided in advance of inquiry. Since all parties to the discussion are persons with fundamental rights, democratic dialogue should focus on rational and critical discussion, not the bashing of those sincere democrats who take political positions different from our own.

**Democracy and the Common Good.** In addition to the problem of permanent minorities in a democracy, democrats also face the problem of reconciling the pursuit of individual and group interests with concern for the common good and the public interest. The concern is that people will vote for their own interests or those of their group, and the public interest will be ignored.

There is no easy solution to the problem of how to interest rational individuals in sacrificing for the common good. If the public good in question is a common good, a good for all, it is always rational to contribute less than one's share in the hope that others will pick up the extra. Since everyone reasons in the same way, public goods receive inadequate support. Hence the paradox of public squalor amidst private affluence. Where private goods are concerned, everyone will bid what he thinks the product is worth, for the highest bidder wins and everyone else loses. But where public goods are concerned, it is rational to try to be a "freeloader," which is exactly why labor unions favor closed rather than open shops.

On the other hand, if persons always functioned only as Hobbesian rational egoists, the political order would be impossible. (See the discussion of Hobbes in chapter 1.) If persons were incapable of valuing anything but their own good, human life as we know it might well be impossible. Relationships such as love and friendship, as well as traits such as intellectual honesty, require the taking of an impersonal point of view rather than a narrow egoistic one. Perhaps understanding the foundations of the democratic process itself can provide moral motivation for concern with the public interest. And, as Rawls has argued, since the moral society is likely to win the loyalty of fair-minded citizens, and indeed to promote fair-mindedness, it is likely to be the stable society as well.

More practically, we have seen, as in the case of Hobbesian theory, that it can be rational for people to impose sanctions collectively on themselves in order to make previously irrational behavior rational. It is sometimes in our self-interest to create institutions that discourage us from directly following our self-interest. Since all of us are hurt by significant injury to the environment, to the educational system, or to facilities for cultural and aesthetic expression, perhaps we can agree upon incentives that make it rational for us to help protect such public goods. Thus, automatic payroll deductions for Social Security protect us from our own economic irrationality. To circumvent our own inability to save, we vote for forced saving. Public-interest lobbies, institutional devices such as the ombudsman, and judicious use of tax benefits perform a similar function. The trick is to design institutions that we have some rational incentive to support. These institutions then automatically perform functions that we might not carry out if left to our own devices.

Although this may not ensure protection of the public interest, it is surely less unsatisfactory than Rousseau's method of forcing us to be free. People need not always function as rational egoists, and even when they do, it may be possible for them of their own volition to channel their egoism in a constructive direction. Whether institutional incentives strong enough to protect the public interest and weak enough to leave room for individual liberty can be provided remains a serious problem facing democratic theorists.

## Multiculturalism and Democracy

In recent years, the topic of multiculturalism has been hotly debated. Controversy has arisen in colleges and universities over the change from more traditional to multicultural curricula, while multiculturalists have sometimes criticized the broader society for not giving appropriate recognition to the voices of marginalized groups and for imposing the dominant culture on others. In the view of some critics, multiculturalism requires a new view of justice, focused much less on issues of economic distribution than on a "politics of recognition" that provides a fair and appropriate system in which diverse cultures can be free of oppression.[25]

What is multiculturalism? Like so many "isms," it can mean different things to different people. Therefore, it is important to make sure we are all considering the same idea. Otherwise, a criticism or defense of one person's conception of multiculturalism may not even apply to another's.

The core idea of multiculturalism seems to contain both a descriptive and a normative element. The descriptive component is that American society is becoming more diverse and that, in particular, people of color and previously marginalized groups, such as gay people, are becoming larger and/or more vocal segments of the population. The normative components are the ethical implications that the descriptive components support or suggest. Multiculturalists may differ among themselves as to just what these normative components are and may emphasize different descriptive features as well. Hence, although there is a core concept of multiculturalism—an emphasis on specific forms of diversity and how they should be acknowledged—these core elements can be interpreted very differently by different multiculturalists. Following a suggestion Rawls has made about justice, we might say that there is a core (if perhaps a bit fuzzy) concept of multiculturalism and then there are different conceptions of how that concept is best articulated and developed that are advanced by different multiculturalists. For example, some multiculturalists may promote a kind of cultural relativism, according to which each group has its own internal standards of ethics or rationality that cannot be criticized from the outside. Other multiculturalists may avoid such crude relativism and subscribe to some universal standards of morality, such as human rights. Again, some multiculturalists may emphasize that group differences occur within a common American culture, while others may regard any attempts to promote unity as oppressive attempts by dominant groups to impose a kind of cultural hegemony on others. As one such multiculturalist, Molefi Kete Asante, maintains, "The idea of 'mainstream American' is nothing more than an additional myth meant to maintain European hegemony. . . . There is no common American culture as is claimed by defenders of the status quo. There is a hegemonic culture . . . pushed as if it were a common culture."[26]

Unfortunately, we cannot present a comprehensive examination of multiculturalism here but must stick to its implications for democratic theory. However, we suggest that one good way to approach multiculturalism is to see it as a reaction against assimilation. Assimilation, in its strong form, means the submergence of group identities in a common melting pot. This does not mean that all of us will be alike but rather that our differences will be individual differences rather than group differences. As one proponent of the assimilationist model, Richard Wasserstrom, explains it, assimilation with respect to a given group trait, such as race or ethnicity, means that no one in the assimilationist society will pay any more attention to that trait than we presently do to eye color.[27]

The appeal of assimilation lies in the values of liberty and autonomy. It promises freedom from rigid traditions or the limited perspectives of a particular group and allows individuals to choose for themselves how they will act, what they will believe, and who they will be. According to the assimilationist, groups can be stifling and oppressive, demanding conformity to group positions and adherence to traditions that lack any obvious rational basis.

However, even if assimilationism is attractive as an ultimate goal, some critics point out that we are now in fact members of groups. Many of these groups have been oppressed on the basis of such features as race, religion, ethnicity, sexual preference, and gender. Even if the assimilationist model ultimately is attractive, it is not attainable right now. What we need now, according to such a view, is respect for pluralism and diversity. That is what multiculturalism seeks to provide.

Moreover, as writers such as W. E. B. Dubois have emphasized, different ethnic, cultural, and religious groups may have unique contributions to make to humanity, precisely because the experience of such groups is different from that of others. For example, according to Dubois, "the Negro people, as a race have a contribution to make to civilization and humanity which no other race can make." Therefore, Dubois concludes, "it is the duty of Americans of Negro descent, as a body, to maintain their race identity until this mission . . . is accomplished."[28]

Furthermore, many of those sympathetic to multiculturalism will argue, individuals don't just happen to belong to groups. Often, group membership is a deep aspect of individual identity. As the communitarians emphasized, the individual may be in part constituted by his or her group commitments. One is not just an isolated asocial atom but is a member of a religion, an ethnic community, or some other major social grouping. That is why excluding the voice of a major social group from the college curriculum may be not only disrespectful but also harmful to members of that group. As Charles Taylor notes in a particularly thoughtful essay on multiculturalism, "The projection of an inferior or demeaning image on another can actually distort and oppress, to the extent that the image is internalized. Not only contemporary feminism but also race relations and discussions of multiculturalism are undergirded by the premise that the withholding of recognition can be a form of oppression."[29] On this view, a multicultural recognition of diversity is a prerequisite for a society that is free of oppression and is not simply a means for arriving at an assimilationist ideal in which group differences either melt away or lack fundamental importance.

Multiculturalists have made a valuable contribution in emphasizing the idea of respect for diversity, in promoting greater dialogue among groups, and in insisting on the right of what have come to be called marginalized groups to have a full voice in the discussion. We too have doubts about whether strong assimilationism, the withering away of group differences, is an appropriate ideal toward which society should aim.

On the other hand, we find that some of the interpretations of multiculturalism, at least in some of its more extreme (but not necessarily most thoughtful) forms, have disturbing implications for democracy. For example, the idea that a significant part of our personal identity is constituted by our membership in major social groups may generate the very kind of conformity and internal group oppression that assimilationists warn against. Thus, dissenters within a group may formally or informally be told to conform to the positions of the group's majority or else they will not be considered true members of the group. Thus, women who do not reject traditional female roles may not be viewed as "real" women by some feminists, or assimilated blacks may be regarded as "inauthentic, imitative, copycats, unoriginal, ashamed of their color" by some other African Americans. Similarly, "if a person with a black skin writes a book or poem, he must explicitly show his 'blackness.' Otherwise, he . . . is not 'really' black."[30] In short, group membership can become a prison that forces members to fit a predetermined image rather than giving them the same freedom as others have to choose their own way. This not only harms the individual but also may seriously harm the group since it discourages the kind of internal dissent that forces people to question assumptions and that leads to progress.

Second, to the extent that multiculturalism becomes separatist, it diminishes the kind of dialogue that may take place among groups. If members of different groups conclude that there are no common standards of argumentation, logic, and moral justification that hold across group lines, dialogue itself becomes nearly a conceptual impossibility. The price that marginalized groups pay for this kind of relativism can be quite high. For if there are no common standards, why should members of other groups pay any attention to the critiques that the oppressed make of the existing system, since it is acknowledged that there are no common standards by which such critiques can be evaluated. "Perhaps your argument is good by your standards," a member of the dominant society might reply, "but not by ours." To the extent that multiculturalism rejects common principles of argumentation and justification that apply across group lines, it undermines the case for a social critique of existing institutions that has appeal to groups all across the social spectrum.

Finally, to the extent that multiculturalism undermines the idea of a common society and replaces it with an uneasy aggregate of different groups, how can a democratic society persist? Unless it is moderated by concern for a common society, an extreme emphasis on differences among groups can destroy the moral and social presuppositions necessary for a democracy to work.

Of course, multiculturalism need not have such extreme implications. As we noted earlier, different conceptions of multiculturalism need to be distinguished. Some of these conceptions may be much more defensible than others. We would hope that the positive aspects of multiculturalism, such as appreciation of group diversity, can coexist with elements of liberal morality, such as a concern for fundamental human rights of all people. However, to the extent that multiculturalism leads to a kind of moral paralysis that causes citizens to believe themselves unable to question immoral practices of other groups, ranging from female circumcision to genocide, respect for group differences would have degenerated into a kind of mindless acceptance of whatever evil the powerful in another culture choose to inflict on the powerless. After all, respect for groups and cultures other than our own purports to be a universal value, so to adopt a kind of skepticism about such values would be to reject one of the fundamental assumptions of multiculturalism itself.[31]

Such grounds lead us to recommend, not the strong assimilationism that the multiculturalists reject, but what we would call moderate educational assimilationism, along the lines of promoting a Rawlsian overlapping consensus discussed in chapters 4 and 5. That is, citizens in a democracy need to understand the ethical and practical considerations underlying the democratic system, the different sorts of cases that can be made for liberal democracies, the great works that have shaped the democratic tradition, and of course the arguments of critics of the liberal democracies and possible responses to them. This in turn implies that citizens need to be trained in critical thinking and analysis so that they can make intelligent and informed political decisions. In other words, liberal arts education is a prime prerequisite for the success of democracy. The curriculum of such education needs to be informed by many of the concerns of the multiculturalists, but we hope all would agree that writers such as Plato, Locke, Madison, Marx, Mill, and Rawls, who themselves are a diverse group of thinkers, should be a significant part of education in political theory for citizens of the democratic state.

## Political Obligation

In chapter 1, it was asked under what conditions a state had political authority. As an aid to answering such a question, it was suggested that the proper function(s) or purpose(s) of the state should first be identified. Our investigation so far indicates that the proper function of the state is (1) to protect and, where appropriate, implement the natural or human rights of its citizens; and (2) to provide for the just adjudication of competing claims (including claims of right) among citizens. The second criterion is a procedural requirement. In the view developed here, procedures for adjudicating conflicting claims may fail to honor a claim of right only in order to protect or implement other claims of right. It is the argument of this chapter that democracy is a paradigm procedure for conflict adjudication. As such, it should be a major part of the procedures used in adjudicating disputes in the just state. Also needed is a judiciary to enforce and interpret constitutional provisions and to settle disputes that cannot appropriately be resolved by democratic vote. (We will have more to say about judicial concerns in the next two chapters.)

Of course, not all societies can reasonably be expected to be democratic. They may be so poverty stricken, for example, that efficiency takes precedence over democracy. Or they may have a traditionally accepted hierarchical power structure that cannot be altered without great disruption and harm. But while such excuses may sometimes be valid, they too often function as ideological subterfuges protecting the abuse of power by an elite.

Even at its best, however, democracy constitutes only a just procedure for adjudicating conflicts. Just procedures may lead to unjust results. Depending upon the seriousness of the injustice, various forms of protest, from civil disobedience to revolution (in cases of gross, outrageous, and systematic injustice), may be called for. We will discuss the valuable role of protest within the democratic process in chapter 8. Now, we turn to political obligation in a democracy.

If a state satisfies the criteria discussed above, it is doing what the political order is supposed to do. Consequently, there are good reasons for supporting it. However, it does not follow that it has authority over us and that we are obligated to obey its edicts. Similarly, there may be good reasons for following a low-cholesterol diet, but we need not be under any obligation to do so. What is good to do is one thing. What we are obligated to do need not be what is good to do.

Robert Paul Wolff, in his *Defense of Anarchy*, which we discussed in chapter 1, was perfectly consistent in holding that while there might be good reasons for obeying the edicts of certain states, no one is under any obligation to do so. However, even if Wolff is correct in holding that no state has political authority and therefore no one has a political obligation to obey, it is still important to distinguish good states from bad. Our criteria 1 and 2 are designed to do just that. If they are defensible, they tell us which states we have good reason to support. However, are there any states that we are obligated to obey? Are there any that have authority over us? If so, how do they come to have such authority? Let us consider the issue of political authority and obligation, keeping in mind (as argued in chapter 1) that such obligations need not be absolute and that respect for legitimate authority need not entail blind subservience to its dictates.

## The Theory of Social Contract

The theory of social contract, particularly as developed in the writings of such classical contract theorists as Hobbes, Locke, and Rousseau, contains an account of political obligation. In the contract view, obligations arise from special acts of commitment by agents. Thus, X becomes obligated to pay Y five dollars by promising to do so. Likewise, citizens acquire political obligations by contracting to acknowledge the state's authority. Political authority arises from the consent of the governed, and consent is expressed through the social contract.

However, well-known difficulties face the contract approach. If the act of signing the contract is viewed as a historical one, when did it occur? And since the current generation surely never signed, from whence does its obligation, if any, arise? These questions appear unanswerable if social-contract theory is interpreted literally.

Locke attempted to modify the literal historical interpretation by relying on the notion of "tacit consent":

> every man that has any possessions or enjoyment of any part of the dominions of any government does thereby give his tacit consent and is as far forth obliged to the laws of that government during such enjoyment, as anyone under it; whether . . . his possession be of land . . . or a lodging only for a week, or whether it be barely traveling freely on the highway.[32]

But surely this is unsatisfactory. If even use of public highways is construed as tacit consent, it is far from clear what would count as withholding consent. By Locke's criterion, even revolutionaries plotting to overthrow a government have tacitly consented to obey it merely by their use of public roads. Surely, this Lockean account of tacit consent is too broad.

However, it is far from clear that narrower criteria of tacit consent are any more satisfactory. For example, suppose it is maintained that voting is a necessary and sufficient condition of tacitly consenting. Unfortunately, this criterion seems to be too narrow. Voting can hardly be a necessary condition of consenting, for we surely would want to say that many of those who fail to vote nevertheless (tacitly) consent. If a person who would have voted fails to do so because of illness on election day, it is surely plausible to think that such a person consents to political authority. (Indeed, if we take this condition seriously, it follows that since only about half the electorate vote in United States elections, only about half are under the moral authority of the government.) Moreover, it is doubtful that voting is a sufficient condition of consent. It is at least controversial whether those who vote simply out of habit, or because a boss-dominated political machine tells them to, are consenting to the political order.

Perhaps some criterion of tacit consent can be formulated that is neither too broad nor too narrow. At this point, however, other approaches seem more promising.

Suppose we consider hypothetical versions of the social-contract approach. At first glance, it would seem that such an approach is unhelpful. Even if there were an ideal contract that all rational persons would sign under appropriate conditions, such as behind the Rawlsian veil of ignorance, these conditions are only hypothetical. How can persons be obligated by a contract that they would have actually signed but never did?

This question seems difficult to answer if we appeal to contract theory alone. Perhaps a contractualist could argue that if persons admit that they would have signed a contract under fair conditions of choice, they are acknowledging something like the conclusion that the contract is fair. Then if there is an obligation to be fair, they would seem to be obliged to honor their hypothetical agreement, not because they actually agreed (they didn't), but just because the hypothetical agreement is in fact fair. However, this argument is not purely contractual but appeals to an additional principle that philosophers have called the principle of fairness. Let us consider this principle further.

## Fairness and Obligation

John Rawls has stated the principle of fairness as follows: "This principle holds that a person is under an obligation to do his part as specified by the rules of an institution whenever he has voluntarily accepted the benefits of the scheme or has taken advantage of the opportunities it offers to advance his interests, provided that this institution is just or fair."[33] The intuitive idea here is that if persons voluntarily accept the benefits of a cooperative arrangement, they have indicated to others their intention of playing a role in upholding the arrangement. Without this indication, they could not accrue the benefits, for others would not cooperate without the assurance that everyone will bear their share of any burdens involved. Hence, it is illegitimate—a form of cheating—for anyone to act as a free rider without some special justification.

According to Rawls, the institution must be fair or just if obligations are to arise from participation in it. "It is generally agreed that extorted promises are void ab initio. But similarly, unjust social arrangements are themselves a kind of extortion, even violence, and consent to them does not bind."[34] Rawls's theory of obligation has two parts, then. First, just or fair institutions are to be identified by appeal to an ideal hypothetical contract or, as in Rawls's later writing, by an overlapping consensus of the kind discussed in chapter 5. Second, we become obligated to follow the rules of any particular institution by voluntarily taking advantage of the benefits or opportunities it offers. It is at this second stage that the principle of fairness applies.

Unfortunately, the principle of fairness is itself open to strong objection. As Robert Nozick points out, "the principle . . . would not serve to obviate the need for other persons' consenting to cooperate and limit their own activities."[35] Without a consent requirement, the principle of fairness obliges us to uphold any just or fair institution from which we benefit, even if we would not choose to participate in it. Now, it is true that Rawls's version of the fairness principle, unlike that of H. L. A. Hart, whom Nozick was actually criticizing, can be interpreted as stipulating that benefits must be voluntarily accepted. Nevertheless, even if we read the principle of fairness as requiring voluntary or consensual acceptance of the benefits of the practice, we still need to spell out what counts as consent. Is consent actual, explicit, tacit, hypothetical, or what? Perhaps an acceptable theory of consent in this area might be developed, but it also proves fruitful, we suggest, to follow another line of thought developed by Rawls.

## Obligation and Rights

Nozick's criticism of the principle of fairness could be answered if we could distinguish between institutions that we have a duty to support and those that we need support only if we so desire. Consent would not be required where institutions of the first sort are concerned. Rather, we would have a moral obligation to support or enhance (and, where they do not exist, to help create) institutions of the required sort. Then, once we actually reap the advantages provided by such institutions, we are politically obliged, by application of the principle of fairness, to carry our share of the burdens the institutions impose. In other words, participation in the institutions would be obligatory, and hence consent would not be required.

Rawls adopts just such a strategy by appealing to our natural duties, that is, duties that hold independently of any voluntary act of commitment to a particular institution or person. Thus, we have a natural duty not to be cruel. If one were to be discovered dipping helpless babies in strawberry jelly and then feeding them to army ants, one could not excuse oneself by declaring, "I have never consented to the institution of avoiding cruelty." So, according to Rawls, we have a natural duty to support just institutions. In the contractual version of his theory, emphasized most fully in *A Theory of Justice,* Rawls holds that we have this duty because such a conclusion would be accepted by rational persons deliberating behind the veil of ignorance.[36]

Given the lack of agreement over just which principles would be accepted behind the veil, let alone over whether the contract approach is warranted, it would be helpful if conclusions similar to Rawls's could be derived from a human rights framework. We believe that they can. Human rights impose obligations on others. These obligations require us not only to refrain from interfering with others but also to do our share in supporting institutions that provide social and material prerequisites of an at least minimally decent human existence. Now, it is the function of the state to protect and implement claims of human right. Since we are obligated to respect such claims, and since the just state is the most efficient means of implementing them, we are obligated to support the just state.

On both the Rawlsian and the human rights view, we have a natural duty to support the just state. Once we are part of such an institution, we have a special duty, based on the principle of fairness, to carry our share of the burdens, for example, by obeying the laws such institutions impose. Natural duties bind us to support a legitimate political order. The principle of fairness creates the political obligation to acknowledge the authority of some particular political framework.

However, the problem of consent cannot be fully avoided. Citizens are not slaves. While they have an obligation to support the just state, which just state they support is up to them. That is, while citizens have an obligation to support the just state, which particular state they have an obligation to support depends upon which one they actually participate in. Furthermore, citizens normally have the right to leave one state and join another if they so wish.

Moreover, although obligations to the just state are genuine, they need not be absolute. Remember that by a just state we mean one that respects fundamental rights and has a just procedure for adjudicating conflicts among rights. However, a procedurally just political-decision procedure may yield unjust decisions. While the requirement of respect for rights mitigates the degree to which injustice can exist, some injustices might be quite significant. In such cases, decent persons may find themselves with conflicting obligations. There is no a priori reason to believe that the obligation to follow the dictates of political authority will always take precedence. However, if the argument of this section has force, there is a prima facie obligation to obey. If political obligation does not imply blind subservience, neither is it a myth. Rather, it arises ultimately from our obligation to respect others as rights bearers equal to ourselves.

## An Overview

In chapter 1, we asked the following questions:

1. Under what conditions should the state's claim to authority be accepted?

2. How wide should that authority extend?

3. What are the obligations of a citizen to the state and its laws? What is the proper response of political authority to lawbreaking, on the one hand, and to injustice, on the other?

We have approached the first question by attempting to identify the function(s) of the state. In our view, it is the function of the state to protect, enhance, and implement the natural or human rights of its citizens and to provide for just adjudication of conflicting claims that may arise among the citizenry. Given this account, question 1 might be answered as follows: A state has authority over its citizens and they a prima facie obligation to respect that authority if and only if the state is not in serious violation of the above criteria and the citizens benefit by the advantages provided by the state, that is, by having their rights protected or implemented, or through the use of adjudication procedures.

The remaining chapters discuss the implications and consequences of this theory. In chapter 7, our concern will be with the nature and scope of individual liberty. We will examine how the right to liberty constrains the democratic process. Democracy, on our view, is justified by the commitment to respect our fellow citizens as bearers of equal fundamental rights. Hence, each individual is to have an equal voice in the decision process, even if is expressed indirectly through the institutions of modern representative democracies. However, liberty protects citizens' status as individual agents with the abilities to choose and plan their own lives. It is to a discussion of individual liberty that we now turn.

## Notes

1. See the exchange between Felix E. Oppenheim and Virginia Held in *Political Theory* 1, no. 1 (1973): 54–78, for a discussion of whether value-laden or value-free definitions of terms like "democracy" are more valuable.

2. See Brian Barry, *Political Argument* (New York: Humanities Press, 1967), 58–66, for a discussion of majoritarianism.

3. See, e.g., Felix E. Oppenheim, "Democracy: Characteristics Included and Excluded," *Monist* 55, no. 1 (1971): 29–50, for a narrower account of democracy. Oppenheim would claim that (c) is a characteristic of a liberal society, not a democratic one.

4. However, some theorists have argued that democratic rights are of little or no significance in an inegalitarian, "one-dimensional" society because they make the established order appear just when it really is unjust.

5. John Stuart Mill, *Considerations on Representative Government* (1861), in *The Philosophy of John Stuart Mill,* ed. Marshall Cohen (New York: Modern Library, 1961), esp. 401–6.

6. See our discussion of Mill's utilitarianism in chapter 2.

7. Emile Durkheim, *Suicide,* in many editions.

8. See David B. Truman, *The Governmental Process* (New York: Knopf, 1951); Robert Dahl, *A Preface to Democratic Theory* (Chicago: University of Chicago Press, 1956); and Robert Dahl, *Who Governs? Democracy and Power in an American City* (New Haven: Yale University Press, 1961).

9. Dahl, *Preface to Democratic Theory,* 137, 146.

10. Robert Paul Wolff, *The Poverty of Liberalism* (Boston: Beacon Press, 1968), 152–53.

11. Eugene Lewis, *The Urban Political System* (Hinsdale, Ill.: Dryden Press, 1973), 147.

12. Dahl, *Preface to Democratic Theory,* 138.

13. Wolff, *Poverty of Liberalism,* 159.

14. Jean-Jacques Rousseau, *The Social Contract* (1762), trans. Maurice Cranston (Baltimore: Penguin Books, 1968), bk. 1, chap. 6, 60. Citations are to this edition.

15. Ibid., bk. 2, chap. 3, 72.

16. Ibid., bk. 2, chap. 7, 64.

17. S. I. Benn and R. S. Peters, *The Principles of Political Thought* (New York: Free Press, 1965), 319.

18. See Barry, *Political Argument*; and Virginia Held, *The Public Interest and Individual Interests* (New York: Basic Books, 1970), for discussion of the ideas of the common good and public interest.

19. This position is argued for in an excellent book by Peter Singer entitled *Democracy and Disobedience* (New York: Oxford University Press, 1974).

20. John Rawls, *A Theory of Justice* (Cambridge: Harvard University Press, 1971), 221–22.

21. Plato, *Republic,* bk. 8, 558, quoted from the translation by Benjamin Jowett (New York: Modern Library, 1941), 312.

22. Carl Cohen, "The Justification of Democracy," *Monist* 55, no. 1 (1971).

23. See the discussion of rule utilitarianism in chapter 2.

24. See *Shaw v. Reno (Shaw I),* 509 U.S. 630.113 S. Ct. 2816, 125 L.Ed. 2d 511 (1993), and the series of subsequent decisions in *Shaw v. Hunt (Shaw II)* decided in 1996.

25. See, e.g., Iris Marion Young, *Justice and the Politics of Difference* (Princeton, N.J.: Princeton University Press, 1990).

26. Molefi Kete Asante, "Multiculturalism: An Exchange," in *Debating P.C.: The Controversy over Political Correctness on College Campuses,* ed. Paul Berman (New York: Dell, 1992), 305, 308. Originally published in *American Scholar* (Spring 1991).

27. Richard Wasserstrom, "On Racism and Sexism," in *Today's Moral Problems,* ed. Richard Wasserstrom (New York: Macmillan, 1979), esp. 96–97.

28. W. E. B. Dubois, "The Conservation of Races," in *Negro Social and Political Thought, 1850–1920: Representative Texts,* ed. Howard Brotz (New York: Basic Books, 1966), 491.

29. Charles Taylor, "The Politics of Recognition," in *Multiculturalism,* ed. Amy Gutmann (Princeton, N.J.: Princeton University Press, 1994), 36.

30. Bernard R. Boxill, "Separation or Assimilation?" in *Campus Wars: Multiculturalism and the Politics of Difference,* ed. John Arthur and Amy Shapiro (Boulder, Colo.: Westview Press, 1995), 242. Originally published in *Blacks and Social Justice* (Lanham, Md.: Rowman & Littlefield, 1992).

31. For a discussion of this point, see Robert L. Simon, "The Paralysis of 'Absolutophobia,'" *Chronicle of Higher Education,* 27 June 1997, B5–B7. Gutmann warns that failure to criticize other cultures or other social groups on relativistic grounds has the effect of immunizing the powerful within such groups from criticism. See Amy Gutmann, "The Challenge of Multiculturalism in Political Ethics," *Philosophy and Public Affairs* 22 (1993): 171–206.

32. John Locke, *Second Treatise of Government* (1690; reprint, ed. Thomas P. Peardon, Indianapolis: Bobbs-Merrill, 1952), chap. 8., sec. 119.

33. Rawls, *A Theory of Justice,* 342–43.

34. Ibid., 343.

35. Robert Nozick, *Anarchy, State, and Utopia* (New York: Basic Books, 1974), 95.

36. Rawls, *A Theory of Justice,* 333 ff.

## Questions for Further Study

1. Explain the utilitarian case for democracy. What are its strengths and weaknesses? Explain Mill's defense of democracy based on self-realization. In what way does it differ from classical utilitarian arguments?

2. In your view, is pluralism a form of utilitarianism, or does it differ from utilitarianism? Defend your conclusion.

3. What are some of the criticisms that can be made of pluralism as a normative defense of democracy? How do you think pluralists might best reply to these criticisms? Is their reply successful? Defend your view.

4. How does Rousseau's justification for democracy differ from that of the utilitarians? How does it differ from that of the pluralists? How would Rousseau criticize the pluralists? How might they best respond? In your view, which side, if any, has the better argument?

5. What is the argument for democracy based on equality of fundamental rights? How would a proponent of that argument reply to the objection that not everyone is equally capable of participating in the political process? Is that reply successful? Justify your view.

6. What important values might the process of cultural assimilation promote? How would some multiculturalists criticize the ideal of strong assimilation? How might they reply to the criticism that emphasis on cultural diversity and group difference undermines social unity? Is it possible to have diversity and unity, or are the two incompatible? Justify your view.

7. Sometimes when citizens ignore burdensome duties to their fellow citizens, they are accused of breaking their promise. "You accepted the benefits of living in our country," they are told, "so in effect you promised to accept the burdens." What, in your view, are the strengths and weaknesses of this form of argument? Is some version of it sound?

8. In your view, is democracy the best form of government, or is the belief that democracy is the best form of government just a Western bias? Can citizens of the Western democracies legitimately criticize the governments of other, nondemocratic countries for being nondemocratic or for violating democratic rights? Or is such criticism a form of cultural imperialism that is morally wrong? (Can one criticize Western bias as wrong if one also takes the position that moral standards themselves are nothing more than biased expressions of specific limited cultural perspectives?)

## Suggested Readings

### Books

Braybrooke, David. *Three Tests for Democracy: Personal Rights, Human Welfare, Collective Preference.* New York: Random House, 1968.

Cohen, Carl. *Democracy.* Athens: University of Georgia Press, 1971.

Gutmann, Amy, ed., *Multiculturalism*. Princeton, N.J.: Princeton University Press, 1994.

Gutmann, Amy, and Dennis Thompson. *Democracy and Disagreement*. Cambridge: Harvard University Press, 1996.

Levine, Andrew. *Liberal Democracy: A Critique of Its Theory*. New York: Columbia University Press, 1981.

Locke, John. *Second Treatise of Government*. 1690. (Widely available in a variety of editions.)

MacPherson, C. D. *Democratic Theory: Essays in Retrieval*. New York: Oxford University Press, 1973.

Mill, John Stuart. *Considerations on Representative Government*. 1861. (Widely available in a variety of editions.)

Nelson, William. *On Justifying Democracy*. Boston: Routledge & Kegan Paul, 1980.

Pennock, Roland, and John W. Chapman, eds. *Liberal Democracy*. Nomos 25. New York: New York University Press, 1983.

Rawls, John. *A Theory of Justice*. Cambridge: Harvard University Press, 1971. Chaps. 4 and 6.

Rousseau, Jean-Jacques. *The Social Contract*. 1762. (Widely available in a variety of editions.)

Simmons, A. John. *Moral Principles and Political Obligation*. Princeton, N.J.: Princeton University Press, 1979.

Singer, Peter. *Democracy and Disobedience*. New York: Oxford University Press, 1974.

## Articles and Essays

Benhabib, Seyla. "Deliberative Rationality and Models of Democratic Legitimacy." *Constellations* 1 (April 1994): 26–52.

Christiano, Thomas. "Democracy." In *Encyclopedia of Ethics,* edited by Lawrence C. Becker and Charlotte B. Becker. New York: Garland Publishing, 1992.

Dahl, Robert A. "Procedural Democracy." In *Philosophy, Politics, and Society,* 5th ser., edited by Peter Laslett and James Fishkin. New Haven: Yale University Press, 1979.

Fishkin, James. "Symposium on the Theory and Practice of Representation." *Ethics* 91, no. 3 (April 1981). The entire issue is devoted to representation.

Gutmann, Amy. "The Challenge of Multiculturalism in Political Ethics." *Philosophy and Public Affairs* 22 (1993): 171–206.

Hook, Sidney. "The Philosophical Presuppositions of Democracy." *Ethics* 32 (1941–1942): 275–96.

*Monist* 55, no. 1 (1971). The entire issue is devoted to the topic "Foundations of Democracy."

# 7

# Liberty

Although virtually everyone claims to be a friend of liberty in the abstract, many turn out to be only fair-weather friends in the concrete. Although most Americans willingly pledge allegiance to their flag and to the liberty and justice for which it stands, all too frequently in the heat of controversy they lose sight of the very values the flag supposedly symbolizes. This is especially true of liberty. Liberty enables people to act in ways others cannot control. People are left free to act in ways that some might find repulsive, immoral, and subversive. Too often, those affronted react by trying to limit liberty itself.

Thus, fundamentalist religious groups have tried, with some success, to eliminate from the public schools textbooks that do not support certain religious and political values. Similarly, self-appointed guardians of the public's virtue have tried and continue to try, again with some success, to remove controversial books from library shelves. Throughout our history, those who have dissented from official policy often have been faced with economic and even physical retaliation. Without freedom, we would live in a totalitarian state, but often those who exercise freedom in controversial ways face many risks, even in countries where political liberty is most valued and protected.

Other problems concerning liberty arise, even if those involving its infringement are ignored. Thus, even the staunchest friends of liberty disagree over its scope and limits. Your liberty to swing your arm may end where your neighbor's nose begins. But should you be free to take high risks even if the only reason for doing so is to show off to friends? Should attempts at suicide be prevented, or should people be free to end their own lives if they wish? Are there limits to free speech? If so, what are they? If not, does it follow that viciously racist or anti-Semitic speeches are protected by law? Can colleges or universities promulgate and enforce speech codes prohibiting what has come to be called "hate speech" directed against various minority groups? If colleges can prohibit hate speech, can religious or political groups prohibit speech—for example, certain kinds of rap music—that they consider anti-Christian, antifamily, or antifemale? Can behavior be prohibited simply because it is offensive to others? If so, how offensive must it be? On the other hand, if offensiveness is not a good justification for prohibiting a behavior, does it follow that even behavior that deeply disgusts virtually all who witness it must be allowed?

In chapter 6, it was argued that democracy constitutes a fair process for adjudication of conflicting rights claims. Our concern here is to delineate the scope of one kind of such claim, the claim to individual liberty, and also to indicate how the right to liberty can act as a needed constraint on the democratic process. Consideration of the scope and limits of individual liberty will also enable us to demarcate the proper limits of the state's authority over the individual. It is to such questions concerning liberty that we now turn.

## The Concept of Political Liberty

Our concern is with political liberty. Thus, disputes over liberty of other kinds need not concern us. For example, there has been some dispute over whether humans have free will or whether the laws of nature are restrictions on human liberty. Are humans unfree to jump over the moon, or do they simply lack the ability to do so? Are our personalities, and hence our choices, determined by our environment and our genetic heritage? Do humans have free will? Fortunately for us, no stand need be taken on these issues here since our concern is purely with political liberty. Political liberty seems to be associated with the presence or absence of constraints imposed directly or indirectly by persons or associations of persons. Thus, a mountain range may render inhabitants of a valley unfree to leave, but it is not their political liberty that is restricted.

There is some temptation to identify liberty with the ability to satisfy one's wants and desires. Suppose that Jones is locked in a room but wants nothing more than to remain there. Is Jones free? After all, Jones can do exactly what he wants to do. If Jones is free, then are the subjects of a ruthless dictatorship, under which criticism of the despot is not permitted, also free so long as they actually support the government and do not want to criticize the dictator?

One difficulty with the view that one is free if one does as one wants is that wants themselves can be coercively imposed. John Stuart Mill, in his essay "On the Subjection of Women," suggests that even if women behave as they want, they are not free if what they want to do is itself the result of coercion:

> All causes, social and natural, combine to make it unlikely that women should be collectively rebellious to the power of men. . . . Men do not want solely the obedience of women, they want their sentiments. . . . They have therefore put everything in practice to enslave their minds. . . . When we put together three things—first, the natural attraction between opposite sexes; secondly, the wife's entire dependence on the husband, every privilege or pleasure . . . depending entirely on his will; and lastly, that the principal object of human pursuit . . . and all objects of social ambition, can in general be sought or obtained by her only through him, it would be a miracle if the object of being attractive to men had not become the polar star of feminine education and formation of character. . . . Can it be doubted that any of the other yokes which mankind have succeeded in breaking, would have subsisted till now if the same means had existed, and had been so sedulously used, to bow their minds to it?[1]

If Mill is correct in claiming that the wants of many women have been formed coercively, then surely such women are not free even if they are doing what they want to do. One might as well say that we can liberate prisoners simply by getting them to want to remain in prison.[2] On the other hand, we must be careful of dismissing others as "brainwashed" or "socialized" just because we reject their views. Thus, the tendency of some feminists to dismiss criticism by women who hold more traditional values than they do as being the result of social indoctrination too often functions as a device for avoiding the need to deal with objections and to take opponents seriously as persons. Nevertheless, it surely is too simple to say that people are free simply because they can do what they want, since it is at least possible that what they want is the result of coercion and oppression.

A second unacceptable consequence of the view that one is free if what one does is what one wants to do has been pointed out by Joel Feinberg. Consider, Feinberg asks us, "the case in which Doe can do one thousand things including what he most wants to do, whereas Roe can do only the thing he most wants to do. On the [freedom as the ability to do as one wants] model, Doe and Roe do not differ at all in respect to freedom."[3] Surely such a consequence is unacceptable. But since any account of freedom that has such an unacceptable consequence is itself unacceptable, the account that identifies freedom with doing what one wants must be rejected. Accordingly, liberty ought not to be confused with being able to do as one wants. The willing slaves of a dictator may be happy, but they are not free! But what is liberty? Some valuable suggestions are found in Sir Isaiah Berlin's important paper "Two Concepts of Liberty."

## Berlin's "Two Concepts of Liberty"

In "Two Concepts of Liberty," Berlin attempts to distinguish negative from positive liberty. The first, negative liberty, is involved in the answer to the question "'What is the area within which the subject . . . is or should be left to do or be what he is able to do or be, without interference by other persons?' The second . . . is involved in the answer to the question 'What, or who, is the source of control or interference that can determine someone to do, or be, this rather than that?'"[4] Negative liberty concerns the absence of external constraints imposed by others. Positive liberty concerns self-mastery, or control over one's own fate. Let us examine negative and positive liberty more closely.

**Negative Liberty.** According to Berlin, you lack negative liberty "only if you are prevented from attaining a goal by human beings."[5] Negative freedom is the absence of coercion. Coercion "implies the deliberate interference of other human beings."[6] Such interference prevents action that the agent otherwise could have performed.

Is Berlin correct in maintaining that for negative liberty to be violated, constraints must be deliberately imposed?[7] This identification of constraint with coercion or deliberate interference seems unfortunate. If Bradley accidentally locks Adler in his room, Adler is just as unfree to leave as he would be if Bradley's behavior were deliberate. Similarly, if through a series of actions whose consequences were unforeseen, our economic system develops in a way that closes significant options for most people, surely their liberty has been restricted. Lack of intention may well mitigate personal responsibility. But freedom can surely be restricted unintentionally. Hence, we suggest that constraints on negative liberty need not be deliberately imposed.

Negative liberty is the absence of constraint imposed by others. Such liberty is embodied in the notion of civil liberties, which are barriers against interference by the state. Lockean natural rights, as we have seen, were concerned primarily with negative liberty. What then is positive liberty?

**Positive Liberty.** Berlin tells us that the "positive sense of the word 'liberty' derives from the wish on the part of the individual to be his own master. I wish my life and decisions to depend on myself, not on external forces."[8] Positive freedom, according to this account, is self-mastery. One might be subject to no constraints imposed by others yet lack positive freedom. For example, if one is neurotically indecisive, then even if no one else prevents one from attending a movie, one may be unfree to go because of inability to make up one's mind. Likewise, compulsive desires, overwhelming depression, and perhaps even ignorance can restrict positive liberty.

Berlin believes that the concept of positive liberty is dangerous. Demagogues might claim that just as the neurotic is in the grip of irrational desires that prevent free choice, so too might the citizenry need to be forced to be free of their "irrational" desires for democracy. Once demagogues take this position, they may ignore the actual desires of the citizenry in order to "bully, oppress, torture [the citizens] in the name . . . of their 'real' selves."[9] Berlin is quite right to point out the fallacy here: namely, that of equating what we might want if we were not what we are with what we do want, and then assuming that if we are forced to promote the former, we are being liberated. This fallacy may lie behind the claim of some totalitarians that the citizens of a dictatorship have true freedom in spite of their protests to the contrary. It may also lie behind the claim of some allegedly progressive political movements that discount criticism on the ground that their opponents have been so corrupted by the existing system that they are incapable of critically examining it.

Berlin's essay is a warning against the appeal to positive liberty, with all the abuses to which such an appeal may lead. The idea of "forcing people to be free" in the name of their deeper selves certainly can lead to terrible abuses of human rights. Indeed, positive liberty can be, and has been, perverted in just the way Berlin points out.

However, the fault may lie more in the misuse of positive liberty than in the logic of the concept. Surely, there is nothing absurd in the claim that mental illness, exhaustion, or even lack of knowledge constrains one's decision-making ability and obstructs autonomous deliberation. The danger lies either in the misapplication of the claim, as when radical social critics mistakenly dismiss the arguments of opponents by claiming that the opponents have been brainwashed by the system and have lost the power to examine it critically, or in the additional step of claiming that the opponents must be coerced in order to be freed. This additional step is the one that we should be especially wary of taking, although sometimes, as in the treatment of the psychotic, we may be warranted in taking it. Be that as it may, the fault seems not to lie in the claim that there are constraints on self-mastery but rather in the further claim that the victim should be forced to be free.[10]

That is, we should first of all be very careful not to dismiss the critical arguments of opponents on the grounds that they lack positive freedom, for this not only deprives them of their standing as moral agents but also insulates our own view from criticisms that they might make that often will deserve consideration. In fact, such a device can be used as a political weapon to avoid criticism in the first place. Second, even in the probably infrequent cases when political opponents do lack positive liberty, it does not follow that they should be forced to be free. Berlin is right to warn us of the dangers of this road to tyranny. Rather, we need to consider noncoercive measures to raise critical awareness, such as increased exposure to education and to the argument of others. Perhaps there are occasions when people need to be forced to be free, as when a drug addict is made to go "cold turkey," but we need to keep in mind the abuses that might follow from such a conclusion when it is wrongly drawn. Refusing to consider others as responsible moral agents and reducing them to the status of slaves of their passions or of the social system to which they belong can be a way of depriving them of human dignity and human rights.

Having said that, we acknowledge that the concept of positive liberty. while easy to misapply, is not inherently defective. There can be, and have been, cases where human freedom has been severely restricted not by clear-cut external barriers to liberty, such as chains and iron bars, but by molding the victims' wants and desires to produce "happy slaves" who accept their plight regardless of its lack of justification or the damage it does to their self-respect and self-interest.

Berlin's comments suggest a rather sharp distinction between positive and negative liberty. But perhaps the distinction, while useful, is not very sharp or clear-cut. After all, compulsive desires, neuroses, ignorance, and the like frequently arise from the action or inaction of others. If so, it is perhaps more useful to distinguish between internal and external constraints on liberty than between two kinds of liberty.[11] This suggests that ultimately there is only one concept of liberty, with positive and negative components. Let us consider this suggestion further.

## Liberty as a Triadic Relation

Perhaps the clearest account of a unitary concept of liberty is the highly influential analysis advanced by Gerald C. MacCallum Jr. He argues that liberty claims are best understood as expressing triadic relations: "whenever the freedom of some agent or agents is in question, it is always freedom from some constraint or restriction on, interference with or barrier to doing, not doing, becoming or not becoming something."[12] On this view, liberty claims are to be analyzed according to the schema: "X is (or ought to be) free from Y to do or become (or refrain from doing or becoming) Z."

According to this account, the simple claim to be free must always be understood as elliptical for a more complex claim that specifies whose freedom is at stake, what it is from, and what it is for. For example, both advocates and critics of the use of steroids by athletes to increase athletic performance may appeal to considerations of liberty. Proponents of such use may appeal to the freedom of athletes from regulation so that they can decide what risks they will accept in order to obtain the rewards of athletic success. Critics may also appeal to the freedom of athletes, but in their case, it will be the freedom to compete in a drug-free arena without being required to take harmful drugs in order to remain competitive. Both sides may appeal to liberty, but each is concerned with a different set of constraints and with different goals. Different sides in a debate can each appeal to liberty. But if the structure of the actual liberty claims at stake is made clear, important differences between the sides that their common rhetorical appeal to freedom may obscure can be brought out into the open.

Thus, according to the triadic analysis, the difference between negative and positive liberty turns out not to be a difference between two kinds or concepts of liberty at all. Rather, the distinction is between two different ways of filling in the variables in the above triadic schema. Negative freedom can best be understood as freedom from external constraints, while positive freedom concerns freedom from internal ones.

What might X, Y, and Z stand for? X is to be understood as ranging over not only individuals but groups, corporations, states, and other kinds of institutions. Z ranges not only over actions but also over deliberations. Thus, as a result of imposed psychological blocks, a member of a group that has been subject to systematic discrimination may be unable to conceive of becoming a physician or an attorney. In such cases, it seems correct to say that such a person is unfree even to consider these alternatives.

Much controversy arises over the range of the Y variable. Many theorists, anxious to extend the scope of liberty, view poverty, ignorance, lack of opportunity, and lack of health as constraints on liberty. They are then able to justify the efforts of the welfare state to correct such conditions as required by concern for liberty. Other theorists argue, however, that liberty ought to be distinguished from the conditions under which liberty is significant or valuable. Suppose, for example, that Smith will not be admitted to college because he does not realize that he must take certain college preparatory courses in secondary school. In the first view, Smith may be considered unfree to attend college. His ignorance is a constraint on his freedom. In the second view, he is perfectly free to go. No one is stopping him from taking the appropriate courses. Unfortunately, because of his ignorance, his freedom is not of much value. But he is nevertheless free. Proponents of the second interpretation, particularly the kinds of libertarians we discussed in chapter 4, often criticize the activities of the welfare state as actually limiting liberty through excessive regulation. In this view, the welfare state spends so much time trying to improve the conditions of liberty that liberty itself gets lost in the shuffle.

This dispute seems largely verbal, however. While our sympathies lie with exponents of the broader interpretation, because they correctly point out that such "conditions" of liberty as ignorance and poverty often result from human action, the truth of their point does not depend on the language used to describe it. Certainly, if we consider poverty a constraint on liberty, then if we value liberty, we will want to eliminate poverty. But equally, if we believe that poverty diminishes the value or significance of liberty, then, if we value liberty, we will still want to eliminate poverty. Someone who distinguishes between liberty and the conditions of liberty need not be a defender of a laissez-faire free-market economy. Similarly, one can adopt the broad interpretation of liberty while defending laissez-faire. One would simply maintain that liberty from centralized government regulation is more important than liberty from poverty, ignorance, or lack of opportunity. Accordingly, whether one adopts the broad or the narrow interpretation, the verbal issue of what is a constraint on liberty and what is a condition of liberty should be distinguished from the substantive issue of what conditions must be altered if liberty is to be extended (made more valuable).

This is not to deny that the choice of conceptual frameworks may have important consequences. Given the favorable connotations of "liberty," it is probably easier to muster political support for elimination of what are termed constraints on liberty than for efforts to increase the value of liberty that one is already believed to possess. On the other hand, in some contexts, blurring the distinction between liberty and conditions under which liberty is of value may result in concern for negative rights being unduly subordinated to concern for implementation of positive ones. Hence, the intelligent choice of conceptual schemes requires thorough investigation and evaluation of the consequences of adoption in particular contexts.

The following conclusions emerge from this discussion of the concept of political liberty:

1. Liberty claims are often elliptical and need to be filled in as indicated by the triadic schema.

2. Liberty should not be confused with other values, such as want satisfaction, with which it can conflict.

3. Restrictions on liberty need not be deliberately imposed.

4. Conditions such as poverty and ignorance can (depending upon one's choice of vocabulary) restrict liberty or significantly lower its value.

With these points in mind, some of the political and social issues concerning the scope and limits of individual liberty will now be considered.

## Liberty: Its Scope and Its Limits

Liberty is of great value because of its intimate connection with human dignity and self-respect, with autonomy and individuality, with free inquiry, and with a host of other values.[13] To be always at another's beck and call, to be always dependent on someone else's permission for action, to be always under constraints that severely limit one's ability to act (or even to choose to act) is incompatible with the development of self-respect and retention of human dignity and autonomy. It also precludes the kind of growth and exploration that inquiry requires.

However, one person's liberty can conflict with another's. Moreover, other values can conflict with liberty. One individual's liberty can conflict with another's welfare. Moreover, individual liberty may be threatened by the state. It is not surprising, then, that those in the liberal democratic tradition have been concerned with demarcating the proper scope or range of individual liberty. The problem is that of deciding just when it is justifiable for individuals, groups, and institutions to impose limits on choice or action. For example, should someone be free to watch pornographic movies at home? At a movie theater? In a kindergarten classroom? Should free speech be extended to those who support racist and totalitarian ideologies? Does freedom include the freedom to advocate the elimination of freedom? Virtually all parties to the discussion agree both that some degree of liberty is desirable and that liberty is not without limits. As a prominent Supreme Court justice once noted, your freedom to swing your arm stops where my nose begins. But where should the line between permissible and impermissible exercises of liberty be drawn in more complex cases?

What is wanted is a criterion for distinguishing those areas in which restraint on others is permissible from those in which such restraint is illegitimate. Perhaps the most important criterion of demarcation was proposed by John Stuart Mill in his eloquent defense of individual freedom, *On Liberty*. In *On Liberty*, Mill declares that

> the sole end for which mankind are warranted individually or collectively in interfering with the liberty of action of any of their number is self-protection. That the only purpose for which power can be rightfully exercised over any member of a civilized community, against his will, is to prevent harm to others. His own good, either physical or mental, is not a sufficient warrant.[14]

This passage has long been cited in defense of civil liberties and individual freedom. Each person, it asserts, is to be granted a sphere of inviolability in which to do as he or she wishes. The sphere is limited only by the like sphere of others. Paternalistic coercion for the good of the agent is ruled out. Interference with one person is justifiable only when necessary to protect others from harm. Self-regarding actions—those that affect only the agent—may not be interfered with. Other-regarding actions—those that may lead to harm to others—may legitimately be regulated in the interests of public safety.

Sometimes, the significance of a proposal becomes clearer if we understand what it is attempting to rule out. In asserting what has come to be called the "harm principle," Mill is ruling out paternalistic interference with the liberty of persons for their own good. Thus, if the harm principle is in effect, physicians cannot treat a patient without the patient's consent, even if they believe the patient might die if left untreated. So long as patients are competent, interference with their liberty without their informed consent, even to preserve their lives, is unjustified according to the harm principle. But paternalistic interference is not all the harm principle prohibits. It also forbids interference with behavior that is merely offensive to others or with behavior that others believe is immoral but that is not harmful to third parties. Thus, even if the majority of the population finds homosexual relations offensive or immoral, the harm principle forbids any prohibition on this kind of sexual conduct simply on the grounds of its offensiveness or alleged immorality.

If Mill is correct in suggesting that the only permissible grounds for interference with liberty is prevention of harm to others, it becomes crucial to understand what counts as harm. How are we to understand "harm"? For if we do not know what is to count as harm to others, we cannot apply the harm principle.

Perhaps physically hurting or causing someone pain is the criterion of harming. However, one can hurt or cause someone pain without harming them, so this proposal fails. For example, a dentist may hurt someone when filling a cavity, but the dentist is helping and not harming the patient. Likewise, someone may be harmed without being physically hurt or being caused to experience pain—for example, by having valuable possessions stolen.

Harm seems to be a broader notion than physical hurt or pain. We will assume here that interests delimit harm. To harm X is to damage X's interests.[15] Since it normally is not in one's interest to be physically hurt or caused to experience pain, physically hurting and causing pain normally are ways of harming. But they are not the only ways. Insulting, excluding, discriminating against, and degrading are other ways of harming that need not involve physical hurt or pain. While the concept of an interest is far from clear, an interest at least seems to be something necessary for carrying out our actual or potential desires, or for securing our good. Understood in this way, the harm principle states that interference with anyone's action is justifiable only when necessary to prevent damage to the interests of others.

But is the distinction Mill attempts to draw between self- and other-regarding actions viable? Aren't all acts really other-regarding? Even reading a book in the privacy of one's own home can change one's character in a way ultimately detrimental to others. Thus, Mill's contemporary, James Fitzjames Stephen, maintained that "the attempt to distinguish between self-regarding acts and acts which regard others is like an attempt to distinguish between acts which happen in time and acts which happen in space. Every act happens at some time and in some place, and in like manner every act that we do either does or may affect both ourselves and others."[16]

Mill is not without reply to this objection. He acknowledges, for example, that acts performed in the privacy of one's home might constitute a bad example for others who learned of them. The problem this raises for Mill's position is that the distinction between self- and other-regarding actions seems to collapse if even acts performed in private contexts can affect others. Mill rejoins, however, that if the example is truly a bad one, others, seeing the harm it causes the agent, will not follow it.[17] This reply, however, seems weak since it rests on a questionable empirical claim; even worse, it seems irrelevant since if we presume that others are generally judicious, there may be no need to delineate the proper bounds of liberty to begin with.

Perhaps a better rejoinder available to Mill is that the original private act does not cause harm directly. Rather, harm is caused by other individuals who choose to follow the bad example of the original agent. On this view, for an act to be other-regarding, it must cause harm directly and not merely indirectly influence another free agent to choose to do wrong. In a similar fashion, Mill denies that long-range, indirect consequences of an act render it other-regarding. He distinguishes harmful consequences of neglect of a duty from remote, long-range consequences of ordinary human actions. If we were to interfere with the latter, no sphere of liberty would exist at all. Hence, "No person ought to be punished simply for being drunk: but a soldier or policeman should be punished for being drunk on duty."[18] It is only the immediate, direct risk of harmful consequences, not merely an indirect effect or influence on others, that renders an act other-regarding.

Whether or not the distinction between self and other-regarding acts can be defended along such lines is controversial. However, even if these replies are satisfactory, the harm principle still faces many serious objections of other kinds. We will consider attempts to override it in three areas: offensive acts and the enforcement of morality; paternalistic interference; and interference with freedom of thought and discussion.

## Offensive Acts and the Enforcement of Morality

**Offensive Acts.** The self-/other-regarding distinction has been attacked by appeal to the idea of an offensive act. The claim here is that offensive acts may be prohibited simply because they are offensive to others. If this claim is true, Mill's harm principle must be modified, since it allows interference only with harmful acts, not with offensive ones.

However, there are difficulties with the view that offensive acts may be prohibited just because they are offensive. How many people must be offended? How offensive must the act be?

It would seem that, on this view, almost any act might be subject to prohibition, since almost any act might offend someone. For example, should we prohibit a philosophy professor from discussing criticisms of the classical proofs for God's existence because some believers might be offended? Should we prohibit homosexual relationships because some people are offended by them? Should we prohibit certain forms of music or art because those styles offend some people? It would seem that the idea of prohibiting acts just because they are offensive is too broad, since almost any act might be offensive to some groups or individuals, and the idea is objectionable besides, since it leads to the prohibition of conduct, such as free discussion in philosophy class, that ought to be allowed.

Sometimes, of course, offensive acts also are harmful. For example, degrading epithets directed at a minority group on a college campus may not only be offensive to many people but also may harm those targeted by making them feel unwelcome or threatened, thereby decreasing their capacity to work effectively. We will discuss the case of hate speech more fully later in this chapter, but we acknowledge that where offensive action is also harmful in ways that violate the harm principle, regulation of such behavior may be permissible. However, it remains unclear that offensive actions may be regulated on grounds of their offensiveness alone.

But while there is danger in allowing regulation of offensive acts simply because they are offensive, is it plausible to say offensiveness *never* is a ground for regulation? People may be deeply offended at witnessing what they regard as immoral or obscene acts and behavior. A deeply religious person may be significantly pained by seeing or hearing about what he regards as a sacrilegious speech, work of art, or play. Virtually anyone in contemporary Western societies would be disgusted by public defecation. In at least some such cases, the offense given not only can be upsetting but also can induce rage, affect health, and perhaps even alter the course of a person's life—as when someone makes it her or his life work to stamp out pornography. Does acceptance of Mill's harm principle imply that we must be prepared to be constantly offended in the name of liberty?

Perhaps individual liberty can be reconciled with the desire to be safe from constant offense. A first step at reconciliation would involve distinguishing easily avoidable from unavoidable offensive acts. If witnessing the act or behavior that is regarded as offensive can be avoided with a minimum of effort, it is not unreasonable to expect those who object to make the minimal effort required. Surely, liberty is of great enough value to outweigh the minimal effort required to avoid being offended. Thus, having sexual relations on the subway may be legally prohibited. Sex between the proverbial consenting adults in private should be beyond the scope of the law. Again, nudity in a posted area that may be easily avoided by those likely to be offended surely is far easier to justify than allowing nudity on major public city streets.

How exactly is the boundary between avoidable and unavoidable actions to be drawn? Just how easy must an act be to avoid for it to be classified as avoidable, and exactly how hard must an act be to avoid for it to be classified as unavoidable? It is doubtful that any precise formula can be constructed that then can be applied to cases in a mechanical fashion. In practice, the boundary should be established by democratically enacted statute, as applied by the judiciary. However, there are limits on how far democracy may go here. These limits are set by the value of liberty itself. In view of the importance of individual liberty, the burden of proof is on those who would limit it to show at least (a) that the allegedly offensive behavior cannot be easily avoided; (b) that it is not feasible to provide a restricted area where the behavior in question need not be witnessed by the general public; (c) that the behavior is widely regarded as deeply offensive in the community as a whole; and (d) that the allegedly offensive behavior is not the expression of an ideology or ideal that ought to be protected under the heading of free speech. We also should remember that since any act may offend someone, we cannot prohibit all offensive behavior without surrendering liberty entirely.

In practice, the courts often have appealed to the standard of what the community in general finds offensive, obscene, or revolting. The trick, which may not yet have been performed satisfactorily, is to characterize the relevant community properly. Presumably, one should not define the community so narrowly that the showing of the very same movie is allowed in one and prohibited in the other of two neighboring suburbs. Yet one might not want to define the community so broadly that what is permissible on Forty-second Street in New York City must also be permissible in an Amish community.

The guidelines sketched above should be interpreted as placing a heavy burden of proof on those who would restrict liberty in order to minimize offense. Protecting liberty normally is more important that protecting people from being offended. This is a moral judgment concerning the importance of liberty that we hope is warranted in view of the arguments for human rights in chapter 3, as developed in later sections of this chapter.

**The Enforcement of Morality.** In 1957, in Great Britain, the Wolfenden Report concluded that homosexual behavior between consenting adults in private should not be subject to criminal sanction. In the spirit of Mill's harm principle, the report argued that the law should not favor particular patterns of behavior or ways of life unless necessary to protect others. The Wolfenden Report reflects the view of those liberals who follow Mill in maintaining that the widespread belief that a practice is immoral, even if true, is not itself a reason for imposing criminal penalties. In this view, crime and sin are not coextensive categories. Prohibition and punishment, on the view as developed by Mill and defended by many liberals, may be used to prevent harm to others but not simply to enforce prevailing moral standards.

This liberal view was attacked in Mill's time by James Fitzjames Stephen and at the time of the Wolfenden Report by the distinguished British jurist Lord Patrick Devlin.

Let us consider Devlin's case for the enforcement of morality, for it raises important issues of contemporary concern. For example, does society have a right to prohibit gay people from marrying each other because the majority holds the view that gay marriages are immoral?

*Devlin on Enforcing Morality.* The foundation of Lord Devlin's position lies in the claim that society has a right to protect its own existence. He then maintains that a common public morality is one necessary condition of a society's survival. But certain acts, even though they may not harm other individuals in Mill's direct sense, undermine the public morality. Accordingly, society has the right to regulate such acts in self-defense: "society may use the law to preserve morality in the same way as it uses it to safeguard anything else that is essential to its existence."[20]

Devlin does not maintain that every act widely believed to be immoral should be legally prohibited. In fact, he favors maximal tolerance consistent with the security of society.[21] The position Lord Devlin takes, then, is that "without shared ideas on politics, morals and ethics no society can exist."[22] This central core of the public morality, which is essential to society's very existence, can and should be protected by criminal sanctions. Contrary to some critics, Devlin does not view morality as a "seamless web," every strand of which is to be protected.[23] All he need be committed to is that some elements of the public morality are so essential to society's existence that sins against them are to be counted as crimes as well. In this way, Devlin's position has some resemblance to that of the communitarians whose views we discussed earlier, since, in effect, he is defending the right of the community to preserve essential elements of its way of life through its legal system.

*Hart's and Dworkin's Counterattack.* There is a serious problem for Devlin, however, which critics have not hesitated to exploit. The problem is this: How are those elements of the public morality essential for society's survival to be distinguished from those elements unessential for society's survival?

Devlin would respond that the proper test is the reaction of the "reasonable man." The reasonable man or woman should not be confused with the rational one:

> He is not expected to reason about anything, and his judgment may be largely a matter of feeling. . . . For my purpose, I should like to call him the man in the jury box, for the moral judgment of society must be something about which, any twelve men or women drawn at random might after discussion be expected to be unanimous.[24]

It is this feature of Devlin's position that has drawn fire from such liberal legal theorists as H. L. A. Hart and Ronald Dworkin. Hart and Dworkin raise the banner of objective morality against Devlin. Thus, Hart maintains that if all Devlin means by "morality" is widely shared feelings of indignation, intolerance, and disgust, there is no justification for giving such prejudices the status of law. Rather, Hart asserts that "the legislator should ask whether the general morality is based on ignorance, superstition, or misunderstanding . . . and whether the misery to many parties, the blackmail and the other evil consequences, especially for sexual offenses, are well understood."[25] In a similar vein, Ronald Dworkin maintains that Lord Devlin has not distinguished moral convictions from personal prejudices. At the very least, moral convictions must be based on reason rather than emotion, must be arrived at autonomously, and must pass minimal standards of evidence and argumentation. The trouble with Devlin's position, Dworkin tells us, "is not his idea that the community's morality counts, but his idea of what counts as the community's morality."[26]

In other words, Hart and Dworkin fear that society's worst prejudices and most irrational phobias may be supported under Devlin's banner of the enforcement of a public morality. On the other hand, does it follow that, merely because Devlin's position can be abused, it is never justifiable to legally prohibit acts simply on grounds of their immorality?

*Reflections on the Debate.* In our view, Hart's and Dworkin's criticism of Devlin surely has force. Devlin, for example, seems committed to a view that would permit prohibiting interracial handholding if a randomly selected jury in a segregated, racist society would find such behavior intolerable. Surely, Devlin's critics are right in contending that the "reasonable man" is not the proper source of wisdom on the nature of the public morality. But then Devlin is left without a means of distinguishing essential from unessential elements of the public morality. He relied on the "reasonable man" to make the distinction, but that reliance is unwarranted.

However, Devlin and his critics do seem to agree on one point, namely, that if essential aspects of the public morality could be identified, they should be protected by law. But surely there are enormous problems about identifying the essential aspects. Social scientists might tell us what people believe is essential, but this would not show whether such beliefs are correct. Who is to be the final arbiter? Do we want physicians making the decision? Philosophers? CEOs of major corporations? Labor leaders? No answer of this kind seems convincing.

Perhaps we ought to appeal to the democratic process, the decision of the majority of all the people. But doesn't this bring us right back to Devlin's "reasonable man" standard, one that these critics have already rejected as inadequate?

One suggestion, one that we ourselves made in an earlier edition of this book, is that the whole issue can be avoided. Both Devlin and his critics make an assumption that can be rejected, namely, the assumption that a society is entitled to protect itself through the criminal sanction from any kind of assault on the essential elements of common public morality. Perhaps society has no such right. That is, it is always an open moral question whether any society ought to survive, where "survival" is understood merely in terms of "survival of an essential public morality." Perhaps the shared morality ought to be changed, even if this means bringing a new society into existence. According to this suggestion, Devlin—and perhaps even Hart and Dworkin—does not clearly distinguish between legitimate and illegitimate methods for bringing about change. Respect for others forbids forcing change down their throats. Society surely has the right to protect its members against coercion. On the other hand, as Joel Feinberg points out:

> a citizen works legitimately to change public moral beliefs when he openly and forthrightly expresses his own dissent, when he attempts to argue, persuade and offer reasons and when he lives according to his own convictions with persuasive quiet and dignity, neither harming others nor offering counterpersuasive offense to tender sensibilities.[27]

Thus, if one is really committed to democratic change along lines developed in chapter 5, one must be prepared for public debate and decision on what the public morality ought to be.

While we still think that this point has considerable merit, we note that it does not settle the issue of whether it is ever permissible to prohibit action solely on grounds of its alleged immorality. It is one thing to say that the nature of public morality should be debatable. It is quite another to say that no element of the public morality can be legally protected. Thus, a prohibition of gay marriages can be debatable and legally enforceable at the same time. Similarly, even liberal academics probably would want to enforce the moral standards necessary for preservation of academic communities, such as respect for evidence and scholarship and censure of plagiarism, while acknowledging that those standards can be criticized and discussed within the academic community. But, some social conservatives may argue, if the academic community has the right to enforce its academic ethic in the name of preserving academic communities, why doesn't the broader community also have the same right to preserve its most sacred standards? If this rejoinder has force, Devlin's views may not be so easy to dismiss as liberal critics, including ourselves, have thought.

However, we also need to make sure that the force of the Hart-Dworkin critique has been properly appreciated. Their point may well be not simply that it is hard to distinguish the enforcement of morality from the enforcement of personal or community prejudice. Rather, it may be that if some factor like harm to others is not involved, the appeal to morality is in principle nothing more than an appeal to prejudice. That is, what distinguishes a moral argument from mere personal preference is that moral argument appeals to reasons that can be impartially appreciated and approved. But then such reasons must be provided. Devlin's response is that the continued survival of the community is such a reason, but there must be a moral case that the community is worth preserving. Does a community founded on racism and bigotry automatically merit preservation? Ultimately, it seems that the kinds of reasons that must be provided involve such factors as human welfare, preservation of rights, and protection from harm and not simply enforcement of morality itself.

Thus, briefly consider the debate over whether gay marriages ought to be permitted by law. Gay rights advocates often defend the claim that such marriages ought to be legal on grounds of equality and antidiscrimination. Why should gays have fewer rights than anyone else simply because of sexual preference? Isn't the right to marry a human right? Are opponents simply homophobic?

If opponents simply were to argue that gay marriage should be prohibited because it is immoral, without giving any further reason for their view ("Why is it immoral?" "It just is!"), it would appear that they were trying to enshrine their personal prejudices in law. However, opponents may have other arguments that they can present for public debate. For example, they might argue that marriage is a special institution with some specific function—namely, to promote monogamous relationships most suitable for rearing of children—and deny that homosexual couples could fit into this paradigm. The point here is not whether or not such an argument is justifiable but rather that it appeals to factors such as the harm that might be caused to individuals, a factor that fits within the framework of the harm principle itself.

Thus, while we are not prepared to rule out the immorality of an act or kind of act as a ground for prohibiting it, especially where a community tries to protect what it regards as its core values, we conclude that a heavy burden of proof rests on proponents of such prohibition to show that their conception of immorality is not merely personal prejudice or preference. Moreover, if the core values of a community cannot be defended through public debate in democratic forums, it is not clear that the community's code should be preserved. Accordingly, unless this heavy burden of proof is met, the immorality of an act or kind of act is not by itself grounds for prohibiting it through the legal system. However, it may be that in some cases the burden of proof can be met. Thus, we view the harm principle as providing the framework for discussion about the grounds for limiting liberty, a framework that may be abandoned only for the weightiest of reasons, but not as an absolute, exceptionless principle that must be adhered to no matter what.[28]

## Paternalistic Interference

Paternalistic interference is interference for the benefit of the agent whose liberty is infringed upon. Its aim is the good of the person coerced, or at least the prevention of harm to that person, not the prevention of harm to others. According to the harm principle, paternalistic interference is unjustified, at least where competent adults are involved. But is such a view acceptable?

Examples of allegedly paternalistic interference range from suicide prevention and involuntary confinement of mentally ill but not dangerous patients, to passage of statutes requiring motorcycle riders to wear helmets and automobile occupants to wear seat belts, to refusing to serve ice cream to dinner guests who suffer from high cholesterol in spite of their expressed desires to the contrary. To be sure, such interference need not always be paternalistic. Accident victims may have to be cared for at the public expense, for example, so the statutes requiring helmets and seat belts can be viewed as protecting the public from undue medical costs. For the moment, however, let us consider whether such statutes, and other similar kinds of interference, are justifiable when they are paternalistic in character. Perhaps this issue can best be explored by considering in detail a kind of intervention that is often regarded as both paternalistic and justified, namely, intervention to prevent suicide.

**Paternalism and Prevention of Suicide.** Suicides are not always or even usually self-regarding. Loved ones, dependents, and associates of the victim frequently are liable to harm. Accordingly, in a number of cases, intervention may be justified on other-regarding grounds. However, even here, it is doubtful that extensive, lengthy interference with freedom is justifiable on other-regarding grounds alone. The loss of liberty may outweigh the benefits received. (In any case, a person who is repeatedly suicidal is unlikely to be helpful to family, friends, and associates.) So, while remembering that suicide prevention often can be justified on other-regarding grounds, it is also well to remember the costs of ruling that a person's life is really not his or her own but is under the control of others. The case that is of interest here, however, is that of suicide that does not harm others. Is purely paternalistic interference with a potential suicide justifiable?

Most of us will be moved in two apparently conflicting ways on the issue of the legitimacy of suicide prevention. On the one hand, at least in cases where either there are no dependents or dependents are unlikely to be seriously harmed, we are inclined to say that a person's life is that person's own business. At least in cases where suicide is unlikely to involve harm to others, interference seems to imply that the agent in question is really like a child, unable or unwilling to make responsible decisions. On the other hand, it does seem callous simply to stand by, allowing other humans to take their lives. It looks as if our compassion is at war with our libertarianism here. Is there any way to reconcile the two?

One strategy of reconciliation is to restrict the applicability of the harm principle so that it allows at least some kinds of suicide prevention. Mill himself suggests one such approach when he declares that: "It is, perhaps, hardly necessary to say that this doctrine is meant to apply only to human beings in the maturity of their faculties. . . . Liberty, as a principle, has no application to any state of things anterior to the time when mankind have become capable of being improved by free and equal discussion."[29] This passage suggests a position according to which intervention with another's action in order to prevent suicide is justifiable where there is reason to believe the agent in question has not made a rational, responsible decision.

How might one fail to make such a decision? For one thing, a person might be in the grip of an abnormal, highly emotional mental state, such as extreme anxiety or depression. While a person is in such a state, suicide might seem a desirable alternative. However, if the person were to return to normal, suicide no longer would seem acceptable. Surely it is justifiable to intervene in such cases in order to make sure that a person's decision to commit suicide is one that has been given sufficient consideration and examination. To allow a fleeting desire or an unusual emotional state to bring about such an irrevocable decision is to ignore the agent's own rational plan of life that might be adhered to if a person were given further opportunity for reflection. As one proponent of intervention has declared of the proverbial businessman on the ledge of a tall building, "He is on the ledge rather than in his office because he wants to jump. But he is on the ledge rather than in the air because he wants to live."[30] Intervention, at least for the purpose of allowing due consideration and time for cessation of abnormal moods and impulses, seems fully acceptable. Moreover, the potential suicide might not just be suffering a fleeting depression or an abnormal mood. Such a person may be highly neurotic, mentally ill, or in the grip of a recurring compulsive desire. In such cases, it may be doubted whether the person involved has decided to commit suicide at all; suicide becomes more like something that happens to one rather than something one does.

Care must be exercised, however, to avoid two kinds of mistakes. First, it should not be concluded that simply because a person is a potential suicide, that person necessarily fails to be rational or responsible. This would be to rule out by definition the possibility of a rational, responsible suicide. Such a move is trivial, for it can alter only what we call the facts and not the facts themselves. We would simply have to invent a new word to refer to rational, responsible agents who take or attempt to take their own lives. The claim that no suicides are rational or responsible would be true, but only tautologically so because of linguistic fiat. The danger here is that of mistaking linguistic legislation for fact and, on the basis of such a confusion, interfering with the freedom of autonomous agents. Second, one must be wary of too extensive interference in the lives of potential suicides. Thus, it seems incompatible to say both that a patient's mental state is fleeting or abnormal and that the patient must be confined for long periods of time. Intervention of some preliminary sort may be justified in all cases of potential suicide as a failsafe device, designed to allow the agent to think through his or her situation or to provide counseling. But the assumption that an agent is not rational or responsible can be overridden in particular cases. Indeed, when the person in question is suffering from a painful terminal disease, failure to allow suicide may not only unreasonably infringe on liberty but also may be just plain cruel.[31]

On the other hand, as recent discussions of the permissibility of euthanasia have brought out, making suicide, including physician-assisted suicide, too easily obtainable, may put pressure on people to end their lives who otherwise would not. If Jones and Smith have committed suicide to spare their families the pain of watching them deteriorate from a terminal illness, their friend and contemporary Taylor may feel pressure to take the same option, even though she in fact wants to live as long as possible.[32]

However, the burden of the discussion so far is that individuals who are competent and autonomous ultimately have the moral right to control their own lives, so long as they do not harm others. But can't this reasoning be carried too far? For example, does it imply that a person should be allowed to contract into slavery? Suppose, for example, that some individuals would be willing to become slaves in return for financial benefits for their families. It might seem that such an act should be permitted under some circumstances. Interference might be justified to ensure that the agent is rational and autonomous. But once such a conclusion is established, if the subject freely contracts into perpetual slavery, there would seem to be no grounds for interference.

While some extreme libertarians might be willing to allow even slavery contracts, we suggest that the reasoning justifying such contracts and the reasoning suggesting that suicide sometimes may be permissible are not really parallel after all. The decision to commit suicide, especially when motivated by a desire to escape the ravages and indignities of a painful terminal illness, can itself be an expression of autonomy and dignity. Without these, the subject believes, life is not worth living. To contract into slavery, however, is to choose a life without autonomy or dignity. While one can commit suicide out of respect for such values, the decision to become a slave represents their abandonment. Hence, we suggest that the harm principle is overridden in cases where the agent would choose such extreme degradation that the very values of human dignity and respect for persons, which lie at the foundation of the harm principle itself, are irrevocably abandoned.

Moreover, we also suggest that it is highly unlikely that a person would voluntarily enter into slavery. Rather, slavery contracts are most likely to be signed by poor people anxious to protect their families from the ravages of poverty at almost any cost to themselves. It is at best extremely doubtful that such contracts in such circumstances could be entered into freely rather than under duress. (It is also possible, however, that suicide also might seem attractive because of external pressures, such as terminally ill patients' desire to spare their family the costs of medical care, and for this reason it is important that strong procedural safeguards are in place to prevent subtle forms of coercion.)[33]

**Extension to Other Cases.** This discussion of suicide prevention suggests that the following are acceptable principles of paternalistic interference.

1. One may paternalistically interfere with another in order to insure that that person's behavior is autonomous.

2. One may paternalistically interfere with the behavior of nonresponsible persons, e.g., children, the severely depressed and disturbed.

3. One may paternalistically interfere with the behavior of others in order to prevent acts (a) that irrevocably commit the agents to situations or ways of life that are seriously harmful to them, and (b) that commit such agents to abandonment of the very values of rationality and autonomy that justify the concern for liberty in the first place.

These principles constitute guidelines that indicate the sorts of considerations relevant to justification of paternalistic interference. Each, we suggest, is compatible with the harm principle. Principle 2 states the limits of applicability of the harm principle while principle 1 allows interference for purposes of checking that the limits have not been exceeded. Principle 3 indicates that the harm principle is limited by the same values that justify it.

How might these principles apply in practice? We can give only some brief suggestions here that indicate how the principles might apply to more complex cases. Mountain climbing, for example, although risky for the participants, could not be justifiably interfered with. Normally, mountain climbers are autonomous rational agents. Although the decision to climb may be momentous, in the sense of (3a), it surely does not represent an abandonment of autonomy and rationality or self-respect. The decision to participate in an activity that, although dangerous, requires great skill, gives participants a sense of achievement, and exposes them to the beauty and majesty of our world, is not only an intelligible decision but often may be an admirable one as well. On the other hand, a more plausible, if not fully satisfactory, case can be made for legislation that requires that seat belts be worn in motor vehicles. The failure to wear such belts is more often a matter of lack of proper habits than conscious choice. Finally, (3) does seem to sanction interference with activities that will lead to drug addiction. Heroin addicts, for example, certainly seem to run afoul of both (3a) and (3b).

In *On Liberty*, Mill maintained that

> the human faculties of perception, judgment, discrimination, feeling, mental activity and even moral preference are exercised only in making a choice. . . . The mental and the moral, like the muscular powers, are improved only by being used. . . . He who lets the world, or his own portion of it, choose his plan of life for him, has no need of any other faculty than the ape like one of imitation.[34]

Those who find a society of apelike mimics abhorrent have good reason to be skeptical of paternalistic intervention. However, such skepticism admits of justified exceptions where paternalism is designed to protect the autonomy of the agent in the long run.[35]

## Freedom of Thought and Discussion

The second chapter of *On Liberty* is entitled "Of the Liberty of Thought and Discussion." It is perhaps the most eloquent and moving defense available of virtually absolute freedom of thought and discussion. In this chapter, Mill claims that interference with thought or discussion in itself is almost never warranted. "If all mankind minus one were of one opinion, mankind would be no more justified in silencing that one person than he, if he had the power, would be justified in silencing mankind."[36]

**Mill's Defense of Freedom of Thought and Discussion.** How might the harm principle apply to freedom of thought and its natural extension, freedom of speech? Exactly how Mill himself thought the harm principle would apply in this area is unclear. Perhaps he believed that virtually no harm to others could arise from freedom of thought and discussion. Such a view seems implausible, however. After all, speech can have effects. Thus, a radical tract can lead to a violent revolution, or the lyrics of a popular song can make a life devoted to drugs and violence seem attractive to vulnerable young people. Surely, in some such cases, the effects of speech are clearly harmful. Although it is possible to argue that such effects are indirect and hence outside the scope of the harm principle because the harm is mediated by the choice of autonomous agents, as when a person decides to take heroin after listening to a song glorifying drug use, another more plausible reading of Mill is possible.

Remember that Mill is a utilitarian. As a utilitarian, he needs to establish the usefulness of freedom of thought and discussion apart from any appeal to abstract rights or justice. If he were to reason as an act utilitarian, he might be able to argue that allowing freedom generally or normally is more useful than prohibiting it. However, as critics have rightly pointed out, this would not lead to any strong principle of liberty in this area but at best only to a presumption in its favor. As James Fitzjames Stephen pointed out in Mill's own time, the question whether liberty is a good or bad thing appears as irrational as the question whether fire is a good or bad thing. It is both good and bad according to time, place and circumstances. . . . We must confine ourselves to such remarks as experience suggests about the advantages and disadvantages of compulsion and liberty in particular cases.[37]

Stephen's point is that utilitarians cannot have a general principle supporting freedom of thought and expression but must look at whether allowing such freedom on each particular occasion produces better consequences than suppressing it. But such a contextual approach hardly amounts to a robust defense of liberty, since whether or not liberty is protected depends on contingent circumstances. Our Bill of Rights would hardly provide fundamental protections if each right were amended so that we could exercise it only when it was useful for the rest of society to allow us to do so.

However, remember that Mill is often taken to be a rule utilitarian. If Mill can show that the rule or practice of allowing freedom of thought and discussion has utility and that judging in each individual case whether to allow such freedom has disutility, he will have made a strong case for the general principle that freedom of thought and discussion should be inviolate. Moreover, such a defense might have great value for those who are not utilitarians but who, like ourselves, argue from a human rights perspective. This is because if Mill is a rule utilitarian, he construes utility rather broadly and in fact ends up appealing to some of the same factors that lead to a defense of fundamental individual rights. Let us examine this approach further.

Perhaps Mill's strongest and most famous argument along such lines is that freedom of thought and discussion are valuable because of their intimate connection with rationality. To be rational is at least in part to use procedures that enable us to detect our errors and arrive at more warranted belief. Mill held that thought and open discussion are the principal procedures that allow us to attain such a goal:

> [T]he particular evil of silencing the expression of an opinion is that it is robbing the human race, posterity as well as the existing generation—those who dissent from the opinion still more than those who hold it. If the opinion is right, they are deprived of the opportunity of exchanging error for truth: if wrong, they lose what is almost as great a benefit, the clearer perception and livelier impression of truth produced by its collision with error.[38]

Without freedom of discussion, and the open exchange and criticism such discussion involves, we are deprived of the chance of having our errors corrected and condemned to hold the views we do hold as prejudices, without rational foundation. This is precisely why it is important to present our views in rational debate before intellectually diverse critics. Just as a sports team proves its mettle by defeating worthy opponents, a belief or claim is tested by seeing if it can survive the criticism of worthy critics. Free discussion is the mechanism for detecting and correcting error and for providing support of, and understanding for, those views that emerge unscathed from critical inquiry. Institutions and practices that permit and encourage free inquiry and discussion provide the framework within which our views can be supported or refuted. "Complete liberty of contradicting and disproving our opinion is the very condition which justifies us in assuming its truth for purposes of action."[39] On the other hand, if an opinion is protected from criticism by suppressing all dissent, its adherents have no basis for claiming it to be justified, for they have not submitted it to be tested in the first place.

Mill's first premise of his defense of freedom of thought and discussion is that such freedom is necessary for the correction of error and appreciation of truth. As a utilitarian, Mill also must establish a second premise, namely, that correction of error and appreciation of truth are useful in some utilitarian sense of that term. Presumably, Mill would argue that the process of inquiry would allow society to avoid serious error by exposing mistaken reasoning or dubious assumptions. Hence, it is more likely that a free society will choose optimal policies than it is that an unfree society will make such choices. Moreover, Mill also argues forcefully that freedom of thought and discussion leads to a diversity of points of view, which in turn produces inventiveness and independence among the citizenry. New ideas produced by an inventive and independent people lead to social, technological, scientific, and intellectual progress, which in turn benefits the society as a whole.

**Assessment of Mill's Argument.** While we are sympathetic to Mill's approach as developed above, we question whether rule utilitarianism alone provides the strongest defense for liberty of thought and expression. First, as we saw in our discussion of utilitarianism in chapter 2, there is the danger of rule utilitarianism collapsing into act utilitarianism owing to the weight of thousands of exceptions. That is, should exceptions to the rule permitting liberty of thought and discussion be allowed on utilitarian grounds alone? Moreover, does utility itself provide a firm enough foundation for freedom of thought and discussion? Are we really sure that a free society will always be happier in a utilitarian sense than an unfree one? Those who believe freedom is a human right might want to place it on a more secure foundation.

However, it is important to remember that Mill is not always best read as if he supported traditional utilitarian theories. In fact, we suggest that one of Mill's best arguments is not in the mainstream utilitarian tradition at all. Rather, although he often equivocates, Mill suggests that the development of critical, autonomous individuals, not simply pleasure in a hedonistic sense, is the intrinsic good to be produced. For Mill, "The worth of a state in the long run is the worth of the individuals composing it."[40] Social institutions are to be judged according to the kinds of individuals they develop. Thus, even if freedom does not always produce the most favorable attainable ratio of happiness to unhappiness, free discussion does promote the creation of critical, autonomous individuals. Such people are developed, Mill believed, through participation in free and open critical discussion and inquiry. Since the goal is development of an atmosphere in which such individuals can grow and flourish, Mill held that an absolute prohibition on interference was justified.

Whether Mill ever unequivocally adopted such a position is unclear, although he surely was attracted by it. In any case, we suggest that a stronger defense of liberty of thought and discussion can be made along such lines rather than through appeal to quantitative considerations of utility.

A further line of argument for a human right to liberty that is independent of utility also can be developed with help from Mill's suggestion that critical inquiry is the medium through which our opinions are justified. According to this line of argument, the right to individual liberty is best justified by showing it to be a precondition for the promotion and protection of personal autonomy. Whether or not liberty best promotes the overall general happiness, without it individuals cannot determine the course of their own lives. Freedom of thought and discussion is a particularly important aspect of human liberty. The exchange of ideas that it protects provides the framework within which we can make informed and intelligent choices, influence the views of others by appealing to their own rational capacities, and function as autonomous moral agents within a community of equals.

Finally, as Mill argued, a framework of rights that guarantees liberty of thought and discussion provides the very background within which claims can be examined and criticized. Without such a framework, it is doubtful that our views can be properly examined, since they might well be insulated from serious challenge. To use the analogy we developed earlier, they would be like teams that always avoided competition with opponents who might provide a challenge. Just as such a team could not claim to be excellent, untested and unchallenged opinions have no reasonable claim to be justified. Liberty, then, constitutes the framework within which other claims can be rationally evaluated. It is a fundamental element of any acceptable political order, for without it we are in no position to examine critically the major choices before us or to examine rationally the moral foundations of the political order itself.

This implies that the best remedy for bad, misleading, erroneous, and oversimplified speech is more speech. Debate, discussion, and inquiry provide the context in which flaws in our own positions or those of others can be detected and pointed out. If speech is restricted, such flaws might never be detected and our system of belief never improved.

But even if freedom of thought and discussion is of fundamental value, it does not mean that such liberty can never be limited by other considerations. Liberty is not license. To aid in understanding both the importance and the possible limits of liberty of thought and discussion, we will briefly consider a particularly controversial issue involving individual liberty: the recent attempts by some colleges and universities to prohibit, through the passage of campus speech codes, what has come to be called hate speech.

## Liberty and the Restriction of Hate Speech

Unfortunately, recent years have seen a series of deplorable expressions of hate speech against racial, religious, and ethnic minorities, as well as women and gay people, on many of the nation's campuses. While we will not attempt to provide a precise definition here, and doubt whether necessary and sufficient conditions can be provided, by "hate speech" we mean roughly the verbal or written expression of visceral hatred against distinct social groups, such as African Americans or Jews, employing epithets and slurs in a hostile, intolerant manner. For example, in January 1987 at the University of Michigan "unknown persons distributed a flyer declaring 'open season' on blacks . . . referred to as 'saucerlips, porch monkeys, and jigaboos.'"[41] Soon afterward, a student disc jockey allowed racist jokes to be broadcast on an on-campus radio station, and a Ku Klux Klan uniform was displayed at a demonstration protesting the earlier events. Similar episodes directed against various social groups, denigrating their race, religion, gender, or sexual orientation, have taken place at far too many academic institutions throughout the country.

In an attempt to prevent some incidents and to protect members of the target groups from them, some academic institutions promulgated speech codes designed to prohibit and punish hate speech on campus. Such codes restrict freedom of speech but do so to protect people from denigration based on their group membership. Does hate speech fall outside the realm of protected speech, or are speech codes an unjustified limitation on freedom of expression?

**Speech Codes and Hate Speech.** To focus our discussion, it will be useful to consider an actual speech code. Let us examine the code that was adopted by the University of Michigan in response to the incidents described above and that was challenged in the courts by an instructor at the university.

The code adopted by the University of Michigan applied specifically to educational and academic areas such as "classroom buildings, libraries, research laboratories, recreation and study centers" and probably to university housing, although various public parts of the campus were exempted, as were publications sponsored by the university, such as the campus newspaper.[42] In areas covered by the policy, persons were subject to disciplinary action for

> Any behavior, verbal or physical, that stigmatizes or victimizes an individual on the basis of race, ethnicity, religion, sex, sexual orientation, creed, national origin, ancestry, age, marital status, handicap or Vietnam veteran status and that
>
> a. Involves an express or implied threat to an individual's academic efforts, employment, participation in University sponsored extra-curricular activities or personal safety: or
>
> b. Has the purpose or reasonably foreseeable effect of interfering with an individual's academic efforts, employment, participation in University sponsored extra-curricular activities or personal safety: or
>
> c. Creates an intimidating, hostile, or demeaning environment for educational pursuits, employment, or participation in University sponsored extra-curricular activities.

To help explain the code to members of the campus community, Michigan published an interpretive guide that contained the following examples of prohibited behavior:

- A flyer containing racist threats is distributed in a residence hall.

- Racist graffiti are written on the door of an Asian student's study carrel.

- A male student makes remarks in class like "Women just aren't as good in this field as men," thus creating a hostile learning atmosphere for female classmates.

- Students in a residence hall have a floor party and invite everyone on their floor except one person because they think she might be a lesbian.

- A black student is confronted and racially insulted by two white students in a cafeteria.

**Evaluation of the Michigan Code.** What factors might colleges and universities that develop such speech codes cite as a justification? The first and perhaps most important consideration is protecting the victims from harm. While many people may maintain that "Sticks and stones will break my bones but names will never harm me," in fact the opposite seems true where hate speech is concerned. Racial epithets, for example, can cause great psychological stress to those at whom they are directed and make them fearful for their lives as well. This can affect their ability to work and function effectively as full members of the college community. "The symbols and language of hate speech call up historical memories of violent persecution and may encourage fears of current violence. Moreover, hate speech can cause a variety of other harms, from feelings of isolation, to a loss of self-confidence, to physical problems associated with serious psychological disturbance."[43]

In addition to harming students, hate speech can also wrong them by denying them equal opportunity to benefit from the academic institution they attend simply because of their race, religion, sexual orientation, ethnicity, or some other educationally irrelevant factor. In other words, the targets of hate speech are being discriminated against. Moreover, the kind of discrimination in question is especially invidious, since hate speech in effect states or implies that its targets are not fully persons and are not equal members of our moral community. In effect, hate speech, like racism, excludes its victims from the human race and from full and equal membership in the moral community. Surely, proponents of speech codes will argue, academic institutions have not only the right but also the duty to protect their students from being harmed and dehumanized. Therefore, they conclude, the imposition of speech codes like that implemented at Michigan is justified.

Is that conclusion warranted? Consider the case of *Doe v. Michigan,* in which a graduate student at Michigan who wished to remain anonymous, and who therefore is known as John Doe, successfully challenged the university's speech code in court. Doe's speciality was the study of the biological basis of individual differences in personality traits and mental abilities.

> Doe said that certain controversial theories positing biologically-based differences between the sexes and races might be perceived as "sexist" and "racist" by some students and he feared that discussion of such theories might be sanctionable. . . . He asserted that his right to freely and openly discuss these theories was impermissibly chilled.[44]

In fact, as the courts pointed out, Doe had a basis for his fears since, as we have seen, the guide to the code published by the university specifically cited remarks made in class, such as "Women just aren't as good in this field as men," as violations of the code.

At this point, those disposed to favor the code might deny that Doe has the right to question the abilities of major social groups in class. After all, doesn't that create a hostile classroom environment in which members of those groups may have trouble learning, precisely because their confidence in their own abilities has been undermined?

But then what other issues and questions also would be out of bounds? Could a critic of affirmative action say that it lowers the standards of those admitted to the school, since that also might insult or undermine the confidence of beneficiaries of affirmative action policies? Could a philosophy professor maintain that adherence to a religion was an irrational superstition, since such talk might create an intimidating or unfriendly atmosphere for religious fundamentalists? Could a psychiatrist argue that homosexuality was a disease?[45]

Proponents of the code might rejoin that their intent was not to create a politically correct atmosphere in which controversial issues could not be discussed but to prohibit slurs and insults directed against groups. However, it is not clear that the Michigan code draws an effective line between controversial political discourse and purely emotive slurs and epithets. In fact, the code prohibits verbal behavior that creates an "intimidating, hostile, or demeaning environment for educational pursuits." Unfortunately, words such as "intimidating," "hostile," and "demeaning" are just too vague to provide a reasonably clear boundary between controversial, possibly offensive intellectual discourse, which must be permitted if we are to have genuine intellectual disputes on important topics, and pure cases of hate speech that proponents of the code would assert fall outside the boundary of intellectual discussion.

A major problem with the Michigan speech code, then, is that it is both too vague and too broad. It is too vague because it is not clear how words such as "hostile" and "intimidating" are to be applied and too broad because it appears to rule out controversial (and possibly highly offensive) comments on issues that are under intellectual discussion.

Would the code be more defensible if it could somehow be amended to apply only to clear ethnic slurs, insults, and epithets? Even then, problems remain. We have already seen that there are problems with the view that speech or behavior should be prohibited or sanctionable simply because it is (or is believed by the majority to be) morally wrong or offensive. Yet speech codes, such as those of the University of Michigan, appear to prohibit and sanction racist, homophobic, anti-Semitic, and sexist speech simply because such speech is immoral or offensive.

But surely racist, homophobic, anti-Semitic, and sexist speech is wrong. Why shouldn't it be prohibited, then, on grounds of its wrongness? As we have seen, however, there are at least three major problems with enforcing morality in this way. First, where do we stop? Suppose the majority thinks homosexual behavior is morally wrong. Can it prohibit and punish such behavior? One problem with enforcing morality is deciding whose morality is to be enforced. Second, can we clearly separate genuine moral positions from purely emotional reactions without appealing to some additional factor such as harm to others, unfairness, or violation of rights? As Hart and Dworkin argued against Devlin, without such a check, the criterion of enforcement of morality can too easily degenerate into enforcement of the prejudices of the majority. Third, as Mill argued, if we do not subject our views to challenge, we are in no position to assert that they are justified. Consider Doe's point that men and women may not have equal capacities to engage in all areas of inquiry. How can we be justified in rejecting such a view without even examining it?

In addition, while there is an intuitive distinction between ethnic slurs and epithets on one hand and intellectual discourse on the other, it is not always easy to say where one ends and the other begins. Valuable debate is not always fully civil or polite. While we agree that civil debate is most likely to be productive, sometimes individuals believe that they can get their point across only by being shocking or outrageous. It seems dangerous to us to cede to officials of major organizations, whether they are speaking for the state or for the university, the power to draw lines here, since it will often be their own conduct that is at the center of the dispute.

In addition, it is important to note that the Michigan speech code is not viewpoint neutral.[46] For example, it does not prohibit or sanction the use of epithets by feminists against traditionalists or by radicals against flag-waving patriots. Is dismissing someone's arguments by calling him "homophobic," or a "heartless Republican," or a "pro-life dogmatist brainwashed by the church," or a "religious fanatic," or a "godless atheist who will burn in Hell" using epithets or slurs? Is dismissing the viewpoints of rural southern citizens by contemptuously referring to the "Bubba vote" or calling them "rednecks" allowable? Should the university favor one set of political positions and disfavor opposing views by prohibiting one set of alleged slurs while allowing others? As Judge Avern Cohen maintained in his opinion in *Doe*, "What the university could not do . . . was establish an antidiscrimination policy which had the effect of prohibiting certain speech because it disagreed with the ideas or messages sought to be conveyed."[47] The *Doe* opinion then goes on to quote with approval an important passage from the United States Supreme Court's decision is an earlier case protecting free speech when the Court maintained that "If there is any star fixed in our constitutional constellation, it is that no official, high or petty, can prescribe what shall be orthodox in politics, nationalism, religion, or other matters of opinion."[48]

The problem with speech codes such as that examined in the *Doe* case is that they are overbroad, vague, and arguably partisan rather than content neutral. While we agree that the harms caused by hate speech are real and serious, we do not believe for these reasons that codes such as the one at Michigan are justifiable forms of response.

**Speech-Acts, Narrow Speech Codes, and Civil Rights.** While the Michigan code may be defective in the ways cited, perhaps we have not done justice to the case for some sort of regulation of hate speech. Thus, while we have emphasized the value of liberty, what about equality? As we have seen, hate speech results in some members of the academic community being treated as moral inferiors, as not full human beings. Aren't the targets of such speech entitled to some protection?

Moreover, considerations of free speech may not be all on one side. If members of less powerful groups are harassed by hate speech, they may feel threatened. As a result of such intimidation, they may be less likely to participate in the public life of the institution, or even to attend. Hence, their contributions to open discussion are lost, and we have a less diverse set of participants in debate than would otherwise be the case. In other words, by not limiting hate speech, we reduce the value and effectiveness of free and open inquiry far more than a narrowly tailored speech code would.

Such considerations have led some writers to develop a parallel between hate speech and harassment. While the parallel is far from exact—for example, harassment usually is a pattern of behavior, but hate speech may occur only once—it is worth considering further, since regulating harassment is far less controversial than regulating the content of speech and expression. The main thrust of such an approach is that it would not be the content of the speech that is regulated but rather the act of directing certain "speech-acts" at specifically targeted individuals.

Such an approach has been developed by Andrew Altman, a philosopher and law professor, who emphasizes the connection between his argument and the speech-act theory developed earlier in the twentieth century by J. L. Austin at Oxford. Austin's main point was that by saying certain things in certain contexts, we also were performing certain acts. For example, by saying "I do" during a wedding ceremony, the bride or groom marries. By saying "I promise" in the appropriate circumstances, one promises.

Altman starts off with the comments of such writers as Mari Matsuda, who claims that "racist speech is particularly harmful because it is a mechanism of subordination."[49] Altman suggests that such a comment is best understood not as merely maintaining that racist speech causes harm (what Austin would call perlocutionary force) but as asserting that such speech in the context of hate speech *is* an act of subordination, just as saying "I promise" in the right circumstances is promising (what Austin would call illocutionary force). The illocutionary force is the kind of speech-act one is performing in saying the particular words in a particular context, so that "Duck!" in one context might be a warning ("The golfer on the tee sliced, so duck!") and in another could be a description ("That's a duck, not a swan").

According to Altman, hate speech wrongs its targets by subordinating them, thereby depriving them of their equal standing as persons. However, as we have seen, just because such speech-acts wrong others doesn't mean that the acts can be regulated. Regulation of a narrow sort may be justified, Altman maintains, because of its connection with antidiscrimination and antiharassment legislation: "the wrongs of subordination based on such characteristics as race, gender, and sexual preference are not just any old wrongs. . . . Historically, they are among the principal wrongs that have prevented—and continue to prevent—Western liberal democracies from living up to their ideals and principles."[50] Altman's point is that just as the state can enforce civil rights and antidiscrimination legislation, universities may be permitted to regulate acts of subordination, which are a form of discrimination.

However, Altman's argument leads to a kind of regulation quite different in focus from codes like the Michigan speech policy that are very broad in scope. Discrimination injures specific individuals, as does harassment. Similarly, Altman favors narrowly drawn codes that prohibit specific acts of subordination directed against specifiable individuals. The expression of ideas, however repugnant, is not punishable, but the subordination of identifiable individuals through hate speech is punishable.

The kind of speech policy adopted by Stanford University reflects Altman's approach. As drafted by law professor Thomas Grey, the Stanford policy provides that " 'protected free expression ends and prohibited discriminatory harassment begins' at the point where expression of opinion becomes 'personal vilification' of a student on the basis of one of the characteristics stated in the policy."[51] More specifically, to fall under the policy, speech or other expression constitutes harassment by personal vilification if it

a) is intended to insult or stigmatize an individual or a small number of individuals on the basis of their sex, race, color, handicap, religion, sexual orientation, or national and ethnic origin; and

b) is addressed directly to the individual or individuals whom it insults or stigmatizes; and

c) makes use of insulting or "fighting" words or non-verbal symbols.[52]

Insulting or fighting words and symbols are those " 'which by their very utterance inflict injury or tend to incite an immediate breach of the peace,' and which are commonly understood to convey direct and visceral hatred or contempt for human beings on the basis" of the designated characteristics cited earlier.[53]

**Assessing the Civil Rights Approach.** The advantage of the approach suggested by Altman and expressed in the Stanford code is that it does not prohibit expression simply on the grounds that the majority does not like what is said, or even that the ideas expressed are grossly repugnant or immoral. As we have seen, to limit expression on such grounds is highly problematic. Rather, the approach we are considering limits expression of a narrowly circumscribed sort to protect the civil rights of the victims. Is this approach defensible?

Some critics might object to the very feature of the Stanford code that makes it attractive to Altman and Grey, namely, its narrowness. Thus, the 1987 racial incident at Michigan described earlier in which a flyer was distributed declaring among other things "open season on blacks" might not be covered by the Stanford code since the element of personal vilification and face-to-face insults seems missing. Certainly, more general statements such as the posting of an anti-Semitic flyer or the use of epithets directed generally against homosexuals or people of color also would not be covered for similar reasons. However, any speech policy that does cover such events, such as the Michigan speech code, is likely to be vague, overbroad, and nonneutral, so we do not favor rejecting the idea of narrowly drawn codes on such grounds.

There are two other criticisms of even narrowly drawn speech codes, based on the civil rights model, that we think must be given significant weight. First, considerable leeway is given to those whose job it is to enforce the speech policy to interpret such expressions as "insult," "stigmatize," and "insulting or fighting words." While, unfortunately, there are many clear cases of the use of hate-laden epithets, nevertheless ceding to authorities the discretion to decide where the boundaries of permitted discourse end and violation of the rights of others begins is all too likely to have a chilling effect on speech in other areas. For example, suppose that during an argument on gay rights, some students use offensive language to express their view that gays are promiscuous and lack any kind of sexual morality. Just when do comments such as these constitute harassment or subordination rather than crudely expressed claims that need to be examined and questioned through free debate?

This point, while important, may not be decisive, since other policies, such as those prohibiting sexual harassment or campus disruptions, have similar areas of vagueness. However, even if it is not decisive, the point suggests a second worry. Normally, policies such as those prohibiting sexual harassment or disruption of legitimate campus activities are not partisan. Democrats and Republicans receive the same protection from harassment, and both liberal and conservative rallies are protected against illegitimate interference. However, different kinds of speech codes are not content neutral in the same way. For example, the Stanford code does not include speech that insults on the basis of class, so yelling at students that they are "rednecks" or "white trash" presumably would not be punishable.[54] Thus, the Stanford code does not apply evenly to all uses of degrading and insulting forms of personal vilification.

This degree of partisanship may be defensible, as Thomas Grey has suggested, on the grounds that there are asymmetries of power among groups in our society. Thus, as Grey notes, "there are *no* epithets in this society at this time that are 'commonly understood' to convey hatred and contempt for whites *as such*."[55] Nevertheless, there surely is a case that our colleges and universities should not adopt policies that may punish one group of students for personal vilification using one set of epithets but not punish others for personal vilification using a second set of epithets that also deeply wounds its victims. Even if one agrees with Grey, as we do, that racial incidents directed against, say, African Americans reflect a unique history of oppression in America, it does not follow that educational institutions, let alone the state, should adopt a partisan speech code. Not only is lack of evenhandedness likely to breed resentment and make cooperative social union difficult to achieve, it also elevates a particular set of moral and political perspectives to official status, thereby insulating them to a significant degree from debate and challenge. As we have seen, such protection goes too far since it chills discussion and thereby undermines the very framework of debate under which such a position can be justified in the first place. Moreover, if the neutrality of a framework for discussion were replaced with overt partisanship, it is not necessarily the case that views regarded as progressive would dominate. Once it is permitted to institutionalize an orthodoxy, there is no guarantee that the orthodoxy one favors will win.

Moreover, and probably most important, in evaluating the case for policies restricting speech and expression, we need to keep in mind that the best remedy for bad speech almost always will be good speech rather than repression. Let us consider this point further.

**Good Speech as a Remedy for Bad.** Sometimes policies have unintended consequences that are more significant than the intended ones. In particular, while the imposition of speech policies may be intended to protect members of designated groups from harassment and subordination, they may have broader unintended consequences. For example, individuals may become fearful of expressing controversial views that may offend members of protected groups because they may fear (perhaps wrongly) that the code will be extended in a partisan way to silence their position. They also may fear the reaction of their peers, who may regard them as "virtual" racists, homophobes, or anti-Semites. As a result, not only will genuine personal vilification be targeted, but also a whole range of controversial debate may be eliminated without anyone actually meaning to do so.

Even worse, truly objectionable views may simply be pushed underground. If such views are expressed openly, they can be debated and silenced, but if they are circulated underground, they are more likely to survive until they explode dangerously into the light of day. Generally, our best protection against hateful views is to debate them and expose their flaws, but speech codes unintentionally may make such debate virtually impossible.

Finally, the kind of protection provided by speech codes may be viewed as paternalistic by those it is designed to protect. African Americans, Jews, gay students, and others may much prefer to stand up for their rights in open debates rather than be protected by the institution.

For these reasons, we suggest that even narrowly drawn speech codes are at best the last resort in the liberal democratic state. However, while we categorically reject the imposition of broad speech codes such as the one at Michigan, we do acknowledge that narrow codes based on protection of civil rights are more difficult to evaluate. While we are troubled by the power they cede to officials and by their lack of neutrality, we concede that they avoid many of the difficulties of the broader approaches and may in some contexts actually improve the climate for debate by protecting those who might otherwise be intimidated into silence.

However, while individuals are entitled to protection from harassment and subordination, such protection normally should be tied to freedom from threatening conduct and should not be defined in terms of the content of the expression employed. In fact, we can distinguish two separate goals that speech codes might have: (1) protection of individuals from harassment and from what Altman calls subordination, and (2) the prohibition of certain kinds of slurs and epithets. Problems arise when the two goals are blurred together, because it may not be possible to define in a politically neutral way just the language that is to be forbidden. While we do not think it is always desirable or even possible to be neutral, in many contexts neutrality is an important virtue, particularly in colleges and universities, which must provide acceptable forums for broad and vigorous debate.[56] The problem with distinguishing between politically unacceptable and politically acceptable slurs and epithets is that in making the distinction, institutions place the political perspectives of some groups in a privileged position. This is all too likely to limit the degree to which people will challenge the dominant perspective, since they feel it is already officially entrenched and that opposition is sanctionable. It is also important to remember that once neutrality of a framework for discussion is replaced with partisanship, it may be the views that we oppose or find oppressive that become officially entrenched.

Thus, while we think that a total rejection of narrowly drawn speech codes is not warranted by the evidence we have considered, we suggest that proponents of their implementation in a given context face a burden of proof that we believe will be met only on rare occasions. This does not mean that hate speech against African Americans, gays, and other targeted groups should be tolerated but rather that in many contexts the best response is speech itself—for example, widespread condemnation of the acts of hate speech and broad-based expressions of support for the targeted groups. Thus, a widely supported rally endorsing the equal rights of all members of the campus community might be part of an appropriate response to the hate incidents at Michigan. Some highly controversial comments, however, might not consist of mere epithets and slurs but might have intellectual content, such as claims about alleged sex differences in mathematical abilities. These can be explored in the appropriate academic forums.

Political orthodoxies are to be avoided, even if they are our own, for we all lose when the very conditions of free and open debate that make justification possible are limited and eroded.

## The Priority of Liberty

The right to liberty is one among several fundamental rights that the good state ought to protect and implement. However, these rights can conflict. In such cases, where some individuals' rights claims must remain unfulfilled in order that others' can be implemented, the choice is to be made by suitably constrained democratic procedures, as outlined in chapter 6.

Influenced by John Rawls's work, philosophers have been paying increasing attention to what has been called the priority of liberty. Within the liberal tradition, liberty has always been assigned an especially fundamental place. Thus, we have already seen that in Locke's political philosophy, basic rights were rights to liberty from interference by others. Nozick's contemporary libertarianism seems to recognize only the right to negative liberty. Even those whose work defends nonmarket principles of distribution, such as Rawls, either give priority to liberty or argue that economic equality contributes to greater liberty.

In our view, when the right to liberty conflicts with rights to material prerequisites of a minimally decent human life, a choice must be made as to which gets priority. We see no grounds for saying that liberty must always receive priority in all circumstances, at all times, and in all places, although we will argue, as did Rawls, that liberty is particularly fundamental once a minimally decent level of economic well-being has been achieved. However, we point out that since poverty, ignorance, and ill health can constitute barriers to liberty, or at least conditions that rob liberty of its value, there is no necessary conflict between liberty and economic redistribution. Liberty and equality can conflict, but they need not necessarily do so, and making people better off economically may also help enhance the degree of liberty (or the value of liberty) that they enjoy.

However, as we just suggested, our position does provide grounds for assigning a special priority to considerations of liberty. That is, it seems wrong, from a natural rights perspective, to trade away the right to liberty for wealth or community and harmony once one has obtained the material prerequisites of a minimally decent human existence. This is not a psychological assertion about what causes what. Rather, it is a *moral* claim to the effect that autonomy and the freedom to carry out one's choices are more significant constituents of a meaningful human life than is great affluence.

But aren't we just expressing our own personal preferences here? Are such preferences rationally binding on everyone? In response, we would point to two considerations, both of which arise from points made by John Stuart Mill. First, the exercise of liberty is a major, perhaps *the* major, element in living a life of human dignity—of living as a moral person. Would anyone really say that a society of affluent slaves who, while wallowing in luxury, were always at their master's call led a life in which the values of human dignity and respect for persons were exemplified? Similarly, people would not be exercising autonomy if they lived in a rigid community in which traditions were viewed as beyond question or change.

Second, as Mill argued, liberties are essential for rational inquiry. Liberty is required to safeguard access to information, to protect critical discussion, and to allow for the formulation and communication of new points of view. How can citizens in a democracy evaluate foreign policy, for example, if it actually is determined by covert intelligence operations that are not exposed to public scrutiny or evaluation? Once the material prerequisites of a minimally decent human life have been secured for everyone, loss of additional wealth is less likely to hinder inquiry than loss of liberty. Accordingly, as affluence increases, there seem to be good reasons for weighing liberty more and more heavily relative to competing values. These reasons may be overridden on occasion, and perhaps properly so, but they seem at least sufficient to shift the burden of proof to those who would constrain liberty in particular cases.

Thus, fundamental liberties are central to the democratic process, since that process cannot proceed unless the fundamental freedoms of citizens to inquire, discuss, investigate, and argue are preserved. Core or basic liberties will normally be promulgated as provisions of a constitution, exempted from the normal majoritarian voting process, and interpreted and limited, if necessary, by the courts. Other aspects of liberty, more controversial and less central, may sometimes be open to democratic review. However, as liberty is a right, core areas of freedom covered by the right are not subject to the direct democratic process or to limits imposed simply by the pursuit of affluence, utility, or communal harmony.

We see no reason, then, to abandon a modified form of the harm principle. Each person is to be viewed as possessing a right to liberty. This right protects freedom of thought and action, so long as no direct harm to others results. According to our own theory, such harm would be constituted by depriving others of their liberty or by violating their other fundamental human rights. The right to liberty, so understood, significantly limits the scope of the state's authority. States may override the right to liberty only to protect and implement other rights and when such a policy has been arrived at by a just adjudication procedure suitably constrained, such as legitimate proceedings through a court system as defined by a democratic constitution. The right to liberty cannot be overridden on paternalistic grounds, to enforce the moral beliefs or personal tastes of the majority, or to suppress unpopular, merely offensive, or allegedly dangerous ideas. In some cases, such as speech codes designed to protect the civil rights of vulnerable minorities, it will be controversial whether limitations are justifiable. But the mere existence of controversial cases does not undermine fundamental principles; in fact, the cases often arise precisely because fundamental principles sometimes clash. Thus, while controversy will rightly arise over difficult cases, such as the promulgation of speech codes as a weapon against hate speech, we suggest that the fundamental ground rules of freedom and respect for persons that frame the terms of the disagreement should be recognized by all and form the basis of perhaps our most fundamental human right, the right to liberty.

## Notes

1. John Stuart Mill, *The Subjection of Women* (1869; reprint, London and New York: Longmans, Green, 1911), 42–43.

2. This point is made by William A. Parent, "Some Recent Work on the Concept of Liberty," *American Philosophical Quarterly* 2, no. 3 (1974): 151.

3. Joel Feinberg, *Social Philosophy* (Englewood Cliffs, N.J.: Prentice-Hall, 1973), 7.

4. Isaiah Berlin, "Two Concepts of Liberty," in *Four Essays on Liberty* (New York: Oxford University Press, 1969), 121–22.

5. Ibid., 122.

6. Ibid.

7. Berlin seems to have adopted such a position recently. See, e.g., his remarks in the introduction to *Four Essays on Liberty,* xlvii ff.

8. Ibid., 131.

9. Ibid., 133.

10. On this point, see C. B. Macpherson's discussion in *Democratic Theory: Essays in Retrieval* (New York: Oxford University Press, 1973), chap. 5.

11. This is suggested by Feinberg, *Social Philosophy,* 12–14.

12. Gerald C. MacCallum Jr., "Negative and Positive Freedom," *Philosophical Review* 76, no. 3 (1967): 314.

13. See the arguments of chap. 3 in the section "Justification."

14. John Stuart Mill, *On Liberty* (1859; reprint, ed. Currin V. Shield, Indianapolis: Bobbs-Merrill Library of Liberal Arts, 1956), 13. All subsequent quotations from *On Liberty* are from this edition.

15. The connection between harm and interests has been suggested by a number of philosophers. See, e.g., Brian Barry, *Political Argument* (New York: Humanities Press, 1965), 176 f. For a discussion of the connection between harms and interests, see Joel Feinberg, *Harm to Others: The Moral Limits of the Criminal Law* (New York: Oxford University Press, 1984), esp. chap. 2.

16. James Fitzjames Stephen, *Liberty, Equality, Fraternity,* 2d ed. (London: Smith, Elder, 1874), x.

17. Mill, *On Liberty,* 101.

18. Ibid., 99–100.

19. See, e.g., George Gilder, "In Defense of Monogamy," *Commentary* 58, no. 5 (1974): 31–36, for what can be read as an application of Devlin's position to sexual morality.

20. Lord Patrick Devlin, "Morals and the Criminal Law," in *Morality and the Law,* ed. Richard A. Wasserstrom (Belmont, Calif.: Wadsworth, 1971), 34. Originally published in Devlin, *The Enforcement of Morals* (New York: Oxford University Press, 1965).

21. Ibid., 37n, 39–41.

22. Ibid., 33.

23. H. L. A. Hart, *Law, Liberty, and Morality* (New York: Random House, 1966), 51.

24. Devlin, "Morals and the Criminal Law," 38.

25. H. L. A. Hart, "Immorality and Treason," in *Morality and the Law,* ed. Wasserstrom, 54. Originally published in *Listener,* 30 July 1959.

26. Ronald Dworkin, "Lord Devlin and the Enforcement of Morals," in *Morality and the Law,* ed. Wasserstrom, 69. Originally published in *Yale Law Journal* 75.

27. Feinberg, *Social Philosophy,* 39.

28. An interesting kind of case involves the claims of a cultural or religious community to preserve its traditions by law, e.g., by conducting all government business in the "official" language of the group. Prohibition of use of the languages of other cultural groups in government documents, such as ballots, may not reflect the view that use of other languages is immoral but may arise from a desire to preserve and pass on the major traditions of the dominant culture.

29. Mill, *On Liberty,* 13–14.

30. We have been unable to track the source of this remark, which we first heard on a tape of a debate on suicide prevention between Dr. Thomas Szasz and an unidentified opponent. The opponent was the source of the remark.

31. On this point, see Marvin Kohl, *The Morality of Killing: Sanctity of Life, Abortion, and Euthanasia* (New York: Humanities Press, 1974), esp. his discussion of euthanasia.

32. For a thoughtful discussion of the dangers of legalizing physician-assisted suicide, see Leon R. Kass and Nelson Lund, "Courting Death: Assisted Suicide, Doctors, and the Law," *Commentary* 102, no. 6 (December 1996): 17–30.

33. But couldn't procedural safeguards be in place in the case of slavery contracts as well? If we have doubts about whether such safeguards would work, why shouldn't we have similar doubts about physician-assisted suicide where there also is the possibility of subtle forms of coercion influencing patients? Perhaps neither practice should be legally permitted, even if it is morally permissible under some circumstances. For discussion of such problems as they arise with respect to physician-assisted suicide, see Kass and Lund, "Courting Death."

34. Mill, *On Liberty,* 71.

35. Thus, Gerald Dworkin has argued that paternalistic interference is justified if rational, autonomous persons would consent to it in the given circumstances. The limits of paternalism are set

by what might be thought of as an ideal or hypothetical contract. See Dworkin, "Paternalism," in *Morality and the Law,* ed. Wasserstrom, 107–26.

36. Mill, *On Liberty,* 21. Most liberals would agree that speech may be interfered with in certain special cases, such as to prevent a "clear and present" danger from arising. But care must be taken not to construe "clear and present" so broadly that legitimate protest is silenced. In any case, the goal here is to prevent a dangerous action, not to interfere with communication as such.

37. James Fitzjames Stephen, *Liberty, Equality, Fraternity* (New York: Holt & Williams, 1873), 49.

38. Ibid., 21.

39. Ibid., 24

40. Mill, *On Liberty,* 141.

41. *Doe v. University of Michigan,* 721 F. Supp. 852 (E.D. Mich. 1989). Excerpts from this important opinion on speech-act codes have been widely reprinted, e.g., in John Arthur and Amy Shapiro, eds., *Campus Wars: Multiculturalism and the Politics of Difference* (Boulder, Colo.: Westview, 1995), 114–21; and John Arthur and William H. Shaw, eds., *Readings in the Philosophy of Law* (Englewood Cliffs, N.J.: Prentice-Hall, 1993), 537–44.

42. Here we rely on the treatment of the University of Michigan policy found in *Doe v. University of Michigan.*

43. Andrew Altman, "Liberalism and Campus Hate Speech," in *Campus Wars,* ed. Arthur and Shapiro, 124. Originally published in *Ethics* 103 (January 1993)

44. *Doe v. University of Michigan,* as reprinted in Arthur and Shaw, *Campus Wars,* 539.

45. In fact, according to the court in *Doe v. University of Michigan,* at least one student was disciplined or threatened with discipline "because he stated in the context of social work research class that he believed that homosexuality was a disease that could be psychologically treated." Ibid., 540.

46. This point is made by Altman, "Liberalism and Hate Speech," 125–26.

47. *Doe v. University of Michigan,* in *Campus Wars,* ed. Arthur and Shaw, 541.

48. *West Virginia State Board of Education v. Barnette,* 319 U.S. 624 (1943), as quoted in *Doe v. University of Michigan,* ibid., 541.

49. Mari Matsuda, "Legal Storytelling: Public Response to Racist Speech: Considering the Victim's Story," *Michigan Law Review* 97 (1989): 2329–34, 2352; quoted in Altman, "Liberalism and Hate Speech," 126.

50. Altman, "Liberalism and Hate Speech," 128.

51. Thomas Grey, "Civil Rights versus Civil Liberties: The Case of Discriminatory Verbal Harassment," in *Philosophy of Law,* ed. Joel Feinberg and Hyman Gross, 5th ed. (Belmont, Calif.: Wadsworth, 1995), 299. Originally published in *Social Philosophy and Policy* (1991).

52. Ibid., 307.

53. Ibid.

54. This point is discussed by Grey in "Civil Rights versus Civil Liberties," 301.

55. Ibid.

56. For discussion of the role of neutrality in colleges and universities, see Robert L. Simon, *Neutrality and the Academic Ethics* (Lanham, Md.: Rowman & Littlefield, 1994).

## Questions for Further Study

1. What are some of the problems with the claim that if people can do what they want, then they are free?

2. How does Isaiah Berlin distinguish between negative and positive liberty? Why does he regard the notion of positive liberty as potentially dangerous? Do you think that we should dismiss positive liberty as valueless because of Berlin's criticism?

3. Explain the triadic account of liberty. What is its value or importance?

4. Explain the harm principle as defined by John Stuart Mill. What is the importance of the distinction it tries to make between different kinds of actions?

5. Do you believe that it is ever permissible to prohibit an action simply because it offends others? If so, would you prohibit public defenses of atheism on the grounds that some religious people are offended by them? If not, would you allow nudity in public areas even though many people are offended by it? Justify your view on each of these cases.

6. Explain Mill's argument defending freedom of speech and expression and distinguish between utilitarian and nonutilitarian versions of it.

7. Do you think any or all of the following can be justified by a liberal theory of freedom of expression, such as Mill's: the freedom to attack religion as a primitive superstition; the freedom to burn the American flag as a form of political protest; the freedom to fly the Confederate flag at a college football game; the freedom of homosexuals to marry? How would you reply to objections to your view?

8. Do you think your college or university ought to have a speech code prohibiting and punishing "hate speech"? How might such a code best be formulated? Defend your view about whether such a code is permissible by formulating and then replying to what you think is the strongest objection against your view.

## Suggested Readings

### Books

Benn, S. I., and R. S. Peters. *The Principles of Political Thought: Social Foundations of the Democratic State*. New York: Free Press, 1965. Chap. 10.

Berger, Fred R., ed. *Freedom of Expression*. Belmont, Calif.: Wadsworth, 1980. Classic articles on censorship.

Berlin, Isaiah. *Four Essays on Liberty*. New York: Oxford University Press, 1969. See esp. the essay "Two Concepts of Liberty."

Feinberg, Joel. *Harm to Others: The Moral Limits of the Criminal Law*. New York: Oxford University Press, 1984.

———. *Harmless Wrongdoing*. New York: Oxford University Press, 1988.

———. *Social Philosophy*. Englewood Cliffs, N.J.: Prentice-Hall, 1973.

Hart, H. L. A. *Law, Liberty, and Morality*. New York: Random House, 1966.

Mill, John Stuart. *On Liberty*. 1859. (Widely available in a variety of editions.)

Nielsen, Kai. *Equality and Liberty*. Totowa, N.J.: Rowman & Allenheld, 1985.

Oppenheim, Felix E. *Dimensions of Freedom*. New York: St. Martin's, 1961.

Wasserstrom, Richard, ed. *Morality and the Law*. Belmont, Calif.: Wadsworth, 1971. Contains articles by Devlin, Dworkin, Hart, and others discussed in this chapter.

Wertheimer, Alan. *Coercion*. Princeton, N.J.: Princeton University Press, 1987.

Wolff, Robert Paul. "Liberty," chap. 1 in *The Poverty of Liberalism*. Boston: Beacon Press, 1968.


### Articles and Essays

Altman, Andrew, "Liberalism and Campus Hate Speech." *Ethics* 103 (January 1993).

Daniels, Norman. "Equal Liberty and the Unequal Worth of Liberty." In *Reading Rawls: Critical Studies of A Theory of Justice,* edited by Norman Daniels. New York: Basic Books, 1975.

Grey, Thomas. "Civil Rights versus Civil Liberties: The Case of Discriminatory Verbal Harassment." In *Philosophy of Law,* ed. Joel Feinberg and Hyman Gross. 5th ed. Belmont, Calif.: Wadsworth, 1995. Originally published in *Social Philosophy and Policy* (1991).

MacCallum, Gerald C., Jr. "Negative and Positive Freedom." *Philosophical Review* 76, no. 3 (1967): 312–34.

Marcuse, Herbert. "Repressive Tolerance." In *A Critique of Pure Tolerance,* edited by Robert Paul Wolff, Barrington Moore Jr., and Herbert Marcuse. Boston: Beacon Press, 1969.

Matsuda, Mari. "Legal Storytelling: Public Response to Racist Speech—Considering the Victim's Story." *Michigan Law Review* 97 (1989).

# 8

# Law and Order

Up to this point, our discussions have not included any consideration of how citizens who violate the laws of the state should be treated. Our efforts resemble those of a football coach who spends all his time constructing plays for the ideal game but who ignores questions of rule violations and inadequate performance on the playing field. If the theory of the state is to be complete, we must pay attention to how a state ought to deal with citizens who violate its laws.

The legal apparatus of the state, including the police and the courts, is responsible for determining when violations of the law have occurred, for apprehending violators, and for taking measures that encourage both violators and nonviolators to obey the law. Recently, legal institutions in the United States have become highly controversial. The appropriate methods of apprehending and treating criminals have become items of considerable public concern. Charges of police brutality are a recurring phenomenon. Other questions have arisen concerning such practices as wiretapping, the creation of decoys to entrap potential criminals, and the use of police informers. Moreover, concerned citizens have focused on apparent injustices in our practices of punishment. The tragic results of prison rebellions and media exposés of conditions in prisons have raised serious questions about their purpose and organization.

Some psychologists and other social scientists have challenged the legitimacy of the institution of punishment. Other social scientists have conducted studies that indicate great discrepancies in the sentencing of criminals by judges and also strongly suggest that members of certain races or social classes receive discriminatory treatment.

It would take us far beyond the scope of this book to discuss all these issues in detail. Rather, we shall focus our discussion in this chapter on two issues: the legitimacy of punishment, and the theory and justification of civil disobedience.

## Why Law?

One might ask why it is necessary to have a set of coercive rules in the just state. By far the most common argument for the necessity of law is based on the psychology of human nature. There is general agreement that people are political animals, that they need social-political organizations for their protection and self-realization. Such institutions are clearly advantageous. However, to be effective, institutions require rules, and sometimes these rules work to the disadvantage of some individuals participating in the institution. On these occasions, the person whose goals are thwarted by the rule is tempted to ignore his obligations to obey the rule and to yield to immediate self-interest. To overcome this propensity, the rules of the state are backed by sanctions (punishments). Human nature requires that a state have a system of coercive rules to insure that its citizens obey the rules and regulations.

For example, H. L. A. Hart argues that coercive rules are necessary since there are always some persons in the community who will try to avoid obeying the law. Hart declares that coercive rules must contain some restrictions on the violence, theft, and deception to which human beings are tempted, but which they must repress if they are to coexist in proximity to each other.[1]

Human frailty causes another problem that needs legal correction as well. This sort of frailty can arise from the makers of law themselves. In ancient Athens, legal decisions were made by vote in a case-by-case manner. There was not a strong stable body of written law. As a result, decisions were often made in the heat of passion or on irrelevant grounds. The classic case of error in this regard was the sentencing of Socrates on charges of atheism and corrupting the youth. Plato's response to this state of affairs was an elitist political philosophy in which only the wise would be rulers. Aristotle saw that Plato's solution was dangerous since it is difficult to identify the wise and to ensure that power will not corrupt them.

Aristotle's own solution was a stable body of law, especially a constitution, that would establish correct procedures of law and rule out other procedures as legally illegitimate. In other words, a body of law is a practical check on human passions and prejudice, making it less likely that miscarriages of justice will occur.

Of course, to argue on behalf of the need for law is not to argue that law is sufficient as a form of social control. The law and morality have considerable overlap, but they do not coincide. We cannot say, "If it's not illegal, it's not immoral," just as we noted in chapter 7 that we could not say, "If it's immoral, then it should also be illegal."

It also is important to note that law has other important functions besides controlling antisocial behavior through the threat of punishment. As Hart has emphasized in his major study, *The Concept of Law,* law also enables us to perform many activities that would not exist were it not for the legal system.[2] We can marry, make out a will, sell a house, or sign a contract precisely because the law in effect defines what counts as marrying, making out a will, selling a house, or signing a contract. However, in this chapter, our focus will be on criminal sanctions, and it is to an examination of the institution of punishment that we will now turn.

## Punishment

Many persons have accepted without question the idea that the appropriate means for dealing with criminals is to punish them by a fine, imprisonment, or both. In breaking the law, they hold, criminals deserve to be harmed in some way. With this attitude toward punishment already strongly internalized, many will find it strange that philosophers have felt a need to justify the institution of punishment. They will find it even stranger that many philosophers and social scientists think that our current practices of punishment cannot be justified. The arguments against punishment take many forms, but some common threads run through them. One group of critics argues that it is society rather than the lawbreaker that is responsible for crime. Since in this view society is responsible for the conditions that cause crime, punishment is an injustice inflicted on the lawbreakers. Another group of critics is less interested in who is responsible for crime than in our response to crime. They argue that some form of treatment is more appropriate than punishment as a response to criminal acts. Before addressing these critics of punishment, let us begin our discussion by considering the two traditional philosophical arguments in favor of punishment, namely, the utilitarian and the retributive arguments.

## The Utilitarian Justification

If one were an act utilitarian, one would say that an individual is to be punished if and only if his individual punishment would lead to better consequences than his non-punishment. Better consequences in each case are determined by seeing if the pain or harm of punishment is offset by the force that the punishment has in reducing the pain or harm of crime. Punishment is alleged to reduce crime by removing criminals from society, by reforming criminals, and, most important, by deterring other potential criminals. On utilitarian grounds, punishment is justified if the benefits of reducing crime outweigh the pain of the punishment.

One widely discussed objection to this approach has been dubbed the "punishment of the innocent argument" as discussed in chapter 2. The counterexample on which the argument is based involves a town plagued with a rash of heinous murders. The populace is approaching panic. A drifter known by the authorities to be innocent is arrested and executed to stem the panic. This action would be justified punishment on act-utilitarian grounds, since the majority would be less fearful and hence presumably happier, yet most of us would insist that this is not an act of justified punishment at all. After all, an innocent person has been punished. Even if this argument is not foolproof, it has been so persuasive that utilitarians have constantly tried to reformulate their positions to avoid it. (See our discussion of this point in chapter 2.)

The common utilitarian response is to give up act utilitarianism for rule utilitarianism. According to this view, it is the institution of punishment or the rules of the institution of punishment that are to be justified on utilitarian grounds. Individual acts of punishment are justified by appealing to the rules of punishment; the rules of punishment are justified on utilitarian grounds. It is then generally assumed that the legal rule that allows for punishment of the innocent would not pass the utilitarian test, even if individual acts of this kind would. We do not think this assumption has been or can be established.[3] However, our chief argument is the familiar one used throughout this book. The utilitarian theory of justification for the state and its institutions is inadequate because it does not take account of the rights of the individual citizens, as we argued in chapters 2 and 3. With respect to justification, utilitarian theory is not sufficient to justify individual acts of punishment or the rules of the institution of punishment.

Perhaps utilitarianism will serve us better if we distinguish the question of who should be punished from the question of how much punishment should be administered. Utilitarianism may be most plausible, not in determining who should be punished, but rather in determining how much a person should be punished. Jeremy Bentham, whatever his intention, spent most of his utilitarian analysis on this question. Bentham argued that the goal of punishment was deterrence and that in determining the amount of punishment this end must be kept in mind.[4] Punishment should, so far as possible, (a) inhibit one from committing a crime; (b) dispose one to commit a lesser rather than a greater offense; (c) dispose a criminal to commit no more mischief than is necessary; and (d) keep the amount of punishment necessary for deterrence as small as possible. Bentham's position may be summarized as follows: The first rule of punishment is "that the value of punishment must not be less in any case than what is sufficient to outweigh that of the profit of the offence." However, another rule of punishment must always be kept in mind: "The punishment ought in no case to be more than what is necessary to bring it into conformity with the rules here given."

Some illustrative comment might prove useful. It is easy on Bentham's account to see why the punishment for a serious crime is more than for a lesser crime. On utilitarian grounds, a serious crime is defined as one that produces worse consequences than most other crimes. Now if the function of punishment is deterrence, you need more punishment to assure that the more serious crimes will not be committed. We must not be overzealous, however. It is often suggested that kidnapping, rape, and armed robbery should be made capital offenses. To make them capital offenses, however, may well violate Bentham's condition that punishment dispose a criminal to commit no more mischief than is necessary. So long as murder, kidnapping, rape, and armed robbery are all capital offenses, there is no utilitarian reason why a criminal should not kill any of his victims of the three latter offenses. If he is caught, he is no worse off; and if he kills his victim, the chances of his being caught and successfully prosecuted are reduced. On utilitarian grounds, the punishment for kidnapping, rape, and armed robbery should not be death.

Subject to certain significant retributive constraints that will be discussed shortly, we basically accept the utilitarian strategy of basing the amount of punishment on considerations of deterrence.[5] We believe that rules fairly similar to Bentham's should be adopted by a democracy. Our main quarrel is with the utilitarian basis of punishment itself. The focus of this quarrel may be seen by contrasting utilitarianism with its chief rival, retributivism.

## The Retributive Theory of Punishment

Retributivism basically is the idea that criminals ought to be punished because they are guilty, not simply because society finds it useful to punish them. Retributivists claim that the criminal deserves punishment and often also claim that the punishment should fit the crime. While critics often equate retributivism with a primitive desire for revenge, retributivists themselves defend their theory by appeal to social justice. Revenge, on their view, is the expression of the emotion of the individual, while punishment, administered after a fair judicial finding of guilt, helps restore equity. Surely, it would be unjust if criminals were not punished and were allowed to gain from their crimes.

Immanuel Kant is one of the major classical retributive theorists.[6] It is useful to begin with his theory because it contains many propositions that retributivists defend and because it is so uncompromising. The basic propositions of Kant's theory are:

1. Punishment can be inflicted only on the ground that a person has committed a crime.

2. Judicial punishment can never be used merely as a means to promote some other good for the criminal.

3. If a person commits a crime, that person ought to be punished. In fact, it is immoral not to punish the criminal.

4. The degree and kind of punishment are determined by the crime committed.

One should note that to Kant the commission of a crime is a sufficient condition for the infliction of punishment. Kant's comment in this regard might be considered by some as quite shocking:

Even if a civil society were to dissolve itself by common agreement of all its members . . . the last murderer remaining in prison must first be executed so that everyone will duly receive what his actions are worth and so that the bloodguilt thereof will not be fixed on the people because they failed to insist on carrying out the punishment.[7]

Those guilty of a crime must be punished if justice is to be done. Some retributivist theorists, but not Kant, give proposition 3 an additional twist. They argue that criminals not only ought to be punished but indeed have a right to be punished. Sometimes this is expressed by saying that the criminal has willed punishment or that he has contracted for it. One way of explaining this proposed condition is to take the overall perspective of the present book. We view political institutions as means for implementing individual rights and for resolving conflicts of rights. Presumably individuals concerned with these rights would choose to live in such a society as we have described. However, in accepting the benefits of such a society, justice requires that one accept its obligations as well. Thus, there is a sense in which the criminal has willed punishment and indeed even has a right to it. Hence, we add another item to our list of propositions that retributivists might hold:

5. If a person commits a crime, the person has a right to be punished.

Our list of five propositions indicates that retributivists may come in many forms and share the label "retributivist" with varying degrees of enthusiasm. A less extreme retributivist would defend fewer conditions. Our interest is not the verbal one of deciding how many or what propositions one must uphold if he is to be called a retributivist. Rather, we wish to discuss the plausibility of the retributivist conditions to discover if any are essential if penal institutions are to be considered just. The first proposition requires that a person be found guilty of a crime before being punished. It protects persons from preventive detention and from any other device that would, in effect, punish them before a crime was actually committed. It also rules out the use of punishment simply to benefit society, prohibiting the counterexamples to act utilitarianism that involved socially beneficial punishment of the innocent.

It should be noted that several states have passed laws designed to keep sex offenders, especially those whose offenses have victimized children, incarcerated even after the sentence imposed by the court has been served. It is also common and sometimes required by statute for officials to notify neighbors when a convicted sex offender moves into the neighborhood. The statutes requiring such notification, often referred to as "Megan's Laws," were instituted after a young girl named Megan was sexually molested and murdered by a convicted sex offender who had moved into the neighborhood unbeknownst to parents of young children.[8] Other states have passed statutes that permit the incarceration of sex offenders after their sentence has been served, usually in mental health facilities. Critics of such laws have argued that they involve the imposition of further punishment for the protection of society over and above the legitimate sentence imposed by the court, but at the time of this writing, it appears that some such statutes may well be found to be constitutional.

The second proposition requires that punishment be meted out in response to the crime and not inflicted simply to promote the good of the criminal. The second condition also protects a criminal from imprisonment beyond the terms of his sentence on the grounds that continued imprisonment is in that criminal's best interest. Thus, further incarceration to rehabilitate the prisoner, as may be the case with incarceration of sex offenders beyond their original sentence, is prohibited.

Proposition 3 seems acceptable so long as it is understood that it does not make punishment obligatory. What condition 3 does is to create a presumption that punishment is appropriate or justified without having to show that any given instance of punishment also promotes utility. If a person makes a promise, he or she ought to keep it. However, sometimes the obligation to keep a promise must yield to a higher moral obligation. As it is with promise keeping, so it is with punishing.

Proposition 4 brings the utilitarian-retributivist conflict into sharp focus. The utilitarians argue that the punishment should be determined by consequences, and hence the punishment should only be great enough to provide deterrence. The retributivists have another answer, which goes back at least to Aristotle. Aristotle argued that the purpose of legal justice was to right wrongs. For Aristotle, this meant the reestablishment of a kind of equality.[9] A crime has upset the moral order, and the punishment is designed to equalize the offense and set the moral order right. In this way one can speak of the punishment fitting the crime. This equality condition has also found expression in the popular notion of *lex talionis,* an eye for an eye, a tooth for a tooth. Despite the expression "an eye for an eye," the equality condition is seldom interpreted to mean that there should be some kind of exact equality. Although you could punish a murderer by taking his or her life, many crimes, such as embezzlement, contract violation, and often libel, to name but a few, don't seem to have equivalent punishments. The point of the equality condition is that more serious crimes should be punished more severely. A violent armed robber should get a more severe sentence than a shoplifter who steals a coat worth $100.

This retributivist proposition is open to strong objection on at least two grounds. First, there are practical difficulties. In many cases the determination of equality is practically impossible. Consider crimes whose chief evil consequences are at least partially psychological, for example, libel, slander, blackmail, even kidnapping, and perhaps rape. How are these crimes to be equalized? In fact, the legal system has established an elaborate system of fines and terms of imprisonment, which, however justifiable on other grounds, seems artificial and ad hoc if justified on grounds of equalizing the harm done or of reestablishing equality in the moral order. Nor is the practical difficulty simply the problem of developing a good yardstick. Consider murder. One retributivist answer is that equalization entails the legal execution of the murderer. But what is equalized? To execute the murderer is to have two dead persons instead of one. The moral order has not been reestablished, unless one simply assumes that morality supports this kind of retributivism. Thus, the second difficulty is that what counts as equalizing the moral order is unclear and often controversial. This is not simply a practical difficulty but a conceptual and moral one as well.

The example of the murderer brings home a significant point. The fact is that crime does upset the moral order and that in a significant sense the injury can never be undone. There is no way the moral indignity can be erased. Nonetheless, there is a sense in which the infliction of punishment must be equal. Given due allowance for the proper exercise of judicial discretion, similar kinds of crimes should be punished similarly. Thus, the retributivist is correct in insisting that fairness prevail in sentencing. Relevantly similar cases must be punished similarly. But the further retributivist claim that there is a unique punishment that "fits" the crime or equalizes the situation is far more questionable and, in our view, is unjustified.

In addition, retributivism places additional moral constraints on utilitarian considerations of punishment. For example, although there may not be a unique punishment that fits the crime, surely punishment should not be inappropriate for the crime. For example, a hard-to-detect but minor crime should not be punished harshly even should it be true that only a harsh penalty would have a deterrent effect (because of the low probability of getting caught). Thus, the retributivist is correct to insist that criminals be treated fairly and not simply used to provide deterrence to make others safer.

In summary, we agree with the retributivists in maintaining that the state has a right to punish criminals, that a person should only be punished if found guilty of a crime, and that punishment can never be used merely as a means for improving the criminal. Moreover, punishment must be appropriate to the crime and consistently applied throughout the criminal justice system. However, we disagree with the retributivist proposition that the state must punish criminals, and we disagree with the retributivist on how to calculate the amount of punishment a criminal deserves.

## Punishment or Therapy?

We are now able to show how radically our point of view on punishment differs from the view of those who propose treatment rather than punishment as the appropriate response in dealing with criminals.

Recent emphasis in the social sciences, especially criminal psychology and penology, has been on the rehabilitation of criminals rather than on measurements of guilt, responsibility, and the notion of making criminals pay for their crime. Some proponents of such a view drop all talk of punishment and speak only of treatment.[10] Crime is considered a type of disease, like malaria or smallpox. The criminal is isolated from society until cured.

But the blurring of the distinction between crime and illness, punishment and treatment is extremely unfortunate for many reasons. First, surrendering the language of guilt and punishment threatens human rights. How we talk does make a difference. For example, once crime is regarded as a disease, it is easy to leave the term of treatment indefinite. Presently, one serves a fairly definite term for the crime of armed robbery. However, if committing armed robbery is like being afflicted with malaria, one is cured only when a group of specialists representing the state says one is cured. The danger to civil liberties presented by such a practice should be obvious.

Moreover, the favorable connotations of treatment make it easy for the state to abuse treatment. Since treatment is supposed to be humane, there is a temptation to avoid taking seriously the rights of the one being treated. The procedural safeguards of the criminal trial are not part of the operating procedures of hospitals. In this regard, it is instructive to note that it was common practice in the former Soviet Union to commit dissident intellectuals to mental institutions as punishment for their intellectual heresies. By calling such people mentally ill, one may "treat" them without even the pretense of a fair trial.

Yet another danger is that those who emphasize the benefits of treatment have a propensity to "treat" people before a crime is actually committed. After all, if someone has a disease that manifests itself in a propensity to commit antisocial acts, shouldn't that person be treated at the earliest opportunity? Somehow the fact that the person has not actually committed the crime for which he is being treated gets lost in the shuffle.

Finally, the proportional relation that now exists between a crime and punishment would be lost if crimes were treated like diseases. As Herbert Morris has pointed out: "With therapy attempts at proportionality make no sense. It is perfectly plausible giving someone who kills a pill and treating for a lifetime within an institution one who has broken a dish and manifested accident-proneness. We have the concept of 'painful treatment.' We do not have the concept of 'cruel treatment.'"[11]

A second reason to avoid blurring the distinction between crime and illness, punishment and treatment focuses on the loss of individual responsibility that such a view presupposes. We usually do not blame someone for becoming sick. Normally, illness is something that happens to an individual; it is not something that the person does (although illnesses caused by such bad health habits as smoking may be exceptions). By viewing crime as a disease, one implicitly adopts a model that denies human responsibility for crime. On this point, those who utilize the therapy model for treating criminal behavior are at one with those who view crime as caused by society rather than by the individual criminal. An example of this latter view appears in the writings of Benjamin Karpman. He says:

> It is our basic tenet that the criminal is a product of a vicious, emotionally unhealthy environment in the creation of which he had no hand and over which he had no control. In so far as society has done nothing or not enough to alleviate the developing anti-sociality of the child, it may truly be said that it deserves the criminals it has and that the criminal is society's greatest crime.[12]

This is not the place for us to argue the merits of the claim that human beings have free will. In fact, free will itself has been understood differently by different theorists, being thought of as lack of causal determination by some philosophers, acting in accord with one's basic character by others, and in various other ways as well. It is a presupposition of nearly all moral philosophy that human beings are at least responsible creatures in some significant way. Surely their background does have important ramifications for how people behave. In some cases of criminal action, we might agree that the individual's background is a decisive causal factor. However, in many cases we believe that people are responsible for their actions. To treat them in any other way would undermine their self-respect and sense of human dignity. We can illustrate our point by again quoting from Herbert Morris:

> Alfredo Traps in Durrenmatt's tale discovers that he has brought off, all by himself, a murder involving considerable ingenuity. The mock prosecutor in the tale demands the death penalty "as reward for a crime that merits admiration, astonishment, and respect." Traps is deeply moved; indeed, he is exhilarated, and the whole of his life becomes more heroic, and, ironically, more precious. His defense attorney proceeds to argue that Traps was not only innocent but incapable of guilt, "a victim of the age." This defense Traps disavows with indignation and anger. He makes claim to the murder as his and demands the prescribed punishment—death.[13]

Perhaps those remarks are sufficient to indicate why we reject the views of those who seek to substitute therapy for punishment and the views of those who would deny individuals all responsibility for their actions. In a just state, failure to obey the law is prima facie evidence that the lawbreaker is being unfair to his fellow citizens. He is not willing to play by the rules when they work to his disadvantage. When faced with such acts of lawbreaking, an institution of punishment that respects individual liberty and whose rules for determining guilt and innocence are in accord with democratic procedures and the demands of justice is certainly justifiable. There is nothing necessarily immoral about punishment when administered to guilty individuals who are responsible, competent agents. The rules of punishment reflect essentially political decisions. The social sciences, by investigating the effects of various rules of punishment on recidivism, deterrence, and so forth, may help us to make enlightened rather than unenlightened decisions. Whether the rules are just depends upon whether the rules conform to the canons of justice. The rules are also constrained by what we shall call the retributivist rule of legal justice: Punishment may be inflicted only on those guilty of committing a crime.

For similar reasons, as noted in our discussion of retributivism, we have grave doubts about the moral legitimacy of suggestions for preventive detention. The idea behind preventive detention is to incarcerate people before they actually commit a crime. Preventive detention involves incarcerating persons because they are likely to commit crimes, even though they have not actually done so, or jailing persons for a crime for which others who commit the same crime have not been jailed, on the grounds that the person who is jailed is more likely to commit additional crimes. In both cases, persons are being jailed for what they are likely to do rather than for what they have done.

Surely the same arguments that apply against punishing the innocent apply here. However, that does not mean that we should stand idly by and allow persons to be victimized. Society may encourage, and arguably require, potential child molesters to seek treatment so that they will not commit a crime. (This requirement is justified to the extent that the criminal is regarded as extremely likely to commit a sex offense again, therapy is regarded as helpful, and the treatment does not involve incarceration.) Society may keep the potential child molester under surveillance and perhaps inform the neighborhood of the presence of such a person. Society also should provide speedy trials and police protection for victims and witnesses. Much can be done without preventive detention. However, justice may have costs. Despite the protections outlined above, on occasion the failure to use preventive detention will mean that some people will be harmed who otherwise would not have been harmed. Perhaps this is one of those cases where there is a genuine conflict between justice and utility, and we come down on the side of justice. As we said before, punishment may be inflicted only on those guilty of committing a crime.

In summary, the following propositions concerning punishment seem most defensible:

1. No one can be punished unless found guilty of committing a crime.

2. The rehabilitation of criminals should not be confused with the punishment of criminals. The rehabilitation of criminals should have deterrence as one of its goals. All compulsory rehabilitation must be confined to the term of the criminal's sentence.

3. The amount of punishment is determined by the judicial system. More serious crimes should usually receive more severe punishments. The effectiveness of various punishments as deterrence should also play a major role in determining the amount of punishment.

4. If the rules for the infliction of punishment are to be just, they must be in accord with the principles of justice as outlined in chapter 4 and with the principle of legal justice 1 above.

Not all instances of lawbreaking fit this violation-of-fairness model. Later in this chapter, we will consider civil disobedience as an example of intentional violation of the law that its proponents claim is just. Before leaving the topic of punishment of criminal behavior, however, we will consider a particularly controversial topic, namely, capital punishment.

## Capital Punishment

The laws of certain states, as well as those of the federal government as currently interpreted by the Supreme Court, allow capital punishment—the death penalty—for certain major offenses. These laws were rewritten after the Supreme Court had declared many earlier statutes allowing capital punishment to be cruel and unusual punishment in violation of the Bill of Rights (Amendment 8 of the United States Constitution).[14] Once state laws were rewritten to pass constitutional muster, the number of executions in the United States has escalated sharply, particularly in the state of Texas. Can laws that permit capital punishment be justified? Should capital punishment be prohibited?

Utilitarians would evaluate statutes permitting capital punishment on the basis of their consequences. Utilitarian proponents of capital punishment maintain that such punishment is needed to deter individuals from committing particularly heinous crimes. However, critics of capital punishment, including utilitarian critics, question whether capital punishment does deter, pointing out that states without capital punishment, such as Maine and Minnesota, do not have higher murder rates than those, such as Texas, that do have capital punishment.[15] Of course, it is very difficult to estimate just which factors influence the murder rates. Perhaps Maine would have an even lower murder rate if it allowed capital punishment and Texas would have an even higher one if it did not. Thus, whether or not capital punishment actually deters is controversial.

On the other hand, retributive supporters of capital punishment are sympathetic to Kant's idea that death is the punishment deserved by criminals who commit certain kinds of crimes. Perhaps the best contemporary example can be found in the Colorado jury's decision to give convicted Oklahoma City bomber and mass murderer Timothy McVeigh the death penalty.

However, critics of the death penalty, including some retributivists, argue that the practice of imposing the death penalty, as well as the laws that permit its imposition, is seriously unjust. First, critics argue that the death penalty is applied unfairly and in a discriminatory manner. For example, evidence suggests that a black person who murders a white person is far more likely to get the death penalty than a white person who murders a black person.[16] Second, critics argue that there is no remedy for a mistaken execution, one in which an innocent person who was mistakenly believed to be guilty is killed. Finally, some critics also argue that the death penalty is always wrong and that it is never justified for the state to take a human life and reduce itself to the same level as the murderer.

These arguments raise complex issues, but they do not strike us as decisive refutations of the permissibility of capital punishment. While the first, which charges discrimination on the basis of race, probably is the most serious, the concern that lies behind it might be met by reforms in the way capital punishment is assigned rather than by its elimination. Perhaps capital punishment should be mandatory for those who commit certain especially terrible crimes, regardless of race. Perhaps more whites should be executed. Perhaps each state should be monitored and allowed to execute criminals only if the overall assignment of capital punishment in its courts is found to be fair and non-arbitrary. Thus, it is not self-evident that possible bias in the way capital punishment presently is administered counts against allowing it at all. However, we acknowledge that if bias cannot be eliminated by reasonable methods within a reasonable amount of time, the case for capital punishment is significantly weakened, and the practice probably should be eliminated.

The critics' second and third arguments also do not strike us as decisive. While the capital punishment of the innocent, unlike that of other wrongly convicted individuals, is final and cannot be rectified, individuals sentenced to death have many avenues of appeal open to them. While we do not think that all reasonable persons will agree, proponents of capital punishment are not obviously wrong to say that the greater injustice is committed by allowing a great many vicious murderers to live than by risking the rare execution of an innocent person. We agree that it is better to let a number of guilty persons go free than to execute an innocent one. But is it better never to execute a guilty person in order to avoid the rare execution of an innocent person, even if the legal system contains many safeguards designed to prevent such an evil? Even if capital punishment does deter and so does prevent harm to potential victims of crime? In our view, whatever our personal feelings about capital punishment, there is no decisive argument that clearly establishes which alternative is worse. Therefore, it is open to the people, through proper democratic procedures, to decide for themselves whether capital punishment should be permitted.

Finally, we reject the argument that it is always wrong for the state to kill or allow killing. The state allows killing in self-defense and may be actively killing in times of war. While people's intuitions clearly differ about capital punishment, critics are not entitled simply to dismiss the intuition of the retributivists that justice requires administering the death penalty for certain kinds of vicious crimes.

We suggest, then, that the death penalty is not wrong in principle, although it may turn out to be wrong in practice if it cannot be administered in a fair and unbiased way. On the other hand, we doubt that the retributivists can establish beyond a reasonable doubt that administration of the death penalty is morally required. Therefore, we conclude that whether or not the death penalty is allowed should be determined by democratic procedures, so long as the death penalty is applied in a fair, nondiscriminatory, and nonarbitrary manner.

## Civil Disobedience and Protest

Is the citizen, particularly the citizen of a democratic state, under an absolute obligation to obey the law, even when such a citizen believes the law in question to be unjust? One of the most important moral questions that any individual might have to face concerns the limits of obedience owed to the state. During the past half century, the question of civil disobedience has been a central question in political philosophy.

In the 1950s, the atmospheric testing of nuclear weapons by the United States and other atomic powers was considered dangerous to all inhabitants of the globe and thus became an object of protest. The distinguished philosopher Bertrand Russell was one of the leaders in the protest against such testing. During the early 1960s, the injustice of many state laws governing the relations between races, particularly between blacks and whites, was called to public attention. By using such techniques as the sit-in, Dr. Martin Luther King Jr. and other black leaders sought to overturn various laws segregating the races. The black struggle for equal justice gained sympathetic support for a time from most Americans, particularly when television newscasts showed scenes of white policemen hosing, beating, and in other ways maltreating nonresisting black and white men, women, and children. With the active involvement of the United States in the Vietnam War, civil disobedience focused on resistance to the war. Indeed, doubts about the United States's moral position on this war became so widespread and resistance so broad-based that an American president was denied an opportunity to seek a second term and the United States was forced to begin a slow, painful withdrawal from Vietnam. More recently, some of the protests on college campuses urging colleges and universities to divest their holdings in companies doing business in South Africa raised issues of civil disobedience, and the divestment movement as a whole may have helped bring apartheid to an end in South Africa.

In light of such events, one might think that the question of civil disobedience is of only recent concern. This is not at all the case. The ancient Greek dramatists were true craftsmen at raising the moral complexities of civil disobedience. Sophocles' Antigone represents the epitome of the Greek dramatists' concern. The towering figure of Socrates, however, provides a starting point for philosophical debate on the question. Rather than escape from a death sentence Athens imposed upon him, Socrates insisted to the end that the state was entitled to obedience and submitted to the penalty with equanimity and even good cheer. Not all men and women have followed Socrates' acceptance of obedience. Henry David Thoreau and Mohandas K. Gandhi are but two of the many well-known figures to choose a different response to alleged state injustice. The debate on the legitimacy of civil obedience is a long, emotional, and as yet unresolved one.

Liberalism, including the version defended in this book, requires that civil disobedience be a prominent area of concern. After all, the core of liberal theory is that within a fair framework provided by the rules of justice and respect for the individual, decisions should be made democratically. The state provides a fair framework for decision making, rather than enforcing a particular conception of the good life or promoting a specific form of community. In our version of this approach, democracy constrained by a theory of natural rights and by specific principles of justice provides at best a just procedure for implementing rights claims and for adjudicating conflicts that arise among them. However, just as criminal trials sometimes set guilty people free or even convict innocent ones, so a state operating according to just procedures, including democratic voting, sometimes creates unjust results. With this thought in mind, we must now confront the question of whether or not citizens should break the law if they believe the law is unjust or to protest injustice committed by the state.

## The Nature of Civil Disobedience

We begin by asking how civil disobedience differs from other kinds of lawbreaking. What is civil disobedience anyway? Intuitively, the act of robbing a bank for personal profit is quite different from the act of refusing to keep classified material secret because one thinks the public will be harmed by such secrecy.

This suggests that the key for distinguishing civil disobedience from ordinary lawbreaking is that the motivation for civil disobedience is moral concern. One breaks the laws as a moral protest against some action of the state. We shall define civil disobedience as the act of intentionally violating a valid law for the purpose of registering a moral protest against the state. By emphasizing "intentional," "valid law," and "moral protest," acts of civil disobedience can be distinguished from other acts of lawbreaking that superficially resemble it. First, it is important to distinguish civil disobedience from accidental or unintentional violations of the law. Suppose someone aids a seriously ill person by driving him to the hospital in an unregistered car.[17] Even if the driver knows that driving an unregistered car is against the law, the driver is not engaging in civil disobedience. The driver is not challenging the morality of the laws against speeding. If an act of lawbreaking is to be an act of civil disobedience, the act of lawbreaking cannot be simply a by-product or side effect of other actions.

Second, civil disobedience must be distinguished from law testing. Law testing occurs when one challenges a law to see if it is really valid. The strategy of the law tester is to have some higher court—for example, an appeals or supreme court—declare the rule invalid or unconstitutional. If this strategy is successful, the lawbreaker has not really broken the law and is not a civil disobedient. Indeed, the protestor has performed a valuable legal service by expunging an invalid rule from the legal system. Much of the civil rights activity of the late 1950s and early 1960s was not civil disobedience at all. It was law testing, not lawbreaking. The strategy was to show that segregationist statutes and certain rules restricting voter registration and occupational choice were illegal under the Constitution, that is, that such rules were not laws at all.

One possible difficulty for this account of civil disobedience is presented by the law tester. The difficulty for the law tester is that of error. The highest court may decide that the law being tested is valid. In this case, the protestor did really break the law, but breaking it was not a case of civil disobedience. The lawbreaking was not intentional. Of course, this lawbreaker is no ordinary criminal, either. Perhaps it is best to call such a person an unsuccessful law tester.

The distinction between the law tester and the civil disobedient is not merely verbal. The justification for testing a law is easier to establish than the justification for civil disobedience. For the former, the justification is within the legal system itself. The interested party is really doing nothing more than unmasking a fraud by showing that what pretends to be law is not really law at all. Even unsuccessful law testers are somewhat heroic; they suffer consequences, sometimes serious ones, for their unsuccessful stand. It seems to us a mistake to consider Martin Luther King Jr. solely as a prime example of a civil disobedient. Rather, another of his great contributions to American society was an unmasking of many frauds by showing that so many rules that had held a people in bondage were not really laws at all.[18] The civil disobedient, on the other hand, by intending to break a valid law has greater problems with justification. There is at least a prima facie obligation to obey the law, and the civil disobedient must show that this prima facie obligation is overridden.

In our account of civil disobedience, the civil disobedient claims that the prima facie obligation to obey the law is overridden by the fact that the state allegedly has passed an immoral law or allegedly is pursuing an immoral policy. The civil disobedient breaks the law to register his moral protest. Is such activity really justifiable?

## The Justification of Civil Disobedience

There are several arguments designed to show that one should not break valid laws as a means of registering one's moral protest against the state. One such major argument has its basis in the moral imperative that one ought to obey the law. Some critics of civil disobedience seem to believe that the mere validity of this imperative is sufficient to show that civil disobedience is not justified.[19] Of course, this is not correct. For such a position to be correct, the moral imperative that one ought to obey the law would have to be supreme, that is, whenever this imperative was in conflict with another moral imperative, the moral imperative that one ought to obey the law would have priority. It is one thing to grant that "One ought to obey the law" is prima facie binding. However, any attempt to make it a supreme moral principle would need considerable additional argument. The civil disobedient accepts the prima facie obligation, at least in a reasonably just democratic state, but maintains that in certain cases the prima facie obligation is overridden by a higher ethical principle.

It is unfortunate that the defenders of the supremacy of the principle that one ought to obey the law give no argument for their position. One implication of their view is that one of our political obligations overrides all our other obligations. In a significant sense, the state is supreme. On the other hand, if, as we argue, the moral claims of the individual are supreme, then those who defend the supremacy of "One ought to obey the law" are defeated at the outset. Since we hold that the state should implement or protect the rights of individuals, the state is subservient to the individual. Moreover, even when the state is empowered to resolve conflicts among individual rights, the powers of the state in this regard are not unlimited. They are constrained by principles of morality, principles that are inconsistent with the supremacy of "One ought to obey the law." "One ought to obey the law" could only be a prima facie obligation because the law, if obedience is justified, must be in accord with the principles of morality and justice. This does not mean that one always is justified in disobeying an unjust law, because there surely is a prima facie duty to conform to the dictates of a democracy, but it does suggest that it is not necessarily wrong to disobey an unjust law to protest its injustice.

The critic of civil disobedience can salvage an important point, however. If "One ought to obey the law" is an ethical imperative and if moral-action guides have supremacy over other kinds of action guides—that is, if the moral point of view is supreme—then the only kind of claim that can defeat "One ought to obey the law" is another moral claim. Nonmoral claims will not do. What is established is that the only basis for the justification of civil disobedience is a moral justification. What the critic has not done is to show that this moral justification is impossible.

Another argument against civil disobedience is based on a version of the principle that people ought to keep their promises. One of the classic statements of this position is presented by Socrates in Plato's *Crito*. Socrates presents the arguments of the state by personifying the laws, which speak as follows on behalf of Athens:

> Although we have brought you into the world and reared you and educated you, and given you and all your fellow citizens a share in all the good things at our disposal, nevertheless by the very fact of granting our permission we openly proclaim this principle, that any Athenian, on attaining to manhood and seeing for himself the political organization of the state and us its laws, is permitted, if he is not satisfied with us, to take his property and go away wherever he likes. If any of you chooses to go to one of our colonies, supposing that he should not be satisfied with us and the state, or to emigrate to any other country, not one of us laws hinders or prevents him from going away wherever he likes, without any loss of property. On the other hand, if any one of you stands his ground when he can see how we administer justice and the rest of our public organization, we hold that by so doing he has in fact undertaken to do anything that we tell him. . . . You have been content with us and with our city. You have definitely chosen us, and undertaken to observe us in all your activities as a citizen, and as the crowning proof that you are satisfied with our city, you have begotten children in it. Furthermore, even at the time of your trial you could have proposed the penalty of banishment, if you had chosen to do so—that is, you could have done then with the sanction of the state what you are now trying to do without it. But whereas at the time you made a noble show of indifference if you had to die, and in fact preferred death, as you said, to banishment, now you show no respect for your earlier professions, and no regard for us, the laws, whom you are trying to destroy. You are behaving like the lowest type of menial, trying to run away in spite of the contracts and undertakings by which you agreed to live as a member of our state.[20]

Socrates' argument, as stated by the laws, can be paraphrased as follows:

1.  In return for certain benefits, the citizen promises to obey the laws of the state.

2.  Should the citizen feel that the laws of the state are unjust, he can try to convince the state of its error by following certain procedures.

3.  Should the citizen believe that this contract with the state is a bad one—for example, that he does not benefit or that the laws are unjust—he is free to leave at any time.

4.  Hence, the citizen has a contract with the state in which the individual citizen receives personal benefits in return for a pledge, or promise, of obedience.

5.  The contract is in effect a mutual promise between the state and its citizens.

6.  One ought to keep one's promises.

7.  Therefore, one either ought to obey the laws of the state or go elsewhere. (Obey it or leave it.)

Let us begin our discussion of the argument by indicating where it applies and where it does not. First, it will not count if the contract analysis of the relation between the individual and the state is wrong. Second, this argument will have no force if the contract is entered under duress or if there is no escape clause. We are in essence defending a freedom condition that the contract must meet. Most people would agree to obey the laws of the state, indeed surrender all personal liberty, if they were hungry enough and if the state provided food and shelter. Consider a holdup victim who has promised the armed robber to tell the police nothing about his crime. Suppose the victim then tells the police everything, and as a result the robber is captured. Surely the thief has no right to say that the victim was morally unjustified in telling the police since in so doing he broke a promise. A contract made under duress is not a contract at all. In other words, since the state is supposed to provide great advantages for the individual, if the contract argument for obedience is to be accepted, then there must be some options for those who feel they are not receiving the advantages or do not want them. Socrates tries to provide these options by procedures for registering complaints and ultimately for emigration. Our analysis has tried to indicate the necessity for those conditions.

This leads to our third and final point. The contract itself must be a moral one. If Smith promises Jones that Smith will murder Green, Jones cannot hold Smith in violation of his contract should Smith not murder Green. Similarly, any contract between an individual citizen and the state must be of a moral nature if the contract is to have binding force. The kinds of constraints put on a contract depend on the moral theory that one holds. According to our theory, no contract is morally obligatory if it denies the natural rights of the citizen signees or resolves conflicts between rights by unjust procedures.

The individual citizen may also be excused from obeying the contract when the state has failed to live up to the provisions in the contract that apply to it. After all, a contract places responsibilities and obligations on both contractors. The systematic failure of one party to carry out its obligations removes the moral obligation on the other party.

We can now summarize the conditions that must hold if the critic of civil disobedience can appeal to the principle "You ought to keep your contracts": (1) the contract analysis of the relation between the individual and the state must be appropriate; (2) the contract must not be made under duress and must have escape clauses; (3) the contract must be morally acceptable; and (4) the state must live up to its contract obligations.

A further complicating feature must now be discussed. How are disputes as to whether or not the contract is being violated to be resolved? For example, who is to decide if the state is living up to its contract obligations? If the authorities of the state are to give the definitive answer to this question, the citizen becomes subservient to the state. The citizen must submit and has no justification for civil disobedience. To allow the state supremacy at this point is to concede that the contract argument against civil disobedience is successful. Of course, one could argue, as would we, that ultimately it is the individual citizen who must decide if the contract is being violated. This maneuver would be quickly challenged by the opponents of civil disobedience on the basis of the following two arguments: (1) since normative statements are not objective factual statements, the individual citizen has no objective basis for his normative judgments; (2) to allow each citizen to pass judgment on the laws of the state would create the grounds for anarchy. Let us consider each of these arguments in turn.

**The Argument from Moral Skepticism.** We have previously claimed that there is at least a prima facie moral obligation to obey the law and that this obligation can only be overridden by a superior moral obligation. Now the critic of civil disobedience could ask, what could such superior moral obligations be? The traditional appeals to individual conscience, the inner light, the law of God, and the public good all fail on the same ground. When conflicts arise between consciences, between different theological conceptions of God's word, between different conceptions of the public good, there seems to be no way of resolving these disputes. It is just the sincere conscience of one person against another. Thus, it is claimed that there is no way civil disobedients can justify their civil disobedience. This situation is even more awkward in a democratic state. If one opinion cannot be justified over another, then there is no reason to accept the view of the civil disobedient over that of the majority. At least the majority has the force of greater numbers; one might as well obey the laws of the state.

This argument has been a rather popular one and raises questions about the foundations of this book. It is obvious that we believe value judgments can be justified. For the sake of argument, however, let us accept the premise that conflicts of value cannot be objectively resolved. (However, see the criticisms of skepticism in the introduction.) This admission will not allow the critic of civil disobedience to carry the day.

If you follow moral skepticism consistently, whatever is true of the value judgments of civil disobedients is also true of those of their opponents. If moral judgments cannot be defended, then the moral judgment that we ought to obey the law cannot be defended either. It is self-contradictory to say that moral judgments cannot be defended, so therefore you have a moral obligation to obey the law. The fact that the civil disobedient lives in a democracy does not change this conclusion one iota. The civil disobedient may well have the overwhelming majority aligned against him, but they are in no position to provide reasons for their moral positions if we take moral skepticism seriously. There may be nonmoral reasons for following the majority if moral skepticism is true, but there can be no moral reasons for following the majority if moral skepticism is true. Hence, the argument against civil disobedience from moral skepticism fails.

**Civil Disobedience and Anarchy.** One of the most frequent criticisms of civil disobedience is that it provides the basis for anarchy. Indeed, some alleged civil disobedients have argued from anarchistic premises. Thoreau is probably one of the best examples. Here are some remarks from his essay "Civil Disobedience":

The only obligation which I have a right to assume, is to do at any time what I think right. ...There will never be a really free and enlightened State, until the State comes to recognize the individual as a higher and more independent power, from which all its own power and authority are derived and treats him accordingly. ... In fact, I quietly declare war with the State, after my fashion, though I will still make what use and get what advantage of her I can, as is usual in such cases.[21]

It is these explicit principles of anarchy that many critics of civil disobedience find so abhorrent. Moreover, they argue that anarchistic consequences are implicit in all acts of civil disobedience. Whether citizens disobey a law because of their belief that it is immoral or because of their belief that the state has violated its own contract, they are pitting their own authority against that of the state. But if the civil disobedient can do that, every citizen is entitled to do so as well and the state would be undermined. Anarchy would reign.

We believe the argument from anarchy to be unsuccessful for two basic reasons. First, in a just democratic state the necessity for civil disobedience would not reach a level where anarchy prevailed. Most citizens would perceive that, on the whole, state decisions are just; and given that states are of necessity imperfect dispensers of justice, most citizens would also agree to accept occasional injustices. In essence, as Rawls has argued, a just state is likely to be stable, and a certain amount of deviation from perfect justice must be accepted.[22] In a reasonably just state, the argument of anarchy is based on a false set of empirical premises. In an unjust state, the argument from anarchy is no defense at all. Given that the state is unjust, it is not at all clear that anarchy ought not to prevail.

Second, the argument from anarchy reflects a fundamental misperception of the role of civil disobedience in the just state. We take the position, adopted by several recent writers on the topic, that genuine civil disobedience is supportive of the state. It strengthens the state rather than undermines it. Since this is our chief argument in defense of civil disobedience, we shall develop it in some detail. Our strategy, then, for answering the opponents of civil disobedience is to show that their most plausible arguments are based on a misperception of the act of civil disobedience itself.

**Civil Disobedience as a Support for Democratic Institutions.** The democratic state constrained by general and particular principles of justice may be generally reliable but, nonetheless, imperfect in performing its function of implementing the natural rights claims of its citizens and of resolving disputes among rights claims. In such a state, justified acts of civil disobedience would not occur with great frequency. Nonetheless, in a state where the achievement of justice is at best imperfect, we believe that civil disobedience has a central place.

First, civil disobedience gives an opportunity for individual citizens to make a moral appeal to their fellow citizens when they believe that the institutions or practices of a state have violated their rights. Civil disobedience is then a means for seeking a redress of grievances. The potential benefits of civil disobedience do not accrue solely to the civil disobedient, however. There are also substantial potential benefits for the state. The civil disobedient may well be able to show that certain state actions are unjust. Hence, the disobedient will provide the catalyst for reform. Given that the purpose of the state is to provide justice, a civil disobedient who succeeds in pointing out an injustice in civil procedures is a good citizen and not an ordinary lawbreaker. Even if the civil disobedient should fail in the attempt to convince the state that an injustice has been done, the disobedient still fills the role of good citizen. Because of such disobedience, the state is forced to reexamine its policies and to be ever vigilant against situations where state activities do create injustice. A state that is constantly challenged is more likely to be a just one. As rigid patterns of thought need to be challenged and reexamined if the best kinds of intellectual activity are to prevail, so must the patterns of the state be challenged if the ideal of justice is to be approached. The civil disobedient serves as the analogue of an intellectual gadfly. In this sense, our view of civil disobedience is clearly in the tradition of Socrates. The civil disobedient is not an enemy of the state; rather, the civil disobedient, as Socrates argues, is a good citizen:

> If you put me to death, you will not easily find anyone to take my place. It is literally true, even if it sounds rather comical, that God has specially appointed me to this city, as though it were a large thoroughbred horse which because of its great size is inclined to be lazy and needs the stimulation of some stinging fly. It seems to me that God has attached me to this city to perform the office of such a fly, and all day long I never cease to settle here, there, and everywhere, rousing, persuading, reproving every one of you. You will not easily find another like me, gentlemen.[23]

To take this perspective on civil disobedience, however, is to be committed to constraining the form that civil disobedience must take if it is to be justifiable. If an act of disobedience is to be justified, (1) it must be public; (2) it must be nonviolent; (3) the civil disobedient must be willing to take the punishment the legal system may impose for disobedience; and (4) the law being violated must be identical with, or related to, the policy or law against which the moral protest is lodged. To the extent that any of these conditions is violated, the act of civil disobedience in question is harder to justify. It is hard to see how violations of the first three conditions can be justified at all.

Thus, if civil disobedience is designed to call attention to a possible injustice so that the state might correct its procedures, then the act of civil disobedience must be open and public. Such openness is an indication that the lawbreaking of a civil disobedient is nonetheless a political act of good citizenship. Clandestine lawbreaking, on the other hand, is directed against the political community; it is antipolitical. In such cases, one breaks the rules of society and tries to go undetected. Such action, if universalized, would threaten the state itself. Willingness to break the law openly is one of the characteristics that distinguishes the civil disobedient from the thief in the night.

This perspective on civil disobedience as an act of good citizenship also enables us to defend the traditional prohibition against violence. Our argument here is twofold. First, violence can be seen as an attack on the democratic state itself. Its goal is not to appeal or persuade but to force. Second, violence does not promote the atmosphere for a public discussion and reexamination of state policy. Violence tends to precipitate still more violence. Violent civil disobedience is likely to provoke violent response. Violent clashes among the citizens of the state tend to undermine both the institution of law and the state itself. The violent society is best epitomized by Hobbes's state of nature. In the state of nature, there can be neither government nor law. In other words, the violent disobedience of a particular law tends to set in motion a causal chain that undermines the conditions that make a state possible and valuable. For these reasons, the state could consider violent disobedience of its laws to be an attack on the state itself.

We emphasize that if the justification of civil disobedience is to be found in the civil disobedient's intention of provoking a reexamination of a state policy with an aim toward improving justice, violence is self-defeating. Violence is also unjust, since it violates the rights of others; it makes public rational discussion impossible; and hence it obliterates a civil disobedient's claim that his lawbreaking is morally superior to that of the ordinary criminal.

Similar remarks support our contention that in justified civil disobedience, the civil disobedient must be willing to take the penalty. This willingness to accept the penalty indicates that the person is not at war with the state nor with fellow citizens. Rather, the civil disobedient is accepting his position as one among equals. The civil disobedient gives evidence of not taking unfair advantage in the sense of receiving the benefits of the state without paying the costs.

Finally, the civil disobedient should believe that there is a connection between the law being violated and the law or policy being protested against. To broaden the attack from the unjust law or policy to any law remotely connected with the offending law or policy is to attack the state itself. If, on balance, the state performs its functions adequately, protest should focus on the unjust laws or policies. In most cases, protest should not be a broad attack on the state. The policy must be wicked indeed if it justifies a broad attack on all the policies of the state. Of course, in some cases, policies may reach that level of wickedness; the Nazi policy of exterminating the Jews is a case in point. (In any case, Nazi Germany was not a democracy, and our discussion does not apply directly to it.) However, unjust laws or policies of a state may be attacked without attacking all the policies of that state. The point of limiting civil-disobedient acts is to prevent a confusion between civil disobedience and stronger forms of protest. If this confusion is to be avoided, there must be some connection between the law being broken and the law or policy being protested against. To the extent that this condition is violated, the act of civil disobedience in question is harder to justify.

Not all philosophers have accepted these constraints. In attacking a position that is somewhat similar to ours, that of John Rawls, political theorist Brian Barry has said:

> The essence of Rawls's high-minded conception of civil disobedience is the slogan 'This hurts me more than it hurts you.' The protesters are to break the law, but do it with such delicate consideration for others that nobody is inconvenienced. Why, then, bother to break the law at all? As far as I can see from Rawls's account, any public form of self-injury would do as well to make it known that one believed strongly in the injustice of a certain law: public self-immolation or, if that seemed too extreme, making a bonfire of one's best clothes would be as good as law-breaking. Civil disobedience à la Rawls is reminiscent of the horrible little girl in the 'Just William' stories whose all-purpose threat was 'If you don't do it I'll scream and scream until I make myself sick.'[24]

We think this attitude quite mistaken, however. Constraints on civil disobedience are the marks that are presented to establish that the lawbreaking in question is justified and hence stands apart from ordinary acts of lawbreaking. These constraints provide evidence that the intention of the lawbreaker is really the intention of a moral person who respects fellow citizens as bearers of equal rights and as equal members of the political community. By adopting these constraints, those who claim that civil disobedience is unjustified can be answered. The type of civil disobedience under consideration here does not promote anarchy, nor do those practicing it claim any special status for their own moral views. Rather, civil disobedients ask only for an opportunity to present their case outside established channels, and for this privilege they pay special costs.

Finally, if we view civil disobedience as an integral part of the political structure, the contract argument against civil disobedience is circumvented. In fact, the ideal contract might contain a provision allowing civil disobedience so long as the moral constraints upon it are observed. The necessity for civil disobedience is accepted in a democratic state that provides only imperfect justice. By interpreting civil disobedience as an act of good citizenship, we establish the grounds for its justification.

In this chapter, the role of conscientious disobedience in a democracy has been examined. We have emphasized not only that such disobedience can sometimes be justified but also that it serves a valuable moral function in a democratic society. Since just procedures need not lead to just results, there is a continual need to reexamine the results to which such procedures lead. By contributing to such constant reevaluation, the civil disobedient often betters the legal and political orders to which we all belong.

## Notes

1. H. L. A. Hart, *The Concept of Law* (Oxford: Clarendon Press, 1961), 189–95.

2. Ibid., chap. 3.

3. One theoretical argument against this position is provided by David Lyons. He tries to show that ultimately rule utilitarianism reduces to act utilitarianism. See David Lyons, *Forms and Limits of Utilitarianism* (Oxford: Clarendon Press, 1965).

4. Jeremy Bentham, *Principles of Morals and Legislation* (1789), chaps. 13, 14.

5. For a contemporary defense of a utilitarian theory of punishment based on the claim that utilitarianism is most consistent with our practices regarding punishment, see Steven Soderholm, "On Wrongs, Rights, and Responsibilities: A Utilitarian Defense of Punishment" (Ph.D. diss., University of Minnesota, 1996).

6. Immanuel Kant, *The Metaphysical Elements of Justice,* trans. John Ladd (Indianapolis: Bobbs-Merrill, 1965), 99–108, 131–33.

7. Ibid., 102.

8. "Megan's Law" originally referred to a New Jersey statute, the Act of Oct. 31, 1994 (N.J. Laws 128). In 1996, a version became a federal law as well (Megan's Law, Pub. L. No. 104–145, 110 Stat. 1345, 16 May 1996). Thus, the term "Megan's Law" can be misleading, as there are several "Megan's Laws." The federal version requires states to create their own version of Megan's Law or lose federal funding.

9. Aristotle, *Nicomachean Ethics,* bk. 5, chap. 4.

10. See Karl Menninger, "Therapy, Not Punishment," in *Punishment and Rehabilitation,* ed. Jeffrie G. Murphy (Belmont, Calif.: Wadsworth, 1973), 132–41.

11. Herbert Morris, "Persons and Punishment," in *Punishment and Rehabilitation,* ed. Murphy, 48.

12. Benjamin Karpman, "Criminal Psychodynamics: A Platform," in *Punishment and Rehabilitation,* ed. Murphy, 131.

13. Morris, "Persons and Punishment," 40.

14. See esp. *Furman v. Georgia,* 408 U.S. 238 (1972), and *Gregg v. Georgia,* 428 U.S. 153 (1976). In the former, the Court invalidated Georgia statutes allowing capital punishment, and some justices argued that capital punishment is always "cruel and unusual" and hence prohibited by the Constitution. In the latter, the majority argued that capital punishment does not inevitably violate the Constitution, although it might do so under certain circumstances.

15. Amnesty International, *United States of America: The Death Penalty, A Human Rights Issue* (New York: Amnesty International, 1989), 10–14.

16. See, e.g., Gregory D. Russel, *The Death Penalty and Racial Bias: Overcoming Supreme Court Assumptions* (Westport, Conn.: Greenwood Press, 1994); and Amnesty International, *United States of America: Developments on the Death Penalty in 1995* (New York: Amnesty International, 1996), 21–24.

17. This example is from R. B. Brandt, "Utility and the Obligation to Obey the Law," in *Law and Philosophy,* ed. Sidney Hook (New York: New York University Press, 1964), 51.

18. Of course, Martin Luther King Jr. and other civil rights advocates did engage in civil disobedience and indeed would have engaged in additional civil disobedience if the laws they were testing had been upheld.

19. E.g., this seems to be the position of Louis Waldman, "Civil Rights—Yes: Civil Disobedience—No," in *Civil Disobedience: Theory and Practice,* ed. Hugo Adam Bedau (New York: Pegasus, 1969), 106–15.

20. Plato, *Crito,* trans. Hugh Tredennick, in *The Collected Dialogues of Plato,* ed. Edith Hamilton and Huntington Cairns (New York: Pantheon Books, 1961), 36–37.

21. Henry David Thoreau, "Civil Disobedience," in *A Yankee in Canada* (Boston: Ticknor & Fields, 1866), 125, 151, 145.

22. John Rawls, *A Theory of Justice* (Cambridge: Harvard University Press, 1971), 567–77, 331–91.

23. Plato, *Apology,* trans. Hugh Tredennick, in *The Collected Dialogues of Plato,* ed. Hamilton and Cairns, 16–17.

24. Brian Barry, *The Liberal Theory of Justice* (Oxford: Clarendon Press, 1973), 153.

## Questions for Further Study

1. State and evaluate the utilitarian theory of punishment.

2. What are the basic propositions of a retributive theory of punishment? Is the list complete? If it is not complete, what should be added? Is the list a good one? Explain.

3. Does it make any sense to say that a person has a right to be punished? Explain.

4. Should people be treated rather than punished? Explain and defend your position.

5. What does it mean to say that punishment should fit the crime? Do you agree? Explain.

6. What are the arguments for and against capital punishment? Which side do you think has the stronger case? Explain.

7. With respect to civil disobedience, evaluate the position that you should either obey the laws of the state or move elsewhere (obey or leave it).

8. Should a democracy have a place for civil disobedience? Should a civil disobedient be willing to accept the penalty for his or her disobedience? Explain your answers.

## Selected Readings

### Books

Bentham, Jeremy. *Principles of Morals and Legislation.* 1789. Reprint, Garden City, N.Y.: Doubleday, 1961.

Dworkin, Ronald. *Taking Rights Seriously.* Cambridge: Harvard University Press, 1977.

Flew, Anthony. *Crime or Disease?* London: Macmillan, 1973.

Hall, Robert T. *The Morality of Civil Disobedience.* New York: Harper & Row, 1971.

Hart, H. L. A. *The Concept of Law.* Oxford: Clarendon Press, 1961.

———. *Punishment and Responsibility: Essays in the Philosophy of Law.* New York: Oxford University Press, 1968.

Haskar, Vinit. *Civil Disobedience, Threats, and Offers: Gandhi and Rawls.* New York: Oxford University Press, 1986.

Honderich, Ted. *Punishment: The Supposed Justifications.* Baltimore: Penguin Books, 1969.

Kant, Immanuel. *The Metaphysical Elements of Justice.* 1797. Translated by John Ladd. Indianapolis: Bobbs-Merrill, 1965.

Singer, Peter. *Democracy and Disobedience.* New York: Oxford University Press, 1973.

Van den Haag, Ernest. *Political Violence and Civil Disobedience.* New York: Harper & Row, 1972.

## Articles and Essays

Barnett, Randy E. "Restitution: A New Paradigm of Criminal Justice." *Ethics* 87 (1977): 279–301.

Cohen, Marshall. "Liberalism and Disobedience." *Philosophy and Public Affairs* 1 (1972): 283–314.

Cottingham, John. "Punishment." In *The Encyclopedia of Ethics,* vol. 2, edited by Lawrence C. Becker and Charlotte B. Becker. New York: Garland Publishing, 1992, 1053–55.

Dworkin, Ronald. "On Not Prosecuting Civil Disobedience." *New York Review of Books,* 6 June 1968.

Farrell, Daniel M. "Paying the Penalty: Justifiable Civil Disobedience and the Problem of Punishment." *Philosophy and Public Affairs* 6 (1977): 165–84.

Schoeman, Ferdinand D. "On Incapacitating the Dangerous." *American Philosophical Quarterly* 16, no. 1 (1979): 27–35.

Wertheimer, Alan. "Should Punishment Fit the Crime?" *Social Theory and Practice* 3 (1975): 403–23.

———. "Punishing the Innocent—Unintentionally." *Inquiry* 20 (1977): 45–65.

———. "Deterrence and Retribution." *Ethics* 86 (1976): 181–99.

Woozley, A. D. "Civil Disobedience and Punishment." *Ethics* 86 (1976): 323–31.

# 9

# An Evaluation of Affirmative Action

Systematic and pervasive discrimination directed against whole groups of people is a particularly serious and abhorrent form of social injustice. In our own society, racial minorities and women are among those who in varying degrees have been, and continue to be, victims of such systematic injustice. Slavery, racial segregation, and continuing discrimination against African Americans in the United States constitute especially significant forms of injustice. What should be the response of a society such as the United States, which claims to be dedicated to the ideal of human equality and respect for human rights, to such injustice in its own domain?

While some would say that the just society simply should stop discriminating, others respond that that is not enough. In addition to eliminating discrimination, the state may be required to take affirmative action to ensure that the victims of past discrimination can take their full place as equals in society.

Affirmative action is in large part a response to the long, cruel, and shameful history of racial discrimination in the United States. As we will see, affirmative action can take many forms. However, a particular form of affirmative action that has proven especially controversial is preferential treatment. Proponents of preferential treatment argue that the proper response to systematic discrimination is to extend special preference to members of victimized groups in the distribution of jobs, as well as in the selection of applicants to scarce positions in medical and law schools and other graduate and university programs.

Affirmative action, particularly the assignment of preferences according to race, has been the subject of considerable debate in the political arena and in the courts. To its critics, such a practice constitutes invidious discrimination in reverse. White males such as Allan Bakke have argued before the Supreme Court that preferential treatment in favor of racial minorities is a form of reverse discrimination that deprives white men of equal protection of the laws. In the 1978 *Bakke* decision, a divided Supreme Court claimed, by a 5-4 majority, that racial preference is not in itself unconstitutional. But, by a different 5-4 majority, that same Court decided that the particular form of racial preference extended by the University of California Medical School, which rejected Bakke, was not constitutionally permissible.[1] The constitutional status of preferential treatment is still far from clear, in spite of the *Bakke* decision, precisely because the Court was so divided that no clear and widely accepted principled basis for the ruling emerged. Controversy over preferential treatment has continued throughout the 1990s, as the Supreme Court has somewhat narrowed the conditions under which remedial preferences may be employed but has not rejected the overall case for them. In 1996, voters in California approved a proposition presented to the electorate of that state that prohibited the

State of California from employment preferences based on race in its own hiring, although, as of this writing, the exact constitutional status of the proposition remains unclear. What is clear is that affirmative action, at least in some of its forms, is highly controversial and is likely to remain so for the foreseeable future.

Is affirmative action for blacks, Asian Americans, Hispanics, women, and other victimized minority groups justified? Are charges warranted that affirmative action, when it includes preference based on such factors as race, ethnicity, or gender, is a new form of invidious reverse discrimination? In this chapter, we will consider whether society's responsibilities to the victims of social injustice require preferential treatment in their favor. But before turning directly to the substantive issues at stake, a number of preliminary points, often ignored in the heat of political debate, need to be clarified.

## Distinctions and Clarifications

Debates over affirmative action often are doomed to inconclusiveness because different forms of affirmative action policies are not distinguished. "Affirmative action" is a name that has been applied to a cluster of policies, generated in part by Title 7 of the Civil Rights Act of 1964, and especially by a series of executive orders issued by President Lyndon Johnson. The label of "affirmative action" has been applied since then to significantly different forms of policy. It is important to keep these differences in mind if we are to avoid confusion. Thus, two individuals might both claim to be in favor of affirmative action, but they may use the expression to mean very different things.

A policy of distributing scarce positions among applicants is one of nondiscrimination if such factors as race, religion, sex, or ethnic background are not taken into consideration in the selection process.[2] Affirmative action, on the other hand, requires more than nondiscrimination. In its least controversial sense, affirmative action refers to positive procedural requirements that employers or admissions officers must use to ensure that their pool of candidates is representative of some larger body, such as the pool of qualified candidates in the nation, region, or in some smaller group from which the institution normally recruits. Such procedures might include open advertising of positions, inclusion in such advertisements of a statement of employer interest in hiring minorities or women, and greater internal efforts to make sure that applications of minorities and women are not dismissed because of perhaps unconscious bias or stereotyping. Policies such as these constitute the *procedural* form of affirmative action.

Affirmative action of a second sort requires employers or admissions officers to make numerical projections of the percentage of women or minorities who would be hired or selected under a fair and unbiased selection procedure. If such a goal is not met, the institution normally is expected to shoulder the burden of proof of explaining the failure. Although critics have argued that such numerical goals in fact turn into quotas, the intent of this form of affirmative action is not to prefer anyone on the basis of such factors as race, ethnicity, or gender but to specify a target against which actual hiring procedures can be measured. The target is simply the result that a fair hiring procedure would produce. Thus, if 30 percent of the Ph.D.s granted by universities in a given field are earned by women, then on this conception one normally would expect institutions that hire from such an applicant pool to select women for roughly 30 percent of their new positions. Let us call this the *regulative* form of affirmative action.

*Preferential treatment*, on the other hand, is a form of affirmative action that requires that positive weight be given to race and/or sex in the selection process. The degree of preference can be weak if it is used only to break ties between otherwise equally qualified candidates, or it can be strong if used to favor an otherwise less qualified candidate.

Finally, some may consider race, ethnicity, or gender a kind of qualification in some contexts. For example, some might argue that the hiring of women or minority group members in colleges and universities contributes to intellectual diversity and provides models for female and minority students, which promotes their academic success. On this view, the candidate preferred on the basis of race, ethnicity, or gender may not be preferred over a more qualified candidate. Rather, race, ethnicity, and gender become a kind of qualification that affirmative action reminds us to consider. Let us call this *meritocratic* affirmative action.

Given these distinctions, a number of points follow: First, to be for affirmative action is not necessarily to be for preferential treatment, and to be against preferential treatment is not necessarily to be against all forms of affirmative action. As we have seen, preferential treatment is only one form that affirmative action may take. Second, to be for preferential treatment is not necessarily to be for quotas. Preferential treatment requires only that positive weight be given to race or sex, not that a fixed number of individuals of a particular race or sex must be hired. Thus, even if individuals are given special credit for belonging to a particular group, it does not follow that they will be more attractive candidates, all things considered, than nonmembers. Finally, preferential treatment, even of the strong variety, does not necessarily involve selection of the unqualified. Indeed, to our knowledge, no serious proponent of preferential treatment favors selection of the unqualified. Rather, preferential treatment is to be applied within the pool of qualified—often highly qualified—applicants.

Linguistically, it is important not to automatically or uncritically equate preferential treatment with reverse discrimination, at least if the word "discrimination" is used to suggest the making of arbitrary or inequitable distinctions. Whether preferential treatment is a form of unjust discrimination must be settled by substantive argument and not by linguistic stipulation. Critics of the preferential form of affirmative action often do claim that it is a form of invidious discrimination in reverse. Let us assess their claim.

## The Reverse Discrimination Argument

Opponents of the preferential form of affirmative action maintain that it ought to be condemned as a form of invidious discrimination in reverse. Stated formally, their argument, the reverse discrimination argument, or RDA, looks like this:

1. Invidious discrimination against racial minorities and women is unjust.

2. Present forms of preferential treatment in favor of women and minorities do not differ in any morally relevant way from past discrimination against minorities and women.[3]

3. Relevantly similar cases must be evaluated similarly.

4. Therefore, present forms of preferential treatment in favor of women and minorities are unjust.

The reasoning in this argument appears to be valid. If the premises are warranted, the conclusion must be warranted. Therefore, proponents of preferential treatment who want to reject the conclusion of the argument must reject one of the premises. But which one?

Premise 3 certainly seems to be acceptable. As we have seen, the principle of universalizability that it expresses is simply a requirement of practical consistency and so is required by the commitment to reason itself. Moreover, premise 1 is accepted by all parties to the debate. Proponents of preferential treatment must show, then, that there is a morally relevant distinction to be made between preferential treatment and invidious discrimination. But how are they to proceed?

One promising strategy is to claim that current policies of preferential treatment, unlike past forms of racial and gender discrimination, are not based on inaccurate and demeaning stereotypes of the people disadvantaged by them and do not express hatred or prejudice. This strategy has been most clearly and forcefully defended by Ronald Dworkin, a distinguished professor of law and thoughtful philosophic critic of values and social policy. Dworkin has argued that advocates of the RDA simply are confused. His argument is an important contribution to the debate, and we will consider it in some depth.

## Dworkin's Critique of the RDA

In his book *Taking Rights Seriously,* and in many subsequent books and articles, Dworkin has attempted to restore the primacy of individual rights in political and legal thought. In jurisprudence, Dworkin argues against what he takes to be the view of legal positivism that judges must use discretion in deciding difficult cases. Rather, he contends that judicial practice at its best involves the enforcement of preexisting legal rights. More broadly, Dworkin views individual rights as political trumps that persons may play to protect themselves against single-minded efforts to implement social and political goals.[4]

However, while Dworkin's theoretical account of rights seems designed to protect the individual, some of his applications of the theory to concrete cases are controversial, even among those sympathetic to his abstract defense of fundamental rights. Thus, one might think that Dworkin would be sympathetic to the charge of reverse discrimination since that charge presupposes that racial and gender preferences violate the rights of white males. But in fact Dworkin is one of the principal critics of the RDA.

In particular, Dworkin has used his account of rights to argue that white applicants disfavored by special admissions programs for minorities in law and medical school cannot legitimately complain that their rights have been violated. In Dworkin's view, special admissions programs for minorities do not violate individual rights. If Dworkin is correct in thinking that special admissions programs violate no individual rights, important consequences would follow. In particular, whites disfavored by the programs, or by other forms of preferential affirmative action, could not claim that their equal rights were violated and so would have few if any grounds for claiming that special admissions programs for minorities are unconstitutional. Reverse discrimination would not be involved.

Instead, the only issues at stake would be resolvable by whatever principles normally apply to questions of pure public policy where no violations of individual rights are at stake. As Dworkin has claimed: "Racial criteria are not necessarily the right standards for deciding which applicants should be accepted by law schools. But neither are intellectual criteria, or indeed any other set of criteria. The fairness—and constitutionality—of any admissions program must be tested in the same way."[5] In effect, Dworkin is claiming that those who equate special admissions programs for minorities with invidious discrimination in reverse are conceptually confused. Such critics are not clear about the nature of invidious discrimination.

To understand Dworkin's argument fully, we need to understand his account of individual rights. Dworkin begins his account of fundamental individual rights by distinguishing between two kinds of rights to equality: "The first is the right to equal treatment which is the right to an equal distribution of some opportunity or resource or burden. . . . The second is the right, not to receive the same distribution of some burden or benefit, but to be treated with the same respect or concern as anyone else."[6] According to Dworkin, "the right to treatment as an equal is fundamental and the right to equal treatment is derivative." Thus, to borrow his example, "If I have two children, and one is dying from a disease that is making the other uncomfortable, I do not show equal concern if I flip a coin to decide which should have the remaining dose of the drug."[7] In this case, equal concern for each child, treatment of each as an equal, would yield an unequal distribution of the drug, or what Dworkin would call unequal treatment.

How does this distinction apply to the controversy over special admissions programs for certain minorities? According to Dworkin, such policies amount to unjust discrimination in reverse only if they violate individual rights. Now, an Allan Bakke has the right to go to law and medical school only if that right is derivable from correct application of an admissions policy that treats all the affected parties as equals. But since any policy "will place certain candidates at a disadvantage . . . an admissions policy may nevertheless be justified if it seems reasonable to think the overall gain to the community exceeds the overall loss, and if no other policy that does not provide a comparable disadvantage would produce even roughly the same gain. . . . An individual's right to be treated as an equal means that his potential loss must be treated as a matter of concern; but that loss may nevertheless be outweighed by the gains to the community as a whole."[8] Dworkin is arguing that the charge of reverse discrimination is a red herring. The kinds of distinctions involved in today's special admissions programs are far different from those characterizing past invidious discrimination against minorities. Thus, Dworkin acknowledges that "in the past, it made sense to say that an excluded black or Jewish student was being sacrificed because of his race and religion: that meant that his or her exclusion was treated as desirable in itself," but he adds that white males such as Bakke are "being excluded not by prejudice but because of a rational calculation about the socially most beneficial use of limited resources for medical education."[9] Since the disadvantage imposed on a Bakke is counted equally in the process of social cost accounting, he has been treated as an equal. Since all candidates, including Bakke, have been treated as equals, the relevant rights of each have been respected. Since no rights have been violated, no reverse discrimination has been practiced, and so, we are told, Bakke and other white males allegedly disadvantaged by preferential affirmative action have no case.

The import of Dworkin's argument, then, is that past invidious discrimination against minorities and women is fundamentally different from preferential forms of affirmative action. Thus, racial discrimination expresses hatred and contempt for the victims, while gender discrimination is based on oppressive and demeaning stereotypes of women. Preferential forms of affirmative action do not stereotype white males and are not based on hatred or contempt for them. Rather, they are based on impartial calculations about the social good in which white males are counted as equals, as important as anyone else to the community as a whole.

## An Evaluation of Dworkin's Argument

The crucial notion in Dworkin's attempt to distinguish preferential treatment from invidious discrimination is that of treatment as an equal. As he officially explicates it, it is a right to both equal respect and equal concern. As he applies it, however, it is equal concern that does all the work. The policymaker is constrained to assign equal weight to the needs and interests of all affected by the policy.

This analysis is an important one and does suggest that the RDA is flawed. Past invidious discrimination and current preferential forms of affirmative action do tend to differ in the ways Dworkin suggests. Therefore, premise 2 of the RDA fails. Preferential treatment, in our view, is not the moral equivalent of past unjust discrimination.

However, that is not to say it is morally acceptable. There are ways of being unfair or unjust or morally problematic other than resembling past invidious discrimination. We suggest that while Dworkin may have defused the RDA, his analysis leaves other problems with preferential affirmative action unresolved. This can be brought out by further consideration of his use of the idea of *treatment as an equal.*

As Dworkin explicates it, the right to treatment as an equal looks suspiciously like the utilitarian requirement that everyone count for one and only one in computing social benefits and burdens. Remember, Dworkin tells us that Bakke's interests are "outweighed by the gains to the community as a whole." If this is all there is to taking rights seriously, one wonders why the emphasis on rights is important to begin with.

Dworkin's perspective in his discussion of preferential forms of affirmative action is that of the utilitarian legislator. As a consequence, the right to treatment as an equal, as he applies it in the discussion, does not satisfy the minimal requirement that he himself endorsed, namely, that rights have a certain threshold weight against the pursuit of collective goals. For the right in question is only the entitlement to be counted equally in determining which goals should be pursued. It does set limits on factors that may be considered in the policymaking process but sets no rights-based side constraints on the process itself.

Perhaps, however, there is a more defensible account of individual rights that emerges from Dworkin's work. Although Dworkin himself sometimes acknowledges that his approach is at least "parasitic on the dominant idea of utilitarianism,"[10] the overall thrust of his writings is to present rights as trumps blocking utilitarian calculations of what promotes the best social policy.

In fact, some of Dworkin's remarks at least suggest that treatment as an equal involves equal *respect* as well as equal *concern.* For example, he sometimes asserts that humans should be respected as beings "who are capable of forming and acting on intelligent conceptions of how their lives should be lived."[11] Insofar as Dworkin is suggesting here that there is a proper way for humans to be treated over and above what any calculation of social benefit might dictate, a nonconsequentialist conception of rights emerges.

Thus, it is plausible to think that basic rights, such as the right to freedom of speech, should be protected, not simply because of benefits accruing to the community from such protection, but also because the autonomy of the individual is threatened in a particularly serious way where such rights are absent. For example, in the absence of free speech and open debate, individuals are deprived of the conditions under which reason functions most efficiently. Their range of intelligent choice has been circumscribed, and thereby disrespect has been shown to their status as choosing, autonomous beings.

This conception of rights as conditions for respecting persons equally as agents seems to us to be defensible and has much in common with our own defense of human rights in chapter 3. Emphasizing equal respect rather than equal concern places central importance upon the agent's capacity to choose and act. Individuals are not regarded merely as loci of desires whose satisfaction is to be maximized by the benevolent utilitarian legislator.

But for this very reason, this conception of individual rights does not easily lend itself to Dworkin's analysis of preferential affirmative action. There is at least a prima facie incompatibility between equally respecting individuals as agents and dismissing an individual from consideration because he or she possesses immutable physical characteristics. Respect for persons as agents implies emphasis on an individual's character, choices, and capacities, while the exclusion based on immutable characteristics ignores these factors as irrelevant. This suggests that what lies behind the charge of reverse discrimination, overstated as it may be, is that preferential selection by race severs the link between a person's fate and a person's character, talents, choices, and abilities on the basis of possession of immutable physical characteristics. Qualities central to an individual's status as a person capable of forming and acting on an intelligent conception of how his or her life would be led count for less than the color of one's skin or one's gender.

If, as we suggested in chapter 3, human rights are best understood as conditions that must be protected if humans are to be respected as rational and autonomous agents, then there are grounds for finding preferential treatment morally problematic. Even though preferential treatment does not stigmatize those disfavored by it in the same way that past racial discrimination stigmatized African Americans, or does not cause the same degree of injury, and so is not justifiably regarded as reverse discrimination, it still is open to the charge of disrespecting persons as such. By conferring or withholding benefits on the basis of race or similar group membership, it requires that factors about individuals such as their choices, decisions, aptitudes, talents, and character—features that reflect their status as rational and autonomous agents—do not determine outcomes. People are deprived on the basis of race of the kind of respect due them as persons.

Proponents of preferential affirmative action may not be persuaded by such comments. For one thing, they might deny that taking such factors as race and gender into account means ignoring such personal qualities as dedication, commitment, aptitude, and talent. Rather, they might argue that because of past and continuing discrimination in our society, women and minorities, particularly African Americans, may have had to make special efforts to overcome disadvantages that white males normally do not face. Thus, preferential affirmative action does respect their dedication, effort, and abilities but views them in light of the disadvantages they faced.[12]

This response will be considered more fully in the discussion that follows. What it suggests, however, is that preferential treatment does need to meet the objection that it disrespects persons as such by discounting their individual circumstances and achievements and viewing them, to a significant extent, simply as members of major social groups, such as women, African Americans, Asian Americans, and so on. This in turn suggests that, contrary to some of Dworkin's comments, preferential treatment by race, ethnicity, or gender is not just another social policy to be justified solely by its utility but that it requires stronger justification. In other words, since social policy should not assign special weight to such factors as race without special justification, preferential affirmative action is justified only if it is necessary to achieve especially significant moral goals.[13] It cannot be justified simply by showing the likelihood of some gains in social utility, since the costs imposed on those disadvantaged by the policy are imposed on morally problematic grounds. Can this burden of proof be met?

## Compensatory Justice and Preferential Treatment

According to the argument for compensatory justice, preferential treatment in hiring and admissions is justified as compensation for past discrimination against group members as such. Often cited here is the familiar analogy of a race between two runners, one of whom is chained to a heavy weight. Surely, if the race is stopped in the middle and the chain cut, it would not be fair simply to let the race resume. Since the previously chained runner already is far behind, fairness requires that the effect of an unfairly imposed handicap be negated. Likewise, advocates of preferential treatment argue that, given past discriminatory practices, implementing equal opportunity is simply not enough. To rest content with equal opportunity would be like expecting people unfairly weighted down in a race to be competitive once the handicap was removed without doing anything to reduce the unfair lead already attained by the runners who were not required to carry extra weight. In the case of the race, not only must the unfair burden be removed but also the effect it has already had on the standing of the runners must be eliminated. Similarly, in the case of past discrimination, compensatory preferential treatment in favor of members of groups that have been unjustly treated is required to remove the unjust advantage gained by others.

If the compensatory approach is correct, the proponents of preferential affirmative action will have provided a sufficiently weighty argument to meet the burden of proof that we suggested they need to bear. After all, compensation is owed to the victims of injustice; they have a right to it. So on this view, preferential affirmative action is far more than sound social policy. Rather, it is required by justice, and therefore to fail to provide it would be a serious wrong.

### The Compensatory Paradigm

Perhaps the classic account of compensatory or corrective justice is found in book 5 of Aristotle's *Nicomachean Ethics*. It will be helpful to consider briefly Aristotle's account, for compensatory defenses of preferential treatment diverge from it in several significant, and perhaps questionable, ways.

According to Aristotle, principles of compensatory justice apply when one party has wronged another. Such principles call for the wrongdoer to provide redress to the victim. Moreover, the penalty imposed on the former, and thus the benefit supplied to the latter, should be proportional to the difference created by the original wrong. The goal is to restore the relative position of the affected parties to what it would have been had the original injustice never occurred.

This Aristotelian paradigm seems intuitively sound. The wrongdoer should not profit from, nor should the victim be disadvantaged by, injustice. Moreover, it fits an important class of cases involving discrimination. For example, if an employer unjustly discriminates against African American employees in promotion and salary, the major elements of the Aristotelian paradigm apply. There is an identifiable wrongdoer and an identifiable victim. There is an identifiable act (or acts) of injustice. The kind and amount of redress that is required is relatively clear. The employees should be paid the difference between the pay that they actually received and the larger amount that they would have received had the rules been applied equally to all. (Perhaps they also should receive an additional sum to compensate for stigmatization brought about by the employer's discrimination.) The workers who have been wronged are not receiving preferential treatment but are only getting what they deserved, that is, what they would have received under a policy of nondiscrimination.

How does the Aristotelian paradigm fit preferential affirmative action? Unfortunately, the fit is not a close one.

## Evaluation of the Compensatory Argument

Preferential treatment departs from the Aristotelian paradigm in at least three important ways. First, in many programs, preference is made on the basis of race, sex, and other forms of group membership rather than on individual victimization. Second, compensation is not provided by wrongdoers but by arguably innocent third parties. Finally, compensation is not proportional to injury. Let us consider each point in turn.

Critics of the compensatory defense should admit that victims of discrimination deserve compensation. But they can go on to point out that if the reason for preferring a victim of discrimination to someone who is not a victim is the injury suffered, then the formal principle of justice that requires that similar cases should be treated similarly implies that any victim of injustice should receive equal preference, regardless of race, sex, or other group characteristics. The only relevant group, from the point of view of compensatory justice, is that composed only of the victimized.[14] This implies that compensatory justice should be neutral with respect to race or gender rather than be race or gender conscious. Preferential treatment violates this criterion and so, according to its critics, is an improper form of compensatory action. Even if virtually all members of a group have been wronged, they should be compensated because they have been wronged and not because they are members of the group. Moreover, nonmembers who also have been wronged may be due compensation as well.

Consider further how the costs of preferential treatment are distributed. Unlike the Aristotelian paradigm, which assigns the costs of redress to the wrongdoer, preferential treatment assigns the cost to arbitrarily selected white males, none of whom may actually be guilty of discrimination. Critics of preferential affirmative action argue that it is unfair to expect such innocent third parties to pay such a price.

Proponents of preferential treatment sometimes reply that although such white males may not be guilty of actual discrimination, they are the innocent beneficiaries of discrimination against women and minorities. On this view, whites, and white males in particular, share in the benefits that accrue to the majority from discrimination against minorities. These benefits include, but are not restricted to, competitive advantages brought about by generally superior education and a sense of esteem and self-worth that has never been undermined by the pervasive message that one belongs to an allegedly inferior and stigmatized group.

However, while this reply deserves serious consideration, it probably is not a fully satisfactory response to critics of preferential treatment. For one thing, even if all white males are beneficiaries of injustice, preferential treatment still does not inflict the costs equitably. Some arbitrarily selected whites are denied admission to graduate training, a job, or a promotion while others are unaffected. Second, it may not be true that all white males are net beneficiaries of injustice. Even if each and every white male has benefited to some degree just from being white, which is disputable, some may be worse off than they otherwise would have been because of earlier discrimination directed against their own ethnic group. In some cases, where the loss outweighs the gain, they too may be entitled to compensation under the Aristotelian paradigm. Finally, while it sometimes is the case that innocent beneficiaries of injustice are required to compensate victims, that is not always the case. If my store does better than yours because yours is closed by arson, it is far from clear that I, rather than the arsonist or an insurance company, am the one who should compensate you for the injury.[15]

Accordingly, it is far from clear that preferential treatment fits the second requirement of the Aristotelian paradigm; namely, that compensation should be made by the wrong-doer. It is plausible to maintain, then, that preferential treatment assigns burdens arbitrarily and inequitably.

At this point, it may be objected that almost any social policy assigns burdens in such a way. After all, if a new highway is built through town, displaced homeowners may be compensated, but the other benefits and burdens may be distributed in a highly arbitrary way. You and I may live near the highway, but you may mind the noise of traffic while I do not. My business, a gas station, may be helped, but yours, a rest home for the elderly, may not.

This rejoinder does have force, but we also need to consider that while ordinary social policy may inflict costs arbitrarily, we are not talking about a normal cost here. Rather, we are talking about disqualification at least partly on the basis of race or gender. That is why the appeal to compensatory justice is so important; it is designed to show not only that reverse discrimination is not at issue but also that fairness is at issue. But is it fair to distribute the costs of compensation on the basis of such factors as race? Critics of preferential affirmative action may argue that while ordinary social policy does sometimes distribute benefits and burdens somewhat arbitrarily, that is different from deliberately distributing them on the basis of such factors as race and gender. Since the whole issue we are debating is whether race- and gender-conscious affirmative action policies are permissible, the proponents of preferential affirmative action may beg the question by assuming that such policies are allowable.

Moreover, there is a third area in which preferential treatment departs from the Aristotelian paradigm. Surely, it is plausible to think that the strength of one's compensatory claim and the amount of compensation to which one is entitled should be, all else being equal, proportional to the degree of injury suffered. A corollary of this is that equal injury gives rise to compensatory claims of equal strength. Thus, if X and Y were both injured to the same extent and both deserve compensation for their injury, then normally each has a compensatory claim of equal strength and each is entitled to equal compensation.[16]

Unfortunately, it is extremely unlikely that a hiring program that gives preference to designated minorities and women will satisfy this requirement of proportionality in compensation because of the arbitrariness implicit in the search for candidates on the open market. Thus, three candidates, all members of previously victimized groups, may well wind up with highly disparate positions. One may secure employment in a prestigious department of a leading university, while another may be hired by a university that hardly merits the name. The third might not be hired at all. The point is that where the marketplace is used to distribute compensation, distribution will be by market principles and hence will only accidentally be fitting in view of the injury suffered and the compensation provided for others. While any compensation may be better than none, this would hardly appear to be a satisfactory way of making amends to the victimized. Preferential action, to the extent that it violates the proportionality requirement, arbitrarily discriminates in favor of some victims of past injustice and against others. The basis on which compensation is awarded is independent of the basis on which it is owed, and so distribution is determined by application of principles that are irrelevant from the point of view of compensatory justice.

**Compensation for Groups.** Perhaps the discussion so far shows that preferential treatment does not fit the Aristotelian paradigm of compensatory justice. Such a result is important, because the Aristotelian paradigm expresses widely accepted principles of fair compensation, principles that are at the basis of much of the law of torts. However, we should not conclude too quickly that the compensatory defense fails. Perhaps departures from the Aristotelian paradigm can be justified.

Thus, it might be granted that if we could apply such ideal principles of compensation, the discussion so far would be conclusive. Ideally, similar injury warrants similar compensation, compensation should be provided by wrongdoers, and compensation should be proportional to injury. Each compensatory claim should be assessed on its own merits, regardless of race, ethnicity, or gender.

However, it might be replied that in the present state of affairs, it is highly unlikely that ideal principles of compensatory justice can or should be applied. Matters are just too complex to permit case-by-case treatment. Consider the factors that might have to be weighed, for example, in providing reparations to African Americans on an individual basis:

> Compare, in this context, the circumstances of a Mississippi sharecropper, a Harlem welfare mother, a Fisk University professor, a successful jazz performer, an unemployed young man living in a Chicago slum, a political leader in Detroit, and a kindergarten child in a predominantly white suburban school. Each would have to prove the amount of his or her damages as an individual. . . . An attempt to individualize the compensation awarded in a program of black reparations would have to weigh so many imponderable elements that . . . the recoveries might in the end be more capricious than accurate.[17]

Influenced by such considerations, one might argue that preferential affirmative action should not be intended to provide compensation to individuals. Rather, compensation should be made on a group basis. But what is it to compensate a group? This question is complex and cannot be examined fully here, but nevertheless some progress can be made in assessing such an approach.

**Statistical Compensation.** One approach to group compensation is pragmatic and administrative. Proponents of this view argue that membership in a group can be a useful proxy for individual claims of injury in contexts where it simply is too difficult to handle claims on an individual basis. Thus, in an article suggesting such a view, James Nickel argues that "if the justifying basis for such [preferential treatment] is the losses and needs resulting from slavery and discrimination, there will be a high correlation between being black and having those needs, and because of this . . . race can serve as the administrative basis for such a program."[18] Nickel allows that "this may result in a certain degree of unfairness" but replies that "it can help to decrease administrative costs so that more resources can be directed to those in need."[19]

We have here a pragmatic justification for preferential treatment in nonideal situations. The argument is that given a statistical premise to the effect that a significant proportion of members of a particular group have been treated unjustly, we are justified pragmatically in acting as if all have been victimized. This argument, like other compensatory arguments that we have been considering, deserves extended consideration but, like the others, may not have sufficient force to justify preferential affirmative action.

There are at least two problems with this pragmatic argument from administrative efficiency. The first is that the proposal may not be so efficient after all. Thus, Nickel acknowledges that his proposal involves some unfairness. For example, individuals who have not themselves been treated unjustly but who are members of groups that have been treated unjustly may be compensated, while individuals who are not members of such groups but who have themselves been treated very unjustly may not get compensated. How do we know that such residual unfairness can be outweighed by the resulting increase in efficiency in distribution benefits to members of designated groups? Aid will not be provided at all for many of those with the strongest compensatory claims, since many will not be members of victimized groups. Rather, it will go to group members instead. In the case of African Americans, this may not be unduly problematic, since the effects of discrimination against that group are so pervasive, harmful, and systematic, but the correlation between oppression of a group and significant harms to individual members may be less when the blanket of affirmative action is extended to other groups.

At the very least, the case for statistically based preference needs to be supplemented by data on the extent of residual unfairness involved and the resulting implications for efficiency. We are not entitled simply to assume that this proposal will increase efficiency when in fact it may actually decrease it.

Second, even if this objection is questionable, a more serious difficulty remains. That is, the statistical approach can also be used to justify disadvantaging women and minorities when it promotes efficiency to do so. For example, it would appear to justify an employer's refusal to interview any women for a job that required great strength on the grounds that most women lacked the strength to be able to do the job.

It is for this reason that the Supreme Court has been very reluctant to allow administrative efficiency to function as an allowable basis for differences of treatment for women and minorities in public programs. As Justice Brennan declared in writing the majority opinion in the sex discrimination case *Frontiero v. Richardson*:

> Although efficacious administration of governmental programs is not without some importance, "the Constitution recognizes higher values than speed and efficiency.". . . On the contrary, any statutory scheme which draws a sharp line between the sexes solely for the purpose of achieving administrative convenience necessarily commands "dissimilar treatment for men and women who are . . . similarly situated" . . . and therefore involves the "very kind of arbitrary legislative choice forbidden by the Constitution."[20]

The problem, then, is this: If proponents of the compensatory defense of preferential treatment want to justify using race, ethnicity, and gender to assign benefits and costs on grounds of administrative efficiency, how are they to avoid assigning equal weight to efficiency-related arguments when they count against women and minorities? On the other hand, if they would agree that administrative efficiency does not justify disadvantaging individual women or minority group members, doesn't consistency require them to say the same thing about preferential treatment?

Even this objection may not be decisive, however, for proponents of the statistical argument might reply that in view of the discrimination that has been so pervasive in American history, statistical arguments used to disadvantage racial minorities and women normally ought to be invalidated, but such arguments might more generally be allowable when only dominant groups, such as white males, are disadvantaged.

However, this rejoinder seems only to raise the issue of the permissibility of using race- and gender-conscious policies at a new level, so at best it begs the question against critics of preferences. Accordingly, we regard the statistical argument as interesting but at best inconclusive. It simply is not sufficiently strong to meet the burden of proof that must be shouldered if preferential affirmative action is to be justified.

**Collective Compensation.** Maybe the above objections seem to have force only because the kind of collective compensation that we have considered is still too individualistic. Perhaps the object of compensation should be groups themselves; that is, groups considered as collective entities and not merely as sets of individuals. On this approach, objections based on fairness to individuals that do seem to count significantly against the compensatory approaches considered so far would be irrelevant since compensation to groups and not to individuals is at issue.[21]

This line of defense is not without promise and may have application in some other contexts, such as reparation by the United States for wrongs done to Native Americans, compensation by Germany to Jews or to Israel for the evils of the Holocaust, and reparations to black Americans for the evils of slavery and segregation. However, whatever the worth in such contexts of the notion of compensation to groups, it seems especially problematic when used to justify preferential affirmative action.

In particular, it is unclear how compensation to a few individual members of a group who are given some degree of preference for selection compensates a whole group considered as a collective. Not only do proponents of this line of argument need to show that some groups are entitled to compensation as groups, but also they need principles indicating how such compensation is to be distributed to individuals. Preferential affirmative action distributes benefits to individuals, but it is unclear why this counts as compensating a group as such. Indeed, it is plausible to think that if a group has been injured as a collective, compensation ought to be made to the group collectively, through its institutions, and not to individual members arbitrarily selected by some hiring or admissions process. For example, if the institutions of a religious group, such as churches, have been taxed unfairly, perhaps because of prejudice against its beliefs, it is plausible that compensation ought to be in the form of tax relief to the churches, not payments to arbitrarily selected individual adherents.[22]

A similar point can be made about responsibility. While the notion of collective responsibility for an evil may well be coherent, preferential affirmative action imposes costs not on a group, such as white males, as a whole but on arbitrarily selected individuals.[23] Moreover, some of these individuals may themselves be disadvantaged and have gained little from past discrimination, while some white males who may have gained considerably from past discrimination against others incur no costs whatsoever. This hardly seems fair or just.

There are other problems associated with the defense of preferential affirmative action as a kind of collective compensation. For example, have all the groups covered by affirmative action been injured as groups in the same way and to the same degree? Should relatively affluent and well-educated groups, such as Jews and Asian Americans, be eligible for compensation in light of a past history of discrimination? Or if we say that they have already overcome the effects of past injustice, should we say the same of blacks of West Indian descent, who do as well as the national average in terms of employment, income, and years of education?[24] It is tempting here to say that preferential treatment is needed only for those groups that have not yet "made it" in America. But can such a move be made within a compensatory framework, whose goal is to pay what is due for past wrongs? In other kinds of cases, we do not deny that the victim of another's negligence is owed compensation just because she is wealthy and does not need to be compensated.

We suggest that until a plausible theory of group compensation is provided, the burden of proof is on its advocates, at least when there is danger of conflict with other important values, such as fairness to individuals. In summary, preferential affirmative action should not be based on the relatively unclear idea of group compensation, an idea that may well have application in some contexts but that raises many serious ethical issues in this one. We suggest, then, that the shift from individual to group compensation, conceived of either in statistical or collective terms, does not avoid the problems of the compensatory justification of preferential treatment. If preferential affirmative action is justifiable, it is probably justifiable through appeal to considerations other than those of compensatory justice.

## Noncompensatory Defenses of Preferential Treatment

Preferential affirmative action probably can be defended best on grounds other than compensatory ones. Even if the compensatory defense is inadequate, other defenses might be stronger. We will examine some of the most significant of these noncompensatory approaches to see if they fare better than the appeal to compensatory justice.

### The Appeal to Equality

Perhaps the strongest justification of preferential treatment looks not at the past, as does the compensatory defense, but at the future. That is, it looks at the consequences of preferential treatment. Such a view need not be utilitarian but might be based on concern for rights and social justice. That is, it can be argued that preferential treatment, even if it involves some present unfairness to individuals, is necessary to bring about an egalitarian society. Thus, some might see it as a way of transferring wealth and power from groups that already have it to those that do not. Others might view it as a means for ensuring that members of groups targeted by discrimination have a chance equal to others to develop and carry out their plans of life.

**Preference and Equal Opportunity.** One version of such a consequentialist defense regards preferential affirmative action as a mechanism for implementing equality of opportunity. As one writer on the subject declares:

> Women and blacks want to present themselves as qualified candidates and be assured of having a fair chance. . . . Past practices have shown they do not receive this fair chance and preferential hiring is a way of insuring that chance precisely because preferential hiring requires that the burden of the proof be placed on those who do the hiring—on those who have discriminated against women and blacks in the past—to demonstrate that they are no longer doing so.[25]

But does equal opportunity require preferential affirmative action? Why not simply enforce laws that prohibit discrimination? Then everyone would have the same chance, and no one would receive special treatment.

Proponents of preferential treatment would reply that it is not enough to require everyone to play by the same rules if past discrimination handicaps some of the participants. Former president Lyndon Johnson's famous metaphor of the footrace (which we mentioned earlier) captures this point. Past discrimination, on this view, has denied women and members of many minority groups a level playing field. Preferential affirmative action is needed both as a check against continuing discrimination and as a balance against competitive disadvantages that are the legacy of past injustice.

**Evaluation of the Opportunity Defense.** Equality of opportunity surely is a defensible, even a mandatory, goal. If preferential treatment enhances equality of opportunity, that is a major point in its favor.

Nevertheless, the equal opportunity defense faces significant difficulties. The first major objection, which we will not pursue extensively here, is that a consequentialist must look not only at the good consequences of preferential affirmative action but also at possible harmful ones. The trouble is that preferential treatment may produce undesirable as well as beneficial consequences. Thus, it may exacerbate racial tensions and undermine the self-esteem of the recipients by implying that their qualifications are lower than those of others. Whether or not preferential affirmative action produces an overall benefit after all the consequences are counted is a debatable empirical issue, but an important one.

However, some of the most frequently cited bad consequences, such as anger on the part of white males or loss of self-esteem among recipients, may not be justifiable. For example, perhaps women and minorities have no real grounds for losing self-esteem on the basis of receiving a preference, since without it they would be asked to compete for positions on a playing field tilted against them, which is hardly fair. Again, the goal of preferential affirmative action, greater equality of opportunity, seems required by justice, while some of the negative effects, such as anger on the part of white males, lack the moral significance of the positive gains. Moreover, even if the overall consequences of preferential treatment are, on balance, harmful, such a conclusion would show only that preferential treatment was bad policy, not that it was morally impermissible or especially suspect. Governments and institutions may adopt or even require the implementation of policies whose effects are debatable in the honest belief that more good than bad consequences will ensue in the long run.

Thus, we suspect that the major problem with the equal opportunity defense involves fairness to individuals far more than debate over its actual consequences. In particular, the equal opportunity defense faces many of the same objections that apply to appeals to individual compensatory justice. Thus, some members of preferred groups will not have been denied equal opportunity and many nonmembers will have been denied it, perhaps because of economic disadvantage or the lingering effects of discrimination against immigrant groups that are not counted under affirmative action. Finally, it seems unfair that some arbitrarily selected white males, who may not have enjoyed equal opportunity themselves, should suffer disadvantages while most other members of their group suffer no disadvantage whatsoever.

While this point may not be decisive, it does suggest that the burden of proof should be on proponents of race- and gender-conscious remedies rather than their opponents. We suggest that the argument from equal opportunity does justify the employment of procedural and regulative forms of affirmative action in many contexts, so as to level the competitive playing field. We suggest, however, that preferential forms of affirmative action remain more problematic. While we do not want to say that the equal opportunity defense totally fails to support preferential affirmative action, we think objections based on individual fairness also have force. Accordingly, we conclude that the equal opportunity defense justifies racial, ethnic, and gender preferences only as a last resort, when other forms of affirmative action have not enhanced the competitive position of women and minorities and when residual unfairness to others can be kept at a minimum. For example, it may be more justified in such areas as college admissions, where rejected candidates have a variety of institutions to which they can apply, than, say, in appointment to a position that requires years of training and probationary service. In the latter context, the rejected candidates will have already made a great investment in trying to secure the position and may have no other viable options, so the cost to them of being disadvantaged on the basis of race or gender will be inordinately high.

**Justice for Groups.** A second kind of consequence of preferential affirmative action related to equality concerns justice for groups. Thus, constitutional scholar Owen Fiss has suggested that preferential affirmative action might be justified as a means of eliminating caste from American life.[26] On this view, some groups, particularly African Americans, have been the targets of both legally sanctioned and informal kinds of discrimination and oppression, ranging from slavery to segregation. These practices not only have been destructive to individuals but also have singled out blacks as a special group in American life, a group that for much of our history has shamefully been treated as inferior not only by individuals but also by the state. Black Americans, on this view, have become an undercaste. The preservation of caste violates every principle of justice and fairness. It is of the highest social priority that it be eliminated.

More broadly, leaving aside the rhetoric of caste, preferential affirmative action can be viewed as a means to end the inequality of groups in our society—inequality that has arisen because of past discrimination against, and oppression of, racial minorities and women. Surely, in spite of some residual unfairness to individuals, preferential affirmative action is justified as a means to rid our society of the great injustice of racial inequality. Ronald Dworkin, for example, can be taken as arguing that it is not so much utilitarian considerations that justify overriding the interests of white males as the gains in promoting a more just and equal society that are the relevant consequences.[27]

However, the attempt to secure more equality for groups through preferential affirmative action raises a number of questions. First, which groups should it cover? The rhetoric of caste applies most closely in our view to the situation of African Americans, but does it apply as closely to other groups that are legally designated under federal affirmative action policies? Are women a caste? While women clearly have suffered systematic discrimination in our society, surely many white women also have benefited from discrimination against people of color. Others are affluent or hold positions of importance and power. It is at best unclear whether women should be thought of as a caste. What about Asian Americans or Pacific Islanders, many of whom are recent immigrants to this country?

If we include groups that have been the subject of systematic and pervasive discrimination in the United States, perhaps Jews and white ethnic immigrant groups should be included, even though they do not count under affirmative action guidelines. If we include only groups that are widely believed still to face systematic and pervasive discrimination, legitimate dispute will still arise as to which groups should be included. Again, while African Americans have perhaps the clearest case for inclusion, affirmative action as practiced in the United States includes many other groups as well. But is there a reasonable basis for inclusion or exclusion of groups? Perhaps the greatest impact on inequality in America would be made if the group included was defined in terms of economic disadvantage rather than along lines of race, ethnicity, and gender.

However, the difficulty concerning which groups should be included under the umbrella of affirmative action probably is not insurmountable. Perhaps a more difficult question is whether preferential affirmative action will actually bring about a reduction in inequality among groups. Arguably, it has in fact created a great deal of group animosity and has to some extent stigmatized recipients. This issue is primarily empirical and not philosophical. What are the effects of preferential affirmative action policies? Given that the burden of proof is on the proponents, this objection needs to be taken seriously, since even if is not decisive, it may tilt the balance against the permissibility of preference.

This point has additional force when we add to the equation the issue of fair distribution of the costs of the policy. Once again, it is not society, or even white males as a group, that share the burdens but rather those arbitrarily selected white males who lose out because of preference extended to other groups.[28] This arguably unfair distribution of the burdens might be justified if the expected benefits were relatively certain to be achieved, but that is exactly the point questioned by many critics of preferential policies.

We doubt, then, that the argument for justice for groups by itself justifies preferential affirmative action. Of course, it may be part of a cluster of arguments none of which is sufficient by itself to justify the policy but which, when taken together, make a cumulative case for it. We will consider such a cumulative case in our concluding remarks. First, however, a different sort of argument for preferential affirmative action needs to be considered.

## The Appeal to Qualifications and Efficiency

At this point, some advocates of affirmative action may protest that our whole discussion has been based on a faulty assumption. The assumption is that race- and gender-conscious affirmative action policies are "preferential." As we have been using the term, preferential affirmative action goes beyond the qualifications of candidates and, in effect, gives extra points for race, ethnicity, or gender. But are these points really "extra" in the sense of going beyond qualifications? Or, rather, have we interpreted "qualifications" in too narrow a manner?

On this view, then, forms of affirmative action that give positive weight to race, ethnicity, and gender do not involve the selection of less qualified over more qualified candidates but are relevant to deciding which candidate is most qualified. This argument has promise especially because it appeals to a principle that opponents of preferential treatment are likely to accept; namely, the principle that the most qualified candidate should secure the position. But just how are such factors as race, ethnicity, and gender qualifications?

To understand the response, let us consider the argument as applied to appointment of faculty in colleges and universities. There, it is argued, women and blacks, Asians, and Hispanics, for example, can serve in faculty positions as role models for women and people of color. Because of past discrimination, overt and covert, few members of such groups occupy university positions of authority and influence. But for women and students of color to develop the motivation to succeed in attaining similar positions or related ones in the professions, they must be able to see that people like them can succeed. If they are presented with female faculty and faculty of color, they are given living proof that discrimination can be overcome. Of at least equal importance, they may identify with such models and hence secure the special stimulation that will enable them to succeed.

Especially important in university contexts is the contribution that such faculty may make to *diversity*. A diverse faculty (and student body) is important for a variety of reasons but perhaps especially because intellectual discourse functions best when different perspectives and different points of view are represented. The more students and faculty tend to be the same, the less likely it is that assumptions common to the group will be challenged. Agreement may result, not because of the intellectual merits of a point of view, but simply because a homogeneous group of people fails to see weaknesses that might have been apparent to someone from outside the prevailing consensus. In addition, from the point of view of social justice, diversity may be important because part of education in an increasingly multicultural society such as our own is for different groups to learn to understand each other and get along.

Thus, hiring a diverse group of faculty (and admitting a diverse student body) may be educationally beneficial. If so, contribution to diversity can be a qualification, and recognizing that and counting it in the selection process is actually meritocratic, not preferential.

Diversity, as we have seen, is often appealed to by proponents of race and gender conscious hiring. But just how is "diversity" to be understood? After all, any collection of people is likely to be diverse in some respects, such as in height, and homogeneous in others, such as in religion, or age, or simply in being human. Is "diversity" empty of content, then, since any population is diverse in some respects?

Clearly, claims that a group is or is not diverse are elliptical. They need to be filled in by a specification of the characteristics or qualities that are deemed to be important in the particular context. Thus, as we have noted, in academic contexts, intellectual diversity seems especially important because of its role in promoting intellectual inquiry and discourse.

One way of defending the importance of race, ethnicity, and gender in faculty appointment, then, is to relate it to promotion of intellectual diversity on campus. Members of different groups may bring different viewpoints to discussion and may be more likely than traditional scholars to work in nontraditional areas, such as women's studies and other areas dealing with race and gender. Even when such nontraditional inquiry has been especially controversial, and even dubious, it often has opened up illuminating discussion and challenged received views in ways that contribute to our knowledge. The argument, then, is that a more sexually, ethnically, and racially diverse faculty will be a more intellectually diverse faculty. Is that claim true?

While this sort of argument has been highly influential on many campuses, it also has been the subject of significant criticism.[29] While we cannot cover all the critical points here, the following seem especially important. To begin with, it is far from clear that all members of groups covered by affirmative action share common perspectives on most issues or that their perspective differs from those of others in many cases. Thus, many women are "pro-life" rather than "pro-choice," and these positions are shared by men as well as women. On the other hand, on some issues, such as reactions to the verdict in the criminal trial of O. J. Simpson, there seem to be significant differences between the reactions of whites and blacks. Even in such cases, however, there is considerable overlap between groups. Moreover, isn't it insulting, or at least unjustified stereotyping, to assume that faculty will advocate positions based on their ethnicity, race, or gender? On the contrary, diversity within groups can be very great, and hence in many cases it is doubtful that diversity in group membership contributes significantly to intellectual diversity as well.

Indeed, some commentators have questioned whether an emphasis on groups might diminish, rather than enhance, intellectual diversity. Orlando Patterson is one scholar who has expressed fears that an emphasis on representation of groups can lead to individual conformity. Thus, he suggests that

> the greater the diversity and cohesiveness of groups in society, the smaller the diversity and personal autonomy of individuals in that society. . . . A relatively homogeneous society, with a high degree of individual variation and disdain for conformity, is a far more desirable social order than one with many competing ethnic groups made up of gray, group-stricken conformists.[30]

What Patterson is suggesting is that the greater the emphasis on selection of group members because of the expectation that they will hold different viewpoints from members of other groups, the greater the pressure on group members to conform rather than to shatter the cohesiveness of the group. As a result, there is greater pressure on group members to conform to positions held to be orthodox within the group than on other members of the community. The result arguably is less diversity, the hardening of group lines, an increase in divisiveness between groups, and less intellectual discourse across group lines than otherwise would be the case.

While proponents of the argument from qualifications may argue, perhaps not implausibly, that worries about conformity are overstated, the critics seem correct in pointing out that we cannot just assume that group diversity promotes intellectual diversity. A related point concerns which groups should be represented. It might often be the case that the hiring of a religious fundamentalist, or a political conservative, or a political radical, might contribute more to intellectual diversity on a campus than hiring a member of an ethnic or racial group whose views are already well represented. This point is significant because it raises the question of how far we should go in seeking intellectual diversity. Surely, it seems arbitrary to restrict considerations of diversity to groups designated under affirmative action policies.

Finally, although members of groups favored by affirmative action may often be successful mentors or role models for younger members of the group, critics may object that we should not expect or encourage people to seek mentors along lines of race or gender. After all, the critics may say, would we want white males to identify only with older white males? This criticism may be unfair to proponents of the qualification argument, who may only want to insist that women and students of color can be encouraged to persevere if they see that other people like them have been successful in their chosen fields, not that students should seek advisers only of their own race, ethnic group, or gender. However, the critics may also wonder why race, ethnicity, and gender should actually be qualifications if their connection to student development is relatively loose and undefined.

The argument from qualifications was originally presented as important because it starts from premises that opponents as well as proponents of affirmative action can accept; namely, those that stress the importance of qualifications. But critics may say that this supposed agreement breaks down at the point we have been considering. That is, if contribution to diversity is relevant to qualifications, white males who can contribute to intellectual diversity in a variety of ways might sometimes be favored over women and people of color whose views are not unusual or are already well represented. These critics may maintain, with reason, that they have not yet been shown the special relevance of race, gender, or ethnicity to qualifications in appointment of university faculty.

Of course, there may be reasons for promoting group diversity other than its contribution to intellectual diversity on university faculties. For example, it may promote harmony among groups as members get to know each other and understand each other better, or it may simply reduce economic inequality at the group level. However, to take this line would be to abandon the view that group membership is a *qualification* for certain kinds of employment and revert to our earlier consequentialist arguments about the overall effects of preference. Remember, that assessment would have to take into account possible bad consequences of preferential policies as well as good ones. It is far from clear that the case for preferential affirmative policies based on the probabilities of just which consequences would occur is strong enough to carry the day.

## Affirmative Action without Preference

What has our discussion shown? First, we hope to have shown that there are important considerations that count both in favor of and against preference based on race, ethnicity, or gender. This suggests that people of goodwill can differ on this difficult and complex matter and that to assume automatically that one's opponents have bad motives is unwarranted. Thus, we think the charge that preference is a form of invidious discrimination in reverse is dubious, as is the charge that opponents of preference are supporting policies deliberately intended to keep women and people of color "in their place." As we have seen, worries about unfair distribution of the disadvantages imposed by such policies are legitimate.

Second, we have found no arguments for preferential affirmative action that avoid serious criticism or that are sufficiently strong to meet clearly the burden of proof that we believe proponents of such policies ought to bear. However, this does not mean that affirmative action itself ought to be abandoned or that preference has absolutely no role to play in such programs. Remember that not all forms of affirmative action involve racial, ethnic, or gender preferences. If we are right, the choice is not just between affirmative action or doing nothing. Instead, it may be between more acceptable and less acceptable forms of affirmative action.

## Affirmative Action and Social Policy

We suggest that some forms of affirmative action should be part of a comprehensive effort to overcome the effect of social injustice in America but that affirmative action should conform to principles that eliminate, or at least reduce to a minimum, the problems of fairness raised by preferential treatment. Such an effort may take a variety of forms, but we will make some suggestions concerning principles that ought to regulate such an effort. If we are right, the choice is not a stark one between comprehensive employment of racial, ethnic, and gender preferences, on one hand, and doing nothing, on the other. Instead, there may be a range of policies between those alternatives that avoids the excesses of either preferential treatment or ignoring the effects of past discrimination.

### Procedural and Regulative Elements

To begin with, we have not found fault with either the procedural or the regulative forms of affirmative action. In particular, procedural affirmative action is needed, not only to make sure that selection and hiring processes are fair, but also to make the openness of searches and admissions procedures known to candidates.

Regulative forms of affirmative action, which involve the use of numerical goals, are more controversial, as critics charge that goals tend to become quotas. According to this argument, failure to meet a goal puts a heavy burden of proof on the selection officers to show that their search was fair; and so to avoid that burden, which may be difficult to meet even if the search was in fact fair, preference may instead be extended to members of designated groups.

For this reason, we suggest that the use of numerical goals be somewhat selective. The greater the evidence that an institution or industry has discriminated in the past, or the larger the gap between the percentage of women and minorities among qualified applicants and the percentage actually hired, the greater the case for the use of numerical goals.

## The Compensatory Element

Preferential treatment based on rectification for injustice might well be defensible if it is applied according to relevant criteria. This does not necessarily mean that such policies should be racially neutral or color blind; surely, there is a strong presumption that membership in certain victimized groups confers a compensatory claim (or at least a competitive disadvantage that ought to be rectified). However, it does not follow that those are the only such claims that should be considered. Other individuals, of any race or sex, may also have been victimized or may face severe disadvantages through no fault of their own. When choosing among qualified applicants for a position, it may well be permissible, when other factors are at least nearly equal, to take compensatory considerations into account. Moreover, in deciding who will be disadvantaged by such compensatory treatment, we ought to make sure that those who are asked to bear the costs do not have compensatory claims of their own. It does not follow, however, that we ought to do so along lines of group membership alone. We can benefit the most seriously victimized, regardless of race, while taking into account the special burdens of victimized groups when deciding who are the most seriously injured.[31]

Whether the majority of those who benefit are minorities or whether the majority of those who bear the costs are white males will depend upon the individual characteristics of those considered. Race may be one of the factors to be considered, insofar as it is an indicator of discrimination, but no one would be included or excluded solely on such a basis. While there certainly are problems connected with such an approach, such as how one kind of victimization is to be weighed against another, it still warrants consideration. Preferential treatment need not be considered a zero-sum game between white males and others; it can be reformulated to cut across such categories in a morally defensible way.

## The Meritocratic Element

Standard meritocratic criteria of admissions and hiring ought to be reexamined and broadened where such an extension of standard criteria is justified. Once again, however, this can be done in such a way as to take race into account while recognizing that there are neutral reasons for extension that apply across group lines. (We argued this earlier in the section "The Appeal to Merit and Efficiency.") Thus, in hiring police officers, elected officials may want to take into account the likelihood that officers from minority communities sometimes may be able to relate especially well to the population of such areas and so count race as a kind of positive factor in selection of candidates.

However, the broadening of standard qualifications ought not to be done in an arbitrary way. Thus, hiring officers in colleges and universities may want to include promotion of diversity as a factor in selecting new faculty, but they should keep in mind that there are other, perhaps more important, forms of diversity than simply racial, ethnic, or gender diversity.

## Avoiding Hard Choices

In addition, courts and other relevant institutions can try to avoid situations where women and minorities could be included only by excluding others because of their race or sex. For example, consider the question of whether a firm facing hard economic times ought to lay off those last hired, who may be disproportionately black and female, or violate seniority and fire senior white males instead. Proponents of preferential treatment may argue that the white workers might not have ever gained seniority had they faced competition from women and minorities earlier. Proponents of seniority might respond that it was not the workers who discriminated and that the firm should not change the rules under which the workers have been employed in the middle of the game.

Perhaps we can avoid a zero-sum game here. Before deciding such a case, shouldn't the firm be required to show that no less compelling goal can be sacrificed in order to retain both the minority workers and those with seniority? Perhaps profit margins can be cut. Perhaps all workers, including management, can share a pay reduction so that more workers can be retained. If the employer is a town or other kind of municipality, perhaps nonessential services can be cut back before anyone is fired. Perhaps senior professors at a university should be asked to accept lower raises in pay so that savings can be used to retain more assistant professors, including women and minority group members, but also including young white males. Racial and gender preferences would not have to be employed then in deciding what faculty would be retained, since the pressure to make cuts would itself have been reduced. Such compromise may not always be possible, but perhaps the courts, as well as policymakers, should aim first at reconciling differences through compromise and only last at deciding which group should bear the possibly avoidable costs of social policy.[32]

## Preference

In light of the objections raised in our discussion, should preference by race, gender, or ethnicity ever be employed for remedial purposes? We have our doubts and find the difficulties with the use of preference that we have discussed to be significant, although, as we have noted, we also deny that preferential affirmative action is a form of reverse discrimination. However, since we do not expect all readers to agree that the objections are so serious as to call any use of preferences into question, we suggest the following qualification. If preference is to be extended on the basis of such factors as race, ethnicity, and gender, it should be used (a) in entry-level positions or in admission to educational institutions, and (b) in circumstances where those disadvantaged by preferences are likely to have to bear only minimal costs and have other reasonably available opportunities. This is because the use of preference can best be defended when providing an opportunity to someone who may have had an unequal chance to gain qualifications and when the harm imposed on others is not likely to be serious. Thus, an applicant who has been rejected at a college but who might have been accepted had he been a member of a preferred group normally has a reasonable chance to be accepted at other colleges. The extension of preference seems far less warranted, however, when the favored party already has had many opportunities and the disfavored party—say, an older candidate for a position that acquires extended training—has already invested a lot in acquiring relevant skills and may not be able to find a satisfactory position elsewhere.

Accordingly, reasonable people of goodwill may disagree about the moral acceptability of preferential forms of affirmative action. We ourselves believe that there are serious objections to the use of such preferences. However, a reasonable compromise here might allow the minimal use of preferences but restrict their employment to areas where their use is most justified and where the least cost is inflicted on others.

## Promoting Social Justice

Perhaps the best step the state can take to rectify past injustice is to make sure that present policies are just. In particular, we suggest that we in the United States need to address directly the problems of poverty, particularly in the inner cities, which are tightly interwoven with problems of race and which should not be ignored. While various social critics and commentators have been right to raise questions about whether government programs always are effective and to emphasize that many individuals in poverty should not be viewed simply as helpless victims but need to take responsibility for their lives, we believe that there also is a significant role for action by the state. The judicious use of government aid, as part of a major effort to alleviate the economic misery of disadvantaged Americans, can be more effective as a means to promoting social justice in America than can preferential affirmative action. We believe the arguments of chapters 3 and 4 support the contention that a concerted effort to attack the problems of poverty and race in America is not only warranted but overdue.

## Summary

We have found that preferential affirmative action on the basis of race, gender, or ethnicity does raise serious ethical questions. We have suggested, however, that some forms of affirmative action are more justifiable than others and that affirmative action, although perhaps not preferences, can be part of a program designed to promote social justice in America. The challenge posed by the controversy over affirmative action is to promulgate corrective policies that acknowledge the force of claims to redress while avoiding arbitrary or inequitable treatment. Justice and equality demand no less.

## Notes

1. *The Regents of the University of California v. Allan Bakke,* 438 U.S. 265; 98 Sup. Ct. 2733 57 (1978).

2. Actually, the issue of what counts as nondiscrimination is more complex than the text indicates. Depending upon how one wants to define "discrimination," race, religion, sex, and ethnic background arguably sometimes can be applied in nondiscriminatory ways. Thus, if one goes to a rabbi for information about Jewish religious practices or selects only women to play on a women's college basketball team, then, arguably, one is not discriminating in any invidious way. So, more precisely, a

selection process is nondiscriminatory if it takes race, religion, sex, or ethnic background into account only when they are relevant to the qualifications of applicants. When such factors are relevant and when the purpose of a job or institution is itself discriminatory are matters for further discussion. While these issues are important, they are not directly relevant to our own discussion and so can be ignored in what follows, unless specifically mentioned.

3. This point has been made frequently and early in the debate over affirmative action. For an example in the philosophical literature, see J. L. Cowen's paper "Inverse Discrimination," *Analysis* 33, no. 1 (1972): 10–12.

4. Ronald Dworkin, *Taking Rights Seriously* (Cambridge: Harvard University Press, 1977). Material in this section is reprinted from Robert L. Simon, "Individual Rights and Benign Discrimination," *Ethics* 90, no. 1 (1979): 88–97, by permission of the University of Chicago Press.

5. Ibid., 239.

6. Ibid., 227.

7. Ibid.

8. Ibid., 227–28.

9. Ronald Dworkin, "Why Bakke Has No Case," *New York Review of Books,* 10 November 1977, 15.

10. Dworkin, *Taking Rights Seriously,* xi.

11. Dworkin, "Why Bakke Has No Case," 15.

12. This seems to be the view of Leslie Pickering Francis, "In Defense of Affirmative Action," in *Affirmative Action and the University,* ed. Steven M. Cahn (Philadelphia: Temple University Press, 1993), esp. 35–40.

13. That the burden of proof is on proponents of racial preference has been accepted even by those justices on the Supreme Court who ultimately believe that such preference does not violate the Equal Protection Clause of the Constitution. In fact, our statement of the burden is far less demanding than the Court's, which requires that the use of race in public policy must be necessary to achieve a "compelling state interest."

14. This and related points were first argued in Robert L. Simon, "Preferential Hiring: A Reply to Judith Jarvis Thomson," *Philosophy and Public Affairs* 3, no. 3 (1974): 312–21.

15. A similar point is made and discussed by Robert K. Fullinwider in his book *The Reverse Discrimination Controversy* (Totowa, N.J.: Rowman & Littlefield, 1980), 38–42.

16. This point was also made by Simon in "Preferential Hiring."

17. Boris Bittker, *The Case for Black Reparations* (New York: Random House, 1973), 88. Bittker ends up by defending the case for reparations in spite of the difficulty he raises in the quoted paragraph.

18. James Nickel, "Classification by Race in Compensatory Programs," *Ethics* 84, no. 2 (1974): 147–48.

19. Ibid., 148.

20. *Frontiero v. Richardson,* 411 U.S. 677 (1973), reprinted in *Philosophy of Law,* ed. Joel Feinberg and Hyman Gross (Belmont, Calif.: Wadsworth, 1980), 368–69.

21. See Paul Taylor, "Reverse Discrimination and Compensatory Justice," *Analysis* 33, no. 6 (1973): 179, for an attempt to apply such a position to the defense of preferential affirmative action.

22. A proponent of collective compensation to African Americans and other cohesive social groups can argue that one restores the group to its rightful position by favoring individual members precisely because of the psychological links holding the group together. It is because black Americans, like members of other ethnic groups, tend to identify with one another's achievements that the success of some can encourage others to have aspirations that they otherwise would not have had. Moreover, members who are not directly advantaged can share in the satisfaction of achievement by other members of the group. Finally, successful group members can represent the group's interests in the professions, business, and government.

While such a view is not implausible, it sounds suspiciously like a "trickle-down" theory. Some individual members of the group, selected arbitrarily from the point of view of compensatory justice, will benefit directly from preferential treatment, while others, selected equally arbitrarily, at best benefit only indirectly and to a lesser extent. Many, including many of the most seriously disadvantaged, may not benefit at all. In other words, individuals within the group are treated arbitrarily. An individual who has been less significantly harmed by discrimination than another can benefit far more.

Similarly, costs are still assessed arbitrarily. Arbitrarily selected individuals, not groups, are disadvantaged by preferential treatment. As in the case of benefits, assessment of costs may not be based on any reasonable principle, such as ability to pay or responsibility for past discrimination, but simply on who loses out in the market.

23. See Larry May, *Sharing Responsibility* (Chicago: University of Chicago Press, 1992), for a plausible case in defense of the notion of collective responsibility for the commission of evils.

24. Thomas Sowell, *The Economics and Politics of Race* (New York: Morrow, 1983), 186 ff.

25. George Sher, "Justifying Reverse Discrimination in Employment," *Philosophy and Public Affairs* 4, no. 2 (1975): 163. However, Sher ultimately questions whether this argument justifies selection on a group basis.

26. Owen Fiss, "Groups and the Equal Protection Clause," *Philosophy and Public Affairs* 5, no. 2 (1976).

27. See Dworkin, *Taking Rights Seriously,* 226, 228.

28. Strictly speaking, it isn't only white males who may lose out because of preference. For example, a white woman may lose a position because greater weight is placed on another candidate's race or ethnicity, or the woman may get the position rather than, say, a male Hispanic, because greater weight is assigned to gender.

29. See, e.g., Alan Goldman, "Diversity within University Faculties," in *Morality, Responsibility, and the University: Studies in Academic Ethics,* ed. Steven M. Cahn (Philadelphia: Temple University Press, 1990). Our discussion in this paragraph is heavily indebted to Goldman's earlier treatment.

30. Orlando Patterson, "Ethnic Pluralism," *Change: The Magazine of Higher Learning* 7 (March 1975): 15–16. Goldman, in "Diversity within University Faculties," also argues that contributions to diversity should be evaluated on an individual rather than a group basis.

31. For example, we can give special weight, over and above that given to other forms of educational disadvantage, to those applicants for college admission who have attended schools that, in addition to having poorly funded or otherwise weak educational programs, are de facto racially segregated. Or we can assume that all else being equal, the members of racial minorities, particularly African Americans, have encountered special burdens of racial discrimination. Neither approach dictates that preference will be given to minority applicants over, say, disadvantaged whites, but each ensures that their problems will receive special attention. In this way, we can have a "race-conscious" policy that is not invidious in that (a) it does not exclude anyone from the competition, (b) it allows us to assign appropriate weight to the special difficulties facing all individuals, and (c) it does not require that members of any particular social group actually be selected.

32. Here we adopt a suggestion made by Drew Days at a conference on civil rights, sponsored by the Center for Philosophy and Public Policy, University of Maryland, in October 1984.

## Questions for Further Study

1. Why is it important to distinguish between different conceptions of affirmative action? How would you distinguish the procedural, regulative, meritocratic, and preferential versions of affirmative action from one another?

2. What is the reverse discrimination argument? What do you think is its most questionable premise?

3. Explain Ronald Dworkin's distinction between equal treatment and treatment as an equal. How does Dworkin use this distinction to reply to the reverse discrimination argument? Does Dworkin succeed in refuting or undermining the reverse

discrimination argument? How would you justify your evaluation of his argument?

4. What is the compensatory paradigm? Why is it problematic to view racial and gender preference within some forms of affirmative action programs as applications of the compensatory paradigm? Do you think the compensatory paradigm can be used to justify preferential affirmative action? Defend your view.

5. Can groups as well as individuals be compensated? Explain your view. Can preferential forms of affirmative action be justified by shifting from a model of compensation for individuals to a model of compensation for groups? How would you defend your answer?

6. Can preferential forms of affirmative action best be defended on the grounds that they promote a more just society in the future? How might they bring about such a result? How would you evaluate this approach? How would you defend your evaluation against what you think is the strongest objection to it?

7. Explain the view that the expression "preferential affirmative action" is misguided since the aim of affirmative action is not to admit or hire the less qualified but simply to broaden the idea of what counts as a qualification in ways that include members of diverse groups. Isn't it wrong to call such a practice "preferential," since it calls for hiring the most qualified, properly understood?

8. In what sense are claims that a population is diverse elliptical? Does the desire to promote diversity in universities justify admissions or hiring officers' taking into account such factors as race, gender, and ethnicity when making decisions? Explain your view and indicate how you would reply to what you think is the strongest objection to it.

## Suggested Readings

### Books

Bittker, Boris. *The Case for Black Reparations.* New York: Random House, 1973.

Cahn, Steven M., ed. *Affirmative Action and the University: A Philosophical Inquiry.* Philadelphia: Temple University Press, 1993.

————. *The Affirmative Action Debate.* New York: Routledge, 1995.

Cohen, Marshall, Thomas Nagel, and Thomas Scanlon, eds. *Equality and Preferential Treatment.* Princeton, N.J.: Princeton University Press, 1977.

Dworkin, Ronald. *Taking Rights Seriously.* Cambridge: Harvard University Press, 1977, chap. 9.

Ezorsky, Gertrude. *Racism and Justice: The Case for Affirmative Action.* Ithaca, N.Y.: Cornell University Press, 1991.

Fullinwider, Robert. *The Reverse Discrimination Controversy.* Totowa, N.J.: Rowman & Littlefield, 1980.

Goldman, Alan. *Justice and Reverse Discrimination.* Princeton, N.J.: Princeton University Press, 1979.

Sindler, Allan P. *Bakke, DeFunis, and Minority Admissions: The Quest for Equal Opportunity.* New York: Longman, 1978.

## Articles and Essays

Cohen, Carl. "Race and the Constitution." *Nation* 20, no. 5 (1973): 135–45.

Dworkin, Ronald. "Why Bakke Has No Case." *New York Review of Books,* 10 November 1977.

Ezorsky, Gertrude. "Fight over University Women." *New York Review of Books* 21, no. 8 (1984): 32–39.

Goldman, Alan H. "Affirmative Action." *Philosophy and Public Affairs* 5, no. 2 (1976): 178–95.

10

# Ethics and International Affairs

Do our moral obligations stop at the water's edge? Do individual citizens in the afflu-ent nations have moral obligations to the less affluent and often severely disadvantaged millions of the Third World? Can one nation wrong another? What is the proper role of natural or human rights in foreign policy? Should states aim only at enhancing their national interest, or should their pursuit of national interest be constrained by moral norms?

These and related questions suggest that at least some moral principles might apply across national boundaries. But what are these principles, and upon whom are they binding? Do they apply only to individuals in interpersonal relations, or do they also apply to the conduct of such institutions as the state? For example, are states morally required to sacrifice their national interest in order to meet the demands of morality?

In this chapter, we will explore questions concerning the role of morality in inter-national affairs. Does morality even have any significant role in the international arena? The political realists answer that it does not. Let us begin by considering their views.

## The Challenge of Realism

Political realism is a view about the limits of morality in international affairs. Although it has distinguished contemporary adherents, it was also defended in other eras and was perhaps first described by the ancient Greek historian Thucydides.

In his *History of the Peloponnesian Wars*, Thucydides describes the "Melian dialogue" between the generals of imperial Athens and the leaders of Melos, an isolated island colony of Sparta. The Athenians demanded fealty of Melos, but the independent Melians refused to submit. In Thucydides' account of the negotiations between the two sides, the Athenian generals put morality to one side. According to the generals, the reality of the situation is, "They that have . . . power exact as much as they can, and the weak yield to such conditions as they can get."[1] The Melians refused to surrender until required to do so by force of arms. Thucydides tells us that then "the Athenians . . . slew all the men of military age, made slaves of the women and children and inhabited the place with a colony."[2]

The Athenians, at least on Thucydides' account, are being "realists" in the sense of putting the interest of their city-state ahead of any moral considerations. Can such a dis-missal of morality in international affairs possibly be justified?

## Two Arguments for Realism

For analytical purposes, it will be useful to distinguish descriptive from normative political realism. The former is a descriptive doctrine about how nations do act, while the latter is a normative doctrine about how nations should act:

Descriptive political realism: Nations always *do* act in ways intended to maximize their national interest.

Normative political realism: Nations always *should* act in ways intended to maximize their national interest.[3]

The realist arguments that we will consider are attempts to use descriptive political realism as a crucial part of the justification for normative political realism.

The first argument we will consider might be called the consequentialist argument for realism. According to this argument, which has been defended by such important writers as the late Hans Morganthau, if nations do act to promote their national interest, they will produce more overall good than if they pursue moral goals. Hence, they ought to act in ways intended to maximize their national interest.

According to Morganthau's argument, if nations pursue their moral ideals in the international arena instead of realistically following their interests, their behavior will be unstable, unconstrained, and unpredictable. "What is good for the crusading country is by definition good for all mankind and if the rest of mankind refuses to accept such claims to universal recognition, it must be converted with fire and sword."[4] The fanaticism of Khomeni's Iran and imperialistic attempts to impose the conception of the good life shared by one culture on very different cultures in the name of "civilizing" them might be examples of the kind of crusading moralism against which Morganthau and other realists have warned us. Moralism in international affairs amounts on this view to a kind of fanaticism prone to embarking on dangerous crusades in the name of morality.

On the other hand, the realists continue, if each state realistically calculates its own interests and restricts itself to their pursuit, its behavior becomes predictable, stable, and, above all, constrained. The kind of compromise that often is impossible on matters of deep moral difference becomes a matter of practical negotiation. Accordingly, peace, security, and toleration of national differences are best assured if every state avoids the pursuit of abstract moral ideals and pursues its own national interest instead. According to the consequentialist argument, then, if states do act to promote their national interest, they will promote the overall best consequences as well. Therefore, states should always aim at maximizing self-interest.

In addition to the consequentialist argument, realists often advance a Hobbesian argument as well, designed to show that it is morally permissible for states to promote their national interest even when it might conflict with moral concerns. According to the Hobbesian argument, since descriptive political realism is true, international affairs closely resemble the state of nature as described by Hobbes. Just as individuals in the Hobbesian state of nature act egoistically in the pursuit of wealth and glory, so too do nations act egoistically in the pursuit of national interest. Accordingly, since each nation acts selfishly, no nation can have any reason to expect other nations to behave morally towards it. But then any nation that did act morally would be making itself vulnerable to predatory nations. As Morganthau maintains, "a foreign policy guided by universal moral principles . . . relegating the national interest to the background is under contemporary conditions . . . a policy of national suicide actual or potential."[5] Since moral-ity does not require extreme self-sacrifice, although it may permit it, morality cannot require nations to sacrifice national interest to universal principles in a world where other nations are not prepared to do the same.

Are these arguments for realism defensible? While a thorough examination of realism requires more extended treatment than can be provided here, enough can be said to cast doubt on both the consequentialist and Hobbesian arguments.

## A Critique of Realism

The consequentialist defense of realism amounts to the claim that better conse-quences will be promoted if nations act out of concern for national interest than if they act on moral principle. Realists who defend this argument, however, may have far too simplistic a view both of the concept of national interest and of the role morality might play in international affairs.

Is the Hobbesian argument defensible? Do international affairs resemble a Hobbesian state of nature in which states, rather than individuals, inhabit a lawless world governed only by the needs for survival and power? If so, what moral implications follow?

The claim that international affairs closely resemble a Hobbesian state of nature is controversial and has frequently been attacked—for example, by Charles Beitz in his book *Political Theory and International Relations*.[6] Beitz points to several important differ-ences between the state of nature as described by Hobbes and international relations. In particular, he argues that for Hobbes, each individual in the state of nature is virtually self-sufficient, has a virtually equal capacity to kill any other individual, and has no grounds for reasonable expectation that other individuals would adhere to any set of common norms. However, in the modern world, states are increasingly economically interdependent; small, weak states do not represent serious threats to the greater pow-ers; and general norms of international conduct, including respect for diplomatic per-sonnel and fidelity to treaty, are generally observed. While these factors are not sufficient to show that the international arena is similar to a well-ordered domestic society, for there are important differences of degree there as well, they do cast doubt on the par-allel with the "war of all against all" described by Hobbes.

Beitz's point, then, is that the international system does not closely resemble a Hobbesian state of nature and that therefore descriptive political realism is false. How-ever, even if international relations do resemble a Hobbesian state of nature more closely than writers such as Beitz would concede, the extreme conclusions of the realists do not follow. That is, the premises that (1) no nation can count on other nations to act morally towards it and (2) no nation is morally required to take extreme risks to its national interest do not entail that (3) no moral requirements exist in international affairs. Rather, premises 1 and 2 establish at most that nations are not required to take severe risks, not that they are permitted to do anything that enhances their national interest to any degree. Similarly, individuals in a Hobbesian state of nature may not be morally required to disarm unilaterally. It does not follow that they are permitted to torture, rape, mutilate, or otherwise victimize others without provocation merely for their own momentary gratification.

So far, the assumptions of the realist that (a) international affairs are a Hobbesian state of nature and (b) if international affairs are a Hobbesian state of nature, then any-thing goes, have both been criticized. Equally open to criticism are the realist's assump-tions about the nature of morality and about the nature of the national interest itself, assumptions that underlie the consequentialist defense of realism in international affairs.

According to the consequentialist defense of realism, reliance on morality in world affairs will lead to dangerous and intolerant crusades in the name of ideals. Only reliance on the common standard of national interest will ensure predictability, restraint, and international stability. But at this stage of our inquiry, it probably is unnecessary to point out that the role of morality in world affairs need not be restricted to the kind of crusading moralism rightly rejected by the realists. As we have seen in our discussions in other chapters, moral inquiry need not be dogmatic, rigid, and intolerant. Willingness to compromise on competing values, tolerance of differences, and sensitivity to the consequences of actions are themselves elements of a rational employment of morality in human affairs. It is far from clear that such a sensitive and rational morality, if employed in the international arena, will have the disastrous consequences predicted by realism.

Perhaps equally open to question is the assumption of the realists that the national interest constitutes a clear and objective standard for generating our own policies and predicting the behavior of other nations. We suggest that on the contrary, the idea of national interest is subject to various interpretations and is as open to debate and misunderstanding as are the basic concepts of morality and ethics.

In particular, the realist's argument assumes that the national interest will be understood the same way by all observers regardless of their own normative commitments or ideological frameworks. Only if there is a common understanding of a nation's interest will all observers agree in their predictions about what the nation's self-interested behavior will be. Only if predictions are reliable in this way will the behavior of states seem stable and rational and miscalculation be avoided. Imagine the damage if American policymakers based a prediction that a country that sponsors terrorism in the Middle East would not employ similar forms of terrorism within the boundaries of the United States on a misunderstanding of how the terrorists perceived their interests. Our leaders might let down their guard, believing that continued use of terrorism is not in that group's interest, when in fact the conception of group interest employed by the terrorists is very different from that postulated by American analysts.

In fact, conceptions of the national interest can differ along a variety of dimensions. What is to count as the nation: a majority of its citizens, a set of institutions and laws, or a geographic territory? Is the nation's interest to be identified simply with aggrandizement of power, or might ideal elements also enter in? For example, is the United States's national interest necessarily enhanced by an increase in military strength even if that results in reduced respect for democratic institutions throughout the world? What of nations or groups who identify their causes with the will of God? Secular and religious accounts of national interest may differ radically in a great variety of ways.

Disaster in international affairs, then, can arise not only from crusading moralism but also from one state basing its own foreign policy upon mistaken assumptions about how other states see their national interest. The idea of national interest seems to be a contested one: proponents of different ideologies may well advocate different conceptions of the national interest. If so, the idea of national interest, rather than providing a clear, predictable, and neutral basis for the generation, explanation, and predication of policy, is itself at the center of debate over what policy should be.[7] As the late Charles Frankel, a philosopher and former official of the U.S. State Department has told us:

A national interest is not a chart pinned to the wall from which one takes one's sense of direction. The heart of the decision making process . . . is not the finding of the best means to serve a national interest already perfectly known and understood. It is the determining of that interest itself: the reassessment of the nation's resources, needs, commitments, traditions and political and cultural horizons—in short, its calendar of values.[8]

In short, since the nature of the national interest is open to interpretation and debate, the idea that it can serve as an ideologically neutral standard or a clear basis for justifying, explaining, and predicting the behavior of states seems mistaken.

While we have not considered all possible defenses of political realism, we hope to have shown that since the two principal arguments for realism are open to serious objection, realism itself is far from being an obvious choice. Given our initial intuition that the Athenians violated the requirements of justice in warfare in their treatment of the Melians, the burden of proof would seem to be shifted to the realist. Accordingly, we will go on to discuss concrete moral issues in international affairs. Perhaps the most convincing refutation of realism, once its major defenses have been defused, is to show how morality might actually apply in the world arena. We will begin with a problem facing individuals as much as nations, the problem of famine and world hunger. What are our moral obligations to the severely disadvantaged in other lands?

## World Hunger and the Obligations of the Affluent

The terrible plight of the world's most seriously disadvantaged people raises many issues for public policy. Among those issues are those having to do with the millions of victims of famine and near starvation throughout the globe. Consider the parents who watch their children slowly starve during the almost hopeless retreat along dusty roads from an area struck by famine. Consider the millions whose health is damaged, whose rational capacities may be impaired, because of inadequate diet. What are the obligations of the more fortunate to alleviate such suffering?

Many of the issues raised by this question are empirical and conceptual as well as moral. For example, how extensive is world hunger? Such a question looks like a purely factual one, to be settled by empirical inquiry. However, it also raises an important conceptual issue: How is "hunger" to be defined? By varying our criteria of undernutrition and starvation, we can come up with widely different figures as to the extent of world hunger.

It sometimes is charged that some nations and organizations try to minimize the problem by maintaining that serious starvation is not as widespread as many health organizations claim. On the other hand, some observers, such as Nick Eberstadt, argue that inflated figures hurt the poor.

Food relief and development projects for seventy million people, spread across ninety countries, are a manageable undertaking, and with some international cooperation could be attempted fairly easily. If on the other hand, the number of starving were believed to be a billion the task might seem unmanageable or hopeless and for the governments involved politically dangerous to boot.[9]

As we will see, empirical and conceptual disagreement over the nature and extent of world hunger has implications for the moral analysis of the issue. What are the moral obligations of the more advantaged nations and peoples of the world in light of world hunger? At least one writer, biologist Garrett Hardin, has argued that the more advantaged not only have no obligation to help but may well be morally required not to help. Let us begin by considering his views.

## Lifeboat Ethics and the Tragedy of the Commons

Hardin uses two analogies, that of lifeboat ethics and that of the tragedy of the commons, to make his case. Hardin begins by asking us to imagine that after a shipwreck, we sit with fifty other people in a fairly well provisioned lifeboat. We find our boat surrounded by one hundred other survivors, treading water and asking for provisions. Since "they can all be seen as 'our brothers,' we could take them all into the boat, making a total of one hundred fifty in a boat designed for sixty. The boat swamps, everyone drowns. Complete justice, complete catastrophe."[10] Perhaps we could at least let an additional ten people into the boat, for, after all, its carrying capacity is sixty. Hardin replies that "If we do let an extra ten into the lifeboat, we will have lost our 'safety factor,' an engineering principle of critical importance."[11] Our own security would be thrown into great danger.

The analogy to world hunger is fairly clear. If those of us in the affluent countries rescue the starving, we will all be swamped as world population grows and more and more people continue to need our aid. Those rescued will reproduce, so by saving some starving people now, we will be responsible for even more starving people later, until we are all overwhelmed by needs far too extensive to be met at all. By limiting suffering now, we would have produced even more suffering later. Aid would make the situation drastically worse, not better.

Hardin's argument is reinforced by the example of the tragedy of the commons. "If a pasture becomes a commons open to all, the right of each to use it may not be matched by a corresponding responsibility to protect it. . . . [T]he considerate herdsman who refrains from overloading the commons suffers more than a selfish one who says his needs are greater."[12] In short, everyone has an incentive to overload the commons. If I refrain from overloading, I will be exploited by those with no scruples. Since everyone reasons the same way and no one wants to sacrifice his or her welfare pointlessly, everyone overloads and the commons is eventually destroyed. Similarly, the simple provision of aid, as if it came from a global commons, will encourage more and more irresponsible behavior on the part of the recipients, until the global commons is exhausted and we are all reduced to the level of the severely disadvantaged.

Are Hardin's arguments decisive? Should we apply his lifeboat ethic to world hunger? What are the real implications of the tragedy of the commons? Let us consider Hardin's position in some depth.

Unfortunately for his perspective, Hardin's position rests on some very debatable factual and moral assumptions. For one thing, Hardin makes the empirical assumptions that if aid is given to disadvantaged nations so as to minimize or prevent starvation, population will rise, and if population rises, the standard of living will fall still further. Each of these assumptions faces serious difficulties.

Even if aid is given to a developing country to prevent starvation, that aid can be accompanied by birth control devices and instruction. Aid does not have to be all of one type. Indeed, aid might be given only to those countries that are willing to implement birth control policies, or at least such states may be given priority in receipt of aid. (Such a selective policy might seem objectionable on humanitarian grounds, but one might want to go half way with Hardin here and reply that one should give aid only where it actually will do some good.)

Perhaps of greater importance, there is evidence that indicates that when a developing nation becomes better off, its rate of population growth tends to decrease.[13] This may be because children are considered a resource in a poor nation; they bring in income and care for parents in old age. In a poor country, it pays to have many children, since only a few will survive to maturity. However, as the country becomes more affluent, a higher percentage of children survive, and the family tends to have resources that it might rather invest elsewhere than in child care. There is less incentive to have many children as a form of old-age insurance. The better off the developing country becomes, the less its population may grow.[14]

Finally, even if population in developing nations does grow, it does not necessarily imply that the standard of living will fall. Highly populated Japan, as well as the Benelux countries, has shown that efficient use of human capital can produce a high standard of living along with high population density.

Hardin, of course, might reply correctly that while his empirical assumptions are not self-evident, neither are those of his opponents. Perhaps provision of aid will only generate more problems. Even a lowered rate of population growth in some developing nations may not be enough to help so long as the size of the population grows. Be that as it may, it is important to see that Hardin's predictions are controversial and should not be taken as self-evident.

His moral assumptions are highly controversial as well. The moral theory upon which his argument seems to be based is some version of utilitarianism. It is because the alleged consequences of famine relief would be bad that Hardin rejects such aid. However, if, as we have argued, natural or human rights constrain the pursuit of utility, appeal to utilitarian consequences does not settle the case, particularly when Hardin's own predictions about the probable consequences of providing aid are open to question.

Thus, some proponents of an approach to morality that makes rights and justice more fundamental than utility may question whether those on the lifeboat—the citizens of the more affluent states—have any right to be there. Are their secure places the result of exploitation of the less affluent nations through colonialism or just the result of the luck of being born in the right place at the right time? In either case, the fact that some are fortunate enough to be in the well-provisioned lifeboat does not mean that they are morally entitled to their favored status.

A more moderate critic might acknowledge that many of those in the developed nations do have rights to their position, rights that they have either earned or legitimately inherited or that are human rights. For example, the right to liberty may protect us against great interference with our lives, even if it is simply moral luck that we have enough to eat and someone born in Somalia does not. (Similarly, even if I, through an accident of birth, have healthy kidneys and you do not, it does not follow that you can appropriate my kidneys without my consent; you are blocked by my right to personal liberty.) However, the moderate critic will still want to argue that the idea of positive rights to a minimal welfare floor, which we have defended in chapter 3, supports claims of entitlement of the starving. If there is a natural right to a minimally decent standard of living, the affluent will be morally obligated to make some contribution, even across national boundaries.

Is this kind of approach any more defensible than Hardin's? Let us go on to consider an argument for the view that the affluent of the world have stringent moral obligations to help relieve world hunger.

## The Case for Sacrifice

Peter Singer, an Australian philosopher who has written on a wide variety of social issues, argues that individuals in the developed nations have extensive and demanding obligations to relieve starvation.[15] Singer argues from the following assumptions:

1. Suffering and death from lack of food, shelter, and medical care are bad.

2. If it is in our power to prevent something bad from happening without thereby sacrificing something of comparable moral importance, we ought morally to do it.

Given these assumptions, Singer maintains that since starvation clearly is bad, then we ought to give as much as we can to prevent it, up to the point where deprivation would cost us more than what we give up would benefit the recipient. Premise 2 requires us not merely to make some donation to famine relief but to give to the point of marginal utility, where further giving would hurt us more than it would help the recipients.

In fact, it is a major part of Singer's argument that we should not think of donations to famine relief as a kind of charity. Given our present way of thinking, donations to famine relief are regarded as admirable but optional. The individual who fails to give normally is not thought to have committed a wrong. But Singer's point is that our present way of thinking on the matter is mistaken; it is wrong to fail to give to relieve suffering up to the point of marginal utility. In particular, it is wrong to spend money on luxuries while children starve.

It might be objected that the fact that many of the world's starving live far away and are citizens of other countries blunts our obligation, but Singer would deny this. After all, suppose that I could save a child drowning in a nearby swimming pool by throwing her a life raft and that I could save a child in an underdeveloped country by mailing a check for an amount I do not need. Why should the difference in proximity make a difference to the force of my obligation in either case?

Let us accept this point, at least for now, and consider assumption 2, which states that if it is within our power to prevent something bad from happening without thereby sacrificing something of comparable moral importance, we ought to do it. How is this principle to be defended?

Sometimes Singer seems to defend the principle by appealing to example. Thus, he points out that "if I am walking past a shallow pond and see a child drowning, . . . I ought to wade in and pull the child out" even if this means getting my new clothes muddy in the process.[16] However, this example actually does not support premise 2 since the sacrifice involved is relatively minor. It does not establish an obligation to sacrifice something significant, let alone an obligation of the affluent to reduce themselves to near poverty to rescue the starving. To support (2), Singer would have to show that the rescuer has an obligation to risk his or her life, or at least something of great importance, to save the child. Since it is far from clear that such heroic action is morally required, Singer probably cannot defend (2) by appeal to example.

Perhaps it can be defended by appeal to the more general principle of impartiality. If everyone is to count as a fundamental moral equal of everyone else, we have no basis for favoring our own welfare over that of other people. If each counts for one and only one, preventing X from suffering a certain evil is morally required so long as the cost to me is less, even if only slightly less, than the evil I prevent by sacrificing my own interests. Otherwise, I am favoring myself and violating the principle of impartiality.

Looked at in this way, however, (2) looks suspiciously like a variant of utilitarianism, which might be called negative utilitarianism. Unlike standard utilitarianism, it does not require us to promote the good of others, but it does require us to aggregate the avoidance of evil so as to minimize total bad consequences of our acts or practices. If so, it is open to a number of the objections against utilitarianism that we discussed in chapter 2.

In particular, Singer's negative utilitarianism seems to leave little room for individuals to live their own lives, carry out their own projects, and develop in ways they choose for themselves. Rather, it requires individuals to sacrifice control over the direction of their lives so long as by doing so they (perhaps only minimally) reduce the suffering of others. While such sacrifice may be heroic, it is far from clear that it is morally required. For example, if parents decide to save money to pay for their children's college education, it is far from clear that such action is either selfish or immoral. Singer may be correct to say that mere proximity does not change our moral obligations to rescue; but our own commitments, such as commitments to family, friends, neighbors, and perhaps fellow citizens, may conflict with, and sometimes override, our obligations to make heavy sacrifices to rescue strangers.

A proponent of Singer's view might reply that our criticism of (2) rests on a question-begging appeal to the intuitions of our readers. People in our culture, the critic might maintain, have been brought up to think of morality as relatively undemanding, as a set of constraints protecting individual liberty but not requiring much of the individual. Utilitarianism, however, attempts to reform this traditional moral perspective. A more demanding morality, the critic maintains, is more appropriate in a world where suffering is so widespread. To reject utilitarianism on the grounds that it is too demanding is to beg the question, since the rejection is based on appeal to traditional moral intuitions that the utilitarian would reject.

This last-ditch utilitarian defense is a thoughtful one, but we suggest that it does not carry the day. For one thing, utilitarianism itself sometimes is defended by appeal to the intuition that we ought to be benevolent toward others. Perhaps more important, if utilitarianism implies that individual autonomy and the capacity for persons to live their own lives are not significant, it is hard to see how individual freedom and liberty can be accommodated within a utilitarian framework.

Finally, if morality is made so demanding that people psychologically cannot live up to it or are called upon to sacrifice virtually all their nonmoral goals on the altar of moral goodness, morality will come to be seen only as an abstract ideal with no real bearing on human life. The "strains of commitment" of adherence to a strict utilitarian morality may be too great—a point Singer himself has acknowledged in more recent writings.[17]

An interesting distinction made recently by Brian Barry between first- and second-order impartiality may be useful here.[18] First-order impartiality requires us to be impartial in all our everyday transactions with others. Interpreted strictly, it requires, for example, that parents show no preference for their own children in virtually any context—for example, in deciding whose children to play with. Singer apparently relies on this conception of first-order impartiality, which leaves no room for special relationships with others and the network of obligations and rights that such relationships generate. However, the requirement that we should always be impartial in the first-order sense seems unjustifiable precisely because it has such unacceptable consequences. Barry suggests plausibly that, instead, justice requires only second-order impartiality; the idea is that the basic rules and principles of justice should be those that rational people could accept from an impartial perspective. Perhaps one of the rules that could be accepted would allow all parents to save for their own children's college education (rather than be committed to paying equally for the education of all children) or pay special attention to their own children's activities. If so, parents need not be morally required to sacrifice virtually all their savings for famine relief, any more than they must see to it that their children play equal amounts of time with all children. More generally, Singer overlooks the claim that our special relationships with specific persons may block obligations to strangers from even arising. Maybe, as Singer asserts, distance makes no difference to our moral duty, but friendship and family might.

In any case, if, as we have argued, respect for the individual as a choosing, autonomous person is itself a fundamental moral value, a utilitarian ethic of world hunger that does not take such a value into consideration is open to the charge of swallowing up the person in the long-run pursuit of a better world. While, as we will argue, some sacrifice is required in a world where great suffering cries out for alleviation, it is doubtful that the more advantaged individual should be viewed merely as a means for the alleviation of suffering, as Singer's variant of utilitarianism seems to require.

It also is worth noting that Singer's position, like Hardin's, rests on factual assumptions about world hunger. In particular, his discussion seems at least to suggest that world hunger can best be dealt with by individual self-sacrifice on the part of the relatively affluent. If, as recent studies suggest, world hunger is paradoxically due not to severe food shortages but rather to the maldistribution of an adequate food supply, the best long-term solution may well involve political action at the state level designed to bring about institutional change in developing countries.[19] While this perhaps does not eliminate the need for interim help by individuals, it does call into question the assumption that we can make others better off by making ourselves collectively worse off. It is at least arguable, although perhaps self-serving, to maintain that the Western nations need to remain affluent in order to contribute to an expanding world economy and in order to retain the influence needed to promote reform in the distribution of food in the developing world.[20]

## World Hunger and Human Rights

Our discussion suggests that a position on world hunger more demanding than Hardin's but not quite so demanding as Singer's might be worth consideration. In particular, if people have the human right to a minimally decent standard of living, that right, since it is a human right and not a conventional one, applies across national boundaries. On the other hand, if people also possess human rights to liberty and exercise those rights as members of social organizations, they acquire special obligations within those institutions: obligations to children, spouses, coworkers, and fellow citizens. Those obligations may frequently conflict with obligations to aid those in other lands. Moreover, it is far from clear that we as autonomous persons are obligated totally to sacrifice our own life plan in order to benefit others, although it might well be especially praiseworthy should we choose to do so.

Singer has suggested that those who find his original premise 2 too stringent may want to replace it with (2'):

2'. If it is in our power to prevent something very bad from happening without thereby sacrificing anything else morally significant, we ought, morally, to do it.

Premise 2' differs from premise 2 in that it allows a wider range of excuses for non-compliance; we may violate (2) only in order to preserve something of comparable worth, but we may violate (2') to preserve a morally significant but not necessarily comparable goal. The trouble with (2'), however, is that it seems empty without some specification of just what has moral significance.

Perhaps the human rights perspective can help here. As we developed that perspective in chapter 3, it required that individuals be respected as autonomous, rational agents. Natural or human rights are fundamental entitlements that must be protected if humans are to be respected in such a way. Therefore, obligations that arise from the rights of others have greater moral authority than moral considerations such as benevolence. It may be morally good to be benevolent; it is morally required that we honor our obligations. Among the obligations that the rights of others impose on us is the duty to promote the positive rights of others, human rights to minimally decent conditions of welfare without which humans cannot develop or function as rational and autonomous agents.

As Singer argues, it is hard to see why such an obligation should end at the water's edge. On the other hand, the human rights perspective recognizes that positive-rights claims of recipients are constrained by the negative rights of potential donors. If humans are to be respected as rational and autonomous beings, each individual should be left free to develop and follow an autonomously selected plan of life, consistent with reasonable contributions to support the positive rights of others. Moreover, our obligations to our families and to those others to whom we have special obligations may limit our degree of responsibility to help alleviate world hunger or promote a more egalitarian distribution of wealth throughout the world. Singer may be on firm ground, however, when he argues that a mere concern for luxuries, which is not necessarily wrong in itself, does not excuse us from meeting our obligations to those who suffer abroad any more than it excuses us from paying taxes at home.

Finally, it is important to remember that the most effective means of fighting world hunger may exist at the institutional rather than the collective level. Perhaps the best contribution we can make requires not simply financial contributions but also political judgment at the institutional level. Although the proper response of individuals to a particular famine may be to provide relief, it is an open question whether the long-term solution not only to world hunger but also to underdevelopment in the Third World is redistribution. Development policies, which emphasize growth, also need to be considered. Although such programs may themselves raise questions of distributive justice, as when a developing country sacrifices its poorest people in order to save capital for future growth, some combination of development and redistribution may produce morally more defensible results than uncoordinated giving on the individual level alone.

However, the developed nations need to be careful about interference in Third World nations, which can sometimes have unfortunate consequences. For example, market pressure on such countries to switch from crops that can be consumed at home to cash crops for sale abroad is viewed by many experts as one factor that contributes to poverty.[21] At the same time, internal maldistribution and corruption within the developing nations may result in diversion of foreign aid from those it was designed to help to the ruling elite. Ideological narrowness in the Third World, which may lead some developing nations blindly to reject market approaches to problems regardless of circumstances, may also unnecessarily retard development.

Accordingly, while individuals may have responsibilities to provide aid, action at the

institutional level designed to create global systems of equitable distribution may ultimately be what a morally defensible approach to world hunger requires. Be that as it
may, individuals do have obligations to make reasonable contributions, in light of their
own situation, to maintain the positive rights of starving people abroad. These obligations may demand more sacrifice than most of us are willing to acknowledge, although
we doubt that they require as much of us as Singer's position suggests. While we do have
a right, as autonomous rational agents, to a significant degree of freedom as to how we
live our lives, this does not imply that our obligations to others stop at the water's edge.

## Natural Resources and Global Justice

Many of the world's less developed nations have maintained, in the United Nations and
in other international forums, that a new international economic order, designed to distribute more equally the world's wealth, ought to be implemented. On their view, the
current unequal distribution of wealth and resources between the developed nations and
the Third World is inequitable and unjust. International treaties, including the proposed
Law of the Sea Treaty rejected by the United States in 1982, contain provisions calling
for a shift of resources toward the underdeveloped nations. Although recent turns toward
market forms of economy in some Third World countries have muted calls for international redistribution, the gap between the rich and the poor surely should be of as much
concern internationally as within domestic society.

Although the general topic of global justice extends far beyond claims to natural
resources, entitlements to natural resources are a central concern. Should a nation that
lies on rich oil deposits or fertile fields have an absolute and exclusive claim to the fruits
of what may be nothing more than good luck? Should natural resources that lie outside
national boundaries, such as mineral deposits in Antarctica, in the depths of the sea, or
in outer space, be regarded as the exclusive property of the discoverers, or should they
be regarded as part of a global commons, "the common heritage of mankind"? After all,
resource-rich nations may have enormous advantages over resource-poor ones. An individual born into a resource-rich country may, through an accident of birth, have a far
longer, healthier, and more interesting life than an individual born into a resource-poor
nation. Is such a situation fair or equitable?

In this section, we will explore two influential positions on ownership of natural
resources. During the discussion, it will be important to keep in mind the distinction
between natural resources that lie within national boundaries and those that do not,
since different principles may apply in each case.

### Locke and Libertarian Entitlements

Libertarianism, as understood here and discussed in chapter 4, is the political philosophy that holds that rights to liberty are fundamental and that therefore it always is
impermissible to interfere with personal liberty, except to protect liberty itself (or perhaps to compensate those whose liberty has been wrongly violated). For libertarians, the
liberty to appropriate and exchange property is a particularly important one. But how
does property get appropriated in the first place? An answer to that question might shed
important light on claims to ownership of natural resources.

Many libertarians rely on a theory of appropriation proposed by John Locke, whose views we discussed in chapter 3. According to Locke, as long as we are in the state of nature, we are entitled to our body and what we produce with our body through our labor. Accordingly, we can appropriate property by mixing our labor with it. Owners of justly appropriated property can freely exchange it among themselves through the market or can voluntarily transfer entitlements by giving gifts.

If we view international affairs as something like a Lockean state of nature, with nations having rights logically parallel to those of individuals in Locke's theory, then nations can be regarded as being entitled to control resources, just as individual persons have control over their bodies. Moreover, states or other collective entities, such as corporations, can appropriate resources lying outside their own national boundaries by mixing their labor (or that of their agents) with it. For example, an American mining consortium can come to own mineral deposits on the deep-sea bed through deep-sea mining. On this view, since the corporation has invested the resources, technology, and labor in deep-sea mining, it acquires an entitlement to the minerals at the mining site.

This position is a libertarian one, since entitlements to resources arise from individuals or collectives exercising their liberty over their bodies. Libertarians point out that if we could not collectively or individually appropriate property through our free actions, our liberty to control our lives would be significantly restricted. In addition, such free appropriation also may enhance efficiency, since it rewards the productive and the enterprising.

## A Critique of Libertarian Entitlements

Since the libertarian entitlement theory has been examined in chapter 4, the discussion here will focus on its application to appropriation of natural resources rather than on its overall validity. To begin with, even adherents of the Lockean theory of appropriation sometimes will admit that it is vague at crucial points. How much labor must be invested in resources before one can claim them? Why, as Robert Nozick asks, doesn't the laborer lose his labor rather than gain property? For example, if you grew a tomato, made tomato juice from it, and mixed the juice with the Atlantic Ocean, you would lose your tomato juice rather than acquire the Atlantic.[22] Finally, how broad is your entitlement? For example, if you come to own a valuable resource, do you have a right to use it in ways that may harm your neighbors? For example, can you pollute at will simply because your mining operation is on your property? What are the limitations on Lockean entitlements generated by the rights of others?

These are general difficulties with the Lockean theory of acquisition. It is important to see that they count just as much against collective acquisition of property by a socialist state as against individualist acquisition by members of a capitalist one so long as either is defended on Lockean grounds.

Clearly, there is a problem, although not necessarily an unsolvable one, of explaining how property can be justly appropriated in the first place.[23] Rather than deal at length with the general problem, which might be resolved by revision of the Lockean approach or by a more broad-based appeal either to the utility of various rules for acquiring property or to their relevance to preservation of individual freedom, we will consider in depth a particular argument against full appropriation of natural resources. Proponents of this argument maintain that even if the Lockean or some other individualistic approach to appropriation of other kinds of property is correct, none of these approaches applies to natural resources.

## Resource Egalitarianism and the Geologic Lottery

Resource egalitarianism is the view that natural resources are "the common heritage of mankind" and that everyone in the world has an equal claim to benefit from their development. As so defined, resource egalitarianism contradicts the libertarian view, since it denies that natural resources can be fully owned and totally controlled by the appropriators.

The first argument for resource egalitarianism that we will consider is based upon the "geologic lottery." That is, the resource egalitarian can argue that the location of natural resources throughout the globe is a matter of moral luck. The Saudis have done nothing to deserve the huge oil deposits in their territories, nor have Americans done anything to deserve the mineral deposits or fertile soil found within the continental United States. Location of resources is the result of a geologic lottery for which no human is responsible. Since no one is responsible for the location of natural resources, no one can claim to deserve control of them. Therefore, they must be regarded as the common heritage of mankind, to be developed and used for the benefit of all.

According to writers such as Charles Beitz, such a position would be endorsed from a global version of Rawls's original position, an initial situation in which the veil of ignorance (see chapter 4) is extended to cover knowledge of citizenship.

> The fact that someone happens to be located advantageously with respect to natural resources does not provide a reason why he or she should be entitled to exclude others from the benefits that might be derived from them. Therefore, the parties would think that resources (or the benefits derived from them) should be subject to redistribution under a resource redistribution principle.[24]

Moreover, Beitz maintains that such an argument is more defensible than Rawls's similar treatment of natural abilities and talents since "unlike talents, resources are not naturally attached to persons. . . . Thus, while we might feel that the possession of our talents confers a right to control and benefit from their use, we feel differently about resources."[25] Beitz might have added that talents and skills are often developed through hard work, while resources just happen to be located fortuitously for those lucky enough to be born into a resource-rich nation. Hence, we cannot be said to deserve the natural resources we control even if, against Rawls, we can make desert claims based on our own development of our talents and abilities.

### Critique of the Lottery Argument

Is the lottery argument decisive? Before it is accepted, at least three kinds of objections need to be considered. First, it is important to be clear about exactly what the lottery argument establishes. Properly understood, it does not establish that ownership of, or entitlement to, natural resources is either morally or conceptually inappropriate. Rather, it shows, at most, that claims to entitlement or ownership cannot be based on personal or collective desert. However, if ownership is conceived of as a set of rules that, for example, promote utility if generally observed or as a means of implementing the right to liberty, the appeal to the geologic lottery is beside the point.

Even ignoring this point, the lottery argument is open to further objection. In particular, it does not deal with the distinction between actual and potential resources. It is true that no one is responsible for the distribution of potential resources around the globe. No human, for example, placed huge oil deposits in the Middle East. However, oil deposits become an actual resource only given a technology that can utilize them. Given a less advanced technology than now exists, or a much more advanced one, today's valuable oil supplies might be virtually worthless.

What is the significance of the distinction between actual and potential resources? Although no one is responsible for the initial distribution of potential resources, persons and collectivities such as nations can be responsible for turning potential into actual resources. An individual, by inventing a new technology, or a state, by supporting an enlightened policy with respect to science and education, can be responsible for the development of the technology that most efficiently utilizes the available resources. Since the lottery argument applies only to potential resources, it cannot be used to show a priori that claims to actual resources cannot be based on desert. Of course, in specific instances the lottery argument may be found to apply even to actual resources, but it cannot be used generally to discredit desert claims, since some resources may become actual only because of technological developments for which individuals or states can take credit. Thus, whether the lottery argument has force in particular instances depends on the facts of the case at hand.

This point has special application to natural resources found outside national boundaries, such as mineral deposits lying in the deep-sea bed. For the ability to mine and develop such resources depends upon a complex combination of policies influencing technological development, education, and basic research in the sciences—precisely the kinds of things for which individuals and groups can plausibly claim credit.

It is open to the proponent of the lottery argument to reply that no one deserves the good luck to be born into the kind of society that makes efficient use of its human capital. Once this move is taken, however, we seem to be back with the general Rawlsian argument that no one deserves individual talents and capacities. For if a society's development is due at least in part to such factors, and if people have the right to pass on at least some of those benefits to their descendants and to their fellow citizens, then even if one does not deserve to be born into an advantaged position, one may be entitled to some (although perhaps not all) of the inherited initial advantages anyway. So unless the proponent of the lottery argument is willing to extend it from geology to the individual level, an extension that writers such as Beitz try to avoid (perhaps because of the disadvantages pointed out in chapter 4), the appeal to the geologic lottery cannot be used as a general tool to undermine all claims of entitlement or ownership to natural resources.

## Resource Egalitarianism and Positive Rights

We have seen so far that there are difficulties both with an unrestricted Lockean entitlement approach to natural resources and with the view that special claims to natural resources never are justified because all such claims must be based on pure luck. Perhaps a view combining the best elements of resource egalitarianism and libertarian entitlement theory might be worth considering.

While we are not able to present a full theory of how global justice might bear upon appropriation of natural resources, the account of natural or human rights sketched earlier does have implications in this area that may be worth consideration. The ground of such rights is the basic idea that humans are owed respect and concern as rational, autonomous creatures. Part of such respect involves acknowledging the worth of human liberty, including the freedom to join, and act as members of, groups or institutions formed to secure goals that cannot be secured by individuals acting alone. Nations and corporations may at least sometimes constitute such groups. While there is a real problem as to whether unjust nations—those that grossly fail to respect the status of their citizens as free and autonomous beings—should have the same rights and status as reasonably just ones, the liberty of individuals to participate in collectives is the ground for collective claims over natural resources.

Thus, if the function of government is to protect the rights and interests of its citizens, subject to moral constraints of not violating the rights of others, and if this requires territorial integrity, nations have at least a prima facie right to control access to resources within territories. Similarly, if nations or corporations take risks to develop resources in previously inaccessible areas lying outside national boundaries, they may have claims to a profit based upon desert or upon compensation for investment (and the risks that go along with it).

However, none of this implies that such resources ought to be under the absolute control of the developer or the host nation. This is because, in addition to negative rights, each individual has a positive right to a minimally decent standard of living. Although a nation's leaders may well have a duty to put the crucial interests of their fellow citizens first, this does not imply that they can ignore the natural rights of others. Thus, in our view, the affluent nations, and their citizens, are under an obligation to make reasonable contributions to an overall scheme of global justice designed ultimately to create a global welfare floor below which no citizen of the world will be allowed to fall. While such a global welfare floor is at present utopian, there is an obligation to take reasonable steps, in light of other pressing obligations and needs, to help make it a reality. One possible way of doing so is to expect those collectivities—nations or corporations—that develop resources lying outside national boundaries to pay an international tax on profits for such an end. Ideally, the demands of justice, while not so stringent as to limit unduly most individuals' life plans, do apply across national boundaries.

## The Ideal and the Actual in International Affairs

The developed nations have received much criticism not only from Third World countries but also from many of their own concerned citizens for not providing sufficient nonmilitary aid to less developed areas of the globe. It has been claimed that less than 1 percent of the U.S. gross national product is devoted to such aid. Critics charge that this is a shockingly low total, and their point has force even if one adds past U.S. contributions to such international organizations as the World Bank, which the critics sometimes ignore.

While we share the view that an increase in such nonmilitary aid is warranted—and warranted on grounds of global justice rather than charity—we do note that there is a difficulty in jumping too quickly from premises about what justice ideally requires to conclusions about actual policy.

In particular, if global justice is based on individualistic concerns, as it is in our account of natural rights or Beitz's attempt to apply Rawls's theory to international affairs, it is unclear just how it applies in a world of states. That is, global justice as so conceived justifies distributive principles for individuals, but actual distribution in the real world is among states. The problem, of course, is that unjust states may use any wealth they receive for unjust purposes rather than apply it to alleviating the plight of individuals.

Thus, the proposed Law of the Sea Treaty, which in part would have regulated the development of undersea resources and which was rejected by the United States in 1982 in spite of acceptance by virtually all other nations, called for some redistribution of the benefits of deep-sea mining to less developed nations. The U.S. rejection, based in part on professed adherence by the administration of President Ronald Reagan to a Lockean entitlement theory (and perhaps also on economic self-interest), was criticized by those at home and abroad who viewed the deep-sea bed as a global commons to be developed for the benefit of all.

Although these criticisms have some merit, the Law of the Sea Treaty was at best an imperfect instrument of global justice. In particular, it did not require either that recipient countries be internally just or that they use redistributed benefits in just ways. Indeed, given the sorry record of many such states, some of the benefits almost surely would have been used for unjust purposes. It is arguable that the United States should have signed the treaty, although reasons other than those of global justice (such as the need for a stable international arena) seem most compelling. Given the defects of the entitlement theory, the treaty surely was rejected for the wrong reasons. Nevertheless, in view of the distinction between the actual and the ideal, it is unclear that acceptance of the treaty was actually required by considerations of global justice.[26]

In view of these considerations, an enlightened foreign policy would have as one of its principal aims a negative one. We should not act so as to violate, or contribute to violation of, rights abroad. While implementation of a global welfare floor may be beyond our present powers in the actual world, we can try to avoid economic policies that exploit others or support of dictatorships that grossly violate human rights. We can also take reasonable steps, in view of the realities, to implement positive rights. Surely, we can and should do far more in this area than we are doing at present.

Nevertheless, as we have seen, rights can conflict. Although we should be suspicious of politicians who use the contested concept of national interest to justify any policy, however gross, international realities may force unpleasant choices upon us. For example, should we continue support for a repressive but friendly dictatorship if the alternative may be its replacement by an at least equally repressive and hostile opposition?

Philosophy alone cannot settle such hard cases. What is required in addition is thorough knowledge of the facts and wise judgment about different policy alternatives. Nevertheless, moral principle is not irrelevant to international affairs. While the concrete application of moral principles to international affairs raises many difficulties over which good and reasonable people may disagree, such principles do set constraints to which any justifiable foreign policy must conform.[27]

## Humanitarian Intervention

States can intervene, and have intervened, in the affairs of other nations for a variety of reasons ranging from economic exploitation to the desire to impose their own religious or moral ideas on others. Moreover, intervention can take many forms, from direct military action to economic boycotts designed to influence political decisions in other states. In this section, we will focus on humanitarian intervention; that is, intervention carried out for humanitarian purposes such as reducing extreme suffering or protecting against gross violation of human rights in other countries. Recent examples of humanitarian intervention involving the United States include the rescue mission to save starving people in Somalia and NATO's intervention in the Balkans, which continues at the time of this writing.

For much of the period following World War II, humanitarian intervention was relatively rare. In significant part, this was because of the cold war. Both the United States and the Soviet Union needed to be careful about flexing their military muscle abroad, even for humanitarian purposes, since such acts easily could be misinterpreted by the other side. Given the risk of nuclear war, the potential cost of direct intervention tended to be too high. With the end of the cold war and the transformation of the Soviet Union, this point no longer applies. However, just as the risks of direct humanitarian intervention may be less, at least where nuclear conflict is concerned, the risks of superpowers' using their military might for their own profit is great. Moreover, when intervention involves the use of military forces, it may impose significant risks on those who take part. The pictures of mobs dragging the bodies of American troops through the streets of Somalia left a large segment of the American public with distaste for the very idea of humanitarian intervention.

When, and under what circumstances, is humanitarian intervention justified? Is it ever morally required? Is there a duty to intervene? Does that amount to a duty to "police the world," and can that too easily become a rationalization for a new imperialism? Let us consider these issues further.

## The Case against Intervention

According to anti-interventionists, intervention by one state in the internal affairs of other states is (virtually) never justified. A number of arguments are offered in support of such a view.

One line of such arguments makes a case against intervention in the affairs of states that logically parallels much of John Stuart Mill's case against paternalistic interference with individuals. For one thing, external agents are less likely to know what is good for another people than those people are themselves, so interference is all too likely to be harmful to those interfered with, even if the intentions of the interveners are benevolent. For another thing, states, like individuals, are more likely to develop and progress through their own efforts than through external help. Thus, Michael Walzer writes that "the members of a political community must seek their own freedom, just as the individual must cultivate his own virtue."[28] States, like people, must develop on their own if they are not to become mere dependents on the generosity of others.

This kind of approach is supported by concerns of human rights. Intervention may involve one group of people interfering with the association of others. Such coercion may violate the human right to liberty or the rights of individuals to join collective entities, such as the state, to further their own purposes. Thus, intervention, especially for imperialistic or selfish purposes, can violate the fundamental rights of those whose associations are disrupted.

A second line of argument concerns the costs to the interveners. Should we really expect the United States to police the world? How many soldiers must be sacrificed if military action is called for? How many billions should be spent while the needs of many of our own citizens often go unmet? Why is what goes on beyond our national boundaries our concern anyway?

A third line of argument concerns global justice. Wouldn't permitting intervention give too much power and control to strong states and too little protection to weak ones? Just as it is wrong for a strong person to violate the rights of a weak one, isn't it wrong for more powerful states to violate the rights of weaker ones? On the other hand, a principle of nonintervention puts the strong and the weak on the same footing. Each has the right to control its own internal affairs, just as individual persons have the right to control of their own bodies and to a significant degree of liberty as well.

This line of argument is sometimes reinforced by contractualist reasoning. Thus, an anti-interventionist might ask us to imagine a global original position behind a veil of ignorance in which each state was represented. Since the representatives would not know if they came from stronger or weaker states, they would favor a principle of non-intervention in order to avoid the disastrous outcome of invasion by external forces. More broadly, if we are impartial, we would favor a strong principle of nonintervention since we ourselves would not want other countries interfering with our own internal affairs, even if it were for our own good as the outsiders perceived it.

Are these arguments against intervention decisive? If so, do they support a total prohibition against intervention in the affairs of other states, or do they just establish a presumption against it that might be overruled in extreme enough circumstances?

## A Limited Defense of Humanitarian Intervention

The concerns of the opponents of intervention are understandable. They are afraid that powerful states will act like big bullies, interfering in the internal affairs of less powerful states for their own selfish purposes. In light of imperialism, gunboat diplomacy, and a history of American intervention for commercial reasons in Central and South American countries, these concerns are warranted. However, in our view, they do not justify an absolute prohibition against intervention in the affairs of other states.

For one thing, the arguments against intervention presented above are not decisive. First, consider the argument that even intervention designed to benefit the host country has all the defects of paternalism, in particular that it promotes dependency and inhibits growth and development. While that argument may have force when applied to interference with the lives of competent individual adults, we suggest that it has less force when applied to collective entities such as the state. Thus, an oppressive government may actually retard the development of its citizens as individuals by keeping them in a subservient state. As Charles Beitz has pointed out in his discussion of the morality of intervention, the issue is empirical. In some specific cases, interference in the affairs of a paternalistic, tyrannical, or corrupt and inefficient government may promote the development of its individual citizens and even the growth of institutions within the state that give the people a voice in determining their own affairs. Proponents of intervention may reply that progress, to be lasting or significant, must be earned by the people themselves. But Beitz's point is that while such a view often may be correct, it need not apply to every case.[29]

A similar point can be made to proponents of human rights. Although some forms of intervention may indeed violate fundamental entitlements, other forms may be necessary to protect them. This may be especially true when governments have lost their ability to protect their citizens or are themselves the instigators of oppression. Thus, whether or not NATO's intervention in the Balkans proves to be prudent, it surely had the immediate effect of stopping massacres conducted under the banner of "ethnic cleansing" and other war crimes that horrified the world.

What about those who insist that what happens outside our own national borders is none of our business? Perhaps their point is that we have no moral duty or obligation to interfere in the affairs of other states, even for benevolent purposes, especially when serious problems, such as hunger and poverty, remain unsolved in our own country.

While we agree that the bonds of citizenship create special obligations to our fellow citizens and that implementing their basic rights normally takes priority over obligations to citizens of other nations, we deny that this always is the case. On our view as developed in chapter 3, each of us has a duty to respect the human rights of others, positive as well as negative. While the best way of respecting such rights for most people most of the time is to focus on the support and promotion of just institutions within their own state, this need not always be the case. Conditions abroad sometimes may be so extreme, as in the case of famine or terrible oppression, that we must directly focus on protecting the rights of those outside our borders.

Moreover, we do not believe that such a conclusion is dependent on acceptance of our particular account of human rights. Utilitarians, for example, must count the suffering of those outside our borders in their calculations, as Singer's discussion of famine relief brings out. Even rule utilitarians, who concede that meeting domestic obligations first normally is what promotes the most utility, are likely to make exceptions where prevention of mass suffering abroad is feasible. Similarly, nonutilitarians who emphasize the importance of impartial consideration should come to the same conclusion. Surely, when we impartially consider the situation, we would want to be rescued from starvation or terrible oppression under conditions of extreme suffering, even through foreign intervention if necessary. Hence, it is unlikely that impartial, reasonable people would recommend that an absolute prohibition on intervention be adopted as a fundamental component of international morality.

This reasoning suggests, as theorists such as Charles Beitz have argued, that we should reject the superficially attractive analogy of states and individual persons. Individuals are the fundamental bearers of rights, but states are instruments for preserving individual rights. Thus, while each individual has fundamental human rights—or, from the utilitarian perspective, counts the same as others in the felicific calculus—it is far from clear that grossly unjust or ineffective states have similar rights to be free of interference. This is not to suggest that intervention may be easily justified, for even when it is undertaken with benevolent motives, it may wrongly disrupt a legitimate association of individuals; but it is to propose that considerations of justice do not support an absolute prohibition on intervention either.

Of course, in any particular context, it is important to assess the costs of intervention, the form it might take, and the likelihood that it will be successful. Intervention through the use of military force is especially problematic because of the potential in many contexts for violence and wider conflict and because of the sacrifice required of the military personnel involved and, of course, of their families. Normally, as our discussion of Singer's view brought out, we are not morally required to make extreme sacrifices to rescue others.

Thus, intervention must always be carefully considered and judiciously implemented. It should be the exception rather than the rule because of, among other things, the danger of wrongly interfering with the lives and culture of other peoples, the costs of intervention, the danger that things will go wrong and the intervention will get out of control, and the danger that powerful states will create a new imperial realm in which other nations operate only on their sufferance.

Nevertheless, our moral obligations do not stop at the water's edge, and extreme measures may at times be called for. Sometimes this will require genuine sacrifice, but wise leaders will intervene only when the proposed benefits justify the cost.[30] On our view, intervention is justified only to protect human rights from grave abuse or neglect, to protect large populations from extreme suffering, or to prevent some great evil that would afflict large numbers of people. We doubt that there is any precise formula stating the necessary and sufficient conditions justifying intervention. Of much greater value would be wise leaders who judiciously apply moral guidelines to help us steer a course between, on one hand, a blind isolationism that ignores tremendous evil or suffering outside our borders and, on the other hand, the temptation to act as a benevolent world police force, to think we must help whenever there is a chance our interference might do more good than harm. In view of the history of imperialism that has characterized much of our history, as well as that of other powerful or once powerful states, the latter policy is all too likely at best to fail and at worst to disguise our own economic interests. But fear of acting imperially should not prevent us from recognizing our moral obligations to those beyond our borders, even if that sometimes means not fully respecting the claims of their governments.

## Conclusion

In this chapter, we have argued that morality does play a role in foreign affairs. That role is not one of oversimplified moralism, rightly criticized by the realists, but of consideration of complex and often competing moral factors. Thus, in the area of international distributive justice, our discussion suggests that the more affluent nations, and their citizens, have obligations to promote an economically just global order, although these obligations are limited by the rights and deserts of their citizens and by the unfortunate realities of governance in many of the nations of the Third World. Whether our particular lines of argument seem convincing, however, is perhaps less important than our principal conclusion: Morality does not stop at the water's edge.

## Notes

1. Richard Slatter, ed., *Hobbes' Thucydides* (New Brunswick, N.J.: Rutgers University Press, 1975), 379.
2. Ibid., 385.
3. The difference between descriptive and normative political realism, and the use made of the former to justify the latter, was first pointed out to us by Robert Holmes.
4. Hans Morganthau, *In Defense of the National Interest* (New York: Knopf, 1951), 37.
5. Ibid., 35.
6. Charles Beitz, *Political Theory and International Relations* (Princeton, N.J.: Princeton University Press, 1979), esp. 27–66.
7. This argument is developed in Robert L. Simon, "A Limited Defense of the National Interest," in *Values and Value Theory in Twentieth Century America: Essays in Honor of Elizabeth Flower,* ed. Murray G. Murphey and Ivar Berg (Philadelphia: Temple University Press, 1988), 195–214.
8. Charles Frankel, *Morality and U.S. Foreign Policy,* Headline Series 224 (New York: Foreign Policy Association, 1975), 52.
9. Nick Eberstadt, "Myths of the Food Crisis," in *Moral Problems,* ed. James Rachels (New York: Harper & Row, 1979), 299. Originally published in *New York Review of Books,* 19 February 1976.
10. Garrett Hardin, "Lifeboat Ethics: The Case against Helping the Poor," in *Moral Problems,* ed. Rachels, 280. Originally published in *Psychology Today,* September 1974.
11. Ibid., 280.
12. Ibid., 282.
13. See, e.g., William W. Murdoch and Allan Oaten, "Population and Food: Metaphors and Reality,"

in *Social Ethics: Morality and Social Policy,* ed. Thomas A. Mappes and Jane S. Zembaty (New York: McGraw-Hill, 1982), 372–79. Originally published in *Bioscience,* 9 September 1975.

14. See the discussion in Murdoch and Oaten, "Population and Food."

15. Peter Singer, "Famine, Affluence, and Morality," *Philosophy and Public Affairs* 1, no. 3 (1972).

16. Ibid., 231. This example has been discussed by Brian Barry in his essay, "Humanity and Justice in Global Perspective," in *Ethics, Economics, and the Law,* Nomos 24, ed. J. Roland Pennock and John W. Chapman (New York: New York University Press, 1982), 221–25. Some of Barry's comments suggest the lines of our own criticism in the text, although we do not know if this sort of objection was precisely what Barry had in mind or whether he would endorse it.

17. See, e.g., Peter Singer, *Practical Ethics* (New York: Cambridge University Press, 1980), 180–81, where Singer acknowledges that the issue of how much can reasonably be demanded of others is more complex than he indicated in "Famine, Affluence, and Morality."

18. See Brian Barry, *Justice as Impartiality* (New York: Oxford University Press, 1995), chaps. 8, 9.

19. See Amartya K. Sen, *Poverty and Famines: An Essay on Entitlement and Deprivation* (New York: Oxford University Press, 1981), for a defense of the thesis that inadequate food supply in the famine-stricken country is not the principal cause of famine.

20. For discussion, see William Aiken and Hugh LaFollette, eds., *World Hunger and Moral Obligation* (Englewood Cliffs, N.J.: Prentice-Hall, 1977), particularly the essays by John Arthur, Joseph Fletcher, and Michael Slote.

21. See the discussion in Henry Shue, *Basic Rights* (Princeton, N.J.: Princeton University Press, 1980), esp. 42–51.

22. Robert Nozick, *Anarchy, State, and Utopia* (New York: Basic Books, 1974). The tomato juice example is discussed on 175.

23. For discussion of philosophical arguments concerning the justification of property, see Lawrence C. Becker, *Property Rights* (Boston: Routledge & Kegan Paul, 1977). See also Becker's article, "Property," in *The Encyclopedia of Ethics,* ed. Lawrence C. Becker and Charlotte B. Becker (New York: Garland Publishing, 1992) 2:1023–26.

24. Beitz, *Political Theory and International Relations,* 138.

25. Ibid., 139.

26. For discussion of how the distinction between the ideal and the actual might bear on issues of morality and international affairs, see Robert L. Simon, "Global Justice and the Authority of States," *Monist* 66, no. 4 (1983): 557–72.

27. For a fuller treatment of resource egalitarianism and libertarianism, see Robert L. Simon, "Troubled Waters: Global Justice and Ocean Resources," in *Earthbound,* ed. Tom Regan (New York: Random House, 1984), 179–213.

28. Michael Walzer, *Just and Unjust Wars* (New York: Basic Books, 1979), 87.

29. Beitz, *Political Theory and International Relations,* 84–87.

30. Different moral theories lead to different kinds of evaluations of costs and benefits, and even to differences in what counts as one or the other. While utilitarians will look at the ratio of good consequences to bad, presumably measured in terms of happiness or pleasure or preference satisfaction, those concerned with rights and justice will apply different standards, involving justice, fairness, and respect for persons and their fundamental entitlements.

## Questions for Further Study

1. What is political realism? Distinguish descriptive from normative forms of political realism.

2. What do you think is the strongest argument for political realism? What do you think is the strongest objection to it? Is the objection successful? Why or why not?

3. Explain Garrett Hardin's criticism of the idea that people in the affluent nations

have moral obligations to reduce suffering by sending aid to victims of famine throughout the world. Do you think his argument is defensible? How would you reply to what you believe is a strong objection to your own evaluation of Hardin's argument?

4. Explain Peter Singer's argument for the conclusion that people in the affluent nations have moral obligations to reduce suffering by sending aid to victims of famine throughout the world. What does Singer mean by suggesting that the more advantaged should give to the point of declining marginal utility?

5. What do you think is the strongest criticism that can be made of Singer's argument? Do you think the criticism is justified? On your view, do the relatively better-off people in the West have a moral duty to provide some aid to the victims of famine, even if not to the extent that Singer suggests? How would you defend your view?

6. How might a libertarian theory of property rights be applied to acquisition of minerals on the ocean floor or in outer space? Do you think this approach is defensible? Why or why not?

7. What is resource egalitarianism? How is it supported by the lottery argument? Do you think the lottery argument adequately supports resource egalitarianism? How would you respond to what you think is the best criticism of your view?

8. If an American expedition to Mars were to discover valuable minerals there, do you think less developed nations would have a legitimate claim to share in any profits made as a result of American efforts? How would you justify your view, and how would you reply to objections to it?

9. Do you think American military intervention might be justified in order to save thousands of civilians from being massacred in a barbaric civil war? What factors would you consider in your analysis? Would your opinion change if the lives of hundreds of thousands or even millions of civilians were at stake? Do you think you or your friends would have a moral obligation to serve in such a rescue effort if needed?

## Suggested Readings

Aiken, William, and Hugh LaFollette, eds. *World Hunger and Moral Obligation.* Englewood Cliffs, N.J.: Prentice-Hall, 1977.

Beitz, Charles. *Political Theory and International Relations.* Princeton, N.J.: Princeton University Press, 1979.

Brown, Peter, and Douglas Maclean, eds. *Human Rights and U.S. Foreign Policy.* Lexington, Mass.: Heath, 1979.

Hare, J. E., and Carey B. Joynt. *Ethics and International Affairs.* New York: St. Martin's Press, 1982.

Hoffman, Stanley. *Duties beyond Borders: On the Limits and Possibilities of Ethical International Politics.* Syracuse, N.Y.: Syracuse University Press, 1981.

Nardin, Terry. *Law, Morality, and the Relations of States.* Princeton, N.J.: Princeton University Press, 1983.

Phillips, Robert L., and Daniel L. Cady. *Humanitarian Intervention.* Lanham, Md.: Rowman & Littlefield, 1996.

Shue, Henry. *Basic Rights: Subsistence, Affluence, and U.S. Foreign Policy.* Princeton, N.J.: Princeton University Press, 1980.

Walzer, Michael. *Just and Unjust Wars.* New York: Basic Books, 1979.

# Postscript

In *The Individual and the Political Order*, we have examined some of the central issues in political philosophy and have evaluated different approaches to them. We also have tried to defend a version of what we regard as a liberal approach to these issues. It is liberal in that it allows individuals as bearers of fundamental human rights to develop their own conceptions of the good life rather than allowing the state to impose a conception of the good or a vision of community on its citizens.

We are less concerned, however, with whether readers adopt our position, although of course we hope they will, than to have provided a reasonable account of it and especially to have provided a fair account of the views of those with whom we disagree. We believe that much political debate on college campuses and elsewhere in society has degenerated into either a kind of preaching to the converted, where we discuss issues only with those who already agree with us, or a kind of hostile confrontation in which we question the motives of those who take positions different from our own or demonize members of the opposition. We hope that by bringing out the strengths as well as the weaknesses of different approaches to political philosophy, we have helped demonstrate the value of genuine dialogue in which differences are honestly aired and criticisms and objections are faced and discussed.

A number of approaches to modern thought have called into question uncritical acceptance of notions such as objectivity, impartiality, and reasonableness. While these challenges sometimes have made valuable contributions by questioning unjustified assumptions about what is objective, impartial, or reasonable, we need to be careful not to throw out the baby with the bath water. After all, should an argument to the effect that objectivity, impartiality, and rationality are mere illusions be regarded as persuasive? Such an argument would itself have to make some sort of claim to be objectively sound, unbiased, and reasonable, even though there is room, of course, to argue how such criteria should themselves be understood.

Above all, we hope to have shown that rational evaluation of arguments can not only help us to identify those positions that are indefensible because they involve gross violation of fundamental moral principles but also allow us to make progress on difficult moral and political issues and to make judicious assessments of positions that conflict but that each claim some support among reasonable people of good will. We need to make judgments between competing views, even though in difficult cases there may be some support for each of the competing perspectives. When faced with complex moral and political issues, too many individuals today seem to react by throwing up their hands. "Who's to say who is right?" is the typical response of those who are perhaps morally paralyzed by complexity. Many other individuals react with a dogmatic adherence to their own views, regardless of objections to them and regardless of the reasonableness of the different positions of others. We hope that reasoned discussion of the issues provides an alternative both to political dogmatism and to a kind of moral paralysis. We hope that *The Individual and the Political Order* helps to show that the alternative of reasoned discourse is feasible and important, and intellectually stimulating as well.

# Index

abortion: controversy surrounding, 7; and moral values, 94, 105; state regulation of, 17

absolute authority: accorded to the state, 9; Hobbes on, 10–14

abstraction, 110

academic ethic, 157

academic faculty appointments, 202, 217–20

accidents of birth, 84, 88, 90

Ackerman, Bruce, 110

acquisition, 87, 240–41

act utilitarianism, 29, 32, 33, 35–36, 38n8, 38n12

addiction to drugs, 161

advertising, 87

affirmative action, 201–27; avoiding hard choices, 222; as discriminatory, 2; forms of, 202–3; meritocratic affirmative action, 203, 221–22; as more than nondiscrimination, 202, 223n2; as an obligation, 5; procedural form of, 292, 215, 220–21; regulative form of, 202, 215, 220–21; and social policy, 220–23; and speech codes, 166; valid points on both sides of issue, 3. *See also* preferential treatment; reverse discrimination

African Americans. *See* minority racial groups

Altman, Andrew, 168–69

altruism: and Hobbes's view of human nature, 13; innateness of reciprocal, 20n13

anarchism, 15, 194–95

*Anarchy, State, and Utopia* (Nozick), 79

Aquinas, Thomas, 44

Aristotle: on civic participation, 106; on compensatory justice, 208–9; on just distribution, 68–69; on justice as accessible to reason, 43; on law, 180; on pleasure of rationality, 30; on punishment, 184

Asante, Molefi Kete, 133

assimilation, 134, 135

Athens, 180, 229

Austin, J. L., 168

authority: absolute, 9, 10–14; autonomous decision to accept, 15; claims to, 7; horrible deeds committed in name of, 8; justification of, 8;

liberalism legitimating bureaucratic, 111. *See also* political authority

autonomy, individual. *See* individual autonomy

Babeuf, Gracchus, 96n4

Bakke, Allan, 201

Balkans, the, 245, 247

Barry, Brian, 97n26, 113, 197, 237, 250n16

Becker, Lawrence C., 250n23

Beitz, Charles, 231, 242, 247, 248

Bellah, Robert, 101

Benhabib, Seyla, 111, 112, 113

Bentham, Jeremy, 23–28; as act utilitarian, 29; criticisms of, 25–28; on greatest good for the greatest number, 24, 25, 26–27, 29; hedonic calculus of, 25; on human psychology, 24; on natural rights, 45; philosophy as "pig philosophy," 25; on punishment, 24, 181–82; on social contract theory, 24; and utilitarianism, 23–25

Berlin, Sir Isaiah, 147–49

Bill of Rights, 118, 162, 188

birth control, 16, 234

Bittker, Boris, 224n17

blacks. *See* minority racial groups

Brandt, Richard, 32–33, 36, 37, 38n12

Braybrooke, David, 33, 36, 37

Brennan, William, 212

Burke, Edmund, 17

Butler, Joseph, 19n5

capitalism. *See* market, the

capital punishment, 182, 188–89; 198n14

caring, 109

caste, 216

Chamberlain, Wilt, 79–80, 87

checks and balances, 122

child molesters, 183, 187

Cicero, 44

civic republicanism, 105–7

civil disobedience, 189–98; and anarchy, 194–95; conditions of justifiable, 196–97; and democratic institutions, 195–98; justification of, 191–98; of King, 16, 19, 189, 191, 199n18;

civil disobedience *(continued)*
law testing contrasted with, 191; and moral skepticism, 194; nature of, 190–91; of Thoreau, 9, 190, 194–95; for unjust laws, 16
"Civil Disobedience" (Thoreau), 9, 194–95
civil liberties (rights): and hate speech, 169–70; as negative, 147; as paradigm feature of democracy, 118. *See also* individual freedom; individual rights
Civil Rights Act of 1964, 202
classical laissez-faire economics, 76–79
"clear and present danger" condition, 175n36
Clinton, Bill, 9
Cohen, Avern, 167
Cohen, Joshua, 111
cold war, 246
collective compensation, 213–14, 224n22
collective responsibility, 213
common good (public interest): and democracy, 132–33; emotional associations of term, 23; and individual rights, 126–27; and private interest, 129; Rousseau on discerning, 124
commons, tragedy of the, 234–35
communicative democracy, 112–13
communitarians: feminism compared with, 108; on group membership and identity, 134; liberalism criticized by, 96, 101–8; on liberal neutrality, 104–8; on the liberal self, 102–4
compensatory justice, 208–14; collective compensation, 213–14, 224n22; the compensatory element, 221; evaluation of, 209–10; for groups, 211–14; paradigm of, 208–9; statistical compensation, 211–13
competitive market, 31, 76
*Concept of Law, The* (Hart), 180
conscience. *See* individual conscience
consensus, 91–92, 93–94, 105, 123
consent: and fairness principle, 138; Hobbes on mutual consent, 14; and political obligation, 139; in sexual activity, 154; tacit consent, 137–38
constitutions, 93–94
contract, social. *See* social contract
cooperation, social, 90
core values, 157
Cranston, Maurice, 53
crime: deterrence, 181–82, 185, 188, 189; as illness, 185–87; moral order upset by, 184; psychological crimes, 184; sex offenders, 183, 187. *See also* civil disobedience; punishment; serious crimes

critical inquiry, 163
cultural diversity, 107, 133–35, 218–20, 222
cultural relativism, 133, 135
cultural survival, 107–8, 114n10

Dahl, Robert, 123
decision of the majority. *See* majority rule
Declaration of Independence, 44, 46, 47
Declaration of the Rights of Man, 44, 47
deep-sea bed, 241, 243, 245
deliberative democracy, 111–13, 131
democracy: for adjudicating conflict, 136; as appropriate procedure for providing justice, 96; and civil disobedience, 190, 195–98; clarifying meaning of, 117; and the common good, 132–33; communicative democracy, 112–13; communitarians on, 105; deliberative democracy, 111–13, 131; direct democracy, 20n18; and equality, 127–30; and fairness, 130; and fundamental liberties, 173; and the general will, 124–27; and groups, 130–33; as honorific term, 117; the individual as moral foundation of, 130; individual rights constraining, 95, 96; interest-group egoism in, 131; justification of, 118–30; and liberal arts education, 136; Mill on, 120–21; misuses of power in, 17–18; and multiculturalism, 133–36; nonindividualistic defenses of, 121–27; oppressed minorities in, 130–32; paradigm features of, 117–18; participatory democracy, 131–32; Plato's criticism of, 69–70, 128; and pluralism, 122–24; and political obligation, 117–43; Rousseau on, 124–27; utilitarian arguments for, 118–21. *See also* liberal democratic state; majority rule; voting
*Democracy's Discontent* (Sandel), 105
descriptive political realism, 230
deterrence of crime, 181–82, 185, 188, 189
Devlin, Lord Patrick, 154–57
difference principle, 84, 90, 93
dignity, human. *See* human dignity
direct democracy, 20n18
discrimination: and affirmative action, 2, 5, 201–27; in capital punishment, 188; footrace metaphor for, 208, 214–15; as harmful, 152; hate speech as, 165–66; racial segregation, 18–19, 59, 189, 191. *See also* reverse discrimination
discussion, freedom of. *See* freedom of expression
distribution of goods and services: liberalism as too concerned with, 96; Locke on unequal,

49, 50–51; in market system, 77–78, 85, 86; Nozick on, 79; Rawls on, 83; Walzer on, 103–4. *See also* redistribution of resources

distributive justice. *See* justice

diversity, 107, 133–35, 218–20, 222

*Doe v. Michigan,* 166–67

Douglas, Stephen, 105

drug addiction, 161

Dryzek, John, 111

Dubois, W. E. B., 134

Durkheim, Emile, 122

duty. *See* obligation

Dworkin, Ronald: on Devlin on enforcing morality, 155–57; on equal treatment, 96n5, 205, 206–7, 216; on individual rights, 204, 205; on particularity, 110; on paternalism, 174n35; on preferences, 38n10; on reverse discrimination argument, 204–7

Eberstadt, Nick, 233

economics: market approach to economic justice, 76–81; market mechanism as enhancing efficiency, 77, 85; and utilitarianism, 31–36. *See also* market, the

efficiency: market mechanism as enhancing economic, 77, 85; and preferential treatment, 217–20; Rawls's principle of, 83; and statistical compensation, 212

egoism: psychological, 11, 13, 19n5; rational, 132–33. *See also* selfishness

elitism, 58–60; and agency, 63n38; antidemocratic argument of, 128–30; of market critics, 77; of Plato, 70

emotions (feelings), 110, 111

empiricism, 48

entitlements: human rights as, 239; rights as, 42–43

entitlement theory, 79–81; evaluation of, 86–88; and natural resources, 240–41; and property rights, 51, 52

epithets, racial and ethnic, 165–70

equality: democracy as requirement of, 127–30; Dworkin on equal treatment, 96n5, 205, 206–7, 216; egalitarian argument for human rights, 56–57; elitist challenge to, 58–60; justice and, 72–73; justice and equal rights, 73–75; and liberty, 172; Locke on inequality of possession, 49, 50–51; Plato's criticism of, 70; and preferential treatment, 205, 206–7, 214–16; radical egalitarianism, 72; Rawls on, 82, 92; Rousseau on, 124; of voice in democracy, 112. *See also* equal opportunity; resource egalitarianism

equal opportunity: hate speech as denying, 165; and preferential treatment, 214–16; Rawls's principle of, 83, 93; for women, 108

ethics. *See* moral values

ethnic cleansing, 247

ethnic groups. *See* minority racial groups

ethnic slurs, 165–70

Etzioni, Amitai, 101

euthanasia, 46, 159

expression, freedom of. *See* freedom of expression

eye for an eye, tooth for a tooth, 184

faculty appointments, 202, 217–20

fairness: and compensatory justice, 208, 210, 211, 212, 215; as democracy's justification, 130; feminist critique of traditional theories of, 109; in free-market exchange, 51; and Nozick's theory of entitlement, 88; and obligation, 138; in procedure and results, 75; Rawls on, 84, 138; and rights, 42

family, the: communitarians on, 104; family values, 7, 16; Okin on, 108

famine. *See* world hunger

feelings (emotions), 110, 111

Feinberg, Joel, 62n2, 147, 156

feminism: and communitarianism, 108; liberal feminists, 108; liberalism criticized by, 96, 108–14; liberal responses to, 110–14; and Michigan speech code, 167; themes of, 108–10; on traditional women, 135, 146

fighting words or symbols, 169

Fiss, Owen, 216

foreign aid, 244

foreign policy. *See* international affairs

*Fragment on Government* (Bentham), 24

Frankel, Charles, 232–33

freedom. *See* liberty

freedom of expression (speech): as basic liberty for Rawls, 83; "clear and present danger" condition, 175n36; for correction of error, 162–63; and democracy, 94, 118; and fighting words or symbols, 169; limits of, 145; and market mechanism, 76; Mill on, 161–64; and pornography, 3, 17, 101; and rationality, 162; speech-acts, 168. *See also* hate speech

freedom of thought, 161–64

freeloaders, 132

free market. *See* market, the

free riders, 138

free will, 146, 186

Friedman, Milton, 76–77, 85

functionalism, 60, 70, 128
fundamentalists, religious, 91, 112, 113, 145

Galbraith, John Kenneth, 77
Gandhi, Mohandas K., 16, 190
Gauthier, David, 90
gay marriage, 155, 156–57
gay people. *See* homosexuality
general rights, 46
general will, 124–27
geologic lottery, 242–43
Gewirth, Alan, 63n38
Gilligan, Carol, 109
global justice: and foreign aid, 244; and global welfare floor, 244; and humanitarian intervention, 246–47; Law of the Sea Treaty, 245; and natural resources, 240–45
Goldman, Alan, 225n29–30
good, the: communitarian critique of neutrality regarding, 104–8; conflicts over in liberal democracies, 91–92, 111; greatest good for the greatest number, 24, 25, 26–27, 29; liberal neutrality as a good, 101; primary goods, 83, 90–91, 105; Rawls on reasonable conceptions of, 92–93; Rawls's thin theory of, 91; and religious intolerance, 91, 104; social determination of goods, 103, 104. *See also* common good; moral values
"good Germans," 9
goods and services, distribution of. *See* distribution of goods and services
government, the. *See* state, the
Great Society, 18
Grey, Thomas, 169, 170
Grimshaw, Jean, 109, 110
groups: collective compensation for, 213–14; compensatory justice for, 211–14, 224n22; and democracy, 130–33; dissenters within, 135, 219; group rights, 107–8, 114n10; interest groups, 131; justice for, 216–17; legal preservation of traditions, 174n28; multiculturalism, 133–36; plurality of, 122–23; statistical compensation for, 211–13. *See also* minority racial groups
Gutmann, Amy, 108, 111, 141n31

Hampshire, Stuart, 104, 105
happiness: in Bentham's utilitarianism, 24; hedonic calculus for, 25–26, 28
harassment, 168–71
Hardin, Garrett, 234–35
Hare, R. M., 34
harm principle, 151–53; and freedom of

thought and discussion, 161; and liberty, 173; and offensive acts, 153–54; and paternalistic interference, 160; and suicide, 158; and Wolfenden Report, 154
Harsanyi, John, 31–32
Hart, H. L. A.: on coercive rules, 180; *The Concept of Law,* 180; on Devlin on enforcing morality, 155–57; fairness principle of, 138
hate speech, 164; good speech as remedy for bad, 170–71; as harassment, 168–71; as offensive, 153; speech codes for prohibiting, 145, 164–71
hedonic calculus, 25–26, 28
Held, Virginia, 140n1
helmet laws, 158
Hispanics. *See* minority racial groups
Hobbes, Thomas, 10–14; on absolute authority, 10–14; evolution of political theory of, 12–14; on human nature, 10–11, 13; on laws of nature, 11–12; *Leviathan,* 10; Locke's criticism of, 13–14; on mutual consent, 14; political philosophy of, 10–14; on political realism, 230, 231; and selfishness, 11, 13; on state of nature, 10–12, 48, 196, 230, 231; Wolff compared with, 15
Holmes, Robert, 249n3
homeless, the, 131
homosexuality: gay marriage, 155, 156–57; hate speech directed against, 164–71, 175n45; Mill on liberty for, 152; as offensive to some, 153; state neutrality regarding sexual preference, 7; Wolfenden Report on, 154–57
hostile environment, 165, 166
human dignity: and human rights, 58; liberty as connected with, 151, 172; Mill on, 28
humanitarian intervention, 245–49; the case against, 246–47; and the cold war, 246; costs of, 246; as exception, 248; and global justice, 246–47; and human rights, 246, 247, 248; limited defense of, 247–49; as paternalistic, 246, 247
human nature: Bentham on, 24; Hobbes on, 10–11, 13
human rights, 41–65; aim of doctrine of, 41; as applying to all societies, 95; as belonging to human beings as such, 45, 62n12; Declaration of the Rights of Man, 44, 47; egalitarian argument for, 56–57; elitist arguments against, 58–60; as entitlements, 239; as general, 45; humanitarian intervention as violating, 246, 247, 248; as inalienable, 46; and justice, 73, 74; justification of, 56–60; lists of, 47; marriage as, 157; as morally fundamental, 45, 58; and pref-

erential treatment, 207; and republican conception of freedom, 106; the state as protector of, 41, 47, 136; Universal Declaration of Human Rights, 47, 52–56; and utilitarianism, 57; and world hunger, 238–40

Hume, David, 23

hunger. *See* world hunger

ideal utilitarianism, 30

ignorance principle, 82, 88, 95, 128

impartiality: challenges to concept of, 253; feminist critique of, 109, 110; and humanitarian intervention, 247, 248; as ideological, 114; and obligatoriness of sacrifice, 236–38; proper application of, 113; and Young, 112–13. *See also* neutrality

individual, the: communitarian critique of liberal notion of, 102–4; and democracy, 16, 130; as egoistic utility maximizer, 122; nonindividualist defenses of democracy, 121–27; Rawls as ignoring differences among, 90; Rawls on inviolability of the person, 5; respect for persons as ends, 58; self-realization, 120, 179; the state as analogous to, 248; utilitarianism ignoring roles of, 36. *See also* egoism

individual autonomy: as an intrinsic good for Mill, 163; and liberty, 151; natural rights protecting, 45; and paternalistic interference, 160; Rawls on, 92; Rousseau on political authority and, 124, 127; and suicide, 159; Wolff on political authority and, 14–16

individual conscience: as basic liberty for Rawls, 83; and decision of the majority, 16; and political authority, 7–21

individual liberty (freedom): correlative responsibilities of, 106; and liberal democratic state, 16–17; and market mechanism, 76, 85, 86; and natural rights, 45; in Nozick's entitlement theory, 86–87; and other values, 4; Rawls on, 92; Sandel on, 106; scope and limits of, 145, 151–71; state programs as violating, 18. *See also* freedom of speech

individual rights: and the common good, 126–27; communitarians on, 101; in contemporary utilitarianism, 33–34; and democratic vote, 95, 96; Dworkin on, 204, 205; Hobbes on, 12; in Mill's rule utilitarianism, 29; protection of as paradigm feature of democracy, 118; state as protector of, 4, 46–56, 61, 106; and utilitarianism, 27, 37

inheritance, 85

inquiry, critical, 163

instrumentalism, 102

insults: as harmful, 152; speech codes for prohibiting, 165–70

interests: conflicts of in pluralistic societies, 111; good for all achieved by pursuing one's own, 79; interest groups, 131; in Mill's harm principle, 152. *See also* common good; national interest; self-interest

international affairs, 229–52; humanitarian intervention, 245–49; the ideal and the actual in, 244–45; natural resources and global justice, 240–45; political realism in, 229–33; world hunger, 233–40

intervention, humanitarian. *See* humanitarian intervention

Jews. *See* minority racial groups

Johnson, Lyndon, 202, 214

justice, 67–99; Aristotle's theory of, 68–69; clarification of meaning of term, 3; democracy as appropriate procedure for providing, 96; dual theory of, 73–74; entitlement theory of, 79–81, 86–88; and equality, 72–73; and equal rights, 73–75; formal theories of, 68–69; as giving persons their due, 69, 71; for groups, 216–17; liberal justice, 101–16; market approach to economic, 76–81, 85–86; material theories of, 69–76; Plato and Aristotle on rationality of, 43; Plato's theory of, 68–69; procedures versus results, 75–76; promoting social justice, 223; and punishment, 186–87; Rawls on, 81–85, 88–96; retributive justice, 75; traditional theories of, 68–76. *See also* compensatory justice; global justice; procedural justice

Justinian, 44

Kant, Immanuel, 109, 182–83

Karpman, Benjamin, 186

Keynes, John Maynard, 86

King, Martin Luther, Jr., 16, 19, 189, 191, 199n18

Kohlberg, Lawrence, 109

Kozol, Jonathan, 1

Kymlicka, Will, 107

laissez-faire economics, 76–79

law: obligation to obey, 191–94; reasons for, 179–80

law and order, 179–200. *See also* civil disobedience; crime; order and stability; political order

Law of the Sea Treaty, 240, 245

laws of nature, 11–12

law testing, 191

layoffs, 222

level playing field, 215

*Leviathan* (Hobbes), 10

*lex talionis,* 184

liberal arts education, 136

liberal democratic state: authority of, 15–16; conflicts over the good in, 91–92, 111; and individual freedom, 16–17; and justice, 94–95. *See also* democracy

liberalism: and bureaucratic authority, 111; and civil disobedience, 190; communitarian critique of, 96, 101–8; feminist critique of, 96, 108–14; liberal feminists, 108; liberal justice, 101–16; on neutrality, 16–17, 104–8, 109–10; Rawls's *Political Liberalism,* 91–94; on the self, 102–4; welfare liberalism, 18. *See also* liberal democratic state

*Liberalism and the Limits of Justice* (Sandel), 102

libertarians: on centralization and government influence, 76–77; entitlement theory of resource appropriation, 240–41; on state programs, 18; on welfare state, 150

liberty, 145–77; Berlin's two concepts of, 147–49; and equality, 172; forcing people to be free, 148; as fundamental right, 172; Mill on, 151–53, 172; natural liberty, 83; negative liberty, 147, 172; and negative rights, 55; political liberty, 146–50; positive liberty, 147–49; and positive rights, 53; as primary good for Rawls, 83, 89; priority of, 172–73; scope and limits of, 145, 151–71; as triadic relation, 149–50. *See also* civil liberties; individual liberty

lifeboat ethics, 234–35

lifestyles: diversity of, 30; and market mechanism, 76; state neutrality regarding, 7

Lincoln–Douglas debates, 105

literacy, as voting qualification, 73

Locke, John: as empiricist, 48; on equality, 56–57; Hobbes criticized by, 13–14; on inequality of possession, 49, 50–51; on liberty, 172; on natural rights, 48, 50; on negative and positive rights, 47, 56; on private property, 48–49, 240–41; Rousseau contrasted with, 124; *Second Treatise of Government,* 48; on the social contract, 47, 49–50, 51, 137; on the state, 48, 50–52, 56, 61; on state of nature, 48–50, 241; on tacit consent, 137

lotteries, fairness in, 75

Lyons, David, 35–36, 38n8, 198n2

MacCallum, Gerald C., Jr., 149

MacIntyre, Alisdair, 101, 104

Madison, James, 122

majority rule: Benhabib on, 112; and civil disobedience, 16; democracy contrasted with, 118; for enforcing morality, 156; with fundamentalist majority, 113; and individual conscience, 16; and minority groups, 130, 131; Rousseau on, 124; shifting majorities, 122

Mandeville, Bernard, 96n10

market, the: competitive market, 31, 76; criticism of, 77–78, 85–86, 88; democratic voting compared with, 85; and development policies, 239; and economic justice, 76–81; evaluation of, 85–86; individual liberty as enhanced by, 76, 85, 86; Locke on free-market exchange, 51; and selfishness, 96n10; supply and demand, 77

marriage, gay, 155, 156–57

Matsuda, Mari, 168

McVeigh, Timothy, 188

"Megan's Laws," 183, 198n8

"Melian dialogue," 229

mentors, 219

meritocracy, 69–70

meritocratic affirmative action, 203, 221–22

Mexican War, 9

Michigan speech code, 164–67, 175n45

Mill, John Stuart, 28–31; on autonomy, 163; on choice, 161; on critical inquiry, 163; criticisms of, 30–31; on democracy, 120–21; on a framework of rights, 164; on freedom of thought and discussion, 161–64; on hedonic calculus, 28; on human dignity, 28; on individual rights, 29; *On Liberty,* 30, 151, 161; on liberty, 151–53, 172; and panel of experts, 28, 30–31; pleasures distinguished by, 28, 30, 31–32; as rule utilitarian, 29; on tyranny of public opinion, 30; on women's liberty, 146

minority racial groups: affirmative action for, 2, 201–27; and assimilation, 134, 135; and capital punishment, 188; cultural diversity, 107, 133–35, 218–20, 222; dissenters within, 135; elitist arguments against equality for, 59, 60; and hate speech, 153, 164–71; as marginalized by liberalism, 113; multiculturalism, 133–36; and oppression, 111, 130–32; racial segregation, 18–19, 59, 189, 191; separatism, 135; state's responsibility to, 1, 18; unequal distribution of goods for, 86; voting districts for, 130. *See also* discrimination money, 49

Moore, G. E., 30

moral values: conflicts over, 4, 105; core values, 157; enforcing, 154–57, 167; and family values, 7, 16; and human rights, 45, 58; in international affairs, 229–52; and law, 180; lifeboat ethics, 234–35; in political philosophy, 3; and political values, 93, 94; shared values, 17; skepticism regarding, 194; state promotion of, 17; in women and men, 109–10. *See also* good, the; obligation

Morganthau, Hans, 230–31

Morris, Herbert, 185, 186

mountain climbing, 160–61

multiculturalism, 133–36

murder, 184, 188, 189

mutual consent, Hobbes on, 14

national interest: for justifying any policy, 245; and natural rights of others, 244; realist view of, 229–33; varying interpretations of, 232–33

Native Americans. *See* minority racial groups

natural duties, 139

natural law, 44–45

natural liberty, 83

natural resources: actual versus potential, 242–43; as common heritage of mankind, 242; and global justice, 240–45; Law of the Sea Treaty, 240, 245; libertarians on appropriation of, 240–41; within national territories, 244; resource egalitarianism, 242–45

natural rights, 43–46; Bentham on, 45; Locke on, 48, 50; majority rule limited by, 131; and negative liberty, 147; obligations imposed by, 139

negative liberty, 147, 172

negative rights, 47, 53, 54, 55, 61

negative utilitarianism, 237–38

neutrality: communitarian critique of liberal, 104–8; feminist critique of liberal, 109–10; and Michigan speech code, 167; of the state, 7, 16–17, 18, 94, 101, 104. *See also* impartiality

Nickel, James, 211–12

Noddings, Nel, 109

normative political realism, 230

Nozick, Robert: *Anarchy, State, and Utopia,* 79; entitlement theory of, 79–81, 86–88, 241; on fairness principle, 138; on negative liberty, 172; on Rawls, 90; on the state, 97n20

nudity, 154

obedience: to law, 191–94; Wolff on, 15. *See also* civil disobedience

objectivity, 253

obligation: of the affluent toward world hunger, 233–40; and fairness, 138; natural duties, 139; to obey the law, 191–94; and rights, 42–43, 62n6, 139–40. *See also* political obligation

occupational choice, 76, 89

offensive acts, 153–54; disagreement over restricting, 145; Mill on, 151–52

Okin, Susan Moller, 108

Oklahoma City bomber, 188

*On Liberty* (Mill), 30, 151, 161

Oppenheim, Felix E., 140n1, 140n3

opportunity, equality of. *See* equal opportunity

oppression, 111; of minority groups in a democracy, 130–32; of women, 111

order and stability: and independent judgment, 9; and the moral society, 132, 195; of a Rawlsian society, 84, 91. *See also* law and order

organ transplants, 8, 67, 70

other-regarding actions, 151–53

ownership. *See* property rights

pain: in Bentham's utilitarianism, 24; hedonic calculus for, 25; and Mill's harm principle, 152

participatory democracy, 131–32

particularity: MacIntyre on, 104; Rawls on, 110–11; Walzer on, 103

paternalism, 158; acceptable principles for, 160–61; Dworkin on, 174n35; humanitarian intervention as, 246, 247; Mill on, 151; and prevention of suicide, 158–60; speech codes as, 171

Patterson, Orlando, 218–19

perfectionism, 120

physician-assisted suicide, 159, 174n33

Plato, 43, 69–71, 128, 180

pleasure: in Bentham's utilitarianism, 24; hedonic calculus for, 25, 26; Mill on, 28, 30, 31–32

pluralism: and conflict, 111; and democracy, 122–24; on political leadership, 128; Rawls and broad pluralism, 93; Sandel on, 94

police officers, hiring of, 221

political authority: grounds of, 10–17; Hobbes on, 10–14; and individual conscience, 7–21; of liberal democratic state, 15–16; and liberty, 173; and neutrality of the state, 16–17; political philosophy assessing, 9; Rousseau

political authority *(continued)*
   on individual autonomy and, 124, 127; state's claim to, 7–8, 9; utilitarianism on the state's, 37, 46–47; Wolff on individual autonomy and, 14–16. *See also* political obligation

*Political Liberalism* (Rawls), 91–94

political liberty, 146–50

political obligation, 136–40; and democracy, 117–43; and fairness, 138; and rights, 139–40; social contract theory of, 137–38. *See also* political authority

political order: evaluating the, 17–19; natural law in, 45; role of, 94. *See also* law, law and order

political philosophy: clarification of concepts in, 3; of Hobbes, 10–14; human rights perspective in, 61; in justification of political decisions, 3–4; moral evaluation in, 3; political authority assessed by, 9; of Rousseau, 125; the state evaluated by, 7

political realism, 229–33

political values, 93, 94

pollution, 241

population control, 26

population growth, 234–35

pornography, 3, 17, 101

positive liberty, 147–49

positive rights, 47, 52–56, 61, 239, 243–44

poverty: and liberty, 149, 150; obligation to relieve, 5; and political representation, 131; and social justice, 223; and slavery contracts, 160; state amelioration of, 18; war on poverty, 18. *See also* world hunger

power: democracy providing check on abuse of, 119–20, 122, 128; speech codes and asymmetries of, 170

preference utilitarianism, 31–32

preferential treatment: burden of proof for, 224n13; and compensatory justice, 208–14, 221; conditions of, 222–23; constitutional status of, 201–2; distribution of costs of, 209–10; and equal treatment, 205, 206–7, 214–16; as form of affirmative action, 201, 202–3; and group justice, 216–17; noncompensatory defenses of, 214–20; as not a zero-sum game, 221; and qualifications and efficiency, 217–20; and quotas, 203; and reverse discrimination, 203, 222; and self-esteem of recipients, 215

preventive detention, 183, 187

primary goods, 83, 90–91, 105

private contexts, 152

private property. *See* property rights

procedural justice: laissez-faire justice as, 78–79; in liberal democratic state, 94–95; procedures versus results, 75–76

property rights: Locke on, 48–49; market mechanism as guaranteeing, 76; natural resources and global justice, 240–45; as negative, 49; Nozick on, 80–81, 87, 97n14; Rawls on, 83; and redistribution of resources, 1

protest: civil disobedience in, 189–98; and Vietnam War, 9, 119, 189–90

psychological egoism, 11, 13, 19n5

public facilities, equal access to, 74

public interest. *See* common good

public opinion, Mill on tyranny of, 30

punishment, 180–89; arguments against, 180–81; Bentham on, 24, 181–82; as deterrence, 181–82, 185, 188, 189; for enforcing morality, 154; as fitting the crime, 182, 184–85; and justice, 182, 186–87; justification of, 181–85; "punishment of the innocent" example, 27, 32, 181; retributive theory of, 182–85; as revenge, 182; as a right, 183; or therapy, 185–87; utilitarian justification of, 181–82, 184. *See also* capital punishment

qualifications: and preferential treatment, 217–20; for voting, 73

quality of products, 77

Quebec separatists, 107

quotas: and preferential treatment, 203; in regulative affirmative action, 202

racial epithets, 165–70

racial groups. *See* minority racial groups

racial segregation, 18–19, 59, 189, 191

racism: elitist arguments for, 60; and hate speech, 164–71; ignoring the effects of past, 2

rap music, 17, 145

rational-choice theory, 31

rational egoism, 132–33

rationality: challenges to concept of, 253; and emotions, 111; and freedom of thought and discussion, 162; Hobbes on, 11; of justice for Plato and Aristotle, 43; Mill on pleasure of, 30; in Mill's defense of democracy, 120–21; and paternalistic interference, 160; Rawls on reasonable conceptions of the good, 92–93; in Rawls's theory of justice, 82, 83; and suicide, 159

Rawls, John: on civil disobedience, 197; on difference principle, 84, 90, 93; on equality of representation, 128; on fairness, 84, 138; on ignorance principle, 82, 88, 95, 128; on inviolability of the person, 5; on justice, 81–85, 88–96; on stability of the moral society, 132, 195; on natural duties, 139; on overlapping consensus, 91–92, 93–94, 105, 123; on particularity, 110–11; *Political Liberalism,* 91–94; on primary goods, 83, 90–91, 105; on priority of liberty, 172; and resource egalitarianism, 242; responses to his critics, 91–96; Sandel's critique of, 94, 102; on the social contract, 81–82, 88, 95; on the state, 84; *A Theory of Justice,* 81, 88–91; thin theory of the good, 91; on utilitarianism, 35

realism, political. *See* political realism

reason. *See* rationality

redistribution of resources: Locke on, 51; and global justice, 240–45; Nozick on, 79; by the state, 1–2

relativism, cultural, 133, 135

relevant differences, 57, 72–73

religious fundamentalists, 91, 112, 113, 145

republicanism, civic, 105–7

Rescher, Nicholas, 37n3, 71

resource egalitarianism: and the geologic lottery, 242–43; on natural resources as common heritage of mankind, 242; and positive rights, 243–44

resources, natural. *See* natural resources

respect for persons as ends, 58

responsibility, 186, 213

retributive justice, 75

retributive theory of punishment, 182–85, 188

revenge, punishment as, 182

reverse discrimination: Dworkin on, 204–7; and preferential treatment, 203, 222; the reverse discrimination argument, 203–7

rights, 42–43; Bill of Rights, 118, 162, 188; clashes between, 61, 74, 81, 95, 96, 136, 172; as entitlements, 42–43; feminist critique of traditional theories of, 109; general rights, 46; group rights, 107–8, 114n10; justice and equal rights, 73–75; liberty as a fundamental right, 172; negative rights, 47, 53, 54, 55, 61; and obligation, 42–43, 62n6, 139–40; positive rights, 47, 52–56, 61, 239, 243–44; punishment as, 183; special rights, 46. *See also* civil liberties (rights); human rights; individual rights; natural rights; property rights

right to life, 46

role models, 219

Rousseau, Jean-Jacques: on democracy and the general will, 124–27; *The Social Contract,* 124; on the social contract, 124–25

rule of the majority. *See* majority rule

rule utilitarianism, 29; Brandt's reformulation of, 32–33, 38n12; and freedom of thought and discussion, 163; Harsanyi's version of, 31; and humanitarian intervention, 248; Lyons on act utilitarianism and, 35–36, 38n8; on punishment, 181; and rights, 43, 57, 61

Russell, Bertrand, 189

salaries, 77, 85

Sandel, Michael J.: civic republicanism of, 105–7; as communitarian, 101; on debates over substantial moral values, 105; *Democracy's Discontent,* 105; *Liberalism and the Limits of Justice,* 102; on Rawls, 94, 102; on right to liberty, 106

scarcity of goods and resources, 80

Scholasticism, 44

sea bed, 241, 243, 245

seat-belt laws, 158, 161

*Second Treatise of Government* (Locke), 48

segregation, racial, 18–19, 59, 189, 191

self, the: communitarian critique of liberal notion of, 102–4. *See also* egoism; individual, the

self-defense, 188

self-interest: conflicts of, in pluralistic society, 111; discouraging self-interest as in our, 132; in Rawls's theory of justice, 81; and the state, 14, 230

selfishness: Butler on, 19n5; Hobbes on, 11, 13; and the market, 96n10. *See also* egoism

self-realization, 120, 179

self-regarding actions, 151–53

separatism, 135

serious crimes: capital punishment for, 182; murder, 184, 188, 189

sex offenders, 183, 187

sexual activity: between consenting adults, 154. *See also* homosexuality

sexual harassment, 170

sexual preference, 7

shared values, 17

sharing, 103

Sher, George, 225n25

Shue, Henry, 54, 55

Simon, Robert L., 249n7, 250n26–27

Simpson, O. J., 218

Singer, Peter, 236–39, 250n17

sit-ins, 189

skepticism, moral, 194

slavery: affluent slaves and dignity, 172; liberal and communitarian approach to, 105; selling oneself into, 15, 159–60, 174n33

slurs, ethnic and racial, 165–70

Smart, J. J. C., 37n6, 38n12

Smith, Adam, 24

social contract: Bentham on, 24; Hobbes on, 12; Locke on, 47, 49–50, 51, 137; and non-intervention, 247; and obligation to obey the law, 193–94; and political obligation, 137–38; Rawls on, 81–82, 88, 95; Rousseau on, 124–25; and tacit consent, 137–38

*Social Contract, The* (Rousseau), 124

social cooperation, 90

social groups. *See* groups

sociobiology, 20n13

Socrates, 180, 190, 192–93, 196

Soderholm, Steven, 198n5

Somalia, 245, 246

Sophists, 43

Sophocles, 190

speaking skills, 112

special rights, 46

speech, freedom of. *See* freedom of expression

speech-acts, 168

speech codes, 164–71; disagreement over, 145; narrow codes, 168–71; Stanford University code, 169–70; University of Michigan code, 164–67, 175n45

*Spheres of Justice* (Walzer), 103

stability. *See* order and stability

starvation. *See* world hunger

state, the: and absolute authority, 9; as adjudicator of clashes of rights, 61, 96, 136; authority claimed by, 7–8; constitutions, 93–94; role of, 7, 18–19; evaluating the political order, 17–19; Hobbes on, 10–14; humanitarian intervention by, 245–49; and human rights, 41, 47, 136; and individual rights, 4, 46–56, 61, 106; as instrument of mutual advantage, 12; in international affairs, 229–52; and liberty, 173; Locke on, 48, 50–52, 56, 61; moral values promoted by, 17; as neutral, 7, 16–17, 18, 94, 101, 104; Nozick on, 97n20; Plato's ideal of, 128; and political philosophy, 7; and positive rights, 54–55; Rawls on, 84; redistribution of resources by, 1–2; and self-interest, 14; suspicion of, 4, 18; utilitarianism on, 37, 46–47; Wolff on, 15. *See also* law and order; liberal democratic state; political authority; welfare state

state of nature: Hobbes on, 10–12, 48, 196, 230, 231; Locke on, 48–50, 241

statistical compensation, 211–13

Stephen, James Fitzjames, 152, 154, 161–62

steroids, 149

Stoics, 44

subordination, 168–71

suffrage, universal, 118

suicide, 145, 158–60

supply and demand, 77

tacit consent, 137–38

taxation: as disincentive to produce, 78; Nozick on, 79, 86

Taylor, Charles, 101, 102–3, 107, 134

Taylor, Paul, 224n21

teleology, 69

terrorism, 232

*Theory of Justice, A* (Rawls), 81, 88–91

therapy, in place of punishment, 185–87

Thomas Aquinas, 44

Thompson, Dennis, 111

Thoreau, Henry David, 9, 190, 194–95

thought, freedom of, 161–64

Thucydides, 229

tolerance: Rawls on, 91, 92, 95; religious intolerance, 91, 104

tragedy of the commons, 234–35

"Two Concepts of Liberty" (Berlin), 147–49

unintended by-products of action, 55

Universal Declaration of Human Rights, 47, 52–56

universal suffrage, 118

university faculty appointments, 202, 217–20

utilitarianism, 23–39; act utilitarianism, 29, 32, 33, 35–36, 38n8, 38n12; of Bentham, 23–28; on capital punishment, 188; contemporary economic discussions of, 31–36; counterexamples to, 32, 34; criticism of contemporary, 34–36; on democracy, 118–21; and freedom of thought and discussion, 161–63; on greatest good for the greatest number, 24, 25, 26–27, 29; and the hedonic calculus, 25–26, 28; and humanitarian intervention, 248, 250n30; and human rights, 57; ideal utilitarianism, 30; as individualistic, 35; and individual rights, 27, 33–34, 37; individual's roles ignored in, 35, 36; and market economics, 76; of Mill, 28–31; moral objections to, 26–27; on natural rights, 45; negative utilitarianism, 237–38; Nozick on, 79; preference utilitarianism, 31–32; on punishment, 181–82, 184;

on the state, 37, 46–47; as too demanding, 27, 237. *See also* rule utilitarianism

values. *See also* moral values, political values
Vietnam War, 9, 119, 189–90
violence, 196–97
Vlastos, Gregory, 96n7
von Hayek, Friedrich, 76
voting: minority districts, 130; as paradigm feature of democracy, 118; qualifications for, 73; and tacit consent, 137; universal suffrage, 118; weighted voting, 30. *See also* majority rule

Walzer, Michael, 101, 103–4, 246
war on drugs, 7
war on poverty, 18
Wasserstrom, Richard, 43, 58, 62n5, 134
wealth, distribution of. *See* distribution of goods and services
weighted voting, 30
welfare liberalism, 18
welfare state: as disincentive to produce, 78; a global welfare floor, 244; Great Society, 18; liberty as constrained by, 150; and positive rights, 52–56; some recipients as undeserving, 131
well-being: market enhancement of, 77, 85; worsening of for Nozick, 87
Will, George, 17
Williams, Bernard, 34, 59
Williams, Melissa, 111, 113
Wolfenden Report, 154–57
Wolff, Robert Paul: on individual autonomy, 14–16; on pluralism, 123; on political obligation, 136–37
women: affirmative action for, 2, 201–27; as a caste, 216; as differing from men in significant ways, 109; dissenters from feminism, 135, 146; elitist arguments against equality for, 59, 60; hate speech directed against, 164–71; Mill on liberty of, 146; as oppressed, 111; sexual harassment, 170. *See also* feminism
world hunger, 233–40; the case for sacrifice, 236–38; extent and nature of, 233; and human rights, 238–40; lifeboat ethics and tragedy of the commons, 234–35

Young, Iris Marion, 96, 110, 111–14

# About the Authors

**NORMAN E. BOWIE** is the Elmer M. Andersen Chair in Corporate Responsibility in the Departments of Philosophy and Strategic Management and Organization at the University of Minnesota. He served a term as chair of the Department of Strategic Management and Organization. He is the author, editor, coauthor, or coeditor of twelve books and fifty articles on business ethics and political philosophy. He is past president of the Society for Value Inquiry and the Society for Business Ethics and the former executive secretary of the American Philosophical Association. While on sabbatical as a Fellow at Harvard University's Program in Ethics and the Professions in 1996 and 1997, he completed a book entitled *A Kantian Theory of the Firm*.

**ROBERT L. SIMON** is professor of philosophy at Hamilton College. He is the author of *Neutrality and the Academic Ethic* and *Fair Play* as well as articles in ethics, political philosophy, and philosophy of sport. He has held fellowships from the National Endowment for the Humanities, the American Council of Learned Societies, the National Humanities Center, and the Center for Advanced Study in the Behavioral Sciences. He combines his interests in philosophy and sport by serving as an officer of the Philosophic Society for the Study of Sport and by coaching the golf team at Hamilton.